Brand owners from emerging markets are incr........ ,
a key marketing platform and this timely and thoughtful book puts this global
trend into context.

Ravi Venkatesan, former Chairman, Microsoft India

This book provides a comprehensive guide to the many facets of the sponsorship industry. It's an ideal reference for all practitioners – whether experienced
or newcomers; whether buyers or sellers – and sets out commercial figures and
statistics, as well as excellent case studies. If anyone doubted sponsorship as an
effective marketing tool, they will need no convincing now.

Karen Earl, Chairman, The European Sponsorship Association

Ardi has crea... THE sponsorship reference that will remain within arm's reach
for years

Madincea, Founder & Group Managing Director PRISM

Martial
Tel: 01...

A rea...... d and insightful guide to the ever growing world of sponsorship. .... the industry is genuinely coming of age, it's great to have
a book ...... place wraps up all of the key components of the industry in a
clear .... way. A must read.

Andy Westlake, CEO, Fast Track

The L...... Olympic Games were a significant achievement not just in athletic
and o...... terms but also for the global and national sponsors connected with
them. ...... rs are increasingly seeking new ways to connect with audiences
and c...... ments in a personal and engaging way. *Improving the Performance
of Spo*...... ides the blue print for how this can be best achieved; building on
insigh...... work the author undertook for the UK Government in relation to
the L...... Olympic Games. Ardi Kolah has made a very valuable contribution
to our ...... this important and rapidly growing marketing discipline.

Sir Paul Judge, President of the Association of MBAs

An in...... de to the way in which brand owners and rights holders should
now ...... drive their sponsorship platforms ahead of the changes in data
prote...... il impact this dynamic and growing industry.

Darren Verrian, CEO, EU Compliance and Recruitment

Spons...... subset of marketing is a subject that's often treated on a cursory b...... gnored if those teaching marketing are unsure how best to cover
the su...... a robust and interesting way. This book takes a holistic view of
this fa...... ng aspect of marketing. Packed full of examples Kolah has produced
somet...... nat's highly relevant and timely for both brand owners, rights holders
and a...... es that must focus not just on outputs but outcomes from their marketing bu...... . Kolah's six-step sponsorship model is a powerful tool for improving
the pe...... nance of sponsorship and the book is ESSENTIAL READING for anyone that wants   from sponsorship.

...ute of Marketing

The financial services sector is one of the most active when considering its involvement in sponsorship on a global basis. What this excellent book does is to help navigate those responsible for such marketing expenditure to achieve measurable outcomes as well as providing a sound commercial basis for those rights holders that want to succeed in their sponsorship programmes. Written in an extremely accessible way and with the latest case studies and best practice guidance, one of the best sponsorship books for anyone working within the financial services sector.

David Cowan, Managing Director, Financial Services Forum

This is an incredibly comprehensive reference to how you make sponsorship work harder. There's something for everyone here, whether you're new to the sponsorship industry or an experienced old hand. If you're involved in sponsorship programmes in any capacity then this is worth a read.

David Peters, Managing Director, Dentsu
Aegis Network Sport & Entertainment

For a significant marketing channel, we now have a significant marketing handbook which covers key sponsorship decisions with digestible detail and convincing cases.

Professor Vince Mitchell, Sir John E Cohen
Professor of Consumer Marketing, Cass Business School

A thorough and detailed understanding of sponsorship is an integral part of building any brand and Kolah offers readers an educated guide on the subject. *Improving the Performance of Sponsorship* is an outstanding piece of scholarship on a subject of vital importance to every business and this book will undoubtedly prove a valuable tool to marketers and entrepreneurs from start-ups and multinationals alike.

Lord Karan Bilimoria CBE DL, Chairman, Cobra Beer Partnership

This excellent book explores the role of global sponsorship within the overall context of marketing and public relations. The book appeals to marketing and PR practitioners as well as undergraduate and postgraduate students looking to expand their knowledge in this area. The book is easy to read, engaging and packed with up-to-date case studies and is highly commended.

Ray Donnelly, Team Leader, Marketing,
London Guildhall Faculty of Business and Law

This is an essential guide for any marketer with an interest in marketing and sponsorship. The landscape changes constantly, both in terms of compliance and the optimisation of sponsorship returns, and Ardi does a tremendous job of navigating the field – from the basics to the business, legal issues and ethical considerations alike. Highly readable and instantly informative.

Elliot Reuben, Principal Business
Consultant, Salesforce Marketing Cloud

Within the global music and entertainment industry, artists and studios are exploring new ways to drive incremental value from their intellectual property rights. Brand partnerships and collaboration between rights holders, studios and brands is changing the face of the industry where the sum of the parts is the real prize. This excellent book, written in an authoritative and accessible way is highly recommended for all of our MBA students that are forging careers in this dynamic and innovative sector.

Helen Gammons, Programme Director – MBA for Music & Creative Industries, Henley Business School

This book covers the need for achieving a mutually strategic brand fit, the need for genuine collaboration and the adding of real value. Kolah's global view, rich with data and real life case studies, provides true insight into this critical area of brand building in an easy to navigate format. For those involved or merely interested in the subject this book is a must read.

Andrew Marsden, Master, Worshipful Company of Marketors

The voluntary sector needs to diversify in terms of new income streams and commercial sponsorship represents an incredible opportunity to establish long-term relationships on a strong commercial footing with major sponsors. Ardi Kolah's book is essential reading for everyone in the voluntary sector that wants to explore how best to engage in relationships outside of fundraising and corporate giving in order to drive incremental revenues from brand partnerships. Highly recommended.

Richard Leaman OBE, CEO, Guide Dogs

This is a really inspired introduction to sponsorship and the way in which it actually works. Though I wish it had been around 25 years ago, it's a book from which even seasoned fundraisers will benefit and learn.

Colin McKenzie, Director, House of Illustration

Ardi Kolah's latest book is a timely assessment of where the sponsorship industry has got to. It explains succinctly the processes, the challenges and opportunities and there's a wealth of data and case studies to help the reader to understand the subject. I particularly liked the practical approach taken to explaining the need to consider every aspect of the sponsorship process. A useful tool for sponsors and rights holders alike.

Simon Rines, CEO, International Marketing Reports

Sponsorship has come a long way since it depended on the chairman's whim and fancy. But how marketers are actually doing sponsorship and, equally important, how they measure what gets done is often a case of 'hit and miss'. This book provides both experienced practitioners and those new to marketing with an admirably clear and well-structured guide to the key features in the sponsorship landscape. And readers couldn't get a better sponsorship guru. Ardi has the rare gift of combining lucid writing and academic rigour with a truly detailed knowledge of the field – what he doesn't know about sponsorship would probably fill a postage stamp, just.

Daryn Moody, Publishing Editor, Journal of Brand Strategy

Providing absolute currency in today's marketing world, the book is a font of knowledge to help any marketer navigate the increasingly powerful world of sponsorship at all levels, and importantly not just the global deals that grab the headlines.

Howard Kosky, CEO, Markettiers4DC

Sponsorship has now truly come of age as a global marketing tool due to its ability to connect with the values and aspirations of all types of consumers. This new book really captures all the essentials of running successful sponsorship programmes. It highlights the opportunities, the controls and the pitfalls using recent examples from around the world – and it would certainly have been very helpful to have had this book when I was running Olympic and World Cup campaigns for Coca-Cola. Ardi is able to make even the most complex theories understandable and raises crucial questions for the reader to answer as their contribution to the never ending dialogue of how to achieve true marketing success.

Jeremy Stern, Managing Director, PromoVeritas

Having known Ardi for a number of years personally and professionally I know he has a true passion for educating marketers and brand owners on the commercial benefits of sponsorship. He understands that sponsorship is so much more than printing a logo on a shirt or getting a celebrity to endorse a product. This book is a must read for anyone wanting to leverage their sponsorship investments beyond the usual 'slap a logo on it' methods to gain true return on investment through strategic sponsorship activation.

Lena Robinson, Founder, Kiwi Girl Limited and Ex-Group Business Development Director (UK) – Dentsu Aegis Network

There are two sides of the equation when it comes to sponsorship. The body receiving the sponsorship and the body giving the sponsorship. Maximising the benefits and rewards for both in the partnership requires considerable planning and forethought in the relationship. For all those involved or considering sponsorship this is a must have book. There are few books and even training modules that will equip you to improve your investment whichever side of the equation you may be on.

Manjit Biant, Management Consultant

Ardi Kolah is a highly respected expert in the field of sponsorship. His latest book assists rights holders and brand owners reach a deeper appreciation of the strategic value of sponsorship as part of the marketing mix in helping to drive sustainable, profitable growth of these businesses and organisations.

Phil Jones, Founder & Organiser, Podge Events

Improving the Performance of Sponsorship

Without a doubt, sponsorship is one of the most powerful promotional tools we have in the business of brand creation, brand recognition and, ultimately, increasing sales. Moreover, brokering sponsors is a significant business in and of itself something we often overlook. Considering sponsorship is a USD 50 billion a year market – and growing – marketers and students of business ignore its potential at the risk of missing hugely lucrative opportunities. To fail to understand sponsorship is to fail to understand marketing.

If you're looking for an introduction to this topic, most books available address only sports sponsorship: the largest section of the market perhaps, but by no means the only one. Ardi Kolah's *Improving the Performance of Sponsorship* is a guide that examines all types of sponsorship, clearly explaining and defining its mechanics, advising on how to select the right properties, how to sell sponsorship, ethical issues, measurement and key legal principles.

This book is all that keen marketers need for a thorough understanding of how sponsorship works.

Ardi Kolah is a senior visiting lecturer on sponsorship, marketing and public relations at Henley Business School, Cass Business School, Kingston University Business School and the London Guildhall Faculty of Business and Law, UK. He has been working in the sponsorship industry for over 20 years and holds the prestigious UK Sponsorship Award (formerly Hollis Sponsorship Award) as well as being a fellow of several professional institutes and an elected member of the British Academy of Film and Television Arts.

Improving the Performance of Sponsorship

Ardi Kolah

 Routledge
Taylor & Francis Group

LONDON AND NEW YORK

First published 2015
by Routledge
2 Park Square, Milton Park, Abingdon, Oxon OX14 4RN

and by Routledge
711 Third Avenue, New York, NY 10017

Routledge is an imprint of the Taylor & Francis Group, an informa business

British Library Cataloguing-in-Publication Data
A catalogue record for this book is available from the British Library

Library of Congress Cataloging-in-Publication Data
Kolah, Ardi.
   Improving the performance of sponsorship / Ardi Kolah.
      pages cm
   Includes bibliographical references and index.
 1. Corporate sponsorship.   2. Marketing.   3. Branding
(Marketing)   I. Title.
   HD59.35.K647 2015
   659.2'85—dc23
   2014046345

ISBN: 978-0-415-63788-6 (hbk)
ISBN: 978-0-415-63789-3 (pbk)
ISBN: 978-1-315-69602-7 (ebk)

Typeset in Goudy
by Apex CoVantage, LLC
Printed and bound in Great Britain by Ashford Colour Press Ltd

For Fenella, Zara and Aviva, who are my inspiration every day

Contents

List of figures   xii
List of tables   xiv
Foreword   xvi
Introduction   xvii

1 Rewiring our thinking on sponsorship   1

2 The business of sponsorship   10

3 Process of selecting a sponsorship property   45

4 Process of selling a sponsorship property   65

5 Creativity in sponsorship   115

6 Ethical issues in sponsorship   152

7 Legal principles of sponsorship   194

8 Ambush marketing   223

9 Corporate social responsibility and sponsorship   240

10 Measurement and evaluation of sponsorship   266

Index   310

Figures

I.1	Worldwide communications services expenditure, 2014	xix
I.2	Total global sponsorship spending (USD bn)	xix
I.3	Total North America sponsorship spending (USD bn)	xx
I.4	Annual growth of advertising, marketing/promotion and sponsorship (USD bn)	xx
I.5	Incremental new business from major one-off sports events, 2013–22	xxii
I.6	Sports dominate property classes for sponsorship globally	xxiii
I.7	Sponsorship revenue growth by region, 2011–15 (CAGR)	xxiii
I.8	Sponsorship ecosystem in the UK	xxvii
2.1	Football continues to dominate as the top global sports content	14
2.2	Most prevalent business sectors that sponsor arts and culture in North America	17
2.3	Global sponsorship ecosystem	23
2.4	Some of the partners, sponsors and suppliers of London 2012	29
2.5	Number of major sports events across the world, 2013–22	33
2.6	Est. new business opportunities for UK sector across all regions, 2013–22	34
3.1	Celebrity power as a permission-based platform	53
3.2	Matching a celebrity to a brand	55
3.3	Valuable benefits for brand owners looking to purchase sponsorship	59
3.4	Value services provided by rights holder	60
3.5	Objectives for evaluating the performance of sponsorship	60
4.1	Lena's napkin at BAFTA	66
4.2	Typical business and marketing planning cycle	70

4.3 Typical sponsorship lifespan   72
4.4 Integration of sponsorship by the brand
     owner into marketing   73
4.5 Segmentation of potential sponsors   85
4.6 Sponsorship sales ladder   97
4.7 Segmenting sponsorship rights   100
4.8 Negotiation framework   108
4.9 Seven-step negotiation checklist   109
5.1 Most popular ways of activating a sponsorship programme   116
5.2 Unconnected ideas combine to result in a creative fusion   120
7.1 Key intellectual property (IP) rights in a football
     match on commercial TV   209
9.1 Leaders in sustainability (% of analysts polled)   261
10.1 Measurement and evaluation of London 2012   267
10.2 Six-step sponsorship model   270
10.3 Exploitation of sponsorship   273
10.4 Speedo's hierarchy of sponsorship investments globally   277
10.5 Simple calculation of return on investment   286

Tables

I.1	Global spending by region, 2012–15	xxi
I.2	Global sports sponsorship growth, 2006–15	xxiv
I.3	Compound annual growth rate of the UK sector, 2013–22	xxvi
2.1	Classification of typical arts and culture sponsorship areas	17
2.2	Evolution of association sponsorship in the USA	19
2.3	TOP sponsors that got most traction from sponsorship of London 2012	30
2.4	Tier 1 sponsors that got most/least traction from London 2012	31
2.5	Value of incremental new business for UK sector, 2013–22	35
3.1	Sponsorship budget that needed to save 25%	62
3.2	Repurposed sponsorship budget	62
4.1	Secondary sponsors of the BAFTAs	77
4.2	Outdoor exposure for Bournville College (BC), Birmingham (annual average)	88
4.3	Media exposure: launch year 1	89
4.4	Media exposure: years 1–5	90
4.5	Paid for advertising (annual average)	90
4.6	Premium benefits: years 1 and 2	91
4.7	Premium benefits: years 3–5	92
4.8	Intangible benefits illustration	94
4.9	Naming rights sponsorship: year 1	95
4.10	Naming rights sponsorship: year 2	95
4.11	Naming rights sponsorship: years 3–5	95
4.12	Five-year statement of naming rights sponsorship	96
4.13	Types of networking for sales	98
4.14	Bournville College – internal literature/advertising space	104
4.15	Typical accounting periods across global territories	105
5.1	Integrated approach to sponsored content	130
5.2	Top-ranked shows in the USA with product placement	139

5.3	Six simple rules for creating content for mobile and social networks	144
6.1	Gambling brands and sponsorship	165
7.1	Tangible and intangible rights for a sponsor	200
8.1	Examples of non-sponsor marketing for London 2012	228
8.2	Examples of high-profile ambush marketing tactics from the past	232
8.3	FIFA 2014 ambush marketing rankings	233
9.1	UN Global Compact's ten principles	244
9.2	CSR agenda on a country basis	248
9.3	Brands most associated with grass-roots sports, 2013	254
9.4	Motivations of brand owners for incorporating CSR as part of football sponsorship	256
9.5	Typical CSR activities in football sponsorship (UK/Switzerland/Germany)	257
10.1	Link with business and marketing performance	276
10.2	Speedo's objectives turned into selection criteria for sponsorship/endorsement	280
10.3	Where most sponsors tend to do their homework	284
10.4	Return on objectives and return on investment	284
10.5	Speedo brand objectives	288
10.6	Speedo commercial objectives	291
10.7	Speedo relationship objectives	295
10.8	Advantages and disadvantages of research methodologies used in sponsorship	299
10.9	Advantages and disadvantages of using face-to-face interviews	301
10.10	Face-to-face versus telephone interview techniques	302
10.11	Advantages and disadvantages of using telephone surveys	303
10.12	Advantages and disadvantages of using email/online surveys	303

Foreword

Sponsorship is now one of the fastest growing marketing disciplines in the world today – largely as a result of two factors: the ability of brand owners to drive their on-line and offline marketing campaigns using a single platform and the ability to accurately measure a return on investment from such activities.

In the wake of London 2012 Olympic Games, the author was commissioned by the British Government to undertake a forensic examination of the opportunities for the sports marketing and consultancy services sector and the opportunities for growth to 2022. The result of this research and combining his 20 years' experience in sponsorship is this remarkable book.

Ardi Kolah has taken a rigorous approach to understanding how maximize the value of sponsorship across a sport, music, entertainment, culture, education, the environment, broadcast and new media making this one of the most definitive books on the subject.

Highly recommended for all rights holders, brand owners and agencies that need to squeeze more return on investment from their sponsorship activities on a global basis.

Michael Payne, former Marketing Director,
International Olympic Committee

Introduction

The nature of sponsorship

Sponsorship is a subset of marketing and over the last decade has become an increasingly sophisticated tool, capable of being measured in terms of inputs, outputs and outcomes.

It has also become a devalued term, capable of being applied to a charity fundraising event at one end of the scale and multimillion-pound Olympic Games global partner programme at the other.

So it is no surprise that so many who work in the marketing profession are fuzzy about what the nature of sponsorship really is – be it sports, arts, broadcast, environmental, educational or social.

When does advertising become sponsorship and sponsorship become advertising? In fact, should we care? After all, very few consumers stop to think what sponsors bring that genuinely adds value to the object of their desires – be that a player, league, team, event or cause. And yet millions of fans will happily wear apparel plastered with the logos of sponsors that support their favourite player or team without giving it a second thought.

The brand owner, of course, translates this as a commercial opportunity to build deeper customer relationships and a loyalty to its own brand that it could not have acquired through other means or levels of marketing investment.

But even if the above is a reasonable description of what is at play, in reality we have only just begun to scratch the surface of the potential of sponsorship to engage with desired markets and customer segments that creates a deeper relationship with them.

But sponsorship also faces its own PR challenges in times of economic uncertainty.

The fact is that the world is changing at such a pace that it is difficult for any chief marketing officer (CMO) to plan how he is going to drive sales and marketing of products and services over the next 12 months, let alone over the course of the next three years. This presents a challenge in the use of sponsorship, as, by definition, sponsorship tends to be a long-term brand communication, marketing and customer, client and supporter engagement platform and is not really fit for purpose as a 'one-hit wonder'. It is this feature more than most that sets sponsorship apart from advertising.

In addition, rapidly changing global markets and technology are impacting companies and organisations; creating vast oceans of data where marketers are not just swimming in the stuff but are drowning in it! The challenge of keeping afloat is made even more difficult when social media, proliferation of channels, mobile devices, shifting customer and client demographics and changes in data protection laws start to weigh down ever more heavily on those working within the sponsorship industry.

Investment in any form of marketing, including sponsorship, must deliver a return on investment to make it worthwhile in the first place. Some sponsorship managers dress this up as 'return on objectives' or 'return on commitment' from their own employees as a justification of sponsorship.

Frankly, with so many other options available to the CMO, unless a sponsorship or brand partnership programme improves performance in terms of achieving measurable brand marketing, communication and financial objectives, it is unlikely to win support from the board.

So far these introductory observations about sponsorship have come from a sponsorship-industry perspective. Where it starts to get really interesting is to see things through the lens of the customer, client, prospect, supporter and fan. After all, without them, sponsorship would not exist, would it?

Consumer expectations of brands and organisations are at the highest levels they have ever been and are getting steadily higher. To fulfil such demands, brand owners must balance innovation with consistency; quality with value; consumer choice with responsibility; and sustainability with growth. The ethics of not only what companies and organisations do but how they do it is now a matter of legitimate public interest. The standard by which companies and organisations are to be judged must now be about their deeds, not just their fine words, if they are to enjoy a continued high reputation among their desired market and customer segments.

While there are undoubtedly enormous challenges and complexities that need to be addressed in building a robust reputation, conversely, there are also unparalleled opportunities for those brand owners and organisations able to seize the momentum for change where their competitors may fall by the wayside because of an inability to change.

The difference in marketing performance and in particular sponsorship performance will be seeing things that others have missed and doing things that others have not considered. Such improvements in performance in sponsorship can be achieved by listening, collaborating and engaging on the terms of those we want to influence and do business with.

Spending on sponsorship

Sponsorship is a small but growing proportion of the overall marketing and communications industry spend globally (see Figure I.1).

According to the latest research by IEG, sponsorship spending globally is on the increase despite economic volatility across all global markets and is expected to top USD 57.5bn in 2015, an increase of USD 220m (4.1%) compared with 2014 (see Figure I.2).

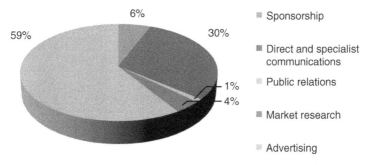

Figure I.1 Worldwide communications services expenditure, 2014
Source: Whitman Howard Equity Research (2014)

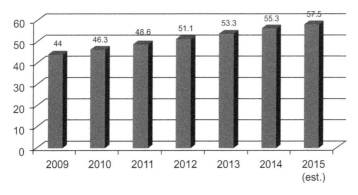

Figure I.2 Total global sponsorship spending (USD bn)
Source: IEG (2015)

North America is expected to perform slightly more strongly than many other global markets and register a 4.0% growth to USD 21.4bn in 2015 (see Figure I.3).

Spending on sponsorship has remained reasonably consistent compared with other marketing expenditure since 2011.

According to IEG, the world's largest sponsorship research organisation, the key factor in projecting healthy sponsorship growth is the unprecedented recognition by senior marketers that sponsorship can help build attention, support and loyalty for brands in an environment that is otherwise hostile to marketing communications (see Figure I.4).

Sponsorship has become elevated to the corporate strategic planning conversation and is more likely to be discussed in the context of integrated marketing programmes that can take advantage of the reach of traditional advertising as well as the emotional and experiential benefits earned through partnerships with sports, entertainment, causes and cultural properties. What used to be identified as 'sponsorship' with discrete budgets and contracts is now far more likely to be

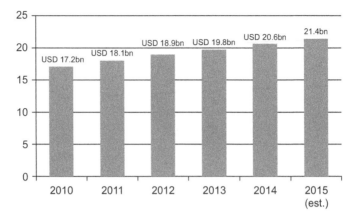

Figure I.3 Total North America sponsorship spending (USD bn)
Source: IEG (2015)

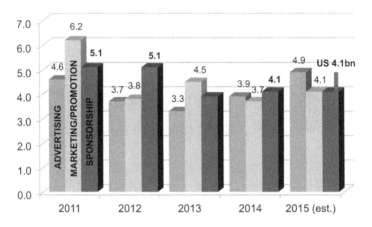

Figure I.4 Annual growth of advertising, marketing/promotion and sponsorship (USD bn)
Source: IEG (2015)

part of a multiplatform, cross-channel programme in which a partnership is just one element and where multiple players have a role in planning, execution and evaluation.

While this development means marketers generally have an appetite and resources for significant investment in B2B, B2C and B2B2C partnerships, they have also raised the stakes, increased the number of internal decision makers and placed many more demands on rights holders to provide value and a return on investment.

Excluding North America spending, sponsors from all other parts of the world spent USD 34.7bn in 2014, according to researchers at IEG. And that number is set to increase by 4% to USD 36.1bn in 2015 (see Table I.1).

Table 1.1 Global spending by region, 2012–15

	2011 spending	2012 spending	Percentage increase from 2011	2013 spending	2014 spending	Percentage increase from 2013	2015 spending (projected)	Percentage increase from 2014 (projected)
Europe	USD 13.5bn	USD 14.1bn	4.7%	USD 14.5bn	USD 14.8bn	2.1%	USD 15.3bn	3.3%
Asia Pacific	USD 11.2bn	USD 12bn	6.7%	USD 12.6bn	USD 13.3bn	5.6%	USD 14bn	5.2%
Central and South America	USD 3.7bn	USD 3.9bn	5.6%	USD 4.0bn	USD 4.2bn	5%	USD 4.3bn	4.8%
All other regions	USD 2.1bn	USD 2.2bn	5.1%	USD 2.3bn	USD 2.4bn	4.3%	USD 2.5bn	4.2%

Source: IEG (2015)

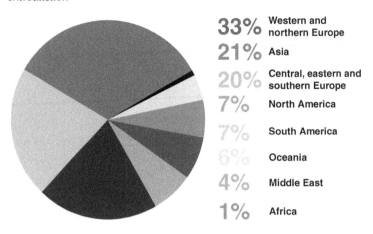

33%	Western and northern Europe
21%	Asia
20%	Central, eastern and southern Europe
7%	North America
7%	South America
6%	Oceania
4%	Middle East
1%	Africa

Figure I.5 Incremental new business from major one-off sports events, 2013–22

Source: Kolah (2013)

Current economic conditions in Europe are a drag on sponsorship spending compared with previous years, although in a recent study undertaken for the British government (see Figure I.5), my research showed that 33% of incremental new business opportunities for the UK sports marketing and consultancy sector in one-off major sports events was to be found in western and northern Europe (see Chapter 2).

While Russian, Indian and Chinese brand owners will contribute to a healthy 5% increase from the Asia Pacific region, growth in sponsorship expenditure is expected to slow to just 2.6% in Central and South America, where the 2014 World Cup and 2016 Olympic Games have secured major sponsorships from brand owners both inside and outside the region, but have failed to spur other local investments that were previously anticipated.

Sport dominates sponsorship globally as a property class

Sport is the dominant property class across the world and, as a result, sports sponsorship is the most reported, recorded and researched sponsorship in the world (see Figure I.6).

According to research by PwC (2013) (see Table I.2), global revenues from sports sponsorships will increase from USD 35bn in 2010 to USD 45.3bn in 2015, registering a 5.3% compound annual growth rate (CAGR).

Accounting for nearly 30% of the total sports market, sponsorship will be a key engine for growth in total revenues to 2015 and beyond, with an average growth rate globally of 5.3%. This is relatively equally shared across the regions, with Asia Pacific having the lowest growth rate of 4.4% and North America the

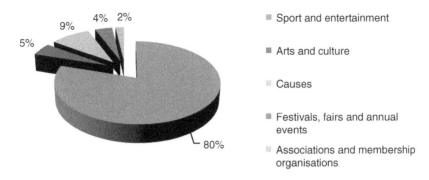

Figure I.6 Sports dominate property classes for sponsorship globally
Source: Kolah (2013)

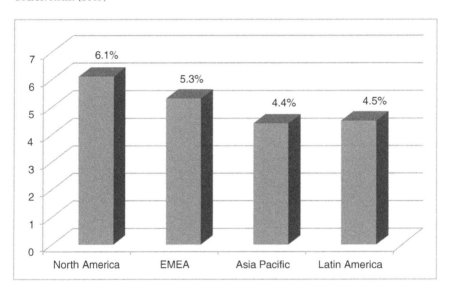

Figure I.7 Sponsorship revenue growth by region, 2011–15 (CAGR)
Source: Kolah (2013)

highest growth rate of 6.1% (see Figure I.7). If major events are excluded from the calculations, the underlying growth rate in the sports market is influenced by media rights as the fastest growing source of income for the sector.

Sponsorship is a key component of the total revenue mix in certain regions with 43.2% of all revenue in Asia coming from sponsorship.

Much of this book is, consequently but not exclusively, about sport, as it has become synonymous with sponsorship and vice versa.

According to industry statistics, the value of the global sports market is between USD 480 and 620bn, which is equivalent to 1% of global GDP. This is a

Table 1.2 Global sports sponsorship growth, 2006–15

Component	2006	2007	2008	2009	2010	2011	2012	2013	2014	2015	CAGR 2011–15
Sponsorships	26,749	29,273	32,494	31,467	34,972	35,132	39,173	40,236	45,559	45,281	5.3
% change	14.2	9.4	11.0	(3 .2)	11.1	0.5	11.5	2.7	13.2	(0.6)	

Source: PwC (2013)

broad definition of the industry and comprises sporting goods, infrastructure construction, licensed products and live sports events. A narrower definition of the market just focusing on the media activities associated with sport, such as sports sponsorship, suggests a total market worth around USD 62bn.

UK perspective on sponsorship

My research for the British government valued the UK sports marketing and consultancy sector at around £550 to £750m a year. On a blended growth rate of 7% over the next 9 years, it is predicted that the UK sector will be worth in excess of £1bn (see Table I.3).

Over the last decade, the expansion of the UK sector has been driven in part by the powerful way that sport can engage with desired market and customer segments on a global basis. The phenomenal success of the London Olympic Games in 2012 put a spotlight on the strength, global experience and talent of the UK sports marketing and consultancy sector in its ability to reach these global audiences.

At the same time, the proliferation of media devices has led to a fragmentation of audiences for mass media such as network television, radio and newspapers. As a result, this has created fresh challenges for media owners, rights holders and brand owners. What is now the best way to reach desired customer segments when the media landscape is so fragmented and mass media channels are in decline?

The heart of future success in engaging with desired audience and customer segments on a global basis is sports and entertainment content (see Figure I.8).

Today's generation of fans and consumers expect to be entertained and have more options available to them than they did even six months ago. They want to be involved in a deeper way and they also want to be kept informed 24/7.

Sport is still the most compelling piece of entertainment content that can deliver global audiences across all media – online as well as offline. A key factor is sport's ability to deliver emotion, excitement, engagement and loyalty in a way that many other entertainment options available to a younger generation struggle to deliver.

Sport is not formulaic or predictable, as the outcome is not always capable of being foreseen. This is what gives sport its high excitement and entertainment value par excellence. The UK sector is part of a sports and entertainment ecosystem, and sports and entertainment content sits at the heart of that ecosystem; fed by sports rights holders, sports bodies and government; brand owners and, of course, sports fans and consumers from around the world. And it is this ecosystem that fuels the future success of the UK sector of sports marketing agencies and advisers; marketing services providers and infrastructure, technology and logistics companies based in the UK.

Table 1.3 Compound annual growth rate of the UK sector, 2013–22

2013 Estimate (£m)	2014 Forecast (£m)	2015 Forecast (£m)	2016 Forecast (£m)	2017 Forecast (£m)	2018 Forecast (£m)	2019 Forecast (£m)	2020 Forecast (£m)	2021 Forecast (£m)	2022 Forecast (£m)	CAGR
550	589	630	674	721	771	825	883	945	1,011	7 %

Notes: Baseline is £550m for 2013

Blended annual growth rate of 7% used to smooth out odd/even years

Source: Kolah (2013)

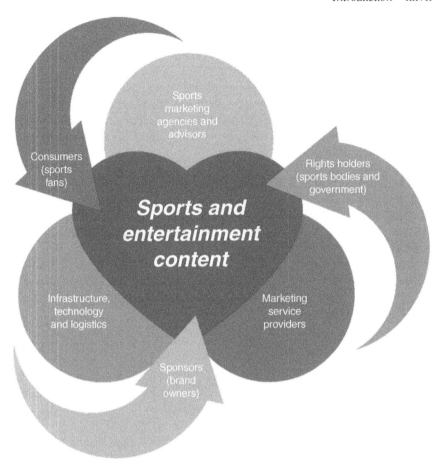

Figure I.8 Sponsorship ecosystem in the UK
Source: Kolah (2013)

About this book

Improving the Performance of Sponsorship is less of a 'how to' book about sponsorship than a way of challenging how we see things working over the next decade, where sponsorship in all its guises continues to go from strength to strength. A lot of what this book discusses is how brand owners involved in sponsorship need to rewire their thinking in order to make sponsorship the most effective component of the marketing mix.

In the right hands, sponsorship is capable of building strong and distinctive brands that can create better customer and client value and help drive sustainable profitable and demand-led growth. But the caveat is that there needs to be genuine collaboration between brand owners, rights holders, consumers and fans.

The digital revolution has forever changed the balance of power that exists between the individual consumer, rights holder and sponsor; making the prospect of collaboration a realistic and achievable objective for any business or organisation. Without this sponsorship would be a dead duck.

If CMOs are to understand and provide value to empowered consumers and fans, they will have to concentrate on getting to know those individuals as well as those market segments. They will also have to invest in new technologies and advanced analytics to get a better grasp of how individual customers, prospects and supporters think and behave.

And in order to cultivate meaningful relationships effectively, CMOs will have to connect with them in ways that are perceived as being valuable. This entails engaging with customers and clients throughout the entire customer life cycle; building online and offline communities of interest among consumers and fans and collaborating with the rest of the organisation or enterprise in this effort so it is part and parcel of how the company or organisation behaves rather than some isolated marketing activity.

In this context, sponsorship can galvanise a shift in the way any business or organisation chooses to engage with its customers, clients, supporters and fans as well as its own employees.

How to navigate this book

The core aim of the book is to assist rights holders and brand owners to reach a deeper appreciation of the strategic value of sponsorship as part of the marketing mix in helping to drive sustainable, profitable growth of these businesses and organisations.

The book can be read from start to finish or readers are welcome to dip into the most relevant chapters reflecting their interest and experience. Each chapter contains a short summary of the chapter contents at the beginning of the chapter in addition to the key points 'at a glance' as well as a series of questions at the end to ensure that all the learning points are captured.

The book has been divided into 10 chapters. Chapter 1 explains what is meant by 'sponsorship', the difference between success and failure, the different perspectives on sponsorship – both for the rights holder, brand owner and audience (external and internal) and the use of social media as a key channel for the activation of a sponsorship programme. Chapter 2 is based on original research carried out on behalf of the British government in mapping the capabilities of the sports sponsorship and consultancy services sector and the opportunities for growth in global markets across the next decade. Chapter 3 examines the fundamentals that sit behind a sponsorship selection such as measurable brand communication, sales and marketing or other objectives; the alignment of values; the strategic fit between the rights holder, the property, brand owner and the audiences that each wants to reach, as well as other strategic and practical considerations, such as the management of expectations on all sides that helps to make the selection process successful and build a long-term relationship between the parties.

Chapter 4 explores the most common mistakes made by even seasoned sponsorship practitioners in the selling process and why it is important to think 'outside in' rather than 'inside out'. Chapter 5 examines an area in which improvement is capable of being made particularly in integrating offline with online channels, including mobile. Chapter 6 is becoming a hot topic for brand owners, as there appear to be more cases coming to light in which unethical practices, such as drug-taking and doping, are becoming much more common. The chapter also examines the place of brands in the classroom and the continuing association of alcohol manufacturers with sport.

Chapter 7 looks at contractual issues surrounding a sponsorship deal as well as the duties and obligations placed on sponsors to ensure that they do not fall foul of legislation that governs the provision and acceptance of hospitality. Chapter 8 examines the two schools of thought that exist on the subject of ambush marketing and the appropriateness of taking this approach in the face of an official sponsor and rights holder. In Chapter 9, we demonstrate how corporate social responsibility (CSR) has risen to the top of the sponsorship agenda for many brand owners particularly involved with major sports events and the chapter examines the business case for giving CSR a sporting chance.

Finally, Chapter 10 looks at what the best practice is for measuring and evaluating inputs, outputs and outcomes from sponsorship activity as well as how to measure the return from CSR.

1   Rewiring our thinking on sponsorship

In this chapter

- The case against sponsorship
- 'Think local, act local'
- Corporate storytelling
- The role of big data in 2015 and beyond

Introduction

The subject of sponsorship is now reported more extensively in the business pages than perhaps it was a decade ago, largely as a result of the eye-catching multimillion deals that happen with regular occurrence around the world. Of course, the Olympic Games, the English Premier League and the FIFA World Cup tend to grab their fair share of global media coverage and news headlines when a sponsor is signed. But, as we shall discuss in Chapter 2, there are now so many different sponsorship properties, options and formats that the sponsorship industry has never been busier, despite the current uncertainty of the global economy as it staggers between stagnation, inflation and deflation in 2015 and beyond.

It is fair to say sponsorship has tended to weather these cyclical storms particularly well compared with other types of marketing expenditure such as advertising and sales promotion, which tend to be cost-cutting casualties when companies have to tighten their belts.

Sponsorship has become much more cost-effective, largely as a result of innovation within the industry that allows a prospective sponsor to get closer to its desired audiences, customers, clients, supporters, partners, fans and employees without having to empty its bank account in the process.

It also reflects a growing confidence in the use of sponsorship as a sales and marketing tool as well as the relatively long-term nature of a sponsorship agreement compared with, say, an eight-week advertising burst. And, as will be discussed in detail in Chapter 10, measurement and evaluation of sponsorship has become a science in its own right.

Talk to any switched-on brand owners in Europe, the USA, the Far East or Australasia and they will have a sponsorship programme that is a key platform for engaging with desired audience and customer segments and integrates with other online and offline channels in order to deliver higher returns for their marketing investment.

Some of those brand managers appear in this book demonstrating current best practice and it is clear from reading the numerous case studies that these market-ers are now much better-equipped to improve the performance of sponsorship in ways that were unachievable in the past. In the digital era, the ability to engage with desired audience and customer segments in a precise way is absolutely critical.

The narrative about any sponsorship relationship now needs to be capable of being sustained under its own momentum; where the relationship between the parties must be transparent and natural rather than contrived. The sponsorship pro-gramme needs to be much more than just a badging exercise for the benefit of the brand owner and should also reflect a genuine partnership with the rights holder.

Ethics in sponsorship has never been more important and is often the subject of intense media scrutiny. What this means in practice is that the bad behaviour of individual athletes, stars, teams and governing bodies strikes at the heart of the reputation of the sponsorship ecosystem.

Given that sport accounts for over 80% of all sponsorship globally, the issue of drug abuse, cheating, match fixing and voting irregularities is never far from the surface, as evidenced by a series of recent scandals that have engulfed the Inter-national Olympic Committee and FIFA and almost destroyed the International Cycling Union in the wake of the Lance Armstrong doping scandal.

Sponsors – quite rightly – expect rights holders, athletes and governing bodies to act in accordance with the highest ethical and professional standards required of them and, of course, the same applies to the sponsors themselves. For example, in November 2014, Championship League side Wigan Athletic appointed as its new manager Malky Mackay, who was also being investigated by the FA for alleg-edly sending racist, sexist, homophobic and anti-Semitic messages during his time as manager of Cardiff City FC, his former club.

In a statement issued to the media on his appointment, shirt sponsor Premier Range said the appointment of Malky Mackay put it in a position that it found untenable:

> Mr Mackay is currently under investigation by the FA for sending text mes-sages that are at odds with the general ethos here at Premier Range – and, it would seem, Cardiff and QPR feel the same as us. The texts Mr Mackay has admitted to sending are wholly unacceptable – and the thoughts expressed within them are a shocking reminder of a past we thought football had left behind. A team that would employ a man who expresses views such these is not the kind of team Premier Range wish to deal with.

Increasingly, there is an expectation that sponsors of major events such as the Olympic Games should also speak out should they see something that is in con-flict with their own values in the same way as Premier Range did.

Staying silent or simply ducking an issue is not the answer, as Coca-Cola found out to its cost when it stayed silent over the issue of draconian laws affecting the rights of the homosexual community that were passed ahead of the Sochi 2014 Winter Olympic Games, at which it was one of the main sponsors. The lesson learned is plain enough: a sponsor should be prepared to stand up and confront discrimination and bigotry, however uncomfortable this may be from a media relations perspective, because it is what customers and even its own employees would *expect* it to do.

Expectations in terms of the performance of sponsorship have also dramatically changed over the last decade; largely as a result of behavioural economics and 'big data', which means that results from major sponsorship campaigns can be tracked and measured with a higher degree of accuracy. 'Advertising value equivalencies', or AVEs, belong in a different era and focus groups are fast heading in the same direction.

Today, sponsors and rights holders make decisions based on real-time data and sponsorship programmes need to be capable of changing direction and 'following the audience' in terms of interests and motivations rather than expecting it to be the other way around.

Sponsorship is much less about being in 'transmit mode' and much more about deepening the level of engagement that it can achieve with desired audience, customer segments, supporters and fans – even on a one-to-one basis. This is best illustrated by the changes that have occurred in the media consumption habits of millennials.

In the UK, 24-year-old fashion and beauty vlogger Zoella (real name Zoe Elizabeth Sugg) now speaks for a new generation of TV viewers. The mainstay of Zoella's channel on YouTube is about friendship, body image, boys and whether to go to university or not, sprinkled between fashion and beauty tips that include hairstyles and 'shopping haul' trips.

Zoella earns a reported £300,000 a year endorsing products as well as having her own branded merchandise in Superdrug. She is attractive to what is known as the 'lost generation' – audiences in their teens and twenties who neither consume conventional media nor watch much TV.

Since 2010 the amount of TV watched by 16–34-year-olds has fallen by 15%, so it is no surprise that brand owners of online games, clothing and beverages are among those seeking to tap into this pop culture via YouTube. Pepsi has put most of its sponsorship activation on digital media such as Facebook and YouTube, rather than relying on more traditional media channels and TV advertising. What is now emerging is a much more sophisticated approach as to how to activate a sponsorship programme, as will be discussed in detail in Chapter 5.

The case against sponsorship

There are a large number of cynics in the business world who believe that sponsorship is nothing more than advertising masquerading under a different label. And they remain unconvinced that the sums involved are justified by returns that are, at best, difficult to measure and evaluate. Well, that may be a narrow or inaccurate view, but it is widely shared and it would be wrong to reject the substance of the charge against sponsorship without first attempting to under-stand the reasons that lie behind this.

With English Premier League football clubs such as Manchester United FC able to draw significant sponsorship fees from the pockets of major global companies, it would be easy to get carried away with the excitement of trying to adorn the team's strip with a shiny new brand logo. But this is exactly what happened in 2014 – the club's commercial pull was so strong that even senior executives got caught up in the excitement of the chase to be associated with it. Sadly, this resulted in a dire consequence for Joel Ewanick, the global head of marketing for General Motors, who found himself out of a job just 48 hours after he had agreed a £175 million shirt sponsorship deal with the club. Presumably Joel Ewanick thought he was acting within his express, usual and implied authority to close such a deal with Manchester United FC, but clearly the board of GM thought otherwise.

The new board of directors at Barclays is also starting to take a different view of its English Premier League investment in sharp contrast to those who have been in charge of driving it forward so successfully since 2001. Senior executives at the bank have not hidden their view from the Football Association that they believe the £40m a year sponsorship has 'zero value' in the UK and have effectively served notice that the bank will not renew the current deal after it expires at the end of 2015–16 Season. The £120m package was 50% higher than the previous deal, which cost £82m at that time, and Barclays is clearly concerned that the battle between BT and BSkyB for broadcast rights is driving up costs all round and this will have a knock-on effect on the price of Premier League sponsorship when it comes to renewal.

It would be easy to dismiss both these examples as a case of attempting to cut costs from marketing budget, but it could also be symptomatic that the rights holder has developed insufficient evidence to demonstrate a significant return on investment for the sponsor. In the case of the English Premier League, the rights holder could have sown the seeds of its own destruction a long time ago, according to British sports journalist and business commentator, Mihir Bose:

> The Premier League would do well to remind itself that the moment of triumph is also the moment of greatest danger, as the Romans were forced to learn.
>
> The tale goes of how a great Roman General returning to Rome having conquered some exotic foreign land was always acclaimed by the crowd. But there was also a man riding next to him in the chariot who warned him that his moment of triumph was also a moment of peril. He should be careful that amid the celebrations he takes steps to ensure the next moment doesn't mark his doom.
>
> Doom for the Premier League has often been predicted and in the last 20 years it has shown a remarkable capacity to prove the soothsayers wrong and buck even the worst recession since the 1930s.
>
> But success shouldn't make it ignore the problems of ownership and finance that clubs face, problems for which there are no easy solutions.

However, these are problems for which solutions must be found. The Premier League has grown because it has seized opportunities and lacking any fixed ideology it has always been flexible enough to move swiftly. However, its success means it now needs to think about a game plan because its success has changed the game.

The old pre-Premier League system of English football, which didn't allow whatever wealth there was then in the game to trickle down and had a sort of democracy of sorts, has gone. But nothing has replaced it. The Premier League has shown itself to be a master tactician. Now it needs to develop a strategic plan to deal with the success it has created. If it fails to develop one on issues such as ownership, then like the Roman General, it may find its moment of triumph carries the seed of its own doom.

It should be remembered that the Premier League sponsorship deal with Barclays was renewed for three seasons from 2013, just days after the bank was fined $453m by US and British authorities for providing false data to help manipulate Libor, the London interbank rate and a key global interest rate. A spokesperson at Barclays was quick to explain that the new CEO Anthony Jenkins feels it is time for the bank to 'shut up for five years and get on with our job' and the introspective review the bank has carried out in recent months has led to the exposure of further reckless behaviour among its traders and the bank faces further multimillion fines from the Financial Conduct Authority as it tries to clear up the mess.

Against such a background, the directors must feel that promoting a tarnished brand on a global basis is probably not the best way to spend what could be £200m as the sponsor of the English Premier League after the current deal expires.

If we dig a little more deeply, clearly Anthony Jenkins is putting his personal stamp on how he wants the bank to start to regard itself, as it may have, to use a well-known expression, 'become too big for its own boots'.

So pulling the plug on 'glamour projects' and focusing instead on much higher levels of technology for customers, far fewer staff and fewer branches marks a new chapter for the bank in trying to rebuild its business, which may also see the loss of 40,000 jobs globally over the next six years. According to brand guru Martin Lindstrom, the views of GM and Barclays come as no surprise, as he remains convinced that most sponsorship does not work, as it often lacks context:

> The vast majority of sponsorship doesn't work because it's aimed at the conscious part of the brain, which neuroscience tells us accounts for no more than 15% of our cognitive capacity. We are bombarded with thousands of direct marketing messages a day, very few of which we are able to take in, let alone process into changing buying behaviour.
>
> The communications industry spends its time measuring awareness and hoping that some value transfer takes place, something that we have never been able to prove. Now we can, and I'm convinced that we'll see the sponsorship model change dramatically as a result.

Marketing people must realise it's not about plastering your logo everywhere, it's about context and about embedding your message within the narrative of the story being told, whether that is a football match or a James Bond movie. Our research into this is extensive and it tells us that when a brand appears in a story at the wrong moment, we don't just ignore it, we delete it from our mind, and such is the irritation of being interrupted.

Rights holders must prove they are about more than just awareness, which isn't so valuable as it was 20 years ago when the sponsorship model was built that still applies today. There are so many poor marketing people out there who must now ask themselves, do we have an emotional strategy? What kind of indirect signals do we want to send? Sponsorship works when we aren't really aware of the signals being sent: the messages get through because our guard is down.

His view is supported by a new piece of research by Sponsorship Intelligence and Zenith Optimedia released in November 2014 which showed the real value of sports sponsorship lies in the combination of direct impact coupled with subtler subliminal benefits from associating with the audience's passions and the ability of consumers to differentiate between brands at point of purchase with sports-themed promotions.

'Think local, act local'

Of course, there was a time when any marketer faced with bringing a major brand into an emerging market would have applied the premise of 'think global, act local', but because digital has made it possible to identify accurately the needs, desires and behaviours of individuals in local markets, 'think global, act local' now looks distinctly out of date.

In the age of interactivity and social media, the ability to touch people's hearts and minds with topical, relevant content is an essential job of sponsorship; hence 'think local, act local' is now much more meaningful.

Success depends on having the right local partners in order to achieve this – which is why buying and selling sponsorship, as we shall discuss in Chapters 3 and 4, are critically important in the sponsorship process. One size does not fit all and sponsorship programmes must take account of local needs and requirements. The brand owner, working in collaboration with local sponsors, must customise the sponsorship programme for the local market. In many instances, this may require hiring local agencies that can activate the sponsorship programme with a deeper insight and knowledge of local customs and behaviours of audiences and customer segments.

Corporate storytelling

Business does not have to be boring, does it? Sponsorship of the Olympic Games, for example, helps to sprinkle the 'magic dust' of the Games on everyday household items and bring a new dimension to corporate story telling.

P&G is a good example of how a global brand can communicate its corporate purpose through the use of storytelling and this is where those with a background in public relations (PR) can really make a difference, where advertising, social media and media relations are used as the 'tent poles' for the sponsorship campaign. The challenge P&G faced as an Olympic partner on a global basis was to make the human-side stories of the mums behind the athletes taking part in the London 2012 Olympic Games interesting enough to get consumers involved – measured by 'likes', tweets and social sharing.

One insight in taking such an approach was that 'reality is more interesting than fiction' – but the reality had to be newsworthy. So P&G took its internal team to spend time in the newsroom of USA Today and then applied what it had learned in order to develop its own news-making and editorial skills. According to Marc Pritchard, P&G's global brand-building officer: 'PR agencies should start to see themselves as documentary film-makers in order to bring the corporate narrative alive.' Many firms now have former news reporters on their team but sometimes fail to utilise this skill set to maximum advantage.

It is a demanding discipline: find the story, make the story and just like the newsroom be 'always on' and ready for the next one, just like the P&G team that saw the oil spill at the Daytona racetrack being cleaned up with Tide and made a story from it. Clearly being 'always on' militates against risks as well as creating opportunities for transmitting the corporate narrative in new and different ways.

The role of big data in 2015 and beyond

Technology is intertwined in nearly every aspect of business today, with information technology fast becoming a primary driver of market differentiation, business growth, and profitability. It is this mindset that is helping to drive innovative thinking in sponsorship. According to recent research by IBM, 'big data' in 2015 and beyond will be about:

- enterprise data (such as a deeper understanding of customer transactions)
- voice over IP (VoIP) developments
- social media extensions
- sensors and monitors in everyday objects.

The result is that sponsors and rights holders must now start to rethink their digital strategies in order to take advantage of the opportunities that 'big data' can deliver. Mobile technologies, social networks and context-based services have all contributed to increasing the number of digital connections with consumers in order to create more detailed views of consumers, consumer attributes and transactions. Individually, these connections may represent new types of user experience, even new sets of sales and marketing channels – where sponsorship is the platform for helping to reach these audiences and customer segments.

However, there is much more that can be done, according to global IT management consultants Accenture, as Marty Cole, Group Chief Executive (Technology), explains:

> It's time for businesses to return their attention to their relationships with consumers. Business success has always been built on relationships and on the relevance of products and services to buyers' needs. Just a few generations ago, consumers were often friends – and certainly neighbors – of the local grocer, pharmacist, and everyone else who provided the things consumers needed. But that model changed with large-scale industrialization and with the introduction of IT. Handcraftsmanship was replaced by mass production. Advice delivered over the counter was replaced by global call centers. A human face making a sale was often replaced by a Web page. That might imply that a growing distance between companies and consumers is inevitable – and over the last few decades, many consumers might agree that they have been treated with greater indifference and far less personal attention.
>
> Yet now, the opposite is true: technology is finally at a point where buyers can be treated like individuals again. Consumers are more than faceless digital transactions, more than a cookie file, transaction history or a demographic profile; they're real people with real differences.
>
> Companies now have rich channels through which to communicate with consumers in a much more personal way. Far-sighted organizations are seeing a golden opportunity to use mobile communications channels, social media, and context-based services to create truly personal relationships with consumers – but digital relationships this time – and to leverage those relationships to drive revenue growth.

Specifically, global brand owners like P&G, Unilever and Samsung are customising the experience for every interaction they have with their consumers regardless of the channel that they wish to use. This so-called 'mass personalisation' includes not only the interactions that companies have with consumers but the interactions that consumers have with each other. The potential payoff is two-pronged: a relationship with consumers that is unique for the brand owner and brand differentiation in a crowded market.

Brand owners now have new ways to learn about consumers based on increasingly digital interactions, whether through email, social media, web pages, online chat, mobile apps or tweets. And by maintaining integrated communications across physical and virtual channels, the performance of sponsorship can be improved, as brand owners are better able to capture, measure, analyse and exploit social interactions with audiences, customers, partners and employees in new and exciting ways.

Chapter 1 at a glance

1. The money that some deals now command has turned sponsorship into a global news story.

2. Unlike other forms of marketing, sponsorship can weather cyclical storms within the global economy better than advertising and sales promotion when it comes to brand owners having to tighten their belts.
3. Sponsors are increasingly expected to enter into difficult discussions over ethics and values particularly when these appear to be at variance with their own.
4. Sponsorship is much less about brand image and awareness but rather should be used to create a deeper level of audience engagement.
5. A global brand should consider employing the skills of a storyteller in order to get its brand messages across – and harness the power of social media in doing so.
6. Sponsors and rights holders need to rewire their thinking about sponsorship strategy around 'big data' and maximise the use of mobile technologies, social networks and context-based services in order to improve the performance of sponsorship.

Questions for discussion

1. How can sponsorship help rights holders and brand owners to listen better?
2. Under what circumstances would sponsorship not be appropriate for a brand owner?
3. Does sponsorship always need to have a 'higher purpose'?
4. What is the starting point for considering how best to embed a sponsorship programme within the sales and marketing cycle?
5. How important is technology in the activation of a sponsorship programme and what considerations need to be made in its use before it is deployed?
6. Why are global brand owners now more confident in using sponsorship than they were only a few years' earlier? What has changed?

Further reading

Berger, J (2013), *Contagious*, Simon & Schuster
Bose, M (2012), *Game Changer – How the English Premier League came to dominate the world*, Marshall Cavendish
Bose, M (2011), *The Spirit of the Game – How Sport Made the Modern World*, Constable
Buckingham, M (1999), *First, Break all the Rules*, Pocket Books
Lovell, N (2014), *The Curve – Turning Followers into Superfans*, Penguin
Meerman Scott, D (2013), *The New Rules of Marketing & PR*, Wiley
Patterson, K, Grenny, J, McMillan, R and Switzler, A (2012), *Crucial Conversations*, McGraw-Hill
Pink, D (2013), *To Sell is Human*, Canongate
Smith, S and Milligan, A (2011), *BOLD – How to be brave in business and win*, Kogan Page
Young, L (2013), *Thought Leadership*, Kogan Page

2 The business of sponsorship

In this chapter

- The time before modern sponsorship existed
- Types of sponsorship property
- UK sports sponsorship ecosystem
- How sponsorship powered the London 2012 Olympic Games
- Global sponsorship opportunities for UK sector in sports and entertainment

Introduction

Today the business of sponsorship has changed from display and exposure of brand messages to something much more interesting and engaging. It is about having great ideas that produce great content!

Sponsorship should now be about content that ultimately attracts audiences, consumers, customers, clients, supporters and fans and can help change perceptions as well as influence purchasing behaviour. Ask yourself the following question: what is more powerful – someone seeing a piece of traditional advertising and telling the person next to them they love it or someone experiencing a continuous and real-time brand story and sharing this with 1,000 Twitter followers who 'love this'?

That is why, when sponsorship is executed with clear, measurable objectives and, with imagination, it can be the most powerful marketing tool in the world today.

The research I carried out in 2013 for the UK government clearly identified global sports and entertainment content at the heart of a sponsorship ecosystem that is fed by rights holders, brand owners and of course consumers, supporters and fans. The continued migration to digital channels requires brand owners to change not just the channels they use but to rewire fundamentally the way they take their goods and services to market.

They need to shift their thinking from one-off marketing campaigns to continuous and real-time stories that contain multiple narratives. And sponsorship gives them the power to achieve this shift in a way that few marketing and communications activities can achieve on their own.

The online dimension to sponsorship is becoming increasingly important in the way that both rights holders and brand owners engage with audiences, fans and customers. For example, 87% of people in the UK spend an average of 15 hours a week online. In 2013 an estimated 2 trillion gigabytes of information were created or replicated online – the equivalent of 250bn HD film. This is what brand owners have to compare with to get what is best described as 'share of engagement' with desired customer segments. Some brand owners are already competing in this space with spectacular results.

In October 2012 and wearing little more than a modified astronaut's space suit to stop him turning into a block of ice with atmospheric temperatures below –70°C, Felix Baumgartner set a new world record for the highest skydive. The 43-year-old Austrian daredevil jumped out of a 770ft helium balloon at about 39km (128,000ft) above New Mexico at the edge of space, descending more quickly than the speed of sound, reaching a maximum velocity of 833.9mph (1,342kph). It took just under ten minutes for him to descend, with the last few thousand feet being negotiated by parachute for a perfect textbook landing. Not surprisingly, the attempt to be the world's first 'supersonic man' was sponsored by high-energy drink Red Bull.

In sponsoring this audacious 'stunt' Red Bull tore up the marketing handbook and rewrote it as a series of tweets, status updates, video clips, memes and amazing digital experiences without the need for a broadcaster on cable or satellite TV. It was a shrewd move by Red Bull as Felix Baumgartner's stunt prompted over 8 million simultaneous live streams of the event on YouTube, which broadcast the mission with a time delay of around 20 seconds.

But it does not always go according to plan.

In 2012, Guido Gehrmann, the personal pilot of Red Bull owner Dieter Mate-schitz, tragically died after crashing in his Bede BD-5 micro-jet while returning from an air acrobatics and motor sports day sponsored by Red Bull at Schlitters in the Tyrol, western Austria. Deaths of similar daredevils connected with Red Bull have led to strong criticism of the company pursuing a marketing strategy that is in a sense without parallel because no other brand owner dares to elevate danger as a part of its core brand communication programme. But perhaps this is why Red Bull spends nearly £1bn a year on marketing and supports over 500 athletes, who range from stuntmen to Sebastian Vettel, Red Bull's F1 Champion. And it would be naïve to think these sportsmen and stuntmen underestimate the personal risks they are taking every time they indulge in such activities.

As I said at the beginning of the book, the difference in marketing performance and sponsorship performance in particular will be seeing things that others have missed and doing things that others have not considered doing.

Red Bull understands, perhaps better than many brand owners, the power of content in pulling audiences towards its brand. It has pursued a single-minded strategy of extreme sports sponsorship that has given it an abundance of one thing – great sports and entertainment content. And with this content it tells the story of Red Bull every day, and we are all part of it. Red Bull's Facebook page has more fans than Australia has people, so it is safe to say that there are a lot of people who are part of its story. The focus is to help extraordinary people to reach their extraordinary goals and many of these are connected to low-risk pursuits, while others are connected to higher risk pursuits, such as free-falling from the edge of space. Whatever our view of the brand, it is clear Red Bull has connected with a global audience that identifies with this spirit of adventure. As brands compete in this digital world, the business of sponsorship has also changed. The idea that 'content is king' is as strong as it ever was, with the addition that 'community is queen'!

This relationship between the brand narrative (content) and audience (community) is not the type of one-sided relationship we used to associate with traditional marketing and sponsorship of the past. It is much more mutual and collaborative; creating a virtuous circle where the community shares brand content, exposing it to more people as a result, with the consequence that more people opt in to receive the brand story through likes, shares and follows.

From a commercial perspective, this gives sponsorship the potential edge over other types of marketing activity. This continuous, real-time story starts to take shape as a joint product of the brand and the audience. A good example of this can be found in the world of advertising, although the lessons learned can be easily replicated within the context of sponsorship. Back in 1987 Unilever brand Magnum was the first handheld ice cream to be marketed as a premium adult offering in the UK. Today, Magnum is one of the world's leading ice cream brands, annually selling over 1bn units worldwide. The challenge facing the brand in 2010 was delivering market share growth in a competitive retail environment.

Retail own labels had stepped up their promotional strategies, focusing on the price point as a key differentiator and attempting to steal market share from Magnum and its variants. Magnum had to convince its customers that it was a premium quality product worth paying the extra for and 'Magnum Gold' was crucial in providing a key brand differentiation against own-label variants. Unilever hoped that the novelty of the first golden ice cream would generate news and 'talkability' to drive excitement and frequency in the ice cream category that until that point had been highly price-conscious.

Inspired by the creative idea of an 'Ocean's 11'-style heist with Benicio Del Toro, 'Magnum Gold' was launched like a blockbuster film – a first for an ice cream category.

The strategy was to drive high awareness and 'talkability' with a heavy burst of activity at the start of the ice cream season. High-traffic spots and films were chosen for a short-burst, high-frequency approach to drive awareness quickly on TV. The UK spots were tailored to drive viewers to the website by adding the pay-off 'story continues?' at the end of the advertisement. Out-of-home (OOH) poster advertising was used to drive 'fame' like a film launch and Magnum booked high-impact outdoor sites during the busy Easter weekend with the focus on London, with additional sites in key cities across the UK.

In London, Magnum booked the IMAX cinema site for two weeks. Other channels such as digital and PR were also used. The OOH poster advertising strategy delivered a huge sales spike, creating a 28% increase in sales of 'Magnum

Gold' as well as driving higher sales of profitable impulse products that resulted in £2m in additional turnover to the category and driving up Magnum 14 places in the Grocer Top 100 UK brands. A Tesco buyer described the campaign as the 'best ice cream activation for years'. The cumulative effect is that Magnum now has 'licence' to talk about fashion, film, design, art and gaming over a 12-month period. This has been achieved through the lens of the brand centred on pleasure, which positions the brand as the authority on 'pleasure+', such as 'pleasure + film', 'pleasure + fashion', 'pleasure + design,' 'pleasure + art' and 'pleasure + gaming'. In this way, Magnum can be relevant to its audiences across several content categories.

Perhaps Unilever should have considered product placement in *Ocean's 11*!

The business of sponsorship is now about doing three things extremely well:

- creating a powerful and compelling narrative that brings the world of the property and the world of the brand together
- moving away from one-off campaigns to the creation of continuous and real-time narratives
- weaving together various strands of that real-time story and experience using the brand essence as the backdrop to that story in a meaningful way.

The time before modern sponsorship existed

Sponsorship as we know it has not been around that long, say 50 years, compared with advertising, which been around in excess of 250 years. And yet sponsorship growth in recent years has consistently outstripped that of advertising, as discussed in the introduction to this book. There are various historical precedents that suggest something of the origins of sponsorship. In ancient Greece, wealthy individuals supported athletic and arts festivals to enhance their social status and during the golden age of the Roman aristocracy, gladiators could be supported or owned for the same purpose.

Many believe the origins of sponsorship can be traced back to the Roman statesman Gaius Maecenas, who lived in Rome was born around 70 BC and was able to support some of the most renowned poets with his enormous fortune.

Six stages of sponsorship evolution over the last 50 years

- 1960s – 'Surreptitious advertising' became popular at sports stadiums as fans were subjected to advertising messages around them.
- 1970s – Sport was slowly incorporated into advertising and promotional activities mainly in the form of perimeter or shirt advertising as part of the wider sponsorship deal.
- 1980s – This marked the start of the professionalisation of sponsorship. Brand owners began to plan and manage their commitments systematically, again typically within sports, and began to start to integrate sponsorship as part of the marketing mix.

- 1990s – This started to open up new possibilities for sponsorship outside sport, such as arts, cultural, social, education and environmental sponsorships. These areas were gaining in importance for audiences, and brand owners quickly started to recognise that. At first, the relationships with these property classes were on the basis of philanthropy and patronage rather than on a commercial basis but this was now starting to change, as those involved with arts, cultural, social, education and environmental activities started to take a much more commercial approach in their dealings with brand owners and started to speak their language of requiring a return on investment. At the same time, there was the growth in sponsorship across all media, including the Internet.
- 2000s – Brand owners started to explore creative ways of integrating sponsorship as part of the marketing mix.
- Today – Brand owners are abandoning one-off-type sponsorship in favour of something more enduring. They are also focused on harnessing social marketing to help drive interest and increasingly must rely on content co-creation with rights holders and fans and be seen to be adding value to the sponsored event/experience. Sponsorship today is much more about creating a powerful narrative in real time, using the brand essence as the backdrop to that story in a meaningful way.

Types of sponsorship property

Sports sponsorship

This is the world's oldest form of sponsorship and as a result it is the most established property class, attracting the largest amount of significant investment from brand owners and accounting for around 80% of all sponsorship globally. And given the popularity of football around the world, it is no surprise that this attracts the highest level of interest from sponsors (see Figure 2.1).

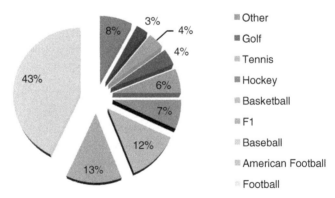

Figure 2.1 Football continues to dominate as the top global sports content
Source: Kolah (2013)

There are several reasons why sports sponsorship dominates the global sponsorship industry:

- In the words of former South Africa President Nelson Mandela, 'sport unites people in a way that politics never can' and it remains one of the most potent ways to engage with a global audience that transcends all ages, all sexes, races, religions, colours, creeds, nationalities, ethnicities and wealth.
- Sport arouses passion in the largest number of people around the world and the global sport that arouses the strongest passion is football – a sport in which the UK is the global leader.
- Sport is highly attractive, as it is a metaphor for teamwork, endurance, personal endeavour, fair play, competitive spirit, excitement, fun, drama and, of course, ultimately winning and being successful as a 'champion' player or team.
- Sport is not formulaic or predictable as the outcome is not always capable of being foreseen. This is what gives sport its high excitement and entertainment value par excellence.
- While the hype over the power of 'big data' has only just started to seep into the oak-panelled boardrooms and onto the pages of the corporate executive agenda, sports rights holders have been at the forefront of exploiting data to gain a competitive advantage for many years. Sport has a lot to teach business and its sponsors.
- Sport is a form of entertainment whose stars are household names and as famous as Hollywood actors.
- Sport can convey the spirit of the game to a brand owner, its products and services in a way that no other sponsorship property class can achieve in the same way.
- A 'live' sport still draws in massive TV audiences, as it is one of the few 'appointments to see' in a world where the vast majority of broadcast media is consumed on a time-shift basis.
- Sport teams, individuals, events and leagues appeal to the widest possible demographic and psychographic of customers and fans irrespective of sex, race, ethnicity, culture or language.
- Sport can connect on a local, regional, national, international and global level without compromising the inherent nature of its ability to hold the interest of the audience in an entertaining way.
- Consumers and fans of sport are more likely to want to receive messages from sponsors than non-sponsors and are more likely to have a higher propensity to purchase products and services compared with non-sports fans.
- Sports sponsorship is one of the most effective global brand marketing, communication and sales platforms. Global brand owners are increasingly looking to capture new customers in emerging markets such as India, China and Russia as a result of commoditisation and oversupply in their own domestic markets, which have become saturated with goods and services. With

this in mind, sports sponsorship offers a unique passion and entertainment platform for brand owners to build deeper bonds with customer segments in less saturated markets.

- The brand owners who spend the most on sports sponsorship are automotive manufacturers, telecoms companies, branded apparel companies, banks, beer companies, airlines, consumer electronics manufacturers, soft drinks companies, gambling companies and insurance companies.

Personality endorsement and sponsorship

Celebrity endorsement of a brand by a world-recognised personality from sports and entertainment can transcend cultural, linguistic and geographical barriers. Such a tactic is a growing part of the sponsorship strategy of many brand owners seeking a winning connection with a celebrity who has pulling power.

In the world of sports apparel, Nike was built on the shoulders of some of the world's most famous sportsmen and women, because they endorsed its products. And around the world, at least one in five advertisements carries the face, voice or testimony of a recognised personality, which is testament to the power of celebrity. However, there are downsides in harnessing the power of celebrity where a rock star, athlete or film star is concerned.

Although it is obvious, it is worth repeating that sponsors can never control the behaviour of the talent in their private lives and, of course, the media makes no distinction between their public or private personas.

As will be discussed in Chapter 6, this can lead to catastrophic results both for the celebrity as well as the sponsor.

Arts, culture and entertainment sponsorship

Arts, culture and entertainment (see Table 2.1) have become more important in recent years, accounting for around 5% of all sponsorship globally. This trend was recognised by brand owners who use arts, culture and entertainment for sponsorship in order to differentiate themselves within their market segment, as well as avoid sponsorship clutter with certain property types, such as sport (see Figure 2.2). Typically rights fees are lower in this property type compared with sport. According to IEG Research, North America-based companies will spend USD 2.13bn to sponsor music venues, festivals and tours in 2015, a 3.8% increase from 2014. In addition, North American sponsors will spend USD 938m on arts and culture, up 1.6% from 2014.

An increase in interest in this property class is due to a number of factors including:

- Brand owners are keen to be seen to be giving something back to the community particularly at a time when governments have reduced resources available to invest in arts and culture.
- Brand owners are using music to support customer loyalty programmes and a sign of cultural expertise is seen as a sign of quality.

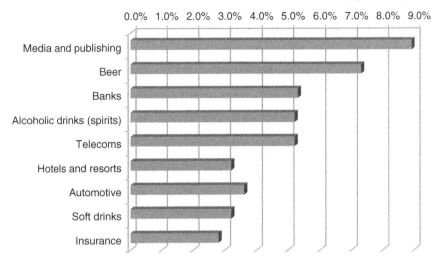

Figure 2.2 Most prevalent business sectors that sponsor arts and culture in North America
Source: IEG (2013)

Table 2.1 Classification of typical arts and culture sponsorship areas

Arts and culture sponsorship category	Appearance
Visual arts	Painting, sculpture, graphic design, architecture, photography
Performing arts	Opera, musicals, cabaret, ballet, theatre
Music	Rock/pop, folk, country, rap, blues, MOBO, classical
Literature	Books, magazines
Media	Film, video, advertiser-funded programming, broadcast, online content
Culture care	Monuments preservation, historic sites

Broadcast sponsorship

Broadcast sponsorship is typically the sponsorship of a TV or radio broadcast on a commercial channel or the channel itself. In the case of the broadcast sponsorship of an event, the sponsor will enter into a separate arrangement with the broadcaster and may therefore be different from the event sponsor. The event organiser may either license the right to broadcast the event to a production company, which will then sublicense these rights to broadcasters, or the rights holder may commission a producer but sell the broadcast rights itself directly to broadcasters. Television and radio rights are commonly sold on an individual territory basis and often before sponsors have been acquired. This is common in the case of TV broadcasts, as a sponsor will usually make TV exposure a condition of entering into any sponsorship agreement.

Broadcast sponsorship of a programme or series will confer on the sponsor rights to associate itself with each programme in 'bumpers' around the opening and closing credits as well as the ad breaks and must comply with strict Ofcom regulations in the UK. In the UK, regulator Ofcom is responsible for ensuring that Section 9 of the Broadcasting Code (2011) is observed by broadcasters as it applies to commercial references in TV programming, which includes sponsorship of TV content by a sponsor. Sponsorship is not permissible on the BBC, as this is funded through the TV licence fee and sponsorship of its programmes would be incompatible with its public service broadcasting remit.

Subject to certain rules, programme and channel sponsorship is permitted where the primary purpose of the sponsor is the promotion of its products, services, trademark or activities. Under the rules in the UK:

- A sponsor can fund a programme at any stage of the production process; for example, a broadcaster may sell the sponsorship of a programme that it has commissioned or produced itself or an advertiser may directly fund the production of content on that channel (advertiser-funded programming).
- In addition, sponsors have the flexibility to fund blocks of programmes, programme segments or entire TV channels.
- In the UK, the rules attempt to strike a balance between allowing a brand owner the promotional benefit of being associated with the content it is sponsoring while at the same time ensuring that sponsorship arrangements do not lead to a blurring of the boundaries between editorial and advertising that surreptitiously or otherwise can be taken as a form of 'viewer deception'. For example, the line is drawn preventing a sponsored programme overtly promoting a sponsor's individual products and services. The rules require broadcasters to retain editorial independence over sponsored content as well as ensuring the audience is told when content is sponsored and prevent unsuitable sponsorship from reaching the small screen.
- Sponsorship of news and current affairs is not permitted. However, short specialist reports that accompany news, such as sport, travel and weather reports can be sponsored, provided that such content itself does not comprise material that constitutes news or current affairs. Such programme inserts should also look distinct from the rest of the news output and this can be achieved by using different presenters and a different set so that viewers are under no misapprehension as to the sponsored content that is being presented within the show.
- There is a list of prohibited categories that may not form part of any broadcast sponsorship and these include political parties; tobacco brands; prescription-only medicine brands; guns and gun clubs; and adult sexual services.

- Brand owners can legitimately get involved in the commissioning and creation of programmes, although such arrangements should not lead to the creation of content that is a vehicle for the purpose of nakedly promoting its commercial interests or the distortion of editorial content for that purpose.
- The broadcaster must ensure that it retains ultimate editorial control over the programmes it transmits in order to prevent the viewer from being exploited by such overt commercialization of TV programme content.

Associations and professional bodies' sponsorship

In the USA, it is common for associations and professional bodies to generate substantial income from sponsorship arrangements. At the same time, many such bodies are also witnessing a decline in sponsorship support in comparison with what they used to get from the private sector. According to IEG Research, a key reason for the decline is the unwillingness of these bodies to move beyond offering 'off-the-shelf' sponsorship packages that continue to focus on signage and other basic benefits (see Table 2.2).

Table 2.2 Evolution of association sponsorship in the USA

Current approach	New approach
'Inside out' and internally focused	'Outside in' and externally focused
Information on 'wants and needs' of the association	Information shared with potential sponsors with their requirements and their corporate objectives
Gratitude for supporting the professional association	Business-like commercial arrangement
Transactional approach, short-term	Relational approach, long-term
Product-oriented	Solutions-oriented
Off-the-shelf packages (gold, silver, bronze)	Bespoke, customised, flexible approach tailored to meet the needs and requirements of sponsor
Valuation of sponsorship package based on price	Valuation of sponsorship package based on value (tangible, intangible and premium) from the point of view of sponsor
Sponsor is responsible for sponsorship activation	Association and sponsor work together to leverage value of sponsorship activation to reach both sets of audience and customer segments
Multifunctional contacts within association	Single point of contact applying key account management (KAM) approach in managing relationship
Measurement and evaluation left to sponsor	Measurement and evaluation is part of sponsorship package delivered to the satisfaction of sponsor, based on a predetermined set of metrics

Environmental sponsorship

This has grown in importance in recent years as issues such as global warming and the exhaustion of natural energy resources have threatened to destabilise the world's delicate ecosystem. However, many sponsors of 'green' issues and technologies will need to have put their own houses in order before attempting to stress their own credentials as being model organisations and companies that have done their bit to reduce the erosion of the ozone layer from CO_2 emissions and other activities that pollute the environment. There are a number of features of this type sponsorship:

- Environmental thinking should be rooted in corporate culture and philosophy.
- Sponsors need to be ready to demonstrate that they are ready to take full responsibility in such a socially important field and be transparent about their own efforts and progress.
- Ecological engagement can create a positive differentiation for brand owners, but quite understandably they are likely to be judged by a higher standard than those brand owners that choose not to align themselves with the environmental message.
- Often the environmental sponsorship could extend to sourcing the raw materials as well as creating sustainable ways of producing those raw materials and the labour required to help maintain a healthy balance with nature.

Education sponsorship

In the UK, there are over 33,400 schools employing in excess of 1 million people supporting almost 10 million pupils. Add to that their parents and you can see how schools touch over half the population. Always looking forward, schools are enthusiastic, innovative and welcome original links with today's businesses and non-commercial organisations. They are, after all, educating the employees of tomorrow. Families have regular contact with schools. They visit them, think about them and care about them. Naturally, sponsors want to reach this community.

Learning also does not stop at the school gates and continues at home, at play and throughout our lives. From social networks to community programmes and from corporate websites to employee engagement, helping people to learn and develop increases their confidence, their perception of a sponsor's brand or their enthusiasm for a particular social cause. On the whole, teachers and parents encourage and support brand owners working in partnership with schools and through appropriate campaigns and projects that deliver suitable and exciting benefits for schools, brands, social causes and families.

In the UK, best practice in this type of sponsorship activity has been defined by the Incorporated Society of British Advertisers (ISBA) and the Consumers' Association (CA) and endorsed by the Department for Education (DfE). Some of the ground rules for this type of sponsorship include:

- All school partnership activities should provide a clear benefit to participating schools.

- Schools should always have the choice to opt into, or out of, any activities.
- Any level of branding must be appropriate to the activity.
- Brand owners should ensure that schools are aware of the social or commercial objectives of all school partnership activities.
- Expressions of opinion should be distinguished from statements of fact.
- Resources or materials should not encourage unhealthy, unsafe or unlawful activities.
- Resources or materials should respect diversity of gender, race, disability and cultural issues, and reflect contemporary UK society.
- Activities should, where possible, be developed in partnership with teachers, pupils, parents and education experts.
- Where possible, the sponsor should seek permission before forwarding materials to the school.
- All activities should respect the unique relationship between parents, their children and schools.

Corporate social responsibility (CSR) sponsorship

CSR sponsorship activities offer the chance for brand owners to demonstrate good deeds to the communities they serve. In comparison with sports and arts and culture sponsorship, CSR sponsorship has some particular features of its own:

- The brand owner supports organisations, causes and projects that make a difference to communities and it does this on the basis of its values and the engagement of its workforce on these issues.
- The motivation for CSR sponsorship is very different from other types of sponsorship as it is not driven by commercial imperatives. It should also not be done to garner media coverage for the brand owner but instead the PR must highlight the work of the organisation, cause, or programme that it is helping to support and the work of others in the community.
- All the evidence indicates that CSR sponsorship has become a key issue for many brand owners competing in a highly competitive marketplace in which strong social credentials based on deeds rather than just words can provide a highly valuable competitive advantage with desired customers and prospects that cannot easily be replicated or copied by competitors.
- Price, quality and functionality are not enough for success. Depending on the market segment, all of these can be replicated within weeks or months. They no longer help to maintain brand differentiation in the longer term. Emotional engagement and values, by way of contrast, are much harder to develop, much harder to replicate and once established, much more embedded and harder to shift. Investing in values and a 'bank of goodwill' pays dividends.
- As brand management evolves, values are becoming the key differentiator. Such 'enlightened self-interest' permeates virtually all the best examples of CSR sponsorship and its relative low cost has helped to make it a compelling proposition for many brand owners.

- Although CSR sponsorship activation costs are usually a lot lower than other types of sponsorship activation activity, CSR sponsorship does requires commitment, imagination and a genuine partnership to make it work successfully. Without this, it risks being labelled a cynical marketing or PR exercise designed to make the public believe that the brand owner is doing its bit for the community when, in fact, it is unashamedly using a charity or cause for blatant self-promotion. And this will backfire.
- CSR sponsorship must be at the heart of a business – it must be about how the brand owner makes its profits not just on how it spends its profits.
- The brand owner needs to look at how customer segments receive information about its brands and not use CSR sponsorship as a way of getting commercial messages transmitted to the market. Instead, the channels used for CSR sponsorship must be used for engaging in dialogue with the audience rather than for traditional 'push' communication activities.
- Given that CSR sponsorship tends to raise the head of the brand owner 'over the parapet' the company needs to respond with integrity to attacks on its reputation where these occur and must not ignore problems or concerns before they morph into serious issues that erode and damage trust, confidence – and, ultimately, its reputation.

UK sports sponsorship ecosystem

Given that sport accounts for around 83% of all sponsorships in the UK, it is no surprise that the heart of the sponsorship market consists of sport and entertainment content that is fed by rights holders, governing bodies, national governments, global brand owners and, of course, consumers, customers, clients, supporters and fans from across the world (see Figure 2.3)

Sports marketing agencies and advisers

The companies and firms in this sector vary the most and tend to deliver a mix of products and services. They typically consist of sponsorship companies, management consultants, PR companies, advertising companies, marketing companies, law firms, media rights advisers, accountants, tax advisers, investment advisers, financial advisers, insurance companies, brand valuation consultants, market research companies, audience research and polling companies, risk management consultants, strategic planning consultants, licensing and merchandising agents, surveyors, planners, sustainability event consultants, events management and player representation and management.

Marketing services providers

The companies and firms in this sector tend to deliver products. They typically comprise overlay specialists, architect firms, engineering companies, social media and digital technology specialists, hardware specialists for venue and stadium

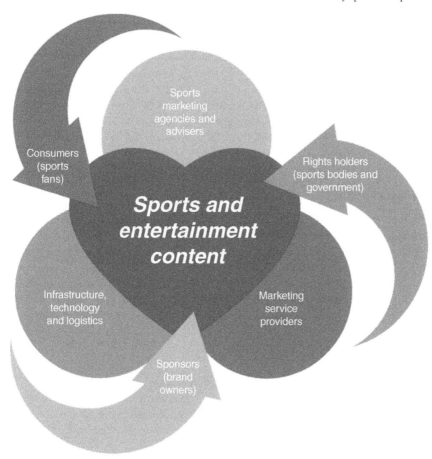

Figure 2.3 Global sponsorship ecosystem
Source: Kolah (2013)

construction, logistics management companies, systems integration companies, data management companies, broadcast production, TV production, technology companies, new media companies, software companies, technology product companies, lighting companies and temporary structure companies.

Infrastructure, technology and logistics providers

The companies and firms in this sector tend to deliver products. They typically comprise facilities management companies, security firms, catering, hospitality, linguistic services, travel and transportation companies, ticketing companies, team building, employee communications specialists, photography, film and photo library services.

Role of sports bodies

Arguably, the UK sponsorship sector could not exist without sports governing bodies overseeing national, international and global sports events on a scale that has helped to build the UK sector into one of the most successful in the world today. As the sector becomes more professionalised in the way in which it does its business, there is more pressure to bring in more money from the private sector. The value of sports rights is the key currency for all sports bodies and one of the most successful in the world is the Premier League, owned by 20 Premier League football clubs.

Role of government

The importance of the active participation and support of government to the sponsorship sector cannot be overemphasised. For example, the London 2012 Olympic Games underlined how crucial the UK government is to the future well-being of the sponsorship sector. Without active support from government lobbying for more major sports events to take place on British soil, the sector would start to resemble an endangered species. The British government is also a key customer segment for infrastructure, technology and logistics providers.

Role of brands

Brand owners (sponsors, supporters and event partners) account for about 80% of sales of products and services within the sponsorship ecosystem. Without the financial investment this segment makes in sport alongside the government, the sports marketing and consultancy sector could not exist as it does today.

Role of sports fans

Sport is all about passion, competition and, above all, world-class entertainment. The support of fans is the oxygen of sport without which the sector would not exist. Fans provide the reason why sponsors want to get involved with sport.

Fragmentation within the sponsorship sector

The UK sponsorship sector is very fragmented, dominated by a mixture of privately owned medium and small companies. For example, the European Sponsorship Association (ESA) has seen a steady decline in its membership (now at 177 members) as a result of a lot of UK sponsorship agencies merging, with the result that one person rather than several represents the interests of that member within ESA.

The sector employs a relatively low number of full-time employees and is minuscule compared with other industry sectors, such as retail. Only 2% of these sponsorship companies are publicly quoted, notably WPP, Chime and Perform

Sports that, which utilise the equity markets for funding. In the vast majority of cases, expansion of sponsorship firms is self-funded through winning more accounts, joint ventures as well as mergers and acquisitions of similar size or smaller players.

Over the last five years there has been an increasing amount of consolidation within the UK sponsorship sector but equally there has also been an increase in start-up businesses entering the sector. According to research by management consultants PwC, although there will be more consolidation within the sector, which has the effect of creating bigger sponsorship groups, at the same time there will also be more niche companies (five employees or fewer) that will be more innovative and specialised and the UK sector will have room for both types of business.

The fragmentation of the UK sector is also a result of the low barrier to market entry, as it is relatively easy and low-cost to establish a sponsorship consultancy business. There tends to be a lack in focus and uniformity of the services offered by the smaller sponsorship companies, particularly as they evolve from start-up. For example, it is still a sector where a one- to three-person sponsorship agency can run a successful business with a few clients.

A review of the handful of large players in the sponsorship sector with revenues in excess of £10m reveals they have dedicated sports and entertainment offerings as part of their wider sponsorship service offerings in non-sport sectors, such as media and entertainment.

In the research that I undertook for the UK government in 2013, about 75% of the 164 companies analysed in this sector were dedicated solely to sports sponsorship and marketing services, while the remaining 25% (41 companies) offered sports marketing as part of a wider range of products and services, such as construction, architectural and legal services.

Very few UK companies have a credible presence in the US sponsorship market, the biggest single sponsorship market in the world.

The US sector is very much a stand-alone market, serviced by US-originated sports sponsorship, marketing and consultancy firms and is highly saturated compared with other less developed markets. The US sector has high barriers to entry and tends to operate with little external competition.

Within the UK, further consolidation within the sponsorship sector is expected over the next decade. There is also a trend for senior executives of big sports sponsorship, marketing and consultancy firms to leave employment to set up their own niche companies, often to be sold at a later date to the same or other sports sponsorship, marketing and consultancy networks.

Domestic and global balance of sports marketing and consultancy business

The phenomenal success of the London 2012 Olympic Games presents a golden opportunity for UK sports sponsorship, marketing and consultancy firms to demonstrate their world-class expertise and experience in time for the Summer Olympic Games in Rio, Brazil, in 2016.

From the research study I undertook for the UK government, it appears much easier for UK sports sponsorship, marketing and consultancy firms to win business with sponsors and to work with the private sector compared with securing work with sports rights holders such as sports governing bodies or government departments. This trend may change where games' organisers and governments in emerging economies such as Qatar, Turkey and South Korea seek international expertise and experience that may not exist locally. This is likely to be a key driver for new business for the UK sector over the next decade and beyond.

According to UK Trade & Investment, around 70 companies had been successful in securing business in connection with the Winter Olympic Games in Sochi, Russia, in 2014, which represented the largest number of contract wins of any foreign nation outside Russia's domestic sports marketing and consultancy sector.

Saturated and unsaturated sports markets

A key challenge for the UK sponsorship sector is the ability of small to medium-size sports sponsorship, marketing and consultancy firms to invest in making trips to emerging markets that are less saturated with competitors or that require expertise and experience that is not available locally, such as India, China, Brazil, Turkey and Qatar. In more mature markets, such as Europe and North America, the decision-making process can be much slower, so sports sponsorship, marketing and consultancy firms need to have more business leads than they did 18–24 months ago in order to filter through those opportunities that offer the best return. Depending on the nature of the products and services, UK sports sponsorship, marketing and consultancy firms may be able to deliver these without the requirement of entering into an arrangement with a local supplier or joint venture partner.

However, in the vast majority of cases, local knowledge and the way things are done from a cultural and linguistic perspective will largely dictate that having a local partner, joint venture partner or wholly owned subsidiary/regional office will be a necessity. For example, the HQ of my old company PRISM (part of WPP) is in London and since 1993 has grown to become the biggest sports marketing network within WPP. It now has ten offices globally, employing 150 people in the UK, Netherlands, Germany, USA, India, Thailand, Africa and Australia.

Future opportunities for growth of UK sector over next decade

The UK sports sponsorship, marketing and consultancy sector will continue to achieve a growth rate of between 5 and 7% annually through to 2022 and will rapidly become a £1bn sector. This forecast is based on a number of factors:

- past performance of the sector
- growth in global sports market

- the London 2012 Olympic Games effect
- further professionalism of the sector
- developing nations' demand for sports marketing services
- increased shift to sponsor-funded events
- digital content opportunities that sports rights holders and brand owners are looking to leverage from sports.

The percentage growth assumption represents a blended rate to factor in that certain years (2014–16) will have an accelerated growth rate due to the 'big ticket' sports events, while odd years will have a correspondingly lower growth rate. The review of annual reports, analyst reports and investor relations presentations for the larger listed/quoted sports sponsorship, marketing and consultancy companies all contain a highly positive trading outlook. Buoyed by the outlook of the sector, many sports sponsorship and entertainment groups are on the acquisition trail and as a result the sector has seen a high level of merger and acquisition activity over the last five years.

A key driver for joint venture partnerships and merger and acquisition activities has been the desire of boards of directors to build scale and resource rapidly so that their companies can provide a global client base with a 'full service' offering and to compete for lucrative contracts with major sports events such as the forthcoming Summer Olympic Games (Rio, Brazil) 2016 and the FIFA World Cup (Russia) 2018.

The UK sports sponsorship, marketing and consultancy sector is one of the most sophisticated in the world. A number of factors will positively impact the future growth of the sector over the next decade, including:

- Super-global economies (such as Brazil, the Middle East, Russia, India and China) and transition economies (such as Turkey and Indonesia) that have the ambition and resources to compete for hosting some of the biggest sports events in the world on their home soil. These economies will need to build their own infrastructure in order to host global sports and non-sport events successfully.
- More sophisticated consulting offers to sponsor brands that more accurately maximise the value of sponsorship and increase the return on investment. This requires dedicated investment in proprietary systems and processes that do not currently exist at present.
- UEFA, in time for the 2013/14 season, implemented a new set of financial criteria called the Financial Fair Play Rules (FFPRs) for football clubs to comply with if they wished to participate in UEFA Champions League and Europa League club competitions. Similarly, the Football Association has announced that it will adopt a version of the UEFA rules, initially for its Championship clubs. The aim of the rules is to ensure clubs in time only spend what they earn. This will generate opportunities for the UK sports marketing and consultancy sector, as the details and application of the rules

are likely to require expert advice and guidance. It is expected that future expenditure focus will shift from on-field to off-field activities and similar FFPRs may also be introduced by other sports. Taken together, this creates new opportunities for sponsorship valuation and research companies in the sector.

*   Continuing to attract top flight talent as part of the ongoing professionalism of the sports sector as well as a desire among brand owners and sports rights holders to embed more effective marketing and commercial practices within their business and organisations.

Where sports sponsorship and marketing were not the only service offering for such global networks, they frequently made the key financial highlights given the sector's strong performance. For example, Chime Communications anticipates an annual 7% growth in the sector, which is supported by analysts' forecasts.

How sponsorship powered the London 2012 Olympic Games

From a purely financial perspective, sponsors (see Figure 2.4) helped to power the London 2012 Olympic Games to a new record by contributing nearly £750m in sponsorship revenues that helped to take the total for revenues achieved to £2.41bn against costs of £2.38bn.

As a result, the London Organising Committee of the Olympic Games (Locog) was able to close its books with a record £30m surplus and make a return of £20m to the Department for Culture, Media and Sport, a £5.3m return to the British Olympic Association (BOA) and £2.6m to the British Paralympic Association (BPA). In addition, a total £1.3m will be donated to London 2012 Games legacy projects as part of an agreement with the National Lottery. The International Inspiration charity will receive £1m and the Join In Trust will receive £300,000. It also meant that an additional £190m of government funding was not drawn down, which allowed Locog to have balanced its books before it was dissolved in 2013.

Fast Track/Opinion Leader research, 2013

Since the conclusion of the London 2012 Olympic Games, Lord Sebastian Coe has become Executive Chairman of CSM Sport & Entertainment, which owns Fast Track, a leading UK sports sponsorship and marketing agency. Research by Fast Track and Opinion Leader shows that the sports sponsorship sector will enjoy a massive boost in the wake of the London 2012 Olympic and Paralympic Games as brand owners commit more resources to sports sponsorship activation. In addition, brand owners are now more likely to want to get involved as sponsors with Paralympic sports and overall sports participation levels are expected to rise over the long term.

International Olympic Committee TOP Partners

Visa, Panasonic, McDonalds, Coca-Cola, lenovo, Atos, P&G, Dow, GE, acer, Omega, Samsung

---

Tier 1 Partners   + Auto partners
                        + Grocery partners
LloydsTSB, British Airways, BT, EDF,
Adidas, BP, Nortel

Tier 2 Sponsors

Deloitte, Cadbury, ArcelorMittal, Thomas Cook, Cisco, UPS, Adecco

---

Tier 3 Suppliers   + 19 other suppliers

Airwave, Atkins, BCG, John Lewis Partnership, Freshfields
Bruckhaus Deringer, Trident

Official Partner Paralympic Games

Sainsbury's

Figure 2.4 Some of the partners, sponsors and suppliers of London 2012

In summary, the research found:

- Nearly 50% of the respondents believed they will now spend more on sponsorship.
- Seventy-five per cent of respondents felt new sponsors will now enter the UK market.
- Eighty-two per cent of respondents agreed that sponsors and potential sponsors had changed their views on sports sponsorship as a direct result of London 2012.
- Seventy-eight per cent of respondents believed new sponsor brands are now more likely to enter the market.
- Researchers expect that brand owners will increase the allocation of activation budgets as sports sponsorship increasingly delivers audience focus, both in-game and out-of-game and across all media platforms.
- Eighty-five per cent of respondents expect an increase in the attractiveness of Paralympic sports to sponsors over the long term given the overwhelming public support that the Paralympic Games attracted, although there is still a long way to go according to the British Paralympic Association.

• 74% of respondents now see women's sports as a more attractive sponsorship proposition.

As Andy Westlake, CEO of Fast Track, observes:

> In an increasingly fragmented communications market, sports sponsorship allows brands to get right within a targeted consumer's sweet spot. The increasing importance of sponsorship to brands is obvious and there's a fantastic opportunity here to back sports whose profiles have risen incredibly.

The research results are consistent with a previous study carried out by Think! Sponsorship in association with *Sponsorship Today*.

Think! Sponsorship/Sponsorship Today, 2013

Overall, the results from this study (see Table 2.3) were that sponsorship by global and national sponsors was a qualified success, although less than half of those surveyed (47.6%) felt that the TOP sponsorship programme (USD 200m) and the Tier 1 sponsorship programme (USD 160–200m) actually offered value for money (See Table 2.4). The consensus view was that Proctor & Gamble's 'Mums' campaign among the Olympic partners (TOP) programme came top of the sponsorship charts.

Coca-Cola, one of the longest-standing sponsors of the Olympic Movement, was one of several sponsors that were involved in sponsoring the Torch Relay and did well as a result, whereas McDonald's and Visa had lower profile activations with consequently less impact as a result. Among the UK national sponsors, both

Table 2.3 TOP sponsors that got most traction from sponsorship of London 2012

Rank	Olympic partner (TOP) sponsors	Respondent votes
1	Proctor & Gamble (P&G)	39.8%
2	Coca-Cola	17.1%
3	McDonald's	16.4%
4	Visa	14.0%
5	Samsung	6.2%
6	Omega	1.5%
7	Atos	<1.0%
8	General Electric (GE)	<1.0%
9	Panasonic	<1.0%
=10	Acer	0.0%
=10	Dow Chemical	0.0%

Source: Think!Sponsorship/*Sponsorship Today* (2013)

Table 2.4 Tier 1 sponsors that got most traction/least traction from London 2012

	Biggest sponsorship winners			Biggest sponsorship losers	
Rank	Brand owner	Percentage	Rank	Brand owner	Percentage
1	Adidas	32.5%	1	EDF	36.5%
2	BMW	23.5%	2	BP	18.6%
3	Lloyds TSB	23.5%	3	BMW	17.0%
4	BA	18.6%	4	Lloyds TSB	13.8%
=5	BP	5.6%	5	Adidas	8.1%
=5	EDF	5.6%	6	BA	5.6%

Source: Think!Sponsorship/*Sponsorship Today* (2013)

Adidas and BMW came top of home-grown sponsors of the London Organising Committee of the Olympic Games. Adidas had its logo present on all Team GB apparel and as a result had very high brand exposure levels that were enhanced by a successful PR campaign associated with the fashion designer Stella McCartney. BMW was successful in having its radio-controlled model Minis feature in moving equipment around the track, a move that appeared to circumvent the clean-stadium policy with supposedly no branding permitted within the line of TV cameras in the stadium other than for the timekeeper Omega and sports clothing brands. The main losers in relation to sponsorship activation were EDF and BP.

Global sponsorship opportunities for UK sector in sports and entertainment

The phenomenal success of London 2012 Olympic Games presents a golden opportunity for UK sports sponsorship, marketing and consultancy firms to demonstrate their world-class expertise and experience before the next Summer Olympic Games in Rio, Brazil, in 2016.

From the sample of 164 companies analysed for the UK government, it appears much easier for UK sports sponsorship, marketing and consultancy firms to win business with brand owners and to work with the private sector compared with securing work with sports rights holders such as sports governing bodies or government departments around the world.

This trend may change where games organisers and governments in emerging economies like Qatar, Turkey and South Korea seek international expertise and experience that may not exist locally. This is likely to be a key driver for new business for the UK sector over the next decade and beyond.

According to UK Trade & Investment, around 70 companies were successful in securing business in connection with the Winter Olympic Games in Sochi,

Russia 2014, which represented the largest number of contract wins of any foreign nation outside of Russia's domestic sports marketing and consultancy sector. A key challenge for the sector is the ability of small to medium-size sports marketing and consultancy firms to invest in making trips to emerging markets that are less saturated with competitors or that require expertise and experience that is not available locally, such as India, China, Brazil, Turkey and Qatar. As Simon Rines, publisher of *Sponsorship Today*, observes:

> For smaller agencies, there's a big risk to hop on a plane and take a week or two off and pay all the expenses to go to these markets in the hope of getting some business. Understandably there's a lot of resistance to do this. Then if you get the work, you need to have international resources to fulfil it. You may have general expertise from the work you've done in the UK, but when you get to India or China then the local business culture can be very different so it's a steep learning curve.

On the other hand, Chris Satterthwaite, CEO of Chime Communications, has very little sympathy with this view and argues that small companies can just as easily make the effort to explore new markets without it breaking the bank.

In more mature markets, such as Europe and North America, the decision-making process can be much slower, so sports marketing and consultancy firms need to have more business leads than they did 18 months ago in order to filter through those opportunities that offer the best return. Depending on the nature of the products and services, UK sports sponsorship, marketing and consultancy firms may be able to deliver these without the requirement of entering into an arrangement with a local supplier or joint venture partner.

However, in the vast majority of cases, local knowledge and the way things are done from a cultural and linguistic perspective will largely dictate that having a local partner, joint venture partner or wholly owned subsidiary/regional office will be a necessity. For example, the HQ of my previous agency PRISM (part of WPP) is in London and since 1993 has grown to become the biggest sports sponsorship and marketing network within WPP. It now has ten offices globally, employing 150 people in the UK, Netherlands, Germany, USA, India, Thailand, Africa and Australia.

My research identified 55 major global sports events taking place over the next decade (see Figure 2.5) that provide business opportunities for the UK sports sponsorship, marketing and consultancy sector outside of the UK that cumulatively are worth £5.9bn in value. The largest number of sports events will take place in western and northern Europe (33%).

However, the main growth drivers of the UK sector over the next decade are not necessarily in those markets with the largest number of one-off sports events but those that offer the most valuable opportunities for the UK sector. My research shows that one-off sports events in Qatar, Russia Brazil, South Korea and France are the top five markets for incremental new business for the UK sector over the next decade.

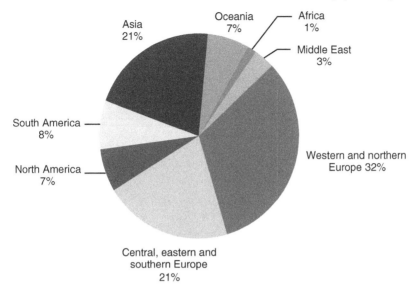

Figure 2.5 Number of major sports events across the world, 2013–22
Source: Kolah (2013)

Key growth drivers for UK sponsorship sector, 2013–2022

Qatar, Russia, Brazil, South Korea and France collectively represent £5bn in incremental revenues for the UK sector or 84.7% of all budgets available to be spent on sports sponsorship, marketing and consultancy services over the next decade (see Figure 2.6). Many countries in the developing world use sport as a catalyst for mega inward investment and tourism. For example, the FIFA World Cup Qatar 2022 is part of a much bigger strategic plan laid out in the 'Qatar National Vision 2030' that aims to put the country on the global map (see Table 2.5).

Sport is also a catalyst for change at a political level and good example of this is Baku, Azerbaijan, which will be the inaugural host of the 2015 European Games.

Global brand owners are increasingly looking to capture new customers in emerging markets such as India, China and Russia as a result of commoditisation and oversupply in their own domestic markets, which have become saturated with goods and services. With this in mind, sports sponsorship offers a unique passion and entertainment platform for brand owners to build deeper bonds with customer segments in less saturated markets. The vast majority of clients of the UK sector tend to be global brand owners that have invested heavily in sports sponsorship and are UK based. However, most small, medium and large sports marketing and consultancy firms expect that at least 50% of their business will come from overseas rights holders and brand owners over the next decade.

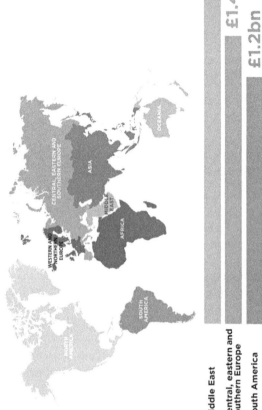

£5.9bn The total spend of new business opportunities for the next 9 years

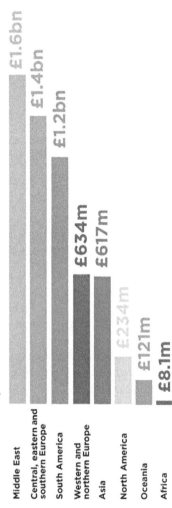

Middle East — £1.6bn
Central, eastern and southern Europe — £1.4bn
South America — £1.2bn
Western and northern Europe — £634m
Asia — £617m
North America — £234m
Oceania — £121m
Africa — £8.1m

Figure 2.6 Est. new business opportunities for UK sector across all regions, 2013–22

Source: Kolah (2013)

Table 2.5 Value of incremental new business for UK sector, 2013–22

Region	Value of new business if 25% of deals secured	Value of new business if 10% of deals secured	Value of new business if 5% of deals secured
Middle East	£421m	£168m	£84m
Central, eastern and southern Europe	£354m	£141m	£70m
South America	£319m	£127m	£64m
Western and northern Europe*	£158m	£63m	£31m
Asia	£154m	£61m	£30m
North America	£58m	£23m	£11m
Oceania	£30m	£12m	£6m
Africa	£2m	£819,000	£409,000
All regions	**£1.5bn**	**£600m**	**£300m**

*Excludes UK

Source: Kolah (2013)

Opportunity rank #1 – Middle East region, 2013–22

The estimated value of potential contracts for UK sports sponsorship, marketing and consulting firms relating to events that have been awarded to host cities and countries in the Middle East region to date is £1.6bn. Key features of market opportunities in the region are:

- The majority of sports marketing and consultancy opportunities in the Middle East will be in Qatar as a result of the 2022 FIFA World Cup, although Saudi Arabia, Bahrain and the United Arab Emirates are becoming more active in wanting to host major sports events in the region. For example, Bahrain and the UAE already host annual F1 races.
- Qatar is consciously engaged in a complete 'makeover' in the region by focusing investment in sporting, cultural and educational facilities and has the ambition to become the universally recognised sports hub of the Middle East and a major destination for world-class sports events.
- Qatar is spending an estimated £138bn on the 2022 FIFA World Cup, approximately 60 times the £2.3bn South Africa spent on the 2010 FIFA World Cup.
- The 'Qatar National Vision 2030' programme is also investing heavily in a number of high-profile mega-projects of interest to the UK sector in areas including transportation and logistics, tourism, health, education and housing.
- After Doha failed to qualify as a candidate city for the 2020 Summer Olympic Games, it immediately launched its campaign to host the Summer Olympic Games 2024. It is also looking to bid to host the FIFA World Cup in 2026. Dubai has also signalled its interest in hosting the FIFA World Cup 2026

- The UAE Football Association has recently made a formal bid, with government backing and financial support, to host the 2019 Asian Cup and will be competing against six nations – Bahrain, the Lebanon, Oman, Saudi Arabia, Thailand and Iran – to host the continent's premier tournament.
- Saudi Arabia and Bahrain have ongoing major sports stadiums and infrastructure projects that also provide the UK sector with unrivalled opportunities to bid for work, particularly as the Middle East has demonstrated a willingness to embrace western concepts and take advantage of expertise outside of the region.

Opportunity rank #2 – Central, eastern and southern Europe region, 2013–22

The estimated value of potential contracts for UK sports sponsorship, marketing and consulting firms relating to events that have been awarded to host cities and countries in the central, eastern and southern Europe region to date is £1.4bn. Key features of market opportunities in the region are:

- Poland and Ukraine are keen to capitalise on the infrastructure built for EURO 2012 and attract sports events to their countries while they are still on the radar of the sporting world. The tournament catalysed a massive shake-up of Poland's ramshackle infrastructure and transformed its image on the global stage, securing a stronger basis for hosting major sports events in the future. Poland is the only EU member to have kept growing throughout the bloc's economic crisis, highlighting the potential for doing business in that country.
- Ukraine has also benefited from improved infrastructure but has a lot more work to do than Poland in order to change its image globally to one that is more positive than at present.
- Russia offers the greatest potential for the UK sector in this region. Over the next few years it will host a plethora of major sports events such as the 2014 Winter Olympics in Sochi, the 2015 FINA World Championships, the 2016 IIHF World Hockey Championships and the 2018 FIFA World Cup. A possible 2024 Summer Olympic Games bid could hail from St Petersburg or Kazan.
- The 2014 Winter Olympic Games became the catalyst for sports development in Sochi, which has already become one of the main sports centres in Russia but it will need guidance to ensure it creates a long-term legacy. This will create opportunities for UK sports sponsorship, marketing and consultancy firms. At the same time, major stadium development is already underway ahead of the FIFA World Cup 2018, with new venues integrating entertainment, leisure and retail features.
- Russia is self-conscious of its negative perception around the world and is taking steps to start to reverse this with the assistance of external consultancy support.

- Several central and eastern European cities are in the frame for bidding for the next Winter Olympic Games, which will be awarded by the International Olympic Committee (IOC).
- In southern Europe, Turkey is rapidly becoming a new sport 'superpower' and is currently undertaking a major infrastructure building programme. Sport has been identified as the key to securing a bright sporting, social and economic future for future generations. The country is using its status as one of the world's fastest growing economies to underpin its commitments for sports development in the capital, Istanbul. Recent political unrest, however, threatens to derail the progress the country has made in becoming a destination for global sports and entertainment events.

Opportunity rank #3 – South America region, 2013–22

The estimated value of potential contracts for UK sports sponsorship, marketing and consulting firms relating to events that have been awarded to host cities and countries in the South America region to date is £1.2bn. Key features of market opportunities in the region are:

- As the host country for the 2014 FIFA World Cup and with Rio de Janeiro having been chosen to host the 2016 Olympic and Paralympic Games, Brazil is set to have an extremely high profile in international sports in the coming years and will already be on the radar of many UK sports marketing and consultancy firms.
- Brazil's Rousseff administration has continued Brazil's ambitious infrastructure programme under the name PAC 2. Over the 2011–14 period, PAC 2 will invest approximately £347bn in energy, infrastructure and housing priority projects while the country also prepares to host both the FIFA 2014 World Cup and the 2016 Olympic Games.
- Local and foreign investors are now coming together hoping to bring Brazil into its place as the next mega-economy, equipped with efficient airports, ports, roads and infrastructure to avoid growth bottlenecks and maintain a sustainable growth rate.
- A study by the University of São Paulo estimated the infrastructure outlays in Brazil ahead of the 2014 FIFA World Cup to be around £11.9bn with £9.25bn coming from Brazilian tax receipts. The expected outlays devoted to hosting the Olympics are an additional £9.92bn, resulting in a total outlay of £21.8bn for both sport events.
- Opportunities for the UK sector will project beyond 2016 and although competition for business is intense in Brazil, there may be better opportunities in less saturated markets in the region, such as Argentina and Columbia.
- UK sports sponsorship, marketing and consultancy firms may find that working directly with the individual cities hosting the 2014 FIFA World Cup matches is a better route than targeting the local organising committees, where

relationships are harder to establish. The 12 Brazilian cities elected to host FIFA World Cup games are Belo Horizonte, Brasilia, Cuiabá, Curitiba, Fortaleza, Manaus, Natal, Porto Alegre, Recife, Rio de Janeiro, Salvador and São Paulo.

- Elsewhere in South America, Argentina is currently bidding for two major events, the 2018 Youth Summer Olympic Games and the 2019 Pan American Games.
- Medellin in Colombia also made the three-city shortlist to host the 2018 Youth Olympics.
- Argentina is also reported to be considering making a bid for the 2023 or 2027 IRB Rugby World Cup.
- It is clear that infrastructure investments in Brazil will be a driving force for economic growth in the longer term. The country will take quite a few steps towards modernisation, become more efficient and lure increased foreign investment. With improved roads, railways and marinas the country will increase its efficiency, which will make it more attractive to do business with.

Opportunity rank #4 – Western and northern Europe region, 2013–22

The estimated value of potential contracts for UK sports sponsorship, marketing and consulting firms relating to events that have been awarded to host cities and countries in the western and northern Europe region (outside of the UK mainland) to date is £634m. Key features of market opportunities in the region are:

- The greatest business opportunity for the UK sector is the UEFA 2016 European Championships (EURO 2016) in France.
- And with UEFA 2020 set to take place in multiple cities across Europe, there will be further opportunities that are not just limited to one country in the region.
- If Madrid succeeds against all the odds and wins its bid to host the 2020 Summer Olympic Games, then there is a strong opportunity for the UK sector to leverage the track record of experience gained from the London 2012 Olympic Games.
- Experience shows that working with Olympic Games bidding cities is an ideal way for the UK sector to start to build strong and lasting relationships with potential future host cities.
- Stockholm and Gothenburg in Sweden aspire to attract more world-class events and would be open to being advised as to how to achieve this.
- Although the outlook for new business on mainland Europe is potentially positive, the fragile state of the European economy is the major negative factor together with the high level of competition in what is one of the most saturated markets in the world for sports sponsorship, marketing and consultancy services.

Opportunity rank #5 – Asia region, 2013–22

The estimated value of potential contracts for UK sports marketing and consulting firms relating to events that have been awarded to host cities and countries in the Asia region to date is £617m. Key features of market opportunities in the region are:

- China, Japan and South Korea in particular all offer attractive opportunities for the UK sector seeking procurement opportunities at major events.
- Meanwhile, both Malaysia and Singapore are also developing major events strategies and also require external support. In March 2013, the Singapore government announced it would boost its spending on sports programming and infrastructure by more than £133m over the next five years to build a strong sporting culture among Singaporeans.
- After a lull in major events hosting after the 2008 Beijing Summer Olympic Games, China has been busy in securing a raft of events over the next few years including the 2014 Youth Summer Olympic Games, the 2014 FIG Artistic Gymnastics World Championships, the 2015 ISU World Figure Skating Championships, the 2015 ITTF World Table Tennis Championships and the 2015 IAAF World Championships in Athletics (Outdoor). While none of these events will require any major infrastructure development, there are opportunities for the UK sector to work with local organising committees and host cities of the events.
- Chinese city Zhangjiakou has confirmed plans for a joint bid with Beijing for the 2022 Winter Olympic Games.
- Over the next few years, Japan will host the 2014 ISU World Figure Skating Championships, the 2014 World Table Tennis Championships, the 2017 Asian Winter Games and the 2019 IRB Rugby World Cup.
- Japan made history by being the first Asian country to be awarded hosting rights for an IRB Rugby World Cup. Hosting the tournament in 2019 is expected to increase the popularity of the sport in the country. The event is estimated to cost £145.1m to stage. With rugby being a developing sport in Japan and Asia as a whole, this presents an excellent opportunity for the UK sports marketing and consultancy sector, which has strong credentials in the sport.
- Tokyo is currently bidding for both the 2019 FINA World Swimming Championships and the 2020 Summer Olympic Games, both of which would offer opportunities for the UK sector if these bids are successful. Fuelled by the city's dynamic atmosphere and youth-driven culture, the bids have an additional important role to play in the process of Japan's spiritual and physical recovery efforts following the earthquake disaster in 2011.
- UK Trade & Investment trade missions to South Korea are helping to stimulate interest in the UK sector's expertise and experience in the construction of the 2012 Olympic Park in East London and how this can be used to win lucrative contracts ahead of the 2014 Asian Games in Incheon,

2015 Summer Universiade in Gwangju and the 2018 Winter Olympics in PyeongChang.

- The infrastructure development of PyeongChang 2018 will be around £4.1bn and £330.7m is estimated to be invested up to 2018 in the 'Drive the Dream' legacy programme.
- India remains an opportunity for the UK sector because of its close cultural and sporting links with the country but the recent problems with India's delivery of the 2010 Delhi Commonwealth Games have dented what aspirations it may have had to host a Summer Olympic Games in the region.
- India does, however, continue to attract cricket events. The 2011 ICC Cricket World Cup was co-hosted by Bangladesh, India and Sri Lanka, and India also recently hosted the 2013 ICC Women's World Cup. India will also host the 2016 ICC World Twenty20, which will also be a big opportunity for UK sports sponsorship, marketing and consultancy firms with credentials in the sport.
- The outlook for the UK sector in sourcing work for major events in Asia is strong in China, Japan and South Korea with opportunities also available in Malaysia and Singapore.

Opportunity rank #6 – North America region, 2013–22

The estimated value of potential contracts for UK sports sponsorship, marketing and consulting firms relating to events that have been awarded to host cities and countries in the North America region to date is £234m. Key features of market opportunities in the region are:

- Opportunities in Canada look positive as a result of the successful Winter Olympic Games held in Vancouver in 2010 and an increase in interest in winter sports. Several other cities are also jostling for the crown as Canada's best sports city and these include Toronto, Ottawa, Montreal, Quebec City, Calgary and Edmonton – all of which could be sources of new business for the UK sector.
- Most suppliers of major events are viewing the 2015 Pan American Games as the biggest opportunity in Canada, if not North America as a whole, over the next few years. The overall budget for Toronto 2015 is approximately £0.91bn split almost equally between the operating and capital development budgets.
- With Toronto considering a possible bid for the 2024 Summer Olympic Games, hosting a successful Pan American Games will strengthen is pitch in the same way that hosting the 2007 Pan American Games was a factor in helping Rio de Janeiro fulfil its Olympic Games ambitions. UK sports marketing and consultancy firms involved in Toronto for the Pan American Games can foster invaluable relationships for the future if an Olympic bid becomes a reality.
- The 2015 FIFA Women's World Cup, the largest single-sport women's event in the world, will not only expand the tournament from 16 to 24 teams from

around the world, but will also mark the first time that a single-sport event has been hosted from coast to coast in Canada. The FIFA Women's World Cup Canada 2015 official host cities are Vancouver, Edmonton, Winnipeg, Ottawa, Montreal and Moncton and these should generate new business for UK sports marketing and consultancy companies.

- Elsewhere in Canada, Quebec City was originally interested in bidding for the 2022 Winter Olympic Games. The city later backed out of its potential bid, saying it would bid for the 2026 event instead. The city hosted the Sport-Accord Convention in 2012, during which the city's major reiterated the city's Olympic ambitions.
- Canada's national policy is to support only two major multisport events in the country in a ten-year period and one large international single-sport event every two years, and that can be viewed as a constraint by some of the cities looking to host events in Canada.
- Over the next few years several major events will be held in the USA, including the 2015 Special Olympics, the largest single event to be staged in Los Angeles since the 1984 Olympic Games and projected be the largest sports and humanitarian event held anywhere in the world in 2015. The 2015 UCI Road World Championships will be held in Richmond, Virginia. For Virginia, the economic impact of Richmond 2015 is estimated to be £104.5m as a result of both event staging and visitor spending in the city.
- Various US cities are considering being the country's representative to bid for the 2024 Summer Games and the 2026 Winter Games but given the saturated sports marketing and consultancy sector in the USA, it is unlikely that this will generate incremental new business opportunities for the UK sector.
- Sports sponsorship and marketing companies that want to work with Mexican sports organisations and brands are better served thinking of the culture and market as an extension of South American culture, rather than as part of North America.
- Mexico may benefit from external expertise if it is to repair its reputation following the Guadalajara 2011 Pan American Games, which suffered from construction delays in the build-up to those Games. In February 2013, Guadalajara did not make the final shortlist to host the 2018 Youth Olympic Games but has announced it may bid for the 2024 Olympic Games. Mexico is also expected to be preparing a bid to host the 2026 FIFA World Cup and is expecting tough competition from the USA for such a bid.
- The outlook for the UK sector sourcing work for major events in North America is positive in Canada and Mexico but opportunities are more limited in North America, where it is a saturated market.

Opportunity rank #7 – Oceania region, 2013–22

The estimated value of potential contracts for UK sports sponsorship, marketing and consulting firms relating to events that have been awarded to host cities and countries in Oceania region to date is £121m. Key features of market opportunities in the region are:

- Australia is hosting the 2015 Asia Cup and the 2018 Commonwealth Games, and is jointly hosting the 2015 ICC Cricket World Cup and 2017 Rugby League World Cup with New Zealand.
- New Zealand offers the best prospects for new business in comparison with Australia, which is a saturated and, to some extent, closed market for the UK sector unless there are existing relationships already in that market.
- New Zealand will host the 2015 FIFA Under-20 World Cup, the 2016 World Bowling Championships and the 2017 World Masters Games. The last event is expected to contribute £29.5m to New Zealand's GDP, including £20.4m in inward investment to Auckland. The return on regional investment for this event is estimated to be 226%, which would represent the highest return achieved by any major event held in the city
- There will be opportunities for the UK sector to work with the cities hosting New Zealand's major events and with organising committees following the Memorandum of Understanding entered into between EventScotland and New Zealand Major Events (signed in 2012), which committed both countries to cooperate in improving capabilities and enhancing one another's reputation as a global destination for international events.
- In reality, given the distances and time zones involved, these opportunities will be dependent on local partnerships and joint ventures or wholly owned subsidiaries of sports marketing and consultancy firms in the region.
- For the 2018 Commonwealth Games in the Gold Coast, the Queensland government is underwriting a £750m investment in the redevelopment of its Parklands Area into a residential and commercial precinct; accelerating community and sports facilities on the Gold Coast; and upgrading transport systems. Spending on these projects is projected to generate £1.38bn in economic benefits and around 30,000 full-time equivalent jobs in the region.
- Melbourne is expected to make a bid for either the 2024 or 2028 Summer Olympic Games as infrastructure is already in place and the only major venue that would need to be constructed would be a rowing and canoeing course.
- The outlook for the UK sector sourcing work for major events in Oceania is stronger in New Zealand than Australia, as the latter has a highly developed major events infrastructure and is less likely to need to work with outside companies.
- While New Zealand gained valuable expertise and experience during the 2011 IRB Rugby World Cup, it will seek external assistance when it co-hosts the 2015 ICC Cricket World Cup and 2017 Rugby League World Cup with Australia.

Chapter 2 at a glance

1. The dominant form of sponsorship is sport and entertainment (80%), where football still dominates sponsorship globally as the world's most popular sponsorship type. Other types of sponsorship are personality and endorsement,

arts and culture, broadcast, associations and professional bodies, environmental, education and CSR sponsorship.

2. The business of sponsorship has moved from its early beginnings as a
    form of 'surreptitious advertising' and then a channel of raising aware-
    ness and promotion (push) to something that is predominately sport- and
    entertainment-driven, where compelling content (pull) sits at the heart of
    successful sponsorship in order to deliver a return on investment (ROI) for
    rights holders and brand owners.
3. The nature of sponsorship has also changed from being short-term to being
    much longer-term (three years on average), where the brand owner can build
    a reputation among its desired audience and customer segments.
4. Investment in sponsorship needs to be part of the marketing mix and inte-
    grated with offline (advertising) and online channels (such as mobile), help-
    ing to weave together various strands of a continuous, real-time story, where
    the brand essence of the sponsor is the backdrop to that story in a meaningful
    way.
5. In the UK, the sponsorship ecosystem has sport and entertainment at its
    core, with sports marketing agencies and advisers, marketing services provid-
    ers and infrastructure, technology and logistics providers making up the sec-
    tor. Feeding this ecosystem are sports governing bodies, government, brand
    owners and fans.
6. New research for the UK government indicates that the sponsorship sector
    in the UK is highly fragmented but successful, and more consolidation within
    the sector is likely over the next decade. The vast majority of sponsorship
    agencies are small to medium-size (£3m–£10m turnover) and currently the
    sector is worth £750m and will grow to be over £1bn over the next decade.
7. There are 55 one-off sports and entertainment events globally that provide
    the best opportunities for incremental new business for the UK sector over
    the next decade where the combined value of that new business is £5.9bn.
8. Although the vast number of single-sport and entertainment events are
    taking place in western and northern Europe (33%), the best opportunities
    for the UK sector are the Middle East (Qatar), central, eastern and south-
    ern Europe (Russia), South America (Brazil), western and northern Europe
    (France), Asia (South Korea), North America (Canada) and Oceania (New
    Zealand).
9. Sponsorship has grown in importance as brand owners increasingly look to
    capture new customers in emerging markets such as India, China and Russia
    as a result of commoditisation and oversupply in their own domestic markets,
    which have become saturated with goods and services.

Questions for discussion

1. How many different types of sponsorship exist and what similarities and dif-
    ferences do they possess?
2. Why is sport the dominant property type in the world today?

3. What have been the main differences in strategy and approach to sponsorship over the last 50 years?
4. How has the business of sponsorship changed from the perspective of the rights holder and the brand owner?
5. What sits at the heart of the sponsorship ecosystem and where are the inputs coming from?
6. What are the essential ingredients required for a successful sports and entertainment sponsorship programme that will help deliver a return on investment for those involved?
7. From a UK perspective, what are the main regions for incremental new business and how much will this be worth to the UK sector over the next decade?

Further reading

Gobé, M (2001), *Emotional Branding*, Allworth Press

Kolah, A (2013), *The Art of Influencing and Selling*, Kogan Page

Kolah, A. (2013), Evolving capabilities for sports marketing and consultancy services in the UK and opportunities in global markets for these services to 2022, Report, Department for Business Innovation & Skills

Kolah, A (2013), *High Impact Marketing That Gets Results*, Kogan Page

McDonald, M, Kolah, A et al. (2007), *Marketing in a Nutshell*, Butterworth Heinemann

Ries, A and Ries, L (2002), *The Fall of Advertising and the Rise of PR*, Harper Business

Zyman, S (2002), *The End of Advertising As We Know It*, Wiley

Zyman, S (2000), *The End of Marketing As We Know It*, Harper Business

Websites

Augmented reality (AR) examples on the Kinetic Worldwide YouTube Channel [accessed 18 June 2013]: http://www.youtube.com/watch?v=InDEcb1VSdU&list=UUUeyWLfV bC8mOGZQ6r2VqMg&index=7&feature=plcp

Department for Communities and Local Government – Guide to Outdoor Advertisements and Signs [accessed 10 June 2013]: http://www.communities.gov.uk

Kinetic Report: The Future of Out of Home Media in the UK – the industry, consumers and technology to 2020 [accessed 24 June 2013]: http://www.kineticww.com

Outdoor Media Centre [accessed 10 June 2013]: http://www.outdoormediacentre.org.uk

WARC Report [accessed 24 June 2013]: Asia's Outdoor Future: http://www.warc.com

WARC Report [accessed 18 June 2013]: Planning for New Interactive Possibilities of UK Out of Home Media: http://www.warc.com

Why QR codes won't last [accessed 10 June 2013]: http://mashable.com/2012/02/15/qr-codes-rip/

3 Process of selecting a sponsorship property

In this chapter

- Strategic decision-making process
- Challenge of integrating sponsorship into the marketing mix
- Negotiating the acquisition a sponsorship property
- Budgeting for sponsorship

Introduction

Why bother with sponsorship? This is the first question I put to my class when embarking on the module that I teach on international sponsorship, endorsement and public relations. Typically, there is always a range of answers from awareness, brand promotion and even corporate social responsibility. Many students fall into thinking that sponsorship is a bit like any other marketing discipline. But, in fact, it is different.

Sponsorship is a commercial agreement, first and foremost. Ignore this reality at your peril. It is a special type of contract with rights, duties and obligations that are not found in any other type of contract in marketing. Fundamentally, sponsorship is about selling more stuff. As a bunch of intellectual property (IP) rights, sponsorship needs to deliver tangible, measurable and incremental benefits and at its heart is the requirement of the sponsor to achieve brand, commercial, and relationship objectives in much the same way as Shell has achieved with its relationship with Ferrari for nearly 100 years.

What I am not saying is that other objectives are less important or in some way inferior. But justifying a marketing programme that is for three years or more requires some robust thinking and a solid business case in order to be accepted at board level.

Frankly, with so many other options available to the chief marketing officer (CMO), unless a sponsorship or brand partnership programme improves performance in terms of achieving measurable brand marketing, communication and financial objectives, it is unlikely to win support from the board.

Consumer expectations of brands and organisations are at the highest levels they have ever been and are getting steadily higher. To fulfil such demands, brand owners must balance innovation with consistency; quality with value; consumer choice with responsibility; and sustainability with growth.

The ethics of not only what companies and organisations do or how they do it, but *why* they do it is now a matter of legitimate public interest. The standards by which companies and organisations are judged are about their deeds not just their fine words if they are to enjoy a high reputation in their desired market and customer segments. While there are undoubtedly enormous challenges and complexities that need to be addressed in building a robust reputation, conversely, there are also unparalleled opportunities for those brand owners and organisations able to seize the momentum for change where their competitors may fall by the wayside because of an inability or lack of enthusiasm for change.

The difference in marketing performance and in particular sponsorship performance will be seeing things that others have missed and doing things that others have not considered. Such improvements in performance in sponsorship can be achieved by listening, collaborating and engaging on the terms of those we want to influence and do business with. Yet one-third to one-half of sponsors have no robust system in place to measure the return on investment (ROI) from sponsorship. And this is bonkers given the often large sums involved. This has meant that sponsorship is often blamed for not delivering results. But the real cause of failure is often that the brand owner has not articulated its objectives in a sufficiently clear way to the rights holder to drive the sponsorship programme in order to satisfy these objectives and consequently deliver the benefits that such a partnership could deliver if wired in the right way.

It also comes down to a debate we used to have at board meetings of the European Sponsorship Association – is sponsorship an expense or an investment? This is not some semantic debate but rather the focus of the sponsorship that is being entered into. Given that sponsorship is a commercial arrangement, there needs to be some form of commercial return, arguably for all parties to the agreement. If this does not form the basis of the partnership, then this arrangement is likely to be corporate philanthropy or charitable giving, donation, corporate social responsibility, gift-in-aid or some other non-commercial activity. It is, however, unlikely to be sponsorship.

So the process of selecting a property must be driven by a clear sponsorship strategy that must be linked to the brand-building, sales and marketing and communication objectives of the brand owner. The sponsorship strategy should also include the overall objective of the sponsorship portfolio; the desired audience and customer segments; the segmentation of those groups in terms of attitudes, values, beliefs, perceptions and behaviours and the touch points at which sponsorship will influence the consumer journey in terms of awareness, consideration, purchase and loyalty.

The biggest sponsorship property in the world for a multi-sport event is the Olympic Games and the Olympic partner (TOP) programme is the highest level of Olympic sponsorship attracting a raft of multinational companies. Each sponsor will pay a significant amount (as much as USD 100m) for the rights to be one of 11 worldwide Olympic partners that will receive exclusive global marketing rights within a designated product or service category, which will make it the most expensive type of sponsorship on the planet.

At this level, 'sponsorship' is perhaps inadequate to describe what, in fact, is a long-term strategic partnership with the IOC, where there is a 'shared destiny' between the rights holder and its global partners for the duration of the agreement. The TOP programme works on a four-year term in line with each Olympic quadrennial and each partner provides goods and services, technology, expertise and cash that help to stage the Olympic Games. The partners are also expected to embody and promote the Olympic ideals of creating a better world through sport. Another important consequence of sponsorship is that every sponsor is expected to support the organising committees involved in the staging of the Games as well as over 200 national Olympic committees (NOC) and their Olympic teams, helping not only athletes to be able to compete in the Games but also people around the world who draw inspiration from these athletes' performances.

And all of this needs to be committed to before the sponsor has even thought about making a single dollar, euro, rupee, yen or pound from the relationship.

In many respects, the Olympic sponsorship programme is really a sophisticated global licensing programme, as the broadcasting of the Games is in a 'clean' stadium without commercial branding and only logos of a certain size are permitted on athletes. As a result, brand owners have to be masters of leveraging the power of the marks associated with the Games across every conceivable channel available rather than during the broadcasting of the Games themselves.

And, increasingly, sponsorship on a global basis is also a way in which the brand owner can connect with its own global workforce in order to inspire them to feel a collective sense of corporate pride, provided that the programme actually engages with the employees to do good deeds in the community.

Strategic decision-making process

The process by which a sponsorship property type is identified and a sponsorship property selected is down to the brand-marketing, commercial and communication objectives of the brand owner/potential sponsor. Typically, a commercial brand owner will face six key considerations when thinking about whether or not to select a particular sponsorship property:

1   How can we cut through the noise and beat the intense competition that we face in our market segment?
2   How do we use sponsorship as part of the brand value proposition and use it to do business on our customers' terms?
3   How does sponsorship help us take an 'outside in' rather than 'inside out' perspective?
4   How do we articulate what we deliver in an emotional and rational way that is totally compelling, memorable and ultimately influences behaviour?
5   How do we use sponsorship to help build relationships that our customer segments actually want to belong to?

6   And what does it take to engage with audience and customer segments more deeply and turn them into brand advocates?

Many research studies have attempted to explain the sponsorship selection process, for example, in terms of 'exchange theory', which describes the process of the rights holder selling exploitable commercial inventory and potential sponsors determining whether the benefit available is valued at the expenditure required.

This, of course, is very transactional and as we discuss in other parts of this book, the focus should be on collaboration and negotiation of what the bundle of sponsorship rights should look like rather than a 'take it or leave it' deal on the table. However, there has been some attempt made by researchers in the USA to evaluate the impact that a popular sponsorship deal such as that with NASCAR can have on the share price of a company or indeed whether a multimillion naming rights deal, as with Fedex Stadium, can signal about the financial security of a company entering into such a deal and how this impacts investor confidence and share price. In the latter example, US researchers viewed a naming rights deal of this magnitude as being a significant informational event that adds value to financial market investors. Such deals on average realised a 1.65% increase in share prices during the period a sponsorship was announced to investors and the media. A key component in the perception of stock value was a winning sports team. Sponsors of venues with teams that held a 65% winning track record realised stock market value increases almost twice as large as those of sponsors of stadiums with teams winning 35% or less of their games. 'High technology firms experienced some of the greatest responses from stock investors of part of stadium naming rights sponsorships,' observes Tom Mueller, assistant professor of communication at Appalachian State University in Boone, North Carolina.

But there is also evidence that sponsors want much more than a bounce in a share price to satisfy the board that the investment in a particular sponsorship is the right thing to do, and now brand owners expect to sit down and collaborate and negotiate for much wider outcomes. It is one reason why NASCAR is starting to rewire the way it sells its sponsorship as it is experiencing a decline in sponsorship revenues, track attendance and TV viewership at the time of writing. Hopefully, by the time this book is published, the sun may be shining on them!

While I was working as Chief Strategy Officer at PRISM – one of the most successful sports and entertainment sponsorship agencies within WPP – we often used a range of tools and techniques to help identify suitable properties for many clients. Given the boom in sport, media and event sponsorship, WPP research agency Millward Brown developed a new research tool called Partner Z to help advertisers evaluate opportunities and plan their spend. The project had been funded by WPP sister agencies Group M, Hill & Knowlton and OgilvyAction and set out to identify which sponsorship vehicles were the best match for any particular brand.

David Muir, head of WPP's media knowledge community The Channel, says: 'The reason we're doing this is that we're seeing global sponsorship spend grow at around 20–30% per annum. As more and more money is spent chasing these opportunities, clients are looking for a more scientific evaluation. They want to know the equities of these properties, and to compare their audiences with that of a brand.'

Partner Z is built around interviews with 51,000 consumers across Europe, the USA and Asia, with brand equity data sourced from the WPP Brand Z study, so it is a proprietary tool for helping WPP agencies do more business with sponsors. With something as big as the Olympic Games, brand owners with deep pockets stand to benefit from an unparalleled opportunity to enhance their corporate reputation, while an association with the Olympic rings and Olympic values enables them to enrich their own brand image. The IOC's Marketing Report, produced in the wake of London 2012, claimed that the Games offered partners:

> [I]nnovative ways to build their businesses, increase sales, connect with the public and develop customer relationships through exclusive marketing programmes and showcasing opportunities. Through internal reward schemes and community outreach initiatives, partners also used the Games to motivate their employees and left a lasting legacy in the communities where they do business.

A review of some of the reasons why global brands were prepared to invest significantly in London 2012 reveals that many were motivated to do so not just by pure sales and marketing objectives.

Case study: Coca-Cola and London 2012

For example, Coca-Cola needs to continually refresh its marketing to young people and brought together the worlds of music and sport in its 'Move to the Beat' campaign, which partnered award-winning music producer Mark Ronson with vocalist Katy B to record 'Anywhere in the World', the anthem at the heart of the campaign. Ronson travelled the world, meeting athletes to record their sporting sounds, providing the beat of the track. And a documentary following Ronson's progress was broadcast worldwide, while the duo was also joined by the athletes in a global TV commercial. Digital activations encouraged teens to interact with the campaign. Desktop and mobile applications featured social media plug-ins, allowing user to fuse personal music and sporting preferences, to create bespoke experiences.

Content marketing also helped to drive home messages about the brand through a daily TV show aimed at bringing the social side of the Games to teens. Coca-Cola Presents: Beat TV was broadcast globally for ten nights of the Games and featured celebrity and athlete interviews, on-air challenges and live music performances from an international repertoire of artistes.

Case study: Atos Origin and London 2012

For other brand owners, such as Atos, the London 2012 Olympic Games was the biggest high-stakes 'advertising billboard' for its brand, as it staked its reputation before the world by taking responsibility for reporting every moment of the Games using its IT systems and infrastructure. Patrick Adiba, CEO responsible for managing the partnership with the IOC, explains:

> The Olympic Games are a complex mix of technology, processes and people. Our challenge for London 2012 was to create an IT solution that allowed the capture and reporting of every moment of the action and supported the world's media in bringing it to the world via television, the internet and social networks – first time, every time.

According to many commentators, London 2012 was the most digitally enabled Olympic Games in history, with more people than ever tuning in to watch on more devices than ever before. Understandably, if Atos can demonstrate how well it performs for something as big as the Olympic Games, then that is a terrific vote of confidence in the company.

Such a reputation outstrips anything Atos could have said about itself through advertising, PR and social media. By delivering a flawless IT ecosystem for the London 2012 Olympic Games, Atos had demonstrated beyond doubt it was world-class.

Other research studies have looked at how a sponsor can be identified strongly with a sponsorship property so that the communication goals help to drive the decision-making process and these typically include:

- enhanced brand awareness
- image transfer from property to sponsor
- creation of more positive attitudes towards the sponsor
- incremental sales of products and services
- higher loyalty levels.

Image transfer is perhaps highly ambitious if desired audience and customer segments fail to identify the sponsor accurately. As we shall discuss in Chapter 10, brand owners may be looking to move the needle with respect to:

- unaided recall
- cued recall
- recognition measures
- data collection (for example, spectators at the event versus TV audience after the event).

Researchers have identified problems for sponsorship managers wishing to know the likelihood of their company or organisation receiving credit as sponsors and achieving their communication goals. What does make a difference is where sponsors increase desired audience and customer segments engagement with the sponsorship property, which in turn increases the chances that they are correctly recognised.

As we shall discuss in Chapter 10, the six-step sponsorship model provides for a review of the brand owner's existing sponsorship policy and strategy, and this may well dictate the process of selecting a sponsorship property. The following are the key elements that should be present in any sponsorship policy and strategy:

- measurable objectives
- audience segmentation (including internal)
- brand essence
- brand fit
- sector match (to the sport, social, arts, culture, education, association, environmental, media property)
- length/duration
- location/geography
- integration with other channels
- impact on behaviour of internal and external audiences.

Assuming that there is a sponsorship policy and strategy – any prospective property will need to measure up against this. In light of experience and in the wake of conducting an existing activity review, the brand owner may decide to update its sponsorship policy and strategy. This often occurs where, for example, technology may have changed and there may now be a focus on content for 4G mobile handsets and user-generated content (UGC) that needs to drive engagement compared with the point in time when the sponsorship strategy was first conceived.

The Norwegian Business School in Oslo has also carried out research to attempt to find explanations for sponsor identification accuracy, the reverse side of the coin and one that influences sponsors in the selection of a property. It stands to reason that if there are risks that the sponsor may not be correctly identified (for whatever reason) with a particular property, then this will clearly have an impact on property selection for that particular sponsor.

In the words of the researchers, 'The fit, relatedness or congruence between the sponsor and object (property) can include sponsor product relevance to the (property), functional similarities, target audience similarities and/or image/ symbolic similarities.' This makes sense, as it would be highly unusual to find a sponsor prepared to select a property where the congruence between itself and that property simply does not exist, although there are plenty of examples of where this has happened with catastrophic results, such as Green Flag's sponsorship of the England football team in 1994.

The researchers also looked at levels of recall that also need to be present in order for the selection of a particular property to be effective. The researchers concluded that a brand owner with less prominence in terms of its market share, for example, should probably seek sponsorship of a lower-profile property 'in order to minimise the chances that a more prominent competitor receives sponsoring credit'.

The research also suggested that brand owners should only choose highly related sponsorship properties and avoid using properties where the connection did not look 'natural'. The issue of sponsor identification appears to plague even high-profile brands such as Adidas, Sony and McDonald's according to recent research carried out by Global Language Monitor (GLM) during the FIFA World Cup in Brazil in 2014. Researchers found that four of the top five brands associated with the Brazil 2014 FIFA World Cup were not official sponsors. Although tyre manufacturer Continental was a sponsor and significantly tops the table of brand owners associated with the FIFA World Cup 2014 when ranked by Brand Affiliation Index (BAI), the study by Global Language Monitor shows Beats, KFC, Bridgestone and Nike – none of which was officially affiliated with the tournament – sit in second, third, fourth and fifth place, respectively.

GLM also identified those brands as direct competitors with FIFA partners Sony and Adidas, and official World Cup sponsors McDonald's and Continental. 'The numbers tell the story and it's a very interesting story indeed,' comments Paul Payack, GLM's President and chief word analyst. 'Global marketers have decided that aligning their brands with the FIFA World Cup is every bit as valuable as the Olympics, and perhaps even more so for certain audiences and demographics.' However, with Nike towering over Adidas in the minds of the public as somehow connected with the FIFA World Cup, the management team at Adidas will need to pull out the stops in order to reverse the dwindling sales that created the need for the company to issue a profits warning in August 2014.

Challenge of integrating sponsorship into the marketing mix

The fact is that the world is changing at such a pace that it is difficult for any chief marketing officer (CMO) to plan how she is going to drive sales and marketing of products and services over the next 12 months let alone over the course of the next three years. This presents a challenge in the use of sponsorship as an integral part of the marketing mix, as by definition sponsorship tends to be a long-term brand communication, marketing and engagement platform and is not really fit for purpose as a 'one hit wonder'.

In addition, rapidly changing global markets and technology are impacting companies and organisations; creating vast oceans of data where marketers are not just swimming in the stuff but are drowning in it! The challenge of keeping afloat is made even more difficult when social media, the proliferation of channels, mobile devices, shifting customer and client demographics and changes in data protection laws start to weigh down ever more heavily on marketers, with the result that integrating any type of sponsorship can be extremely challenging.

The reason is simple. Investment in any form of marketing, including sponsorship, must deliver a return on investment (ROI) to make it worthwhile in the first place. Some sponsorship managers dress this up as a 'return on commitment' from their own employees as a justification of sponsorship. But that is simply not good enough.

As we discuss elsewhere in this textbook, sponsorship is not immune from the rigorous strategic approach that must be taken in deploying other marketing and

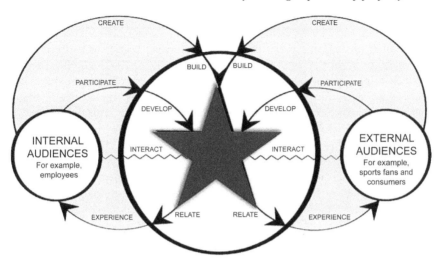

Figure 3.1 Celebrity power as a permission-based platform
Source: Kolah (2013)

communication channels, and ultimately it must deliver outcomes for the brand owner or organisation.

Another challenge facing brand owners is how to integrate a personality endorsement/sponsorship of a high-profile celebrity into the marketing mix. According to the 14th annual IEG/Performance Research Sponsorship Decision-makers Survey, published in 2014, brand marketers said they are no longer as interested in receiving identification on sponsored properties' media buys and collateral materials but ranked category exclusivity as the most important benefit (58%) that can help create awareness and visibility (67%). In this battle for attention, the use of celebrity endorsement can be extremely effective. Reflecting a desire for benefits that deliver more than just visibility, sponsors are also prioritising connections to personalities and talent associated with properties (28%).

The use of a celebrity as a permission-based platform is an area that has been well-researched and many brand owners find celebrities highly useful in engaging with external and internal audiences (see Figure 3.1).

To some extent, the use of a personality appeals to the human desire for belonging to a tribe or to our fascination with the cult of personality – which, to some extent, explains why reality TV shows such as *The X Factor*, *The Apprentice*, *Big Brother* and *I'm a Celebrity* have grown in popularity. The writing was already on the wall over a decade earlier. In *Karaoke Capitalism* (2004), the authors Jonas Ridderstråle and Kjell Nordström explained:

> Mankind has always been and will continue to be tribal, but in new and different ways. Proximity is no longer enough. The reality is that geography, culture and religion no longer automatically overlap. The new tribes are global com-

munities made up of people who actually perceive that they've something in common – no matter where they were born. These biographical tribesmen and women already know each other. They just haven't been properly introduced.

At least one in five ads in the UK carries some type of celebrity endorsement, such as the face, voice or testimony, and this trend is set to continue as brand owners strive to create memorable campaigns. According to Hamish Pringle, former Director General, Institute of Practitioners in Advertising (IPA), a 'genuine' celebrity rather than the type manufactured by the reality TV show *Big Brother* has a clearly defined personality and reputation: the celebrity is known to be extremely good at something beyond appearing in TV commercials and it is their outstanding skill in their chosen field of endeavour that has brought them into the public eye and made them an object of veneration and respect.

Case study: Justin Timberlake, 2014

Pop star, actor, entrepreneur and campaigner Justin Timberlake has been around the brand endorsement block a few times, but MasterCard believed the singer-cum-actor was an effective face for its 'Priceless Surprises' multichannel advertising campaign during the 56th Annual Grammy Awards in January 2014. Ads featured Timberlake himself involved in what MasterCard described as an 'unscripted surprise', while a social media and checkout-connected campaign showered MasterCard customers with surprises right on up to a trip to see Timberlake perform anywhere on his world tour. 'He's very creative; he understands the pulse of his fans so well. He brings insights about his fans with him. And when we created this concept, it was a delightful surprise in how it evolved with him,' explained Raja Rajamannar, CMO of MasterCard Worldwide. MasterCard developed this execution from its earlier 'Priceless Moments', 'Priceless Experiences' and 'Priceless Cities' campaigns.

'I want to move it on or transform it to a marketing platform that is truly holistic . . . inspiring "Priceless" in new and unexpected ways in consumers' lives, big or small. The whole idea was to get consumers involved with our brand. Music is an area of passion for consumers that we're deeply involved in, and the Grammys are the biggest event in music. So it was natural for us to hinge our launch planning around the Grammys,' says Rajamannar.

The decision to align a brand with a personality cannot be undertaken lightly. According to legendary designer and brand guru Wally Olins, there are four vectors through which a brand manifests itself in the use of a personality (see Figure 3.2).

The comparative significance of each vector – product, communication, environment, behaviour – varies according to the nature of the brand. 'Almost all brands are a mix of these four vectors,' explained Olins.

Although not a traditional fast-moving consumer goods (FMCG) brand, Nike has for many years behaved like one. If we apply Olins's lens to the brand, Nike is clearly a communication and product-led brand, which makes it an extremely

Figure 3.2 Matching a celebrity to a brand
Source: Olins (2004)

good fit for personality-driven merchandising. In many respects, Nike built its global brand standing on the shoulders of the world's most famous athletes of their generation – a strategy that continues to this day.

Case study: Nike, 2014

Nike depends heavily on its endorsements and sponsorships to promote itself. According to Reuters, Adidas has the second-largest budget for sponsorships among sports gear companies, but spends about 25% less on it than Nike does.

According to *Sports Illustrated* (2014), Nike easily spends more than USD 750m a year on all sports marketing, sponsorship, advertising and endorsements for athletes, leagues and universities. By tying its products to successful athletes in many sports, Nike has succeeded in boosting its image and creating the impression that the shoes or the clothes play a role in the success of the athlete. Nike went quickly to the lead in basketball shoes following its connection to Michael Jordan and the 1984 Air Jordan shoe line. The company vaulted itself into the top ranks of golf equipment manufacturers when it built its complete product line around Tiger Woods.

Since 2010 the company is tied to almost everything in the athletic department at founder Phil Knight's alma mater, the University of Oregon. It also has deals with many college and pro sports teams that use its equipment exclusively. The company has some unique sponsorship deals with the Indian national cricket team, the national football teams in Brazil and Portugal and clubs such as Manchester United FC. Nike uses these deals to get its logo in full sight on uniforms and inside stadiums throughout the world, which constantly enhances the visibility of its products.

While Nike does not discuss specific amounts spent on individual endorsement deals, these far surpass the next closest competitors such as Coca-Cola, PepsiCo (which includes Gatorade), McDonald's and Subway. Other brand owners that are active in celebrity endorsement include mobile companies such as Samsung and Sprint, financial services such as American Express, Visa and Crédit Suisse, fine watchmakers Rolex, Tag Heuer and Audemars Piguet and other sports apparel companies such as Puma and the Chinese-owned Under Armour.

Nike's roster of sports stars is breathtaking in its diversity and depth – for example, it has 21 skateboarders and 27 snowboarders and some have their own line of Nike apparel and shoes. Nike also has athletes stretching from cricket to athletics and there is always hot competition with its rival, Adidas, to sign up the latest rookie NFL players and NBA players, who have semi-god like status in the USA, where such sports matter most to the consumers and the fans.

Even with the hundreds of athletes signed globally, Nike and Adidas both have signature athletes they build entire marketing campaigns, shoes and clothing lines behind.

Nike claims that it does not look at having a certain percentage of athletes in a given sport or sampling of sports; instead it uses people to track talent to get the right person on board. The company says it looks for pinnacle-level athletes who represent the brand appropriately.

Such an endorsement strategy works both ways. The athlete gets the benefit of being involved in the sports culture that Nike creates by networking talent with other athletes from other sports and they share performance insights that feed directly into new product development for both athletes and consumers – which keeps the money machine working for Nike.

Both Nike and Adidas adopt such a strategy and see this as a partnership model where athletes get to improve their personal standing in terms of global reach and making themselves more attractive to fans outside their home territory. According to David Carter, director of USC's Marshall Sports Business Institute in the US, athletes see their first deal with Nike or Adidas as an arrival point.

And while Nike maintains that the best endorsement it can get is through the performance of an individual athlete or player using its product as it was intended, nowadays connecting athletes with consumers outside competition is a key component, whether through TV ads or social media.

It is four decades since the basketball legend Michael Jordan pulled on his trainers and stepped out onto the court as a pro basketball player. But the world cannot seem to get enough of the Jordan brand, which is owned by Nike, and in order to feed such an insatiable appetite for niche footwear, Nike teamed up with retail chain Footaction in North America to open Jordan-branded stores, the first of which was constructed a stone's throw from the NYC Madison Square Garden, where the NBA legend averaged more than 30 points per game during his playing days.

According to the *Portland Business Journal*, Jordan footwear brings in a cool USD 2.5billion in sales in the USA alone, and the only brand it is behind in market share is Nike itself. These niche shoes, which command hundreds of dollars for a single pair, are so popular that launch events often involve violent clashes among hundreds of consumers eager to get their hands on the first pairs to go on sale. This is an interesting measure of the success of the power of endorsement!

But the use of high-profile sports personalities and celebrities does not come without its risks, as Nike found out when it had to cut itself loose from disgraced cyclist Lance Armstrong, who finally admitted to being a liar and a cheat and was consequently stripped of all of his titles.

Ten principles of celebrity branding

In the process of selecting a celebrity, brand owners should consider the following points:

1 As with branding, brand owners should try to maintain consistency between the celebrity and the brand to establish a strong personality and identity. More importantly, companies should view celebrity endorsements as long-term strategic decisions affecting the brand.
2 Before signing up celebrities to endorse their brands, there are three basic prerequisites: the talent must be attractive, have a positive image in society and be perceived as being relevant.
3 Brand owners must match the values of the celebrity to that of the product or service that they want the talent to endorse so that it strongly influences the audience and customer segments' perception of the brand.
4 Brand owners must monitor the behaviour and public image of the celebrity continuously and take action to protect their reputation when necessary in order to minimise damage to their brand. The agreement with the celebrity should reflect this.
5 Companies should try to bring on board those celebrities who do not endorse other competitors' products/services or endorse very different products/services so that there is a clear transfer of personality and identity between them and the brand.
6 As celebrities command a high price tag, companies should be on the constant lookout for emerging celebrities who show some promise and potential and sign them on in their formative years if possible to ensure a win–win situation.
7 When celebrities are used to endorse brands, one obvious result could be the potential overshadowing of the brand by the celebrity. Companies should ensure that this does not happen by formulating advertising collaterals and other communications.
8 Companies must realise that having a celebrity endorsing a brand is not a goal in itself; rather it is one part of the communication mix that falls under the broader category of sales and brand marketing.
9 Even though it is challenging to measure the effects of celebrity endorsements on brand equity and sales of products and services, brand owners should have a system combining quantitative and qualitative measures to measure the overall effect of celebrity endorsements.

10   Companies should ensure that they hire celebrities on proper legal terms so that they do not endorse competitors' products in the same product category, thereby creating confusion in the minds of the consumers.

Case study: Adidas, 2014

Reinvention of the Adidas brand and its marketing strategy has been critical to its commercial success, and endorsement deals play a major part in this. However, lower than expected margins and lower profits in the wake of the FIFA World Cup 2014 have led to a rapid increase in marketing and sponsorship expenditure across the board and a move to align product innovation with communication, according to the company.

Adidas acknowledges that the markets and industry in which it competes are rapidly transforming, at a pace set by the evolution in how 'sports' are being redefined as part of entertainment. Team sports such as soccer and basketball will always be a fundamental part of sporting competition. Today, however, eclectic, individual, 'no-rules' sports such as snowboarding, inline skating and surfing have grown into significant categories. Activities such as golf, hiking and mountain biking, which used to be seen as lifestyle and leisure activities, are now part of mainstream sports, although Adidas performed poorly in the golf category. To keep up with the competition, Adidas generates at least 60 new foot-friendly designs each year and for the Premier League 2014/15, it is focusing on the 20th anniversary of its Predator football boot in North American and western European markets. The Adidas credo is to regard shoes as feet, which results in a product with superior fit and performance capabilities.

Outside football, Jessica Ennis, MBE, has helped the brand reach a new generation of fans, including stretching the brand into eyewear and other non-apparel and non-shoe product ranges.

Other celebrities who have helped Adidas to become a multibillion business includes 19-year-old pop star Justin Bieber, who is the face of the Adidas NEO range for teenagers. The star is thought to have earned around USD 58m in 2013, with much of his income from endorsement deals. Along with his Adidas endorsement, Bieber endorses headphones, and Proactiv acne cream.

Negotiating the acquisition of a sponsorship property

There needs to be a win–win outcome for all the parties, otherwise the sponsorship programme will fail. Brand owners are now much more sophisticated buyers of sponsorship, but the basics still apply.

As we shall discuss in Chapter 4, there are a number of options available to the brand owner in terms of the type of property it might want to purchase:

- Naming rights sponsorship?
- Presenting sponsorship?
- Presenting sponsorship of a section, area, entry or team?
- Presenting sponsorship of a day, weekend or week at an event?

- Presenting sponsorship of an event-driven award, trophy or scholarship?
- Presenting sponsorship of a related or subordinate event?
- Major/headline sponsorship?
- Supporting sponsorship?
- Official product status?
- Preferred supplier status?

As the IEG/Performance Research Sponsorship Decision-makers Survey (2014) demonstrates, category exclusivity is likely to be of a high value to a brand owner alongside on-site signage and broadcast ad opportunities (see Figure 3.3).

These are all likely to form part of the negotiation process and sponsors are also making it clear that assistance with determining the impact of their sponsorship is also a top priority in terms of the service provided by the rights holder (see Figure 3.4).

Ultimately, brand owners surveyed felt that sponsorship visibility and an increase in brand loyalty were the two most important objectives in terms of evaluating the performance of sponsorship (see Figure 3.5) and this is also likely to form an important consideration in the making of the purchase decision.

Ultimately, there needs to be a climate in which both sides are prepared to negotiate in order to reach agreement. There needs to be:

- a sharing of common interests and some conflicting interests to resolve
- negotiators who have the freedom to meet one another's needs and requirements
- negotiators willing to be explicit to some degree about their wants and needs
- those involved in the negotiation process must be prepared to compromise to some degree in order to reach agreement.

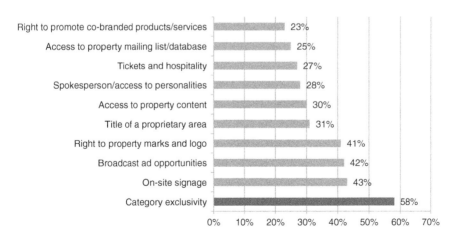

Figure 3.3 Valuable benefits for brand owners looking to purchase sponsorship
Source: IEG/Performance Research (2014)

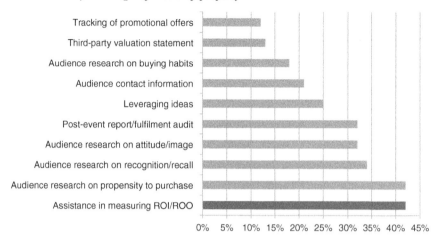

Figure 3.4 Value services provided by rights holder
Source: IEG/Performance Research (2014)

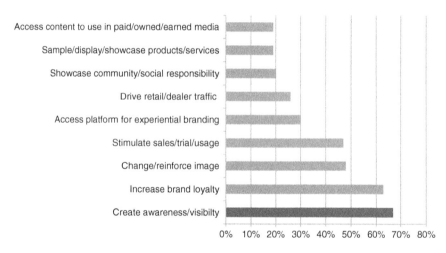

Figure 3.5 Objectives for evaluating the performance of sponsorship
Source: IEG/Performance Research (2014)

British lawyer and negotiator Clive Rich identifies three areas that effective negotiators can handle:

- Attitude: they can manage their own and others' negotiation attitudes.
- Process: they are able to manage the stages – the overall structure – of the
  negotiation.

- Behaviour: they understand and manage their own and others' negotiation behaviour.

Negotiating attitude influences negotiating behaviour and both negotiating attitude and negotiating behaviour influence success in handling the negotiating process. So the three ingredients fit together like the links in a chain.

Process is important in negotiating a sponsorship deal and provides structure for the negotiations. Most people understand that negotiation has a beginning and an end but most people do not realise that there are normally seven stages in any negotiation – and none of these can be skiped without the parties having to revisit it at a later date until they get it right and can then move on.

Budgeting for sponsorship

In the excitement of grabbing a fantastic sponsorship opportunity some brand owners may overlook an important fact of life – that the rights acquired can only become valuable to the business if they are activated and integrated into their sales and marketing activities. The sponsorship fee is a bit like paying the rent for a retail outlet. You have got a great pitch, but unless you have put goods into the shop, it is pretty much useless real estate.

The same can be said about sponsorship. Of course, all sponsorships are different and have varying degrees of activation – say, the FIFA World Cup compared with the sponsorship of a community event. But thinking about how to achieve a return on investment (see Chapter 10) requires thinking hard as to what budgets are already being committed and how these can be used in the activation of a sponsorship property.

In terms of economic downturn, many brand owners will look at slicing budget from activation of their sponsorship investments and keep their fingers crossed behind their backs that no one will notice. As we discuss in other parts of this book, you cannot rely on a sponsorship to be 'self-activating' or depend wholly on the rights holder to do the job for you. I have never read a case study in which this happened. Ever.

There are no hard-and-fast rules either. When I wrote the first sponsorship report for the *Financial Times* back in 1998 I did look at major sponsorship programmes at that time and deduced that for every $1 spent on acquiring sponsorship rights, $2 needed to be spent on activating those rights. For a long time this became something of a mantra in the industry.

Time moves on and so does sponsorship. In those days sponsorship was an incremental investment to the money spent on sales and marketing. That sounds like a luxury, does it not? If the experiences of Nike, Coca-Cola and Adidas are anything to go by, then sponsorship today is a platform for all online and offline activities rather than just a stand-alone activity. What this means is that the brand owner should be focused on making better use of the marketing budget rather than trying to swell it in order to activate a sponsorship programme. Of course, this is easier said than done and does require internal buy-in from all stakeholders involved in the leverage planning process.

Table 3.1 Sponsorship budget that needed to save 25%

Budget item	Amount	Percentage of budget (%)
Sponsorship rights fees	USD 390,000	39%
Incremental leverage spend (approx. 150% of fees)	USD 600,000	60%
Research	USD 10,000	1%
Total	**USD 1m**	100%

Source: Kim Skildum-Reid (2012)

Table 3.2 Repurposed sponsorship budget

Budget item	Amount	Percentage of budget (%)
Sponsorship rights fees	USD 390,000	76%
Incremental leverage spend (approx. 25% of fees)	USD 100,000	20%
Research	USD 20,000	4%
Total	**USD 510,000**	100%

Source: Kim Skildum-Reid (2012)

A great example of this kind of thinking is given by Kim Skildum-Reid. She was advising a client who wanted to reduce the sponsorship spend by 25% and was brought in to identify where sponsorship could be cut (see Table 3.1).

What Skildum-Reid advised was relatively simple but highly effective. A sponsorship stakeholder team was created to help look at activating the sponsorship platform. The team was coached on how to leverage the property creatively by pooling resources and using the sponsorship platform as a catalyst for all marketing. What was also recommended was an increase in the research budget so that this delivered additional insights to improve leverage of the sponsorship property in the future. The result was that the sponsorship budget was reduced by 49% without cutting any sponsorship investment (see Table 3.2).

The difference was a change in approach, better creative execution and closer involvement by a broader stakeholder team.

Chapter 3 at a glance

1 Sponsorship is a commercial agreement with a certain set of rights, duties and obligations that are not found in other types of marketing contracts.
2 Sponsorship needs to be seen as a form of investment rather than cost; otherwise it is more difficult to defend in the marketing budget.
3 Selecting a property must be driven by a clear sponsorship strategy that must be linked to brand marketing, commercial and communication objectives of the brand owner/potential sponsor.

4 Successful sponsorship is dependent on a sponsorship policy and strategy, and it would be unusual to find a sponsor prepared to select a property where congruence between itself and the property did not exist.

5 Research suggests that brand owners should only choose highly related sponsorship properties and avoid using properties where the connection does not look 'natural'.

6 Sponsorship acquisition should also be seen in a competition context and as a weapon for competitive advantage rather than just promotion.

7 The alignment of values between a brand owner and the property is particularly important in the context of using celebrity endorsement for products and services.

8 Typical objectives that are present when a sponsorship property is acquired include enhanced brand awareness, image transfer, creation of more positive attitudes, incremental sales of products and services and higher loyalty levels.

9 Effective negotiators operate across three vectors: attitude, process and behaviour.

10 Brand owners need to budget for the activation of the sponsorship but in order to be cost effective, this relies on apportioning a marketing budget rather than trying to swell it in order to activate a sponsorship programme.

Questions for discussion

1 What considerations does a brand owner need to have when selecting a property?

2 What are the most typical objectives for acquiring a sponsorship property?

3 How should a sponsorship property be integrated into the marketing mix?

4 What budgetary considerations need to be taken into account by the brand owner prior to acquiring the property?

Further reading

Collett, P and Fenton, W (2011), *The Sponsorship Handbook*, Jossey-Bass

Engelsman, R (2012), A comparative study on how sponsorship fit and no sponsorship fit affects consumers' responses to a brand. Dissertation on MSc International Marketing at London Met Business School

Ferrand, A, Torrigiani, L and Povill, A (2007), *Routledge Handbook of Sports Sponsorship*, Routledge

Kolah, A (2006), *Advanced Sports Sponsorship Strategies*, SportBusiness

Kolah, A (2007), *Sponsorship Works: A Brand Marketer's Casebook*, Electric Word

Mueller, T (2011), Professors and practitioners: The practical convergence theory with sponsorship negotiation and management, *Journal of Sponsorship*

Olins, W (2004), *Olins on Brand*, Thames & Hudson

Olson, E and Thjømøe, H (2011), Explanations for sponsor identification accuracy, *Journal of Sponsorship*

Rich C, (2013), *The Yes Book*, Virgin Books

Ridderstråle, J and Nordström, K (2004), *Karaoke Capitalism*, Pearson
Skildum-Reid, K (2012), *The Corporate Sponsorship Toolkit*, Freya Press

Websites

Inside the Games [accessed 23 June 2014]: http://www.insidethegames.biz
International Olympic Committee [accessed 8 August 2014]: http://www.olympic.org/ioc

Reports

International Olympic Committee Marketing Report London 2012

4 Process of selling a sponsorship property

In this chapter

- Best practice in selling sponsorship
- Understanding propositions, experiences, connections and relationships
- Developing a sales strategy
- Essential sales preparation
- Sponsorship sales process
- How to create a winning sponsorship proposal
- How to negotiate with a brand owner to achieve a successful outcome

Introduction

Just before I started to write this chapter, I had the pleasure of a wonderful lunch at my club, the British Academy of Film and Television Arts (BAFTA) in Piccadilly, London, with a great friend of mine, Lena Robinson. Lena is one of the most gifted business development and sales professionals I have ever worked with, when we were together at WPP, and she now runs an incredible business development power-house for agency entrepreneurs called KiwiGirl. Lena is an inspiration for ideas and new ways of thinking. And she shared something very special that I wanted to share with you too. She said: 'People don't buy what you do, but why you do it.'

Lena explained that so many agency heads, rights holders and entrepreneurs get it so wrong when it comes to business development and selling. Lena should know, as she was the global business development director at Vizeum, now part of Dentsu Aegis. 'The goal isn't to sell to people what you have. The goal is to do business with people who believe what you believe,' and Lena drew this on her disposable table napkin (see Figure 4.1).

One of the biggest mistakes that companies and rights holders of all shapes and sizes make is to talk about what they do and how they do it, rather than why they do it. From a sponsorship perspective, this is wonky thinking.

In the Guru in a Bottle® cartoon series of books, website, Twitter feeds and Facebook blogs, I often discuss the need to have a strong focus on audience seg-mentation as a critical component of the selling process. And that means not just demographic and psychographic information about 'target customers or clients' (I really hate using that term, as who on earth wants to be a 'target'?) but, to be

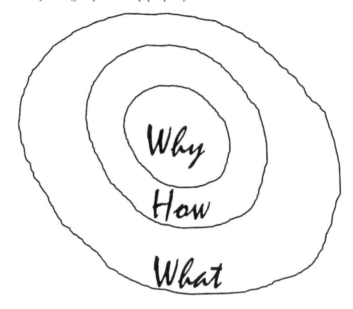

Figure 4.1 Lena's napkin at BAFTA

more precise, it means having a lens on attitudes, values, beliefs, perceptions and behaviours of desired customers, clients, supporters and, of course, sponsors.

Look again at Figure 4.1. It is clear that those who are more successful in business development and selling sponsorship will focus on connecting with potential sponsors and brand partners by sending messages to the limbic part of the brain, where the emotions live, which controls the decision-making process but does not process language.

In other words, selling anything, including a sponsorship opportunity, is about harnessing the power of emotional intelligence – feelings and emotions – rather than being stuck outside of that ring of influence and only appealing to the rational part of the brain.

Just focusing on what the sponsorship opportunity looks like and how it will work simply will not be good enough.

'What you buy shows the proof of what you believe,' adds Lena and, of course, nowhere is this more important than when a sponsor commits to supporting a cause, event, team, personality, league, event or any other type of brand partnership programme.

This insight into human behaviour is much older than you think. 'When dealing with people, let us remember we are not dealing with creatures of logic. We are dealing with creatures of emotion, creatures bristling with prejudices and motivated by pride and vanity,' wrote Dale Carnegie, one of the most famous American entrepreneurs of the 20th century and author of *How to Win Friends and Influence People*.

What is fascinating is that this was written in 1953, well before access to the powerful databases we have today that contain millions of bits of data on just about every aspect of our lives as it is legally possible to hold. What Dale Carnegie said then holds true today. If we only operate on a rational basis in order to try to influence a sponsor to purchase a sponsorship programme, then we will fail, and fail miserably.

The starting point for selling a sponsorship property is not what you may expect. It starts with the issues, challenges, problems and opportunities facing the potential sponsor.

If the rights holder is going to be successful in the pursuit of striking a win–win sponsorship deal, then it must see the whole process from the brand owner's and not exclusively from its own point of view.

Best practice in selling sponsorship

Do your homework!

Prior to making a pitch to a prospective sponsor, you need to have a full understanding of the brand owner you are approaching. This must cover its distribution channels, new product launches, new market competition and previous, current and upcoming sales and marketing campaigns. And that is just the starting point!

'Do a better job of knowing who we are, what we do and what makes us tick. Have a basic understanding of our culture and what our brand stands for,' observes Chuck Browning, head of sponsorships and corporate giving with Farmers Group in the USA.

Listen! And then listen some more!

While it may sound basic, the most successful salespeople are those who are fabulous at listening. And this is an area of competitive advantage in the sponsorship sector, when most prospective sponsors now face the deafening noise of rights holders shouting about their properties.

Listening means understanding the prospective brand owner's marketing and communication objectives, opportunities, challenges and requirements.

'Properties need to hear what I'm saying – those are the people I'm doing business with,' said Lesley Poch, director of strategic partnerships, experiential marketing and events with Panasonic in the USA. 'With everyone constantly pitching us, I explain that I'm not going to advertise in a stadium with Mitsubishi video boards or Sony TVs. Why would I do that?'

This basic lack of understanding of the environment for sponsorship is a serious issue, as context is very often important and can be more important than simply the sponsorship activity itself. And this basic lack of understanding has chipped away at the professional reputation of those selling sponsorship who tend to treat it like an unfocused email marketing campaign.

Other sponsorship decision-makers are quick to agree. 'Whether selling a new sponsorship or working with an existing partner, properties need to listen to what our objectives are, what it is we're trying to accomplish, and translate that information into real opportunities for us,' adds Gillian Fraser, head of sponsorships with BMO Harris.

Treat relationships as a partnership

Sponsorship needs to be a collaborative process in order to be effective for all parties. When working with sponsors, rights holders should adopt the mindset of 1 + 1 = 3. As Fraser says:

> We don't like to be viewed as a chequebook where we write a cheque and walk away. We're very active and engaged in sponsorship, and unfortunately there are some properties that don't like sponsors to be overly involved. We want to be at the table having a conversation. They know their property better than we do, and we want to tap into their mind and use our expertise as a bank to leverage the partnership and make it a win–win for both of us.

Help measure success

It is now expected that a rights holder will collaborate with the brand owner in the measurement of inputs, outputs and outcomes of the sponsorship programme in an 'open book' way. It is vital for the longevity of the relationship that the sponsor's objectives are uppermost in the mind of the rights holder. Browning admits:

> What we really need help with from our partners is a more credible method to measure the value the sponsorship can add to our business. I realize it might sound very basic – and almost silly – but we constantly challenge our partners to help us come up with better measurement tools that help us internally justify our spend.

And he is not alone. According to IEG, 40% of sponsors rank assistance measuring return on objectives (ROO) and return on investment (ROI) as an extremely valuable benefit delivered by the rights holder.

Understanding propositions, experiences, connections and relationships

The first step in creating a sponsorship proposition is to remove the notion that selling sponsorship is simply transactional in nature. Procuring sponsorship is not the same as walking into the supermarket and buying a loaf of bread. As a result, the traditional view of 'selling' is somewhat limited:

Offer to exchange something of value for something else. The something of value being offered may be tangible or intangible. Buying and selling are understood to be two sides of the same coin or transaction. Both seller and buyer are in a process of negotiation to consummate the exchange of values. The exchange or selling process has implied rules and identifiable stages. It's implied that the selling process will proceed fairly and ethically so that the parties end up nearly equally rewarded. The stages of selling, and buying, involve getting acquainted, assessing each party's need for the other's item of value, and determining if the values to be exchanged are equivalent or nearly so, or, in buyer's terms, 'worth the price'.

The traditional view of 'selling' applies where the subject of the transaction is a commodity. So is sponsorship a commodity, like the media buy for a 48-sheet poster site or piece of direct mail?

To some extent, football shirt sponsorship deals, which often make the news headlines, are in reality a media buy rather than sponsorship per se, because the value of the deal is in direct proportion to the amount of media exposure the brand will get as a result of the broadcast coverage. Looked at in this way, a shirt sponsorship deal is a commodity, as the value of the benefit can be measured in hours, minutes and seconds and that is what the brand owner is in effect purchasing – advertising exposure. But I would not describe that as sponsorship in the way that we have been discussing the subject in this book.

The traditional view of 'selling' is also limited in scope in that it does not take account of the relative bargaining positions of the sponsor(s) and the rights holder(s) – and this varies widely between industry sectors as well as property types. For example, the International Olympic Committee (IOC) is arguably the most powerful rights holder on the planet. Governments have been known to bend over backwards to win the right to host a Summer or Winter Olympic Games and national sponsors are eager to acquire intellectual property (IP) rights of association from national organising committees. As a result, the IOC can and does name its own terms, even going as far as laying down highly detailed ground rules as to what it regards as permissible activation and even having a power of veto if it does not like what the brand owner suggests.

At the other end of the scale, a local swimming group may be looking for sponsorship for its team to compete in national competitions and will be grateful to any sponsor prepared to cover travel and accommodation costs with no strings attached.

Irrespective of the level of sponsorship opportunity on offer, the rights holder must see the opportunity on offer through the lens of the prospective sponsor. Think about it. You may be ready to sell a sponsorship opportunity or package, but is the brand owner ready to buy? It is also very important to remember that buying sponsorship has its own purchase cycle, just as selling sponsorship has its own sales cycle.

Figure 4.2 is a useful illustration of how a typical business and marketing planning cycle works.

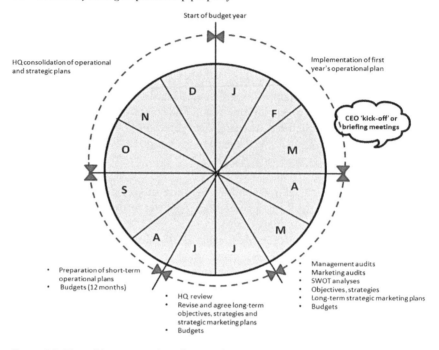

Start of budget year

HQ consolidation of operational
and strategic plans

Implementation of first
year's operational plan

CEO 'kick-off' or
briefing meetings

- Preparation of short-term
  operational plans
- Budgets (12 months)

- HQ review
- Revise and agree long-term
  objectives, strategies and
  strategic marketing plans
- Budgets

- Management audits
- Marketing audits
- SWOT analyses
- Objectives, strategies
- Long-term strategic marketing plans
- Budgets

Figure 4.2 Typical business and marketing planning cycle

The business model defines the way the organisation will sell its products and services, who pays what and the partners and associates to be involved. These are not always obvious and may require prioritisation and selection from within a broader portfolio of existing activities.

The choice of partners, such as licensees, franchisees and associated companies can also affect the way in which the company conducts its marketing – and sponsorship – activities and the resources it is prepared to put behind it.

Once the business or strategic business units (SBU) strategies have been formulated, it is then possible to develop the marketing strategy and plan that could include sponsorship.

Equally, it could omit having a sponsorship component. For example, not all of Shell's SBUs activate the sponsorship with Ferrari F1 in exactly the same way, as some choose to spend a lot less on activation and other SBUs decide to spend considerably more in their own market.

The determination of what goes into a marketing strategy and plan is often an iterative process, where typically functional managers will help shape the marketing strategy and plan but not in return for compromise or delay. They are also unlikely to have strong views either way about the use or absence of sponsorship. And the workflow is likely to run within the brand owner's own internal strategic business and operational planning cycle.

All of these points are useful insight for the rights holder who may be so focused on making a sale that such details can be lost in the process. The success of an approach to a prospective sponsor is dependent on where the brand owner is in this cycle and its propensity to want to enter into a sponsorship deal. Even if the timing of such an approach is right, a decision on the sponsorship proposition could take a frustratingly long period of time, which tends to indicate that the rights holder needs to plan very carefully in advance of making an approach in order to take account of these potentially lengthy timescales.

For example, in the world of sports sponsorship, it can take anywhere between 6 and 12 months to land a five-figure sponsorship deal; 12 and 18 months to land a six–seven-figure deal and around 18 and 24 months to secure a multimillion global sponsorship deal. It is far more profitable to look from the perspective of the potential sponsor, and yet some rights holders will try to 'sell' a generic sponsorship package in the vain hope that, as a numbers game, someone out there will buy it.

This is equivalent of 'spamming' potential sponsors! The tragedy is that the opportunity could be relevant for a handful of them, but given the way in which the proposition has been communicated, it is highly unlikely to create any real interest and is destined to end up in the computer's recycle bin. For example, have you ever seen an advertisement for a sponsorship opportunity 'YOUR LOGO HERE!' Such an approach is guaranteed to turn the stomach of any seasoned sponsorship professional, as selling should not be reduced to what is called 'logo slapping'. This was prevalent in the 1980s, when there was a lot more marketing money sloshing around in the good times. Frankly speaking, rights holders became lazy and made very little effort to provide sponsors with a clear view in terms of a return on investment. It was also partly the fault of sponsors, as they often made no such requests. The result of this laziness and chequebook approach to sponsorship was that the sponsorship industry started to get itself a bad name and with it a poor reputation as expectations fell short and senior managers began to question the efficacy of spending substantial amounts of money without a clear sense of a return on investment.

Although such days are long gone, it is still the case that many rights holders have little or no concept of how powerful sponsorship could be if they stopped to think about how to sell it properly. If rights holders adopt a technique that sales guru Daniel Pink describes as 'perspective-taking', it will help them in their sales efforts, as it involves tuning into the actions and outlook of the potential sponsor.

The key strategy, which works exceedingly well, is to listen – to be in what I call 'receive' rather than being stuck in 'transmit' mode, which as marketers we often struggle with. Reading a poorly crafted sponsorship proposal is rather like being stuck in 'transmit mode' and is doomed to fail.

Selling is also about you – the seller. We need to rewire our thinking about selling. Instead, it is more profitable to influence. In the introduction to this chapter I talked about not simply focusing on the 'what' and the 'how' but also the 'why'. A sponsor is a party that is likely to have a bunch of issues, problems, threats, challenges and opportunities. So it is important to see the world from their point of view to be successful in coming away with a sponsorship deal.

In my experience, there tend to be six common mistakes made when selling sponsorship:

1   The rights holder does not get to understand the brand owner and its competitive situation.
2   Poor timing of the 'pitch' in terms of the brand owner's financial year end.
3   The rights holder's perspective is 'inside out' (about itself) rather than 'outside-in' (about the brand owner).
4   The rights holder focuses on price rather than on value from the perspective of the potential sponsor.
5   No research analysis used by the rights holder to provide a level of confidence about the sponsorship opportunity to the brand owner.
6   No focus on how the sponsorship will achieve a return on objectives and a return on investment for the brand owner.

Every sponsorship programme has a lifespan and irrespective of the property type, a well-leveraged sponsorship will normally hit its peak at the end of year 3 and just before it starts to tail off in effectiveness around the six-year mark, as in the bell-curve in Figure 4.3.

There are always exceptions to a typical sponsorship lifespan: for example, the FIFA World Cup, Premier League, Olympic Games, Wimbledon Tennis Championships, Tate Gallery and other sponsorship programmes. And, of course, there are naming rights deals in the USA that can exceed 50 and even 100 years.

At the end of the day, it is important to keep this in mind when selling a sponsorship property to a brand owner and, of course, it is not about the length of the sponsorship but whether it satisfies key commercial and brand-building objectives in the first place that will grab the interest of a potential sponsor (see Figure 4.4).

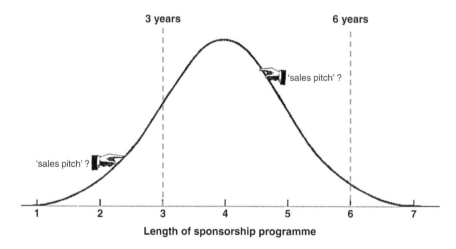

Figure 4.3 Typical sponsorship lifespan

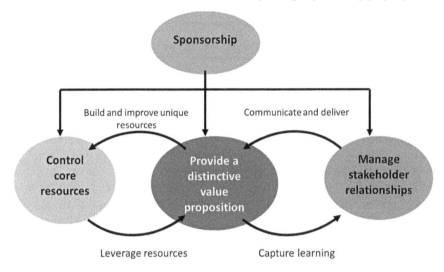

Figure 4.4 Integration of sponsorship by the brand owner into marketing

Exiting early from a sponsorship programme is not an outcome that either you as the rights holder or the brand owner will necessarily want or welcome. The key to ensuring that the sponsorship programme does not end prematurely is to give the sponsor the confidence that the programme delivers tangible value and that it fits with all other marketing activities rather than existing outside of these.

Some of the most effective sponsorships in the world, such as Speedo's sponsorship of swimming or Nike's sponsorship of athletes in just about every conceivable sport that requires some form of footwear, tend to reflect the following arrangement.

Control core resources

The brand owner will need to develop and leverage resources (ideally, proprietary to its own business) that it requires to deliver the value proposition. These resources often include aspects of systems, skills, structures and IP rights that are applied to build and leverage unique competitive advantage and to prevent or inhibit the copying of products/services by competitors.

Provide a distinctive value proposition

The brand owner must develop and consistently deliver a value proposition that is relevant, meaningful, distinctive and attractive to the desired segment so as to earn the consumers' or customers' preference, secure repeat orders/purchases as well as justify a premium price for the goods/services.

Manage stakeholder relationships

The brand owner must engage in genuine two-way communication with its audience in order to communicate effectively and to capture learning in order to enhance its value proposition.

In the right hands, sponsorship is a collaborative marketing platform that allows all of the above to take place. Sometimes, the first year is building an audience for the new sponsor – particularly if it is taking over from the previous sponsor. The second year may be looking to activate more strongly and the third year is seeking to extract as much value from the sponsorship property in terms of over-delivering on key commercial and brand-building objectives.

For this reason, the brand owner may be reluctant to spend heavily in the first year of sponsorship – feeling that there is an overhang with a previous sponsor and better to spend more when that perception has well and truly become eroded from memory. Year 2 is likely to be heavily on social media and offline activation and year 3 may be a lot less if it looks like the objectives have been achieved and that the sponsor is looking to exit from the sponsorship.

This is not a foregone conclusion but it does make a strong case for keeping in touch with the sponsor all the way through the sponsorship programme and for constantly checking that objectives are being met – and suggesting other opportunities for adding value as they arise.

Typical sponsorship propositions

Across the world, there are ten sponsorship propositions that a brand owner may consider for satisfying its commercial and brand-marketing objectives:

1   venue sponsorship
2   exclusive sponsorship
3   multi-sponsor format
4   secondary sponsorship
5   official supplier/partner status
6   personality sponsorship and endorsement
7   broadcast sponsorship
8   editorial sponsorship/native advertising
9   advertiser-funded programmes (AFP)
10 community-linked sponsorship

Venue sponsorship

Venue sponsorship is a relatively new development in the UK, although much more common in Europe and the USA. Notable examples in the UK have included the Reebok Stadium in Bolton (now Macron Stadium), Walkers Stadium in Leicester (now King Power Stadium), the Emirates Stadium in London and the O2 Arena in the London Docklands, which was recently used as a London 2012 Olympic Games venue. In some cases, a venue sponsorship will form part of a naming rights deal: a hybrid of advertising and sponsorship rights where the sponsor's name is physically attached to the stadium or building and sits on top of a pyramid of other tangible and intangible rights.

Exclusive sponsorship

The promotional value of being an exclusive team sponsor, such as Shell and Ferrari F1, can be extremely powerful, given the amount of broadcast media coverage each sport attracts.

In football, Barclays enjoyed exclusive sponsorship of the Premier League and this, in turn, opened up new communication opportunities with fans, customers and prospects on a scale that could never have been achieved in the absence of the sponsorship investment. In 2014 Barclays signalled it was ending the sponsorship.

Case study: McLaren Mercedes and Santander, 2014

In January 2014, McLaren Mercedes announced that Santander renewed its long-term corporate partnership with the team, extending a deal that stretches back to 2007 with driver Jenson Button also playing a key ambassadorial role for the bank for the past 4 years.

Through the sponsorship, Santander used McLaren to establish the brand in the UK and has since released initiatives such as the London Grand Prix 2012 campaign – which was shortlisted for Best Use of PR at the BT Sport Industry Awards 2013.

In his role as brand ambassador, Jenson Button has also fronted major marketing campaigns and employee engagement initiatives, and played a central role in Santander's global Universities Scholarship Programme. The former World Champion will continue to play a 'significant' role in Santander campaigns as the partnership progresses. Keith Moor, chief marketing officer, Santander, said: 'Santander and McLaren have formed a long-term partnership and together we have set new standards in sports marketing. Our decision to renew that relationship is not something that we have taken lightly, but it is based upon a proven track record of achievement and we are pleased to continue to be in partnership with one of the most iconic brands in global sport.'

Multi-sponsor format

Examples include the London 2012 Olympic Games as well as the FIFA World Cup 2014 and the FIA World Championships 2014. These types of sponsorship work particularly efficiently where a brand owner wants to reach a consumer audience on a global basis and relies heavily on broadcast coverage to do the job. In the case of the Olympic Games, which permits no form of branding on athletes or hoardings within the line of camera view, sponsors must be creative in activating their sponsorship rights in other ways, such as on merchandise and at point-of-sale within a retail environment.

From a rights holder's perspective, sponsorship clutter needs to be avoided. For example, the UEFA Champions League currently limits the number of its sponsors to eight in order to deliver a higher level of media exposure for Heineken, PlayStation, MasterCard, UniCredit, Adidas, Nissan, Gazprom and HTC.

Case study: EE and the BAFTA Awards, 2014

The British Academy of Film and Television Arts (BAFTA) has witnessed many changes since its birth in 1947 but its fundamental purpose has remained the same. The Academy was formed on 16 April 1947, when a group of the most eminent names in the British film production industry gathered in a room at the Hyde Park Hotel. The film director David Lean was appointed chairman. Their fundamental aim was 'to recognise those who had contributed outstanding creative work towards the advancement of British film'. Eleven years later, the British Film Academy merged with the Guild of Television Producers and Directors to form the Society of Film and Television Arts. David Lean donated royalties from *The Bridge On The River Kwai* and *Doctor Zhivago* to the Society and these served as an invaluable source of working capital in its early years.

When Her Majesty Queen Elizabeth II made the decision to gift the royalties from Richard Cawston's documentary *Royal Family* to the Society in the early 1970s, it enabled the Society to move from its office suite in Great Portland Street to 195 Piccadilly, which was converted to house two preview theatres and a meeting place for members. In 1976, the opening of the new headquarters was attended by Her Majesty Queen Elizabeth II, HRH the Duke of Edinburgh, HRH Princess Anne and the Earl Mountbatten of Burma. The Society became officially known as the British Academy of Film and Television Arts and BAFTA entered the nation's vocabulary.

There are five BAFTA Awards ceremonies and the BAFTA Film Awards announced in February each year are a bellwether of the fortunes of films that are voted on for the Hollywood Oscars. Over the years, the BAFTAs have grown in stature and significance and are no longer in the shadow of their glamorous cousin in sunny Los Angeles, California. It is notable that the 'royalty' of Hollywood, including Steven Spielberg and Hollywood 'A' stars such as George Clooney, will make the flight over to attend the very British Awards ceremony, which attracts a global TV audience and in many ways is far more prestigious for the independence of its voting members than the enormous amount of lobbying and hospitality that Oscar voting members are subjected to.

The title sponsorship of the BAFTAs was with mobile phone brand Orange for 15 years until 2012 when the company was subsumed within the EE global brand identity that includes T-Mobile, and EE took over the title sponsorship of the BAFTAs in 2013.

Orange was an iconic mobile brand designed by Wally Olins, CBE, and was famous for its stunning use of photography in TV commercials – so there was already a connection with the advertising and film industry. Orange was also famous for introducing 'Orange Wednesdays' when filmgoers could get two-for-one tickets to watch films of their choice, thanks to Orange, or get a discount off the price of a cinema ticket by using their mobile phone.

There is a raft of secondary partnership opportunities available outside the headline sponsorship of EE whereby brands can use the glamour of BAFTA in order to promote their products and services to a global audience. Such is the popularity of the BAFTAs from a hospitality perspective that brand owners are often falling over themselves to want to become brand partners with one of the UK's foremost cultural institutions (see Table 4.1).

As part of the sponsorship deal with BAFTA, brands get to have their products and services profiled with some of the most famous people on the planet and although they are not directly endorsed by the celebrities as a result of this relationship with BAFTA, nonetheless, the association is still a very valuable one, particularly if the brand owner is interested in reaching BAFTA members. At the awards ceremonies, BAFTA works with luxury brands on an invitation-only basis so that nominees get special treatment from these brands with products and services up to and including the award ceremonies. This takes the form of personal services in advance of the events and at the BAFTA style suites.

Style partners also work as a team to maximise their involvement with BAFTA by speaking directly to their customer base and working on promotional initiatives to reach a broader audience.

Table 4.1 Secondary sponsors of the BAFTAs

Category	Brand owner	Designation
Watch	Rue Du Rhône	BAFTA official watch and timing
Jewellery	Asprey	BAFTA nominees' party and official jewellers
Makeup	Lancôme	BAFTA official makeup
Airline	British Airways	BAFTA official airline
Car	Audi	BAFTA official car
Champagne	Taittinger	BAFTA official champagne
Hair stylist	Charles Worthington	BAFTA official hair
Hotel	Savoy	BAFTA official hotel
Men's stylist	Hackett	BAFTA official menswear stylist
Outdoor media	CBS Outdoor	BAFTA official outdoor media
Paper	Paperlinx	BAFTA official paper
Wine	Villa Maria	BAFTA official wine
Beer	Grolsch	BAFTA official beer
Placemat	TCM HD	BAFTA official placemat
Chocolate	Hotel Chocolat	BAFTA official chocolate
Mineral water	Evian/Badoit	BAFTA official water

Source: BAFTA (2014)

The BAFTA Awards also produce high-quality event programmes that are available both in print and offline versions and these also carry advertorial content. The printed versions are collectable souvenirs for guests and another channel for partners to reach desired audience and customer segments.

Advertising includes photo shoots with leading talent, specially commissioned illustrated covers, and articles about selected nominees. A brand owner is able to embed digital links to the online programme to direct readers to a special landing page.

Secondary sponsorship

This describes that status of a sponsor that provides lower-level cash that is counterbalanced by a larger benefit-in-kind or value-in-kind contribution to the rights holder. For example, Heineken enjoys primary sponsorship of the European Rugby Cup (the 'Heineken Cup') with a range of secondary sponsors, including FedEx, Amlin and Adidas, supporting the event.

Case study: Dunkin' Donuts and Liverpool FC, 2014

Dunkin' Donuts is ramping up its marketing activity by sponsoring Liverpool FC as part of a wider move to expand the brand in the UK and Asia. The two-year tie-up marks the brand's first partnership with a Premier League club and will see it develop co-branded campaigns with the team. The Dunkin' Donuts logo will appear throughout the club's Anfield stadium in Liverpool, while it will also supply snacks and beverages to fans on match days.

Dunkin' Donuts says it will work to bring fans closer to the club through 'innovative' promotions across the globe. It is currently deciding what channels it will focus on. However, it has been quick to adopt new marketing channels such as Vine in its US domestic market in recent months.

It is hoping to use the Liverpool FC tie-up to help secure franchise deals in London, the Midlands and eventually Scotland following its return to the UK last year. The company pulled out of the region in the mid-1990s and has outlined a five-year plan to grow its profile across the region. Dunkin' Donuts will activate the deal in other markets where football's popularity is growing, such as Asia and the USA. However, the club's linkage with a product that does not convey a healthy-eating message is going to be controversial, particularly with parents and health professionals concerned about an increase in childhood obesity in Europe.

Official supplier/partner status

Under such an arrangement, an existing sponsor can receive enhanced rights as the 'official supplier' of a product or service category it wishes to associate with the event for marketing purposes. For example, HSBC, Slazenger, Evian, Ralph Lauren, Lanson, G4S, Hertz and Robinsons are the official suppliers to the Wimbledon Tennis Championships, which have a relationship with the All England Lawn Tennis and Croquet Club (AELTC).

Alternatively, 'official supplier' status can be conferred on a brand owner that is not a full-blown sponsor of the event or property. This indicates a lower level of commitment.

For example, 'official supplier' status will almost always include category exclusivity such as kit supply agreements often entered into with sports brand owners such as Nike and Adidas.

Personality sponsorship/endorsement

Many superstars have individual sponsorship deals in place by which they endorse a particular product or service. For example, Hollywood actor George Clooney has a global endorsement deal with Nescafé for a range of its coffee products and coffee machines. And Mercedes-Benz has a multiplatform global marketing partnership with the 16-time Grand Slam champion Roger Federer that covers the use of his image, personal appearances and product placement in a partnership that makes the tennis star a global ambassador for the brand.

Case study: Pepsi and football stars of FIFA World Cup, Brazil, 2014

Footballers including Argentinians Lionel Messi and Sergio Agüero, Englishman Jack Wilshere and Brazilian David Luiz make up a 19-man team that will form part of Pepsi's 'Live for Now' campaign. Not only do the players star in Pepsi's global television commercial but a selection of the players have also featured on limited-edition packaging and point-of-sale (POS) across the globe since March 2014.

Kristin Patrick, global chief marketing officer at Pepsi, said:

> Pepsi has had a tremendous relationship with football, going back nearly 15 years. We've brought together our most impressive Pepsi football roster yet, comprised of players who truly embody our brand spirit. Throughout the year we'll be collaborating with them to bring our fans exciting and engaging content, products and experiences – bringing fans closer to the game they love.

The Pepsi-sponsored players announced they were part of the campaign on social media to kick off a series of year-long activities from January 2014. What is interesting is that such a tactic could be seen as ambush marketing (see Chapter 8), as Coca-Cola is an official sponsor of the FIFA World Cup, Brazil, 2014.

On its Twitter handle #FutbolNow Pepsi stated:

> Pepsi.com is excited to reveal the global 2014 Pepsi superstar football squad as part of the 2014 campaign, inspiring fans the world over to 'Live For

Now.' The line-up unites 19 of the world's greatest players, spanning five continents and nearly 20 countries. Those included, pictured in front of artwork by Brazilian street artist AKN, are: Oribe Peralta, Mohamed Salah, Clint Dempsey, Mario Gomez, Robin van Persie, Gylfi Þor Sigurðsson, Victor Moses, Sergio Ramos, Leo Messi, Vincent Kompany, David Luiz, Sergio Agüero, Tarik Elyounoussi, Jack Wilshere, Peter Osaze Odemwingie, Maynor Figueroa and Kemar Lawrence. Welcome to the 2014 Pepsi #FutbolNow team!

David Luiz, Chelsea player and vice-captain of Brazil's national team, said: 'For me, playing football is about making the most of every second on the pitch and showing your love and character for the game – and for the fans. I can't wait to join fans from across the world and celebrate a big year for football.'

And four-time player of the year and Argentinian captain Leo Messi, adds:

> Football has been my passion since I was a little boy and it's certainly one of the things I live for now. I am so proud to be partnering with Pepsi again and representing the brand globally as part of this star-studded team.

Broadcast sponsorship

Broadcast sponsorship is typically the sponsorship of a TV or radio broadcast on a commercial channel or the channel itself. In the case of the broadcast sponsorship of an event, the broadcast sponsor will enter into a separate arrangement with the broadcaster and may therefore be different from the event sponsor.

The event organiser may either license the right to broadcast the event to a production company, which will then sublicense these rights to broadcasters, or the rights holder may commission a producer but sell the broadcast rights itself directly to broadcasters.

Television and radio rights are commonly sold on an individual territory basis and often before sponsors have been acquired. This is common in the case of TV broadcasts, as a sponsor will usually make TV exposure a condition of entering into any sponsorship agreement, as in the case of UEFA's Champions League. Broadcast sponsorship of a programme or series will confer on the sponsor rights to associate itself with each programme in 'bumpers' around the opening and closing credits as well as in the ad breaks and must comply with strict Ofcom regulations.

Case study: Discovery Channel and India National Defence Academy, 2014

This is an example of broadcast sponsorship on the Discovery Channel in India, where the programme broadcast was sponsored by a raft of India-based brands, including Nokia Lumia 525, Royale Aspira, Hero Maestro, Policy Bazaar and Nano Twist. The following email was sent to subscribers of the Discovery Channel in India on 22 January 2014:

In 1955, soon after World War II, the world's first tri-services military academy with a campus that spans across 8000 acres was established in Khadakwasla – a region near Pune, India. On 26 January at 9pm Discovery Channel will take you inside this unique institution in 'REVEALED: National Defence Academy'. The one-hour special charts out the history of military leadership; and explores the journey of young cadets and officers from all three services (Army, Navy and Air-force) through a gruelling three-year National Defence Academy course. Steeped in tradition and lore, find out what it takes to pass out of this prestigious Academy and to come out serving one's nation with courage and pride. The NDA's alumni have fought and died for India in wars and battles across the globe, always living up to the NDA's motto of 'Service before Self'.

Case study: Vevo and Schwarzkopf, 2014

In January 2014, online music video platform Vevo and haircare giant Schwarz-kopf entered into a six-figure, year-long partnership that will see the hairstyling brand sponsor Vevo's emerging-artist Lift series in the UK. The Lift platform was created for selected emerging artists, allowing them to boost their careers and reach new fans through new content involving their music. The Lift series, which is entering its third year, has previously included artists such as Rita Ora, Labrinth and Conor Maynard.

As part of the deal, brokered by MEC Access, Schwarzkopf's got2b range has been made highly visible, with a continuous presence across Vevo's platform and devices throughout the five Lift cycles planned for 2014. In addition, got2b and Vevo will offer viewers the chance to meet the Lift artists via competitions on got2b's social media platforms and viewers will also be able to go behind the scenes with exclusive videos focusing on hair and fashion styling. Ben Haxworth, head of marketing at Schwarzkopf, explained:

> Sponsorship has been an integral part of our communication strategy on got2b for the last four years, and this partnership with Vevo is a natural evo-lution for the brand as we know that our target audience of 16–24-year-olds are spending an ever increasing amount of time online. Placing got2b around celebrity music content on Vevo is the perfect fit.

Activation includes elements like pre-roll, overlay and display MPU (Web banners) and chances for viewers to meet Lift artists and win goody bags through competitions.

Editorial sponsorship/native advertising

In the September 2013 issue of lifestyle magazine *Shape*, a full-page article carried the headline 'Water works!' under the heading of 'News'. After citing many studies espousing hydration, and a warning from the Center for Science in the

Public Interest against high-calorie sugary drinks, the non-bylined article said that about 20% of Americans did not like the taste of water. 'If that sounds like you, check out the new Shape Water Boosters,' the article reads. 'Just a single squeeze (equal to a half-teaspoon) adds delicious flavor – but not calories – along with a concentrated punch of nutrients that offer some important bonus benefits.'

Accompanying the article were photos of all four varieties of the product, named after those promised benefits: Beauty, Wellness, Slim and Energy.

The US National Advertising Division, the investigative arm of the ad industry's voluntary self-regulation system, ruled that the editorial 'blurred the line between advertising and editorial content in a way which could confuse consumers'. According to the decision, the publisher said that the ad required no disclosure, because a connection between the publication and its branded products was obvious. It also 'contended it would be odd if it could not recommend its own products in the same manner as other companies' products in editorial content'.

Editorial sponsorship is an 'advertorial', although the copy is not generated by the brand owner but by a journalist working for the newspaper, magazine or website.

In January 2014, the *New York Times* (NYT) unveiled its new website design, which helps to push advertorial content, which is now known as 'native advertising'. The *NYT* clearly labels these bits of sponsored content 'paid post' and they have a blue line of demarcation. In a detailed memo timed perfectly to coincide with the holiday break before Christmas 2013, its publisher, Arthur Sulzberger Jr, told staff that the new native advertising platform for the organisation would be digital and very clearly marked. It followed an announcement in November 2013 by Time Inc. that it would dramatically increase the amount of native advertising it carries.

In the UK, the Committee of Advertising Practice (CAP) Code, administered by the Advertising Standards Authority (ASA) applies in such cases. Under the CAP Code, such marketing communications will be seen to be native advertising and potentially not permitted if they are seen as 'an advertisement feature, announcement or promotion, the content of which is controlled by the marketer, not the publisher that is disseminated in exchange for payment or other reciprocal arrangement'.

The question that concerns regulators on both sides of the Atlantic is that of the transparency of such content in the mind of the consumer. Is it clear where the sponsorship of such content is coming from?

Case study: Real Living *magazine and Mark Tuckey, 2010*

Australian lifestyle magazine *Real Living* prominently featured an editorial on designer Mark Tuckey that was sponsored by BMW and also invited readers to visit the BMW website for more content. Separating the church of editorial from the state of advertising is more difficult in digital media; everything is necessarily melded together more closely, and the context or 'furniture', which is hard to miss in a newspaper or during a broadcast, is stripped away as files zip round the Web. The anxiety over transparency is understandable, particularly when it comes to vulnerable markets and controversial products, such as loan companies, insurance schemes, lobbying and gambling products.

Two question marks hang over native advertising:

- Will it become more significant in 2015?
- What is the longevity of the trend for the producers of this content?

Currently, it seems that the curve of enthusiasm for the approach, and ignorance about its benefits or impact, are both at a high, which is the point at which companies make money. This is unlikely to last.

For the consumer, it is the issue of transparency, and EU regulations are likely to become more explicit in this area. It is easy to become very exercised by the potential of native advertising for good and ill. It is arguably a relatively benign part of a much more embedded trend. Every person and institution can now make their own messages and potentially have as much impact as the largest corporation.

Advertiser-funded programmes (AFP)

'Gillette World of Sponsorship' was perhaps one of the most famous advertiser-funded programmes in the world. This weekly international sports magazine show ran for 25 years between 1984 and 2009, offering a topical mix of the best sporting highlights and specially shot features from around the world. It is regarded as the forerunner of successful advertiser-funded programming and the series was broadcast in 180 countries and in flight on 25 airlines. This form of sponsorship goes much deeper than simply an association with a particular programme.

In AFP or 'branded content', the sponsor has input in the selection and treatment of the subject matter, although editorial control remains in the hands of the programme maker. An early example of this type of programming was *Dinner Doctors*, a six-part cooking series on Channel 5 in the UK aimed at young mothers, which included many recipes involving Heinz products, but did not involve any product placement, which is now permissible under the new rules.

And Channel 4 in the UK sees this as another revenue stream:

> The client's contribution could be financial, creative or by allowing producers access to talent or events with which the client has an existing relationship. Creating advertiser funded programming can be a lot more complex and expensive than traditional sponsorship but the rewards can be numerous.

Benefits of AFP include:

- The ability to 'own' a programme, series or format completely, which allows the client to create a sustainable point of difference from competitors.
- Create a deeper brand experience throughout the very editorial fabric of the programme and by planning off-screen activity in line with the production of the programme.
- The ability to exploit content across clients' own platforms and media platforms.

Community-linked sponsorship

To some extent this is corporate social responsibility (CSR) but under a different name. The nature of this type of sponsorship is different from other forms of sponsorship, because it satisfies a range of sponsor objectives that are more community-rather than commercially based. In this respect, a community-linked sponsorship, such as a brand owner funding a healthy-eating programme in schools through educational literature, helps put a 'halo' around the brand rather than necessarily driving incremental sales; although the latter may occur as a result of the activity where messaging about healthy eating extends beyond the school gates and into the homes of families, where it can then influence their purchasing behaviour.

Case study: LifeSkills Programme, 2014

Barclays briefed Hopscotch Consulting to develop a new citizenship programme that would have a high impact and make a real difference to the employability of young people by 2015. Barclays wanted to involve its employees, integrate its community programmes and offer work experience to thousands of young people. The LifeSkills programme was designed following extensive research with teachers, careers advisers and key stakeholders, to give young people in the UK access to the skills they need to make the transition into work. The programme focused on the areas most needed by young people – work, people, and money skills.

The holistic programme gives 11- to 19-year-olds many opportunities to get involved, from lessons in schools, online activities and games, to school workshops and hands-on work experience. Hopscotch Consulting developed ready-to-use teaching resources, all linked to the varied UK curricula and also wrote three themed practical workshops for thousands of Barclays employee volunteers to deliver. Over 10,000 students received their own student log to help with their work experience and teachers received handy tips and guides about preparing their students for the world of work.

The www.barclayslifeskills.com website gives young people the opportunity to build CVs online, explore their strengths and develop new skills. A key feature is the thousands of work experience placements on offer.

LifeSkills launched in April 2013 and already 3,500 schools, colleges and organisations have signed up. It is estimated that 250,000 young people have been engaged with the programme so far. Over 400 workshops have already been booked, and thousands of Barclays volunteers are ready to deliver them. LifeSkills has partnered with the *Times/TES* and has secured high-profile ambassadors, including West Ham FC CEO Karren Brady and TV presenter Jameela Jamil. School engagement continues in September 2014 with an activation pack for teachers featuring quizzes and activities, information on careers, education, information, advice and guidance and a useful directory of careers websites.

Developing a sales strategy

A fundamental component of developing a successful sales strategy irrespective of the sponsorship proposition is to have done a full segmentation of the potential brand owners that could be interested in entering a sponsorship arrangement (see Figure 4.5).

This workflow for the rights holder will typically consist of:

- developing a demographic potential sponsor model using existing data and overlaying external profiles of prospective sponsor companies
- identifying the most likely segments (now and future) and then adding attitude/motivation data
- clustering potential sponsors by their key motivations, and then evaluating their worth and common characteristics
- targeting the best segments by value, clearly defining who they are and what they want.

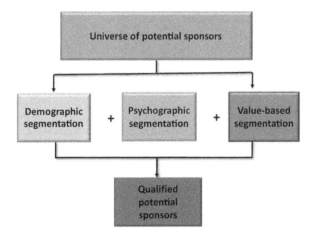

Figure 4.5 Segmentation of potential sponsors

Essential sales preparation

Another fundamental component of success in selling sponsorship is to have conducted a sponsorship audit of all tangible, intangible and premium benefits that will make up the sponsorship package on offer.

Tangible benefits

Put simply, these are the components that can be valued in a measured way. Typically, media values are based on what it would cost the sponsor to buy the equivalent amount of exposure through traditional media. From a venue perspective, tangible benefits will include visible branding to spectators and TV viewers; advertisements in the match day programme, website, Facebook page and sponsored content within Twitter feeds; mentions in the press and radio; and outdoor advertising.

Intangible benefits

These are benefits that cannot be measured as easily on a straight line basis as the tangible benefits of the sponsorship package. Intangible benefits include things such as the audience and image fit of the sponsorship asset, the extent to which the sponsor takes 'ownership' of the asset and the prestige and appeal of the asset.

This is often greater in value to the sponsor – such as EE's deal with Wembley Stadium in 2014, where the enhancement to EE's brand will be immense and arguably worth more to the brand than perimeter advertising at the stadium that appeared on screen during the FA Cup Final between Arsenal FC and Hull City FC in May 2014.

Access to intellectual property (IP) rights such as trademarks and logos as well as corporate social responsibility (CSR) benefits that can flow to a sponsor are also classified as intangible benefits.

Premium benefits

In order to accommodate the market sectors of potential brand partners for a new sponsorship programme, it is important to consider what premium or bespoke benefits can be delivered.

The criteria for premium benefits would be specific to the brand owner in question and ideally outlined during earlier negotiations for the sponsorship. Some examples of this be could showcasing products at the venue or event, opportunities to launch new business ventures in the local community or even new product development.

Case study: Bournville College, Birmingham, 2011

I was asked by the Principal and the Board of Bournville College of Further Education to establish a framework that could realise the commercial value that the

£92m new build on the former Rover car plant site at Longbridge, Birmingham, might afford brand owners coming on board as potential sponsors. What was unique about this project was that I was valuing a building for sponsorship that had not as yet been built!

In order to understand the market value of this opportunity to potential sponsors, an independent valuation was conducted by media agency Sponsorship Intelligence. One key assumption made in the preparation of the sponsorship package was that this would need to be a naming rights proposition in order to deliver the benefits that the new build would represent.

I was also commissioned to make two short films – one before the new build and one after the new build had been completed, and details of these films can be found at the end of this chapter. These films told the story of why the College was looking to build a new state-of-the-art campus and move its location from Bournville, where it had been for over 100 years, to a site less than four kilometres away at Longbridge.

The second film was to give a sense of awe and wonder to potential sponsors and for them to hear the passion of those who were very much part of this remarkable story. The story was told without narration and instead relied on the actual spoken words of those who appeared on the film, including Sir Dominic Cadbury, whose grandfather, George Cadbury, was the inspiration behind the world's first day continuation school, which became Bournville College.

Outdoor exposure

By its very nature, Bournville College's main physical asset is the campus itself, which has become a landmark. Students on campus could be impacted by numerous branded mediums such as directional signage and faculty building branding. I consulted outdoor advertising specialists to use similar student media inventory to reflect this branded campus signage benefit. For example, four-sheet is a small poster and six-sheet is the type of poster you might see at the side of a bus-stop. The other area where outdoor media exposure was valued was via directional roadside signage to the new campus. Directional signs to a landmark building are valuable branding opportunities, as these are subject to strict planning controls and as a result this makes them more valuable.

The level of media interest in the new build was likely to be at its greatest within the first year of operation as well as in the lead-up to its official opening, as this was a local/regional news story. The interest would then be expected to decline gradually between two to five years. As a result, media coverage was conservatively estimated and should the public relations activities over this period deliver more media coverage than forecast, this would help to push up the tangible value of the naming rights deal.

I consulted outdoor media specialists to reveal market rates that equated to road signs in the Birmingham area, to represent the motorists who would be driving by. A price per panel (poster) per fortnight was weighted to represent an annual rate for outdoor exposure.

Table 4.2 Outdoor exposure for Bournville College (BC), Birmingham (annual average)

Benefit	Assumptions	Comments	Annual ROI value £
On-campus signage	Directional signage ×6	Based on typical student union hand-selected campaign – 4 sheets	20,280
On-campus signage	Faculty signage ×2	Based on typical student union regional campaign – 6 sheets	13,520
Road signage	Road signs ×2	Based on 48 sheet rates around BC postcode	20,800
Security guards	Personnel ×5	Based on the uniforms being branded by a logo on one side of the chest	1,250
Catering staff	Personnel ×10	Based on the uniforms being branded by a logo on one side of the chest	2,000
Total			**57,850**

For the branding impact for security uniforms and catering/other auxiliary workers on campus, it was assumed that the value was based on what the sponsor would have to pay if it branded these uniforms itself with its own logo (see Table 4.2).

Media exposure

In this hypothetical scenario, I consulted media analysts with expertise in capturing onscreen exposure for onscreen branding and a range of other events to determine a realistic level of exposure that the potential brand partner for the new site would enjoy. Total brand exposure is translated into the equivalent number of 30-second advertising spots. The total number of spots is then multiplied by the cost of buying such a spot within the programme in question. This gives an 'undiscounted' advertising equivalent value for the sponsor. I then took account of the fact that sponsorship signage cannot deliver as powerful a message as a traditional television commercial can, which has the ability for a brand partner to expose their message solely to a targeted audience, while sponsorship exposure is more peripheral by nature. Therefore, the advertising value equivalent (AVE) is down-weighted in order to produce a figure that more accurately reflects the sponsorship value.

The sponsorship value tends to range from 5% to 50% of the advertising equivalent value, according to Sponsorship Intelligence. The figures used will depend on a number of factors, for example, the size of the source, the location of the source, solus appearances and the number of other sponsors present at the event (i.e., the level of clutter). With respect to radio exposure for the new campus, I established the value of a 30-second commercial and based a verbal mention as the equivalent of 10 seconds of exposure. In turn, this equates to one-third of a 30-second spot.

With respect to print coverage, I valued a sample of related articles clipped throughout the period May 2008 to April 2009, applying a press valuation methodology by Sponsorship Intelligence. For an article to produce a value it had to mention the name Bournville College, on the supposition that a naming rights partner would in future form part of the college name. Within this 12-month period, there were 22 articles that featured Bournville College and/or the proposed new campus at Longbridge. The average article size was 65 column centimetres, average advertising equivalency media value equalled £1,400 and the average sponsorship value (which is dependent on the number and type of sponsor mentions) equalled £925.

With respect to online exposure, I assumed that the number of online features would at least equal the number achieved in print media. I valued a 'typical' online article that might result from each phase of the sponsorship. Under this scenario, an average article would be the equivalent size of five banners and would return an advertising equivalent media value of £225. The typical sponsorship value (which is dependent on the number and type of sponsor mentions) equalled £180 for a launch article (i.e., well-branded) and £25 for running story-type features (fewer sponsor mentions).

The calculations for tangible values were spread over the launch event and year 1 (Table 4.3) and then in subsequent media coverage following the launch, in year 1 to year 5 (Table 4.4).

Paid-for advertising

The values have been based on the Bournville College spend (GBP) figures that were provided to me during the course of the sponsorship audit. All paid-for advertising has been adjusted to reflect the commercial value of this medium to a potential sponsor. The College also provided me with input with respect to all printed matter that could also carry a sponsor's messages (see Table 4.5).

Table 4.3 Media exposure: launch year 1

Category	Phase of sponsorship	Number of projected features	Annual ROI value (£)	Assumptions
Press editorial	Launch period	66	61,050	3× sample period activity
Online editorial	Launch period	66	14,850	Assuming equivalent level of coverage achieved by traditional press media
TV coverage	Launch period	30	18,900	Assuming 1 feature on each regional news programme (BBC, ITV and GMTV) for a 3-day period surrounding launch
Radio coverage	Launch period	50	1,870	Assuming 10 features per station across a minimum of 5 regional radio stations surrounding the launch
Total		**212**	**96,670**	

Table 4.4 Media exposure: years 1–5

Category	Phase of sponsorship	Number of projected features	Estimated ROI value (£)	Assumptions
Press editorial	Normal calendar year	24	22,200	Average of 2 articles per month including topics such as student awards, exam results, events/exhibitions, etc.
Online editorial	Normal calendar year	24	600	Assuming equivalent coverage as achieved by traditional press media
TV coverage	Normal calendar year	16	9,840	Assuming 2 features per term on lunchtime and early evening regional news (BBC and ITV)
Radio coverage	Normal calendar year	8	455	Assuming 2 features per term on at least two regional radio stations
Total		**72**	**33,095**	

Table 4.5 Paid-for advertising (annual average)

Category	Benefit	College spend (£)	Annual ROI value (£)	Comments
Press	Advertising campaign in the *Birmingham Mail* and *Education News*	95,000	47,500	A naming rights partner would feature prominently in advertising undertaken by the college. However, the focus of a campaign would be on the college/courses and not the naming rights partner's products/services. Therefore Maverick has valued this benefit at 50% of the advertising equivalent value, which for this item is the face value spend
Online	Permanent Bournville College website branding	n/a	5,100	Advertising equivalent cost of a banner advert on Oxford College website (17,000 monthly site impressions) is approx. £450 per month (£450 × 12)
Radio	Galaxy and Kerrang campaigns	27,000	9,000	A naming rights partner would receive at least 1 verbal mention as part of the advert. Maverick credit each verbal mention to one-third of the advertising equivalent value, which for this item is the face value spend
Total			**61,600**	

Premium benefits

For the purpose of this exercise, it was assumed that an engineering-based brand owner with a substantial workforce in the Birmingham/Midlands area would be the most likely to want to become the naming rights sponsor of the College, which specialises in maths, physics, engineering and trade skills and as a result the brand owner could find ways of recruiting such skilled labour as well as training this workforce for its present and future needs (see Table 4.6).

BESPOKE IN-HOUSE TRAINING

Course tuition for up to 70 employees of the sponsor. The College to sink cost that would equate to £2,000 per person = £140,000. Consultancy Services – 10 days offered at discounted day rate of £600 = £6,000; – 25 days' access to management centre – external day rate usually charged equates to £250 = £6,250.

Table 4.6 Premium benefits: years 1 and 2

Benefit	Assumptions	Comments	Annual rate £
Bespoke in-house training	The college can tailor a learning programme to fit company HR/talent strategy	Course tuition for up to 70 staff on any timetabled courses available at the college	140,000
		Consultancy services	6,000
		25 days' access to management centre, including all facilities housed at the learning and Resource Institute	6,250
Work experience/ internships	Brand partner saves recruitment for 5× potential employees	Privileged access to students who have studied relevant courses that could benefit company	12,875
Access to campus facilities: conferencing	Brand partner allowed 6× day with access to conference facilities for 80 delegates	Fees for conference hiring within the educational sector in the Birmingham area	27,930
Access to campus facilities: leisure	Brand partner allowed up to 70 annual membership passes for campus leisure facilities	Benefits include: –leisure centre (with fully equipped gym) –hair and beauty appointments –discounted rates at restaurant and flower boutique	46,200
Opportunity to supply fixtures and fittings	College to consider when in discussion with a potential brand partner	TBC – but could include building fabric and/or essential college equipment, i.e., computers, etc.	TBC
Total			**239,255**

WORK EXPERIENCE/INTERNSHIPS

Institute of Civil Engineering endorses suitable internships at £700/intern = £3,500. £500 average finding fee/person for recruitment companies = £2,500. There would also be savings on advertising for jobs – i.e., £675 for an average ad in *Civil Engineering Magazine* × 5 = £3,375. Remaining value is based on company staff time to run intern programme – £100/hr × 35 hours/year = £3,500. Total = £12,875.

ACCESS TO CAMPUS FACILITIES: CONFERENCING

Based on Birmingham University Conference Park rates – £55 per person plus equipment each time (£255); i.e., £4,400 + £255 = £4,655 × 6 = £27,930.

ACCESS TO CAMPUS FACILITIES: LEISURE

Based on membership subscription to equivalent leisure services in the Birmingham area – £660 per annum = £46,200.

Table 4.7 Premium benefits: years 3–5

Benefit	Assumptions	Comments	Annual value £
Bespoke in-house training	The college can tailor a learning programme to fit company HR/talent strategy	Course tuition for up to 70 staff on any timetabled courses available at the college	140,000
		Consultancy services	6,000
		25 days' access to management centre, including all facilities housed at the learning and resource institute	6,250
Work experience/ internships	Brand partner saves recruitment for 5× potential employees	Privileged access to students who have studied relevant courses that could benefit company	12,875
Access to campus facilities: conferencing	Brand partner allowed 6× day with access to conference facilities for 80 delegates	Fees for conference hiring within the educational sector in the Birmingham area	27,930
Access to campus facilities: leisure	Brand partner allowed up to 70 annual membership passes for campus leisure facilities	Benefits include: –Leisure centre –Hair and beauty appointments –Discounted rates at restaurant and flower boutique	46,200
Retail space on campus	An opportunity to have a permanent 1,500m² site on the campus that could offer a retail angle to create revenue.	Based on £65/m² rate at nearby Kings Norton Business Centre.	97,000
Opportunity to supply fixtures and fittings	College to consider when in discussion with a potential brand partner	TBC – but could include building fabric and/or essential college equipment, i.e., computers, etc.	TBC
Total			**336,255**

RETAIL SPACE ON CAMPUS

Although not factored in until year 3, if a nearby business park's rates are realised for at least the rental value, then using an average £65m² on a site approx. 1,500m²; 65 × 1,500 = £97,500.

Intangible benefits

Up until now the discussion has focused on the tangible benefits and the value that these can deliver to a potential brand partner. For the purpose of the exercise, we decided to see this through the lens of a sponsor in the engineering sector. However, a lot of value is actually tied up in the intangible benefits that can be delivered by Bournville College and these are much harder to measure and evaluate.

The intangible benefits refer to those qualitative elements of the sponsorship rights package such as image fit, prestige, location, the extent to which a brand owner takes ownership of a sponsorship asset and factors such as Bournville College's legacy in the community.

Intangible benefits, while difficult to measure accurately, nevertheless provided a highly compelling case for sponsorship investment in the new site. The College's strong links with vocational education provided a solid platform for an engineering company to maximise its association. And given that the College was part of a £1bn regeneration programme for Longbridge with sustainability high on the agenda, the incoming sponsor was assured strong support from the local community. In maximising the value for the potential of sponsorship for the new college campus, a key assumption was made.

Another key assumption that I made was how to put a value on intangible benefits. Intangible components help turn the association between the brand partner and the asset into sponsorship rather than simply advertising, as there is a deeper and richer relationship between the parties.

In the case of Bournville College, the way the benefits fell out, I felt that the intangibles were potentially worth as much as the tangibles (50/50 split). Therefore, by using the value of tangibles as the maximum total, each intangible would be independently assessed out of 10 from the perspective of the potential brand partner. This score is then converted into a percentage that is put against the tangibles to create a monetary value. For illustration purposes only, the prospective engineering brand partner has placed a high importance on exclusivity of the naming rights deal.

INTANGIBLE BENEFITS SCORE EXAMPLE.

So, in this fictitious example of an engineering company, certain factors have scored more highly than others. The factors can change – these are listed as benefits that the engineering company is looking for and this is gleaned from conversations with them. In total, eight factors/intangible benefits were identified as being important to the engineering company. Out of a possible total score of 80, the college scored 54. This provides a value of (54/80 × 100) 67.5% of the possible tangible value of benefits delivered in any one year (see Table 4.8).

Table 4.8 Intangible benefits illustration

Benefit	Comments	Score (1–10)
Brand essence fit with Bournville College	Bournville's strong links with vocational education provide a solid platform for an engineering company to maximise it association with the college	6
Audience fit with target groups	Through being a company that could employ qualified students, supporting their preparation for their careers would seem to be appropriate	7
Corporate social responsibility	Being part of a regeneration project that has resurrected the Longbridge site with sustainability high on the agenda would ensure that the local community would receive the partnership warmly	6
Promotional options	There are unlimited options for a company to promote its products and services on the campus. However, an engineering-based firm with a business-to-business focus will pay less attention to the more consumer-friendly student.	6
Solid performer as an educational institute	With respected and long-standing management at the top, a company will benefit from Bournville's progress against the national benchmark that Ofsted sets to ensure the best standards	7
Optimal geographical location with access to multi-transport hub	Birmingham is well-placed to capitalise on great transport systems which in turn are attractive to regional and national business-related activities	6
Ownership of property (i.e., naming rights element)	This a key area of the sponsorship and being the first company to be involved means there will be no confusion with previous sponsors. There is a real opportunity to create a long-lasting legacy with Bournville, through the establishment of a centre of excellence for engineering	9
Access to intellectual property/official marques	Through the association, the company will be able to use Bournville's marques and logos in its communications and benefit from the striking imagery that the campus will portray	7

Calculation of the total sponsorship package

Given the inputs and outputs that I was able to gather for the valuation model, I was then in a position to calculate the value of the sponsorship package (see Tables 4.9–4.11).

The total value of the naming rights sponsorship was calculated as tangible values £497,540 plus intangible values £335,840 (67.5% of tangible values), providing a total of £833,380.

The media exposure value excluded the launch media value and the exposure from additional benefits excluded retail space values, providing a total of £671,457.

Table 4.9 Naming rights sponsorship: year 1

Benefit	Sponsorship value £
Outdoor exposure	57,850
Media exposure – editorial-driven	33,095
Paid-for advertising	61,600
Launch week exposure	96,670
Exposure from internal literature	9,070
Exposure from additional benefits	239,255
Total tangibles	**497,540**
Intangibles	335,840
Total value of sponsorship rights	**833,380**

Table 4.10 Naming rights sponsorship: year 2

Benefit	Sponsorship value £	
Outdoor exposure	57,850	
Media exposure – editorial-driven	33,095	does not include launch
Paid-for advertising	61,600	
Exposure from internal literature	9,070	
Exposure from additional benefits	239,255	does not include retail space
Total tangibles	**400,870**	
Intangibles	270,587	
Total value of sponsorship rights	**671,457**	

Table 4.11 Naming rights sponsorship: years 3–5

Benefit	Sponsorship value £	
Outdoor exposure	57,850	
Media exposure – editorial-driven	33,095	does not include launch
Paid-for advertising	61,600	
Exposure from internal literature	9,070	
Exposure from additional benefits	336,255	does include retail space
Total tangibles	**497,870**	
Intangibles	336,062	
Total value of sponsorship rights	**833,932**	

The tangibles and intangibles over these three years provided a total of £833,932.

Summary of naming rights sponsorship package value

Years 1 and 2 remain constant while the brand partner establishes itself in the community and the partnership with the College takes shape, except that year 2 onwards does not have the launch value. From year 3 onwards, the real

Table 4.12 Five-year statement of naming rights sponsorship

Year	Sponsorship constant value (£)	Value % increase (year-on-year)	Enhanced sponsorship value (£)	
Year 1	833,380	0%	833,380	includes launch
Year 2	671,457	0%	671,457	
Year 3	833,932	3%	858,950	includes retail space
Year 4	833,932	4%	893,308	includes retail space
Year 5	833,932	5%	937,974	includes retail space
	4,006,634		**4,195,069**	gain over 5 years

sponsorship value would start to rise as the 'halo effect' of the regeneration project really starts to take effect. These years also include the retail space option that would be available to a potential brand partner.

However, the actual rights fees agreed will not change across the 5-year period, thereby benefiting the brand partner by an additional £115,218 worth of value for no additional cost (see Table 4.12).

So, over a five-year naming rights deal, the valuation of brand partnership rights in year 1 is around £833,000; in year 2 this decreases to £671,000 (no benefit from the launch activities that took place in year 1) and then there are incremental increases between years 3 and 5 in terms of the increase in value of the sponsorship rights, largely as a result of the inclusion of retail space in year 3 to £834,000. The total value of the sponsorship rights available to a brand partner are £4.2m over 5 years.

Having justified what the value of the tangible, intangible and premium benefits for a potential naming rights looks like, you are then able to proceed to creating a sponsorship sales package.

Sponsorship sales process

In the vast majority of medium-to-large sponsorship deals being sought, selling sponsorship needs to be consultative and works best when the rights holder and the prospective sponsor collaborate in order to ensure that the sponsorship agreement accurately reflects the intentions of the parties.

The sponsorship sales process looks a bit like the ladder shown in Figure 4.6, where the first step in the sales process starts with prospecting for sponsors and culminates at the top of the ladder with closing the deal with a prospective sponsor.

In the context of sponsorship sales, we need to navigate our efforts towards a successful outcome – a sponsorship sale of the tangible, intangible and premium benefits that can be delivered to a potential sponsor, as the Bournville College case study illustrates.

However, in order to achieve this, we have to do this on the basis of a deep understanding of what potential sponsors will be in the market for such a property.

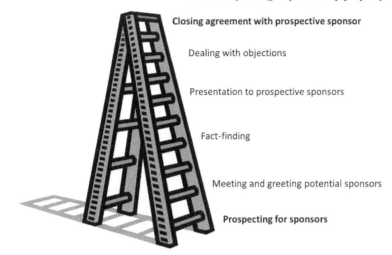

Closing agreement with prospective sponsor

Dealing with objections

Presentation to prospective sponsors

Fact-finding

Meeting and greeting potential sponsors

Prospecting for sponsors

Figure 4.6 Sponsorship sales ladder

Networking for selling

In order to qualify appropriate brand owners as sales leads for the sponsorship opportunity, it is important to network. Word of mouth is important in learning who may be interested in your sponsorship opportunity and what in particular will be of interest for them. But networking needs to be a focused rather than a random activity. It does not just mean turning up to a conference, seminar or trade event in the hope that you may meet a brand owner that could be your next sponsor. It requires more careful planning and execution than relying on chance.

In fact, there are four different types of networking that a rights holder needs to engage with (see Table 4.13).

Each community that the rights holder will want to engage with will need to have some form of narrative or story that will demonstrate to them what the sponsorship opportunity can deliver and why it is relevant for them. In essence what this means is that the rights holder must put its energies into building a dialogue with potential sponsors and focusing on their challenges, issues and opportunities and, in doing so, establish how a long-term relationship will provide a unique solution. For each prospective sponsor and depending on the network that the rights holder is engaged with, there are a number of steps that will need to be taken:

1   Turning the sponsorship proposition into a narrative – a story, advertising, news story, background brief, case study, presentation, letter or face-to-face conversation that is relevant for the prospective sponsor.
2   Need to adopt an 'outside-in' rather than 'inside-out' perspective, so have to start with the potential sponsor's situation, showing that we understand exactly what they seek to achieve.

Table 4.13 Types of networking for sales

Type of networking	Description
Purpose networks	Purpose networks bring people together with a common purpose or passion Purpose networks have: • Self-organising structure • Common purpose • Strong affinity to each other • More value from connections
Social networks	These are online networks such as Facebook, YouTube, LinkedIn, Twitter Social networks bring like-minded people together to share thoughts, ideas, recommendations and information and are a powerful channel for influencing all stakeholder groups, irrespective of whether individuals are part of particular social networks, as these are 'open' to everyone
Customer networks	These are groups of customers/clients who have formed themselves into groups. Such groups could also exist within a trade body, such as the European Sponsorship Association Customer networks have: • Self-organising structure • Shared purpose and values • Strong affinity to one another • Desire for relationships that align with their purpose
Brand networks	Brand networks bring people together with a common affinity to a particular brand, such as organisations known to support a particular team, athlete, cause or event

3 Then need to introduce a reason why this is difficult/demanding – providing a perspective that they have not encountered before, perhaps based on research/insight.
4 Rhetorically pose the key question for them and then the answer – and the context for the sponsorship proposition.
5 Support this message with a number of supporting arguments/evidence and steps to achieve it.

Before making any type of pitch to a potential sponsor, it is prudent to check whether it has a published sponsorship policy that will provide guidance as to what opportunities (if any) it is open to considering. Some brand owners employ sponsorship agencies to sift through unsolicited opportunities that rarely get any sort of conversion, because, if the agency working for the brand owner has been instructed to advise on a property selection, then it will be doing its own due diligence.

So identifying a suitable brand owner and then finding out who the sponsorship, PR or marketing agencies that work for that brand owner are extremely important, as it is much better working up a sponsorship proposal from the 'inside' rather than trying to use a Trojan horse approach.

Creating a sponsorship hierarchy

Depending on the size and complexity of the sponsorship programme, you may want to consider entering into agreements with more than one sponsor. This immediately raises the issue of rights – what IP rights will be granted to a headline sponsor and what IP rights will be granted to sponsors at other levels of sponsorship? How will category exclusivity be managed between sponsors and, of course, how will individual sponsorship packages be valued and sold?

Earlier in this chapter, we discussed the different types of sponsorship propositions with examples of how this worked in practice. When creating a sponsorship hierarchy you may want to segment the rights in the following way:

- Tier 1 – Official sponsor
- Tier 2 –Local sponsor
- Tier 3 – Official partner
- Tier 4 – Official partner/supplier/supporter

Figure 4.7 provides a guide as to what types of brand owner may make a fit with a particular tier of sponsorship, although this will, of course, depend on the nature of the sponsorship, its size, territory and audience, as well as the objectives of any potential sponsor.

Buying sponsorship

This is the other side of the coin, of course – and, in fact, it is probably more important to get this understood before the rights holder or its sponsorship agency wants to commence to sell sponsorship. As I discuss throughout this book, there needs to be a win–win outcome for all the parties; otherwise the sponsorship programme will fail. Brand owners are now much more sophisticated buyers of sponsorship, but the basics still apply.

There are a number of questions that brand owners need to be able to answer with a degree of clarity.

What type of sponsorship are you looking to buy?

This could include any of the following options:

- naming rights sponsorship
- presenting sponsorship
- presenting sponsorship of a section, area, entry or team
- presenting sponsorship of a day, weekend or week at an event
- presenting sponsorship of an event-driven award, trophy or scholarship

- presenting sponsorship of a related or subordinate event
- major/headline sponsorship
- supporting sponsorship
- official product status
- preferred supplier status.

Tier 1: Official sponsor

Telecoms   Soft drinks   Energy   Retail   Banking   Airlines   Petrol and gas

Rights of association, category exclusivity, 'ownership' of a secondary asset, comprehensive branding and accreditation and intangible benefits

Tier 2: Local sponsor

Accountants   Restaurants   Car rental   Hotels   Construction

Rights of association, onsite activation, intangible benefits and very limited branding

Tier 3: Official partner

Broadcast   Merchandise   Ticketing   Venue and stadia

Rights of association, event delivery partners

Tier 4: Supplier/supporter

Made up of smaller level of support from companies, organisations or individuals
No rights of association, but listing on website and in event programme

Figure 4.7 Segmenting sponsorship rights
Source: Kolah (2015)

What level of exclusivity are you looking for?

- category exclusivity among sponsors at or below a given level
- category exclusivity among sponsors at any level
- category exclusivity in event-driven advertising or promotional media
- category exclusivity as a supplier or seller at an event.

What licensing rights are you looking for?

- licence to use the rights holder's logo(s), images and/or trademark(s) in commercial promotion, advertising, or other leverage activities
- merchandising rights (the right to create co-branded merchandise to sell with the rights holder's IP rights)
- product endorsement (the rights holder endorsing the sponsor's products and services).

What type of contract are you looking for?

- one to three years' sponsorship contract
- three years or more
- one year, with the option to renew at the end of the term
- discount for a multiyear sponsorship agreement
- right of first refusal for renewal at the conclusion of the sponsorship contract.

Use of venue/event?

- input in venue, route of the event and/or timing of the event
- use of sponsor venue for the launch, main event, or a supporting event.

On-site opportunities?

- sampling opportunities
- demonstration/display opportunities
- opportunity to sell product on-site (exclusive or non-exclusive)
- coupon, information or premium (gift) distribution
- merchandising (sponsor selling dual-branded products).

Signage requirements?

- venue signage (full, partial or non-broadcast view)
- inclusion in on-site event signage (exclusive or non-exclusive)
- inclusion on pre-event street banners, flags, etc.
- news conference signage
- vehicle signage

- event participant uniforms
- event staff shirts/caps/uniforms.

Hospitality requirements?

- tickets to the event (luxury boxes, preferred seating, reserved seating or general admission)
- VIP tickets/passes (backstage, sideline, pit passes, press box, etc.)
- celebrity/participant meet-and-greets
- sponsorship-related travel arrangements, administration and chaperoning (consumer prizes, VIP or trade incentives)
- access to or creation of what-money-can't-buy experiences
- development of customised hospitality events to suit the interests of the target market (high-end, adventurous, behind-the-scenes, for their families or children, etc.).

Online requirements?

- provision of content for sponsor website (for example, weekly health tips, star athlete's training diary, pertinent articles, behind-the-scenes exclusive content, other exclusive downloadable content, etc.)
- provision of Web 'events' for sponsor website (for example, online chat with a star, webcast, webinar, tweets)
- appropriate promotion of sponsor through rights holder's existing social media activities
- ability for sponsor to add value to rights holder's fans/friends via rights holder's controlled social media
- 'signage' on rights holder's website
- promotion or contest on rights holder's website
- links to sponsor website from rights holder's website.

Loyalty marketing requirements?

This section is about providing benefits that the sponsor can pass on to their desired customer segments in order to reinforce their relationships:

- access to event, parking, or merchandise discounts for customers or a specific customer group (for example, frequent flyers, Gold Card holders)
- access to event, parking or merchandise discounts, or other perks for customers
- exclusive access to an event, area, contest/prize, service, celebrity or experience for all or a specific group of consumers
- early access to tickets (before they go on sale to the general public)
- exclusive access to seating, chill-out areas, etc. for loyal customers.

Database marketing requirements?

- unlimited access to event-generated database(s) (for example, member lists) for direct marketing follow-up (subject to data protection laws)
- opportunity to provide inserts in rights holder's communications online and offline
- rental/loan of event database for one-off communication
- opportunity to run database-generating activities on-site
- opportunity to run database-generating activities on-site as a requirement for attendee admission.

Internal communication requirements?

- participation by employees of the sponsor company/organisation
- access to discounts, merchandise or other sponsorship-oriented benefits
- 'ownership' of part of the event by employees (for example, creating an employee-built-and-run water station as part of a marathon sponsorship)
- provision of a celebrity or spokesperson for meet-and-greets or employee motivation and team-building exercises
- creation of an event, day or programme specifically for employees
- creation of an employee volunteer programme.

Public relations requirements?

- inclusion in all news releases and other media relations activities
- inclusion in sponsor-related and media activities
- public relations campaign designed for sponsor's market and customer segments (consumer or trade).

Media exposure requirements?

- inclusion in all print, outdoor and/or broadcast advertising (logo or name) – see Table 4.14
- inclusion on event promotional pieces (posters, fliers, brochures, badges, apparel, etc. – logo or name)
- ad time during televised event
- event-driven outdoor advertising (billboards, vehicles, public transport)
- ad space in event programme, catalogue, etc.

Market research requirements?

- access to pre- and/or post-event research
- opportunity to provide sponsorship- or industry-oriented questions on event research.

Table 4.14 Bournville College – internal literature/advertising space

Benefit	Circulation	Annual ROI value (£)	Comments
Course brochure editorial branding/ advertising	210,000	6,680	Equivalent to one full-colour page ad rate in the *Times Educational Supplement*, which has a similar target market and circulation of 50,000
Sixth-form prospectus editorial branding/ advertising	12,000	1,390	Equivalent to one full-colour page ad rate in the journal *Further Education Today*, which has a similar target market and circulation of 6,000
Student handbook editorial branding/ advertising	3,000	1,000	Equivalent to one full-colour page ad rate in the *University of Warwick News Letter*, which has a similar target market and circulation of 5,000
		9,070	

Pass-through rights for third parties?

- right of sponsor to pass through sponsorship benefits to third parties (distributors/partners/subsidiaries)
- the right for retailer sponsor to sell-on sponsorship benefits to vendors in specific product categories
- the above is subject to the agreement of the rights holder given that it will have other sponsorship relationships already in place that will have rights that override such considerations.

Provision of benefit-in-kind requirements?

- opportunity for the sponsor to provide equipment, services, technology, expertise or personnel useful to the success of the event in trade for part of the sponsorship fee
- opportunity for the sponsor to provide media value, in-store/in-house promotion in trade for part of the sponsorship fee
- opportunity for the sponsor to provide access to discounted media, travel, printing, or other products or services in trade for part of the sponsorship fee.

Provision of production requirements?

- design and/or production of key sponsor events (hospitality, awards, etc.)
- hiring and/or administration of temporary or contract personnel, services and vendors for the above
- logistical assistance, including technical or creative expertise.

How to create a winning sponsorship proposal

At some point in the discussions, you will be asked to put a sponsorship proposal in writing. Such a question often leads to fear and anxiety, and often sponsorship consultants will be required to help draft such a proposal, particularly if it is asking for a lot of money. Most sponsorship proposals end up in the recycle bin because they are 'inside out' rather than 'outside in'. In other words, the perspective is all wrong!

Another reason they fail is that they take no account of the budget review cycle. In order to time the sponsorship proposal to reach the intended recipient when this review is taking place, it is worth double-checking the financial year-end date (see Table 4.15) as well as also enquiring when a marketing and communications review is likely to take place.

In order to succeed, a sponsorship proposal should be very much like a piece of direct mail. It needs to grab the attention immediately and the only realistic way of doing this is by means of two important ingredients – relevance and timeliness. Should the sponsorship proposal fail these two basic 'tests', it will be going nowhere – and soon. Many sponsorship practitioners have a point of view about what should and should not get included in a sponsorship proposal. My own view is that you need to think of it as a door-opener – it is highly unlikely that any brand owner will choose to make a purchase decision just based on what you send to them.

With that in mind, brevity is also a very powerful third ingredient, as the purpose of the sponsorship proposal has got to be about getting a meeting with the prospective sponsor.

The following is a top ten list of points that ought to be covered in any winning sponsorship proposal:

1   Event/property details – this should be one page and include details on location, attendees/fan base, target demographics, cost and logistics.
2   Overview – where, what, who, how, when, why?
3   Desired audience – segment the audience on psychographic, demographic lines as well as attitudes, values, perceptions, beliefs and behaviours.
4   On-site activities – this can include hospitality, on-site sales, sampling.
5   Media support – list any already committed or planned media support such as TV, radio, press, trade, consumer, specialist, sport, lifestyle, consumer and

Table 4.15 Typical accounting periods across global territories

Territory	Typical accounting period
UK	1 April–31 March
US	1 January–31 December
Japan	1 April–31 March
Australia/New Zealand	1 July–30 June

other media, broadband/Internet, Web, mobile and interactive (for example PS3/Xbox360).

6   Other event/property promotions – signage, website, direct mail, text messaging.
7   Suggested collaborative marketing activities – a brief description of the types of activity that will deliver against the objectives for you as the rights holder as well as the sponsor.
8   Measurable benefits – itemise these briefly, such as tangible, intangible benefits and premium benefits, and also put a monetary value on these from the perspective of the potential sponsor.
9   Measurement and evaluation – explain how the success of the sponsorship programme will be measured and evaluated.
10   Investment required from the brand owner – itemise this in terms of sponsorship fees, value-in-kind (sometimes referred to as benefits-in-kind) and marketing-in-kind support.

According to William Fenton, one of the co-authors of *The Sponsorship Handbook*, pricing continues to be a major problem area in the industry:

> Sponsorship proposals have lots of traps. For example, sponsorship is perhaps more complicated to measure than advertising. So the value of sponsorship is dependent on the sponsor and what's of importance and value for them. As a result packaging and selling sponsorship can end up looking a bit like selling real estate – what price did a similar one fetch? But sponsorship doesn't work like the housing market as prices paid aren't always publicised and very often exaggerated or not disclosed at all.

That said, it is possible to put a value on tangibles, intangibles and premium benefits, as previously discussed in this chapter.

The danger of not taking a rigorous approach to valuation of a sponsorship property is that the rights holder can risk undervaluing the property or the sponsor can risk paying over the odds in terms of the sponsorship fee – neither of which is a desirable outcome. Fenton warns:

> At the lower level of sponsorship, the main error is that people look at the costs of what they're doing. Cost of the event isn't the sponsor's problem and it doesn't equate with the value of the event. People think putting the cost of the event in will impress potential sponsors – that's no way to value a sponsorship opportunity.

The issue of pricing is one of the major drawbacks of sending an unsolicited proposal to a prospective sponsor, which should be avoided at all costs. The danger is that half the time the price will be too high and half the time it will be too low.

As discussed earlier, the more effective alternative to 'pre-packaged sponsorship proposals' is to involve the prospective sponsor in the creation of the sponsorship programme. If a meeting cannot be scheduled without putting something in writing, the initial materials should be short and concise, with just enough information to demonstrate the rights holder's knowledge of the brand owner's objectives.

Rights holders should also be extremely wary of brand owners promising to deliver marketing-in-kind (MIK) or value-in-kind (VIK). The problem with VIK is that it is only of value if it is in the original budget of the rights holder. For example, if an online and offline advertising campaign to support the sponsorship is not included in the sponsorship package and the sponsor wants this but is not prepared to make a substantial contribution to this cost, then the rights holder could find itself out of pocket.

How to negotiate with a brand owner to achieve a successful outcome

Negotiating a sponsorship deal should not become a game of tug of war. If it feels as though it is one step forward and three steps back, then negotiations with the brand owner are not likely to be going in the right direction.

Essential elements of negotiation

- There must be two or more parties.
- They must at least be prepared to reach agreement.
- They must have interests in common and some conflicting interests to resolve.
- Those involved must have the freedom to meet one another's needs.
- Those involved must be willing to be explicit to some degree about their wants and needs.
- Those involved must be prepared to compromise to some degree.

The negotiation framework

There are three areas that effective negotiators can handle:

1   Attitude: they can manage their own and others' negotiation attitudes.
2   Process: they are able to manage the stages – the overall structure – of the negotiation.
3   Behaviour: they understand and manage their own and others' negotiation behaviour.

Negotiating attitude influences negotiating behaviour and both negotiating attitude and negotiating behaviour will influence your success in handling the sponsorship negotiating process (see Figure 4.8).

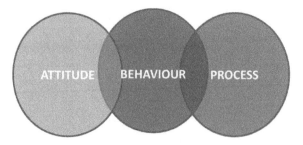

Figure 4.8 Negotiation framework
Source: Clive Rich (2013)

The seven-step negotiation checklist

This seven-step negotiation checklist was developed by Clive Rich, an expert negotiator, and is one of the best methodologies for achieving a successful outcome from any sales process (see Figure 4.9).

Step 1: Preparation

- Who's going to be on your team? Are there any internal stakeholders who need to participate? Do you need any experts?
- What roles are your team members going to play – is someone going to lead, someone else listen and observe, someone look out for opportunities to create a sponsorship solution?
- Who in your team is authorised to make concessions? This is essential: only one member of the team should be authorised to make concessions; otherwise confusion will soon reign.
- Do you need any materials prepared in advance of the pitch sent to the brand owner?
- Who's going to be on the brand owner's team? What roles are they likely to play? Have they worked together before?
- How would you describe the personalities of the people on the other team? What kind of behaviours do they tend to display?
- Is there any history (good/bad) between the parties that is likely to have a bearing on the outcome?
- Is anyone on the other team difficult? If so, why?
- What negotiating attitude do you want to bring to the table and does that contrast with the attitude you think they will bring? Does anybody's attitude need to change?
- What atmosphere do you want for the negotiation and will they want the same?
- Where will the negotiation take place and over what period of time?

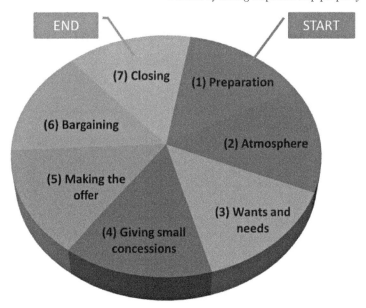

Figure 4.9 Seven-step negotiation checklist
Source: Clive Rich (2013)

- How will you create the agenda – on your own or with the potential sponsor?
- When negotiations start, what are the brand owner's objectives likely to be and what is motivating them (why do they want *those* objectives?) Will different members of their team have different motivations?
- What are your objectives and what is motivating you?
- What concessions are available for you to make to them or for them to make to you?
- What concessions are available that would not cost much but would be particularly valuable to them?
- What is the balance of bargaining power? Who holds the 'aces'?
- In terms of possible outcomes, what is your ideal position on the sponsorship deal (rights, price, payment terms, value in kind, benefits in kind)?
- What is their likely bottom line?
- What is your bottom line, below which you would walk away from the sponsorship deal? The space between your ideal position and bottom line gives you your room in which to negotiate.
- Do you have a Plan B if you can land the sponsorship deal with this brand owner? What is the worst thing that could happen with deal/no deal?

Step 2: Atmosphere

- Warm – very open, friendly, where the mood is relaxed and cooperative.
- Cool – very objective, data-driven, where a methodical process is what is important. There might not be much ill temper with a cool climate to the negotiations but neither will there be too many laughs.
- Hostile – where the rights holder team could feel pressured and the atmosphere could be tense.
- Cheeky – a bit wacky and off the wall, where anything goes, where the more exotic and unusual, the better.

Whatever atmosphere you choose to conduct the negotiations in, there are important issues to be addressed at this stage which help shape the whole of the subsequent negotiation:

- Who will attend the meetings?
- What is the timetable for the negotiation?
- Where will the negotiation take place?
- What's the agenda for the negotiation?
- How much negotiating authority does everybody have?

Step 3: Needs and wants

By using your detective skills, it is your job as a negotiator for the rights holder to look for cues and clues as to what the brand owner's motivation might really be. For example, the potential sponsor may be looking for reassurance that they will not be wasting their time and money. So it is best to use 'open' rather than 'closed' questions to seek clarification of needs and wants.

Step 4 – Small concessions

As the rights holder, what can you give the potential sponsor that may have low value to you but high value to them because it meets a personal need? For example, where the brand owner has 'achievement needs', can you give it:

- Freedom to act?
- Flexibility in the way that they want to work with you as the rights holder?
- A unique sponsorship deal structure?
- An opportunity to innovate or create?
- Development opportunities in new markets and territories?
- A cause they can pursue that has reputational benefits for the brand?
- An enhanced feeling of vision and purpose?

For example, where the brand owner has 'respect needs', can you give it:

- Positive PR?
- Attention?

- Recognition?
- Enhanced reputation in the eyes of their own peer group?
- Your gratitude?
- Display of trust?

For example, where the brand owner has 'belonging needs', can you give it:

- Use of facilities?
- Membership of an exclusive club of sponsors and partners?
- Share of your time?
- Access to your in-house experts and networks?
- Demonstrations of affection and loyalty?
- Joint marketing?
- Access to your infrastructure?
- Access to sales support?
- Use of your intellectual property (IP) rights (e.g., trademarks and image rights)?
- Status or title?
- Opportunity to save face or repair issues of trust with its market and customer segments?

Step 5: Making an offer

Making an offer should not be rushed in the negotiation process, which is often the case. There are six crucial tips for making an offer to a potential sponsor:

- get the timing right
- ask for what you want, but with the caveat of keeping the brand owner's needs in mind and not asking for a ridiculous offer
- sound like you mean it – and do not beat about the bush
- make sure your voice and body language support what you say
- do not be afraid to make the first offer - this helps to 'anchor' the bidding process
- do not give a long list of reasons for the sponsorship offer – just one will do. The temptation of so many rights holders is to create a snowstorm of reasons only to find themselves buried deep beneath a mountain of information that fails to convince a brand owner that this is the right move.

Step 6: Bargaining

- Try to keep some points open, even if you are prepared to agree to them.
- Offer concessions of decreasing size as the bargaining continues.
- Remember to take breaks in the heat of negotiations.
- When you get stuck, increase the size of the pie by creating more value for the sponsor.
- Be patient.
- Create more than one sponsorship solution.

- Think carefully before giving away something for nothing.
- Lead with your conditions and not your concessions.
- When you get stuck and you want to see whether something will work, use hypothetical questions.
- Never negotiate beneath your bottom line.
- Be prepared to take small steps on the way to success.
- See whether there is a way of making what the brand owner wants counter to their own interests.

Step 7: Close and review

If you get to this step, then all the previous hard work and effort will have been well worth it! But there is no deal until the ink is dry on the agreement, so this is a very important last step in the checklist of things that need your careful attention:

- Look for clues that the brand owner's team is ready to close.
- Do they look more relaxed?
- Are they starting to speak more about the future than the present or the past?
- Check for consensus: 'Are we all agreed that. . .?'
- Do not screw up by failing to move from bargaining to close.

At the end of the close of the sponsorship deal, take time to review the negotiation process – consider what went well and what did not go according to plan and how each member of the sponsorship sales team performed across all seven steps and how you could do better in the future. This will ensure that you learn from the experience and indeed this can be done if you were not successful in closing the sponsorship deal. Nothing is ever lost from experience – good or bad – and this could be one of the most valuable lessons to have drawn on in your process of selling a sponsorship property.

Chapter 4 at a glance

1   One of the most common mistakes made by a rights holder is to sell a sponsorship opportunity on the basis of its own needs and requirements rather than positioning the opportunity from the perspective of the brand owner.
2   The rights holder should find out whether the prospective sponsor has a sponsorship policy available in order not to waste its time with a badly thought-through and inappropriate sponsorship opportunity.
3   The rights holder must take an 'outside-in' approach to the issue of selling sponsorship rather than an 'inside-out' approach and put itself in the shoes of the prospective brand partner.
4   Brand owners have a wider range of brand communication and marketing options at their disposal, so a sports rights holder such as football team must provide a robust business case as to what the sponsorship opportunity will

deliver compared with other alternatives that could be chosen by the brand owner.

5   The starting point of any successful sales process is to understand the needs and requirements of the customer – and sponsorship is no different. The rights holder must do its homework and understand how sponsorship may provide a business solution to the brand owner while also not forgetting that it is not what you do or how it works but *why* you do what you do that counts.

6   Rights holders will also need to plan the timing of the approach to potential sponsors carefully – on average it takes about 6 to 12 months to land a five-figure sponsorship deal, 12 to 18 months to get a six–seven-figure deal and around 18 to 24 months to secure a multimillion global sponsorship deal.

7   In terms of what is available for sale – typically, a sports rights holder will have a basket of intangible and tangible assets that will require to be valued in order to achieve a sale price.

8   Pricing is a major issue in the sponsorship industry – some properties are underpriced and some overpriced. The valuation of sponsorship rights should not be calculated on a cost-plus basis alone – it should also take account of the value of those tangible and intangible rights to the sponsor.

9   In today's competitive environment, sponsorship opportunities will most probably need to help drive the sales of a brand owner's products and services as well as help build brand equity.

10   The objectives of the brand owner, therefore, should be the focus of the sponsorship sales process.

11   It is critically important that the rights holder knows and understands what legal rights it has in its possession in order to sell/transfer those rights to a brand owner. Problems often arise when a rights holder attempts to sell tangible and intangible rights where it does not own these and can therefore find itself in breach of contract and in legal difficulties at a later stage.

12   Negotiations between the sports rights holder and the brand owner must be carefully managed and should provide a 'win–win' for all parties; otherwise this could build resentment and subsequent failure of the partnership at a later date.

13   It is preferable that both parties seek the assistance of suitably qualified and experienced lawyers when close to drawing up the sponsorship agreement. Involving lawyers at a relatively early stage in the negotiation process will help to ensure that any agreement will reflect the intentions of the parties to the agreement and will avoid the danger of misinterpretation and legal ambiguity at the point of signing the agreement.

14   Sports rights holders as well as brand owners will need to make sure that they have carried out sufficient due diligence before entering the sponsorship agreement.

15   The rights holder should be proactive in providing creative input in the way in which the brand owner can activate the sports property so that it will achieve its brand communication and marketing objectives, as this will help the sales effort to be more successful.

Questions for discussion

1   What mindset is required for successful selling of sponsorship and where do most mistakes happen?
2   What are the most important skill sets required to be successful at selling sponsorship?
3   What are the ten most common sponsorship propositions?
4   Explain tangible, intangible and premium benefits, and give examples of each.
5   When buying sponsorship, what are the key considerations that a brand owner needs to take account of?
6   What are the key points that need to be covered in a sponsorship proposal?
7   Which of the seven steps in negotiation with a brand owner do you consider to be critical?
8   How do you price a sponsorship package for sale?

Further reading

Carnegie, D (1953), *How to Win Friends and Influence People*, Cedar
Collett, P and Fenton, W (2011), *The Sponsorship Handbook*, Wiley
Kolah, A (2006), *Advanced Sports Sponsorship Strategies*, SportBusinesss
Kolah, A (2007), *Sponsorship Works*, SportBusiness
Kolah, A (2013), *The Art of Influencing and Selling*, Kogan Page
Pink, D (2013), *To Sell is Human*, Canongate
Rich, C (2013), *The Yes Book*, Virgin Books

Websites

Guru in a Bottle [accessed 27 May 2014]: http://www.guruinabottle.com
KiwiGirl [accessed 27 May 2014]: http://www.kiwigirllimited.blogspot.co.uk

Reports

Kolah, A (2013), Global opportunities for sports marketing, infrastructure and consultancy services to 2022, IMR

5 Creativity in sponsorship

In this chapter

- Why creative thinking in sponsorship really matters
- The rule breakers
- Content marketing
- Media sponsorship
- Mobile and social networks in sponsorship
- Using public relations to create brand differentiation in sponsorship

Introduction

Sponsorship is all about 'intelligent activation'. It is not how *much* a brand owner spends on sponsorship activation that counts but *how* that investment is spent. Strategy and creativity go hand in hand.

Splashing the cash or throwing a massive advertising budget at a sponsorship programme does not work as well as understanding the attitudes, values, beliefs, perceptions and behaviours of the various audiences that both the sponsorship and rights holder want to reach and then precisely targeting messages and content for these audiences. In today's hyper-competitive global environment, it is not enough for a brand to be seen or heard. It has to be experienced; which is where creativity has a massive role to play in bringing the sponsorship alive.

And, of course, sponsorship is an important catalyst and component of that experience, as this chapter demonstrates. Creative sponsorship is about forging an emotional and memorable connection with customers, clients, consumers, supporters, partners and employees where they work, live and play. Really creative sponsorship practice is about pursuing uncommon practices, being different and not following the pack, being a thought leader and ultimately it is about being bold.

The 'digital dividend'

Back in 2012 research conducted by the Sports Administration Department at Ohio University in the USA sought to understand where sponsors were directing their dollars on sports-related sponsorships and what they were looking to get out of this. The results showed that a typical sponsor placed digital and social media outcomes at the top of its wish list. Dr Michael Pfahl and his colleagues reported that sponsors wanted activation to be creative and touch a lot of segments of their fan base.

Fast-forward to today, and corporate sponsors are not just more willing to spend more on digital and social media advertising but they are also increasingly seeing sponsorship as a way of achieving an improvement in digital and social media performance. So, when the NBA recently announced the extension of its partnership with Kia Motors on the first day of the 2014–15 NBA Regular Season, the presence of new digital and social media elements were woven into the deal. In particular, one element of the partnership is a digital piece – the 'Top Plays' platform on NBA.com that allows fans to vote on top plays, with the highest-ranking player by fan votes being crowned 'Top Player of the Year'.

Alongside this, the Kia sponsorship involves basketball fans in influencing the direction of a highlights-based commercial, and clips of action on the basketball court are also posted on Twitter and Vine, with the posts receiving the greatest number of retweets and loops earning a spot in the final edit of the commercial.

Today, companies and organisations operate 24-hour Twitter-induced media logic. Transparency, social media and the light speed at which content travels have radically increased the level of unpredictability in communication. As a consequence, sponsors and rights holders must plan and implement communication in new ways.

In the IEG/Performance Research 2014 Sponsorship Decision-Makers Survey, social media were the most popular marketing communication channels used for activating sponsorship, with nine out of ten sponsors including it in their leveraging mix ahead of PR, on-site interaction with fans and traditional advertising (see Figure 5.1).

As will be discussed in Chapter 10, insight and analysis have come to play an increasingly important role in sponsorship activation. Communication must

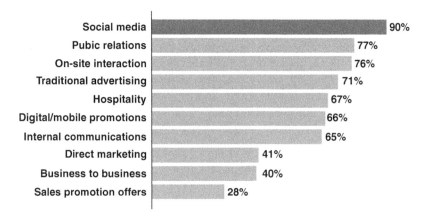

Figure 5.1 Most popular ways of activating a sponsorship programme

Source: IEG/Performance Research Sponsorship Decision-Makers Survey (2014)

become more liquid, and as a result sponsorship agencies need to organise themselves more like the newsroom of a major news-gathering organisation such as the BBC.

Sponsorship activation planning today is much different from the way it was done even five years ago. Instead of searching for 'human truths' or the 'essence of a product or service', a brand owner must put its brands in a relevant social context so that it creates value for the audience as well as those that have an influence over them including the media and society as a whole.

Think differently

'Think Different' was one of the early advertising campaigns for Apple, personally crafted by Steve Jobs, and has stood the test of time for the world's most valuable brand. The advert read:

> Here's to the crazy ones. The misfits. The rebels. The troublemakers. The round pegs in the square holes. The ones who see things differently. They're not fond of rules. And they have no respect for the status quo. You can quote, disagree with them, glorify or vilify them. About the only thing you can't do is ignore them. Because they change things. They push the human race forward. And while some may see them as the crazy ones, we see genius. Because the people who are crazy enough to think they can change the world are the ones who do.

In Steve Jobs's biography by Walter Isaacson, the author writes that Steve Jobs knew that the best way to create value in the twenty-first century was to connect creativity with technology.

In many respects, such a lesson is continuing to be learnt by many sponsors who have woken up to the power of social media as the engine to drive sponsorship activation on a global scale. The reality is that brand owners and rights holders must embrace all forms of technology and also push the boundaries of that technology in the way that Steve Jobs had done at Apple. The key is to use technology to help bring brands to life and deliver meaning for the audience, as well as create a return on investment in the process. In short, it is about shifting technology from the technical to the emotional domain. And, of course, achieving this 'digital dividend' can elude many brand owners as they struggle to change their behaviour to flourish in this digital world, which requires an 'outside-in' rather than an 'inside-out' perspective.

'If it doesn't spread, it's dead' is the mantra that sponsorship agencies now regularly recite to their clients, as the real gains to be had for sponsors are at the confluence of technology and creativity.

Social media

The proliferation of channels and the emergence of a 24/7 media landscape have inevitably led to a rise in the amount of content produced by rights holders and their sponsors.

Although there are almost as many approaches to social media as there are properties, one thing is certain – no sponsor or rights holder can afford to ignore Facebook, Twitter, YouTube, Instagram, Vine and other social networks as a way of amplifying their messages and connecting with diverse audiences.

From videos to mobile apps, augmented reality to online games, social media to picture libraries, sponsors are creating more content, albeit with varying degrees of sophistication. Unsurprisingly, FMCG brand owners tend to be in the vanguard of those leading the way in creating innovative content such as games and apps.

The primary purpose of most rights holders' social media efforts is to strengthen relationships with customers, fans, partners, employees and other stakeholders. Naturally, such initiatives can also serve to provide additional benefits to sponsors, such as delivering more exposure to a passionate and engaged group of fans of a high profile celebrity, team, sports events, rock band, or music event.

But there is a fine line that brand owners need to walk between delivering content to these fans without over-commercialisation of the content that makes it attractive to such audiences in the first place. Twitter and Facebook are useful as channels that deliver content but can also drive fans to the brand owners' own websites, where these audiences can have a meaningful interaction with sponsored content.

The more a sponsor and brand owner invests in social networking efforts, the more it is likely to deliver a return on investment. It is important to determine the optimal level of resources to deploy in the face of limited activation budgets and other alternative channels in order to achieve an improvement in the performance of sponsorship.

'Every consumer loves to attend events but sometimes life gets in the way. And when that happens, we can bring the experience directly to them,' claims Sharon Byers, senior vice president of sports and entertainment marketing at Coca-Cola in the USA. Some of the biggest brands on the planet have fallen over themselves to advertise during the NFL Super Bowl, broadcast every February to over 100m viewers worldwide, paying a record USD 4.5m per 30-second slot in 2015. And that is not counting the production costs associated with such an eye-watering spend, which push the total closer to USD 9.5m.

In 2014 the roll call of brands included Bud Light, Budweiser, Doritos, Go Daddy, Chevrolet, Walt Disney, Beats Music, Bank of America, Hyundai, Cheerios, Squarespace, Radioshack, T-Mobile, Paramount, Volkswagen, Wonderful Pistachios, H&M, Columbia, CarMax, Coca-Cola, Sonos, Toyota, Subway, Jeep, Pepsi, Red Bull, Audi, Intuit, Axe, Chobani, Kia, Sprint, Heinz, Chrysler, Butterfinger, Microsoft, Hyundai, Jaguar, Danone and SodaStream. In the past, the 'big reveal' used to be standard practice for brands but this is not the case any more, as the vast majority of these ads are now shared on social media platforms in advance and in 2014 generated over 80m views on YouTube before Super Bowl Day.

And analysis shows that those brands that had a direct connection with what people do while watching the event, such as those in the food and drinks sectors, tended to score well in social media, generating around 25m tweets during the game in 2014.

Sports and entertainment content is now king

When the manager of Chicago radio station WGN approached a detergent company in 1930 to sponsor a daily 15-minute serialised drama *Painted Dreams,* he could not have envisaged that he was creating the very first piece of sponsored media content in history. Fast forward 90 years and 'content' continues to be the centre of the sponsorship ecosystem, as we discussed in Chapter 2.

The fascination with content is largely born of the proliferation of channels facing a sponsor and the pressure it is under in taking one piece of content and the messages it wants to deliver and making this work across all media platforms. This is no straightforward exercise in copywriting; indeed, increasingly, it is about images, pictures, video and the opportunity for deeper interactivity that this presents. In the global village, creative content is viewed as a key differentiator between competing organisations and brands, and creativity is critical to improving the performance of sponsorship.

Why creative thinking in sponsorship really matters

The attention span of audiences is getting shorter, not longer. As a result, brand owners need to capture share of attention in order to have a chance to capture share of wallet, if the ultimate objective of the sponsorship programme is to drive incremental sales.

Standard content that fails to entertain, inform and engage is unlikely to work. Marketers involved in bringing a sponsorship alive need to go outside their comfort zone. Creativity in the context of sponsorship needs to be about applying a thinking process that opens the mind to new ideas, and new associations between existing ideas, and is fuelled by conscious as well as unconscious insight. In fact, creative thinking needs to transcend the narrow focus of sponsorship activation and should apply to the sponsorship programme as a whole.

Creative thinking can be influenced by a deliberate cognitive process, by the environment around the brand owner and rights holder and even by your own personality, if you are the one who has been charged with coming up with a great idea.

The British marketing guru Peter Fisk says that 'Creativity is best achieved by left and right brain thinking, by combining focus and the big picture, analysis, intuition, logic and emotion.' One technique is to take two unconnected ideas and fuse them together (see Figure 5.2).

Like the Medicis of yesteryear, it is about bringing unfamiliar ideas, situations, talents, challenges and solutions together. Think Ravi Shankar and the early Beatles' stuff. Or even U2 and Apple. Apart from music fusion, one of the simplest ways to think more creatively in business is to apply existing ideas from outside your own market segment.

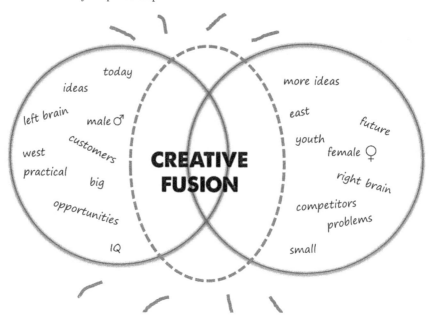

Figure 5.2 Unconnected ideas combine to result in a creative fusion
Source: Creative Genius by Peter Fisk (2011)

Look at what is happening in other sectors, countries or companies and creatively explore how you can apply these ideas to make a sponsorship programme engage in new and different ways. Peter Fisk explains:

> Fusion might also be about more radical crossovers. Whilst it's many years since I studied particle physics, I still use some of the simple ideas in my innovation projects with clients. Understanding atomic structures is a model for thinking differently about how products and services work together. Applying characteristics of astrophysics gives me a categorisation tool for managing portfolios.

One of the most original examples of fusion was achieved by Coca-Cola when it hired top music producer Mark Ronson to create a promotional video celebrating its sponsorship of the London 2012 Olympic Games.

Case study: Coca-Cola and London 2012 Olympic Games

When Coca-Cola looks at sponsorship, there has to be a particular role for the brand to play. If you could just as easily substitute one of the other sponsors for London 2012 into its space, then it is not doing a very good PR job. There has to be something unique for Coca-Cola in helping to triangulate between its brands, the property (London 2012) and the consumer's passions. Any activation that the brand owner gets involved with must not feel generic and must be personalised.

The real value lies in the combination of the direct impact of its sponsorship with subtle and subliminal benefits from associating with their consumers' lives. What Coca-Cola did was to fuse popular DJ culture with sport in order to produce a highly creative music video made by the highly sought-after DJ Mark Ronson that was based on five London 2012 Olympic hopefuls from around the world. Coke prides itself about being able to connect with people around the world – wherever they live, work and play. Peter Franklin, Group Director, Worldwide Sports and Event Management, Coca-Cola explains:

> Oftentimes we have more knowledge of consumer behavior in these territories than the rights holders do and that's an enormously powerful thing to be able to bring to a sponsorship. Our business is about understanding people's behavior in virtually every country in the world – that's what we do. That knowledge can help rights holders with their specific objectives. For example, over a number of years we've been helping the IOC in their aim of reconnecting with youth.

In contrast, sports brand owner Adidas took a completely different creative route by highlighting the underground nature of the London 2012 Olympic Games.

Case study: Adidas Underground and London 2012 Olympic Games

The objectives of the campaign, as part of Adidas sponsorship of London 2012, were:

- to demonstrate the sport/style take on celebrating London during the London 2012 Olympic Games
- to transfer Adidas Originals from the sports pages to lifestyle and mainstream media
- to offer an antidote to large-scale commercial Olympic activities in and around London.

Adidas' in-house marketing team launched a series of live consumer events produced by Sparklestreet Productions during the London 2012 Olympics to create an 'off–schedule' experience, and Adidas took over Village Underground, an East London venue, as a location for this initiative. The premiere of *The Chemical Brothers Don't Think* film, the first event in the series, featured a live performance from the band. The experience was tied back to Adidas by giving attendees an Adidas Originals Firebird track top and painting their faces with an iconic image from the film. VIPs included Matt Smith, Jaime Winstone, Rosamund Pike and Plan B, which ensured media coverage for the event. The second event was a private gig by the Stone Roses, which was their first London show in more than 15 years.

The Adidas in-house team kept the event secret until the day to generate hype and surprise, and invited high-profile music and fashion guests including Paul Weller, Jimmy Page, Miles Kane, Wretch 32, Bobby Gillespie, Maverick Sabre and Daisy Lowe. In addition, Adidas-affiliated Olympic athletes also attended the event, including Pete Reed, Tim Baillie, Etienne Stott and David Florence, as well as gold medallists Jessica Ennis and Sir Bradley Wiggins.

The team worked to secure branded 'Olympic' and Adidas Originals coverage across national media by focusing on the sports and music talent attending its events. This included a one-off photograph of the Stone Roses with Jessica Ennis and Sir Bradley Wiggins that was seeded to press alongside branding board images of VIP arrivals. This type of content would have been impossible had Adidas not pursued its 'Underground' strategy and fused content opportunities in this way.

The PR generated substantial results with over 95 articles outside sport-focused media and across print and online mainstream news titles. This coverage included double-page spreads in *The Sun*, *Sunday Mirror*, *Daily Star* and *Daily Mail* and posts on *Mail Online*, *The Guardian*, *ITV*, *Huffington Post* and Yahoo!, as well as all the lifestyle target titles including *NME*, *Cosmopolitan*, *Vogue* and *GQ*, exceeding projected media coverage by 288%. More than 1,100 people attended the events during the two days and Adidas' UK social media following rose by 25%. From a sales perspective, the campaign delivered an 82% increase in footfall in the Adidas flagship store and online sales rose by 62%. This was an impressive campaign on several grounds: Adidas blended its sports and lifestyle heritage with creative arts, which resulted in the two highly anticipated 'money can't buy' events. The brand owner had used creativity to get cut-through in non-traditional media outlets and it blended sport and style in a credible and engaging way. But this was not without its risks. Underground events can be notoriously difficult to amplify, as they require many ingredients to work together at the same time to be truly successful. This became even more challenging during the London 2012 Olympic Games because of the sheer number of sponsors involved in activation events at that time, all competing for attention.

With the use of unique creative ideas, Adidas Underground secured cut-through in a crowded market. At its core was the visual element of the campaign, which helped to define the Adidas brand and create a powerful emotional connection with the audience.

The rule breakers

Interaction with audiences remains a constant necessity for brand owners and increasingly this needs to be personal, on a one-to-one basis that delivers an ongoing dialogue and interaction. A brand needs to follow a strategy that integrates several factors into the content it creates and this includes clarity on who it targets, how it connects with those audiences, how it delivers a unique experience and how it leverages the content.

One artist who is perhaps best known for breaking all the rules and has extracted significant sponsorship dollars in the process is the twenty-first-century superstar pop idol Lady Gaga, the most followed person on Twitter, with 42.6m followers at the last count!

An inveterate user of Twitter, Lady Gaga has the magic formula of turning followers into super-fans. Her tweets are more than just marketing. They are about allowing fans to have a glimpse inside the life of a superstar. They allow fans to feel they have a one-to-one relationship with Lady Gaga, even though they know they are just one of 42m followers. They allow Lady Gaga to speak directly to fans without having to go through the filter of a TV interview, a newspaper article or magazine spread. They allow Lady Gaga to be genuine.

As one of the biggest-selling artists on the planet, tracks such as 'Poker Face', 'Bad Romance', 'Just Dance', 'Born this Way', 'Telephone' and the latest duet with Tony Bennett, 'The Lady is a Tramp', are freely available on YouTube, having clocked up over a billion views without cannibalising sales at retail.

What Lady Gaga has demonstrated with breathtaking power is that putting a great deal of effort into using social media and modern distribution channels to disseminate her music and videos has been incredibly successful in growing her fan base. According to Forbes, Lady Gaga's earnings in 2014 were USD 33m and have topped USD 100m since 2011. Yet just 24% of her wealth comes from record sales. In fact, even with the some of the best-selling singles of all time, Lady Gaga is estimated to have made USD 25m from record sales. Around 7% of her income comes from endorsement and sponsorship, with 69% from touring and merchandise.

Case study: Absolut Vodka and Lady Gaga, 2014

In order to help drive sales of her latest album 'ARTPOP', Lady Gaga enlisted the support of Absolut Vodka to sponsor artRAVE: ARTPOP Ball, which in turn helped turn ARTPOP into a number-one best-selling album in 2014.

Throughout Lady Gaga's US concert tour, Absolut provided the opportunity for a few lucky fans to watch the performance from the Absolut ARTPOP Lounge – a one-of-a-kind, on-stage bar created to be part of the theatrical set – while sipping custom cocktails such as 'Absolut Gaga' (ginger ale, sparkling cider, grapefruit and Absolut).

Making fans part of the content itself is a great example of breaking the rules. Two lucky fans at each concert on the US tour were chosen in real time to have their seats transformed. Fans also had the chance to win Absolut ARTPOP Lounge tickets to selected shows across the country through the #Absolutgaga contest at www.absolutgaga.com. In addition, fans were encouraged to share creative ideas for how they would transform their community for a chance to win. 'At Absolut, we believe transformative collaborations are the cornerstone of creativity,' explained Joao Rozario, Vice President, Vodkas, Pernod Ricard.

'Absolut – a brand with a rich history of innovative collaborations with artists spanning art, music and fashion – and Lady Gaga, a beacon of creativity and individuality, are coming together to add awe to an already inspiring entertainment experience. 'This show was going to be unlike anything we've ever done before,' said Lady Gaga in a news release issued by Absolut. 'Thanks to Absolut, we've created a special experience where fans can actually sit inside the stage and have their own bar. It's going to be a huge rave in the spirit of art and creativity.'

'We are thrilled to play matchmaker in bringing together two celebrated icons: Lady Gaga and Absolut,' said Russell Wallach, President of Media & Sponsorship, Live Nation. 'This unique collaboration not only gives Gaga devotees unprecedented access to their favourite artist; it seamlessly integrates Absolut into the transformative concert experience.'

From 1 May 2014, fans over the age of 21 could also visit www.AbsolutSummer. com to win a chance to see Lady Gaga live in Sweden, home of Absolut. One national grand prizewinner also won a trip for two to see Lady Gaga's show live in Stockholm, Sweden. The trip included a return airfare and hotel accommodations for five days and four nights, return train journey to/from the airport/central station in Stockholm, spending money and two tickets to the Lady Gaga concert in Stockholm that took place in September 2014. Given Lady Gaga's strong appeal to diverse communities, in May 2014 a dozen LGBT-friendly bars throughout the USA hosted Gaga-inspired runway shows, with fans competing to show who could best transform themselves into their own personal expression of Lady Gaga for the chance to win two tickets to the Absolut ArtPOP Lounge at the ArtPOP Ball in their city. And while witnessing the Gaga transformations, participants and onlookers could purchase another Gaga-inspired cocktail, 'the Absolut Monster', made up of Absolut Mandrin, pineapple juice and grenadine.

By the end of 2014, the artRAVE: ARTPOP Ball world tour has already broken box office records as one of the most attended music tours, having achieved sales in excess of 1m tickets.

Business relationships with the rights holder and the sponsor could increasingly become the norm, where the return on investment for both parties can lead to significant incremental revenues. For example, in 2014, energy drink Burn teamed up with French DJ David Guetta to collaborate on a new film about the artist's life, called *Nothing But The Beat*, which showcased David Guetta's rise from an underground house DJ to global superstar. The film was the largest piece of content marketing ever produced by Coca-Cola (brand owner of Burn) and has been viewed 1.8m times both in cinemas and online. Even more traditional market sectors, such as financial services, can also do things in such a creative way as to achieve cut-thorough in a highly competitive and cluttered sponsorship space.

Case study: ANZ Bank and the LGBT Community, 2014

In order to promote its support of the Sydney Gay and Lesbian Mardi Gras in February 2014, ANZ Bank hired artists from the LGBT community to transform ten of its ATMs into GAYTMs. The bank has a long history of supporting community activities and, as one of the biggest banks in Australia, has supported the festival since 2007. Its cash machines were vividly transformed by the addition of rhinestones, sequins, studs, leather, denim and fur into representations of the LGBT community that included unicorns, drag queens, rainbows and sailors. Even the ATM screens got a makeover, displaying messages such as 'Hello gorgeous' and rainbow-coloured cash-machine receipts carried the message 'Cash Out and Proud'. GAYTMs' operator fees made between February–March 2014 generated by non-ANZ cardholders were donated to Twenty10, a charity that supports young people of diverse genders and sexualities.

This was nothing short of brave of ANZ to support a community that was more used to being victimised than attracting corporate sponsorship at this level and demonstrates that brands can and should be seen as a force for good. ANZ used its sponsorship to showcase its commitment to diversity and inclusivity and was the presenting sponsor of Fair Day, VIP Parade Viewing Area and Mardi Gras Workshop, with around 100 ANZ employees taking part in the parade on the company's float in top hats and tuxedo-style costumes.

ANZ took its commitment further and was also able to drive traffic to its website, where it discussed its commitment to diversity and other activities connected with the Mardi Gras.

Content marketing

At a convention in India on the subject of content marketing in 2014, one of the delegates was Avik Chattopadhyay, head of marketing for Volkswagen. What he had to say would have sent a chill through every advertising agency boss in attendance:

> Cars have virtually been the same for a very long time – with four wheels. But the consumer has changed and so has everything around him, especially the way he thinks and communicates. Today, there's no debate that paid media is gone.
>
> If we do our basic things right, we'll not need paid media at all. There'll be reviews, tweets, shares, and the content that brands may not like but have to listen to, as they come from the consumer. People trust a brand, they believe in its credibility and every brand has to have a higher purpose to it.

At one level, Avik Chattopadhyay makes an interesting point although I think that paid media will never disappear from the marketing mix but it is certainly becoming less significant compared with owned and earned media.

Brand owners like Nestlé, Kellogg's and Cisco are making greater use of content marketing but face a multitude of challenges on the way to connecting with desired customer segments.

'You can't just decide one day you want to do content marketing. Go out and see whom you're trying to reach, what are their passion points and what are the stories and messages you want to convey as a brand. Then choose your tactics,' advises Carolin Probst-Iyer, digital consumer engagement manager at Chevrolet.

Bob Arnold, associate director of global digital strategy at Kellogg's, adds that finding the correct tone of voice is essential to success in this area. 'The biggest challenge is balancing adding value to the consumer and communicating your brand message. The challenge is to do this in a way that you're adding value without being overbearing.'

Orion Brown, senior brand manager at Capri Sun, views so-called 'passion brands' involved in consumers' daily lives as having a creative advantage over other types of brand but warned that such brands have to avoid sounding 'preachy' while encouraging a purchase to be made. 'Identifying the consumer need that a brand meets, then laddering that back up to a higher emotional need helps drive relevant content creation. But even then, brands need to be mindful of not getting too lofty in their brand promise to keep the content grounded and believable to the consumer,' she said.

Other brand owners point to not just the cost of creating compelling content but also the need to have sufficient funds in order to distribute it to the appropriate channels. One of the best examples of owned and earned media is illustrated by Red Bull and the way in which it engaged with millions around the world in most probably the most audacious content-marketing exercise in history.

Case study: Red Bull and Felix Baumgartner, 2012

Wearing little more than a modified astronaut's space suit to stop him turning into a block of ice with atmospheric temperatures below −70 degrees centigrade, Felix Baumgartner set a new world record for the highest skydive from the edge of space in 2012. The 43-year-old Austrian daredevil jumped out of a 770ft helium balloon about 39km (128,000ft) above New Mexico at the edge of space, descending more quickly than the speed of sound, reaching a maximum velocity of 833.9mph (1,342kph).

It took just under ten minutes for him to descend, with the last few thousand feet being negotiated by parachute for a perfect textbook and injury-free landing.

Not surprisingly, the attempt to be the world's first 'supersonic man' was sponsored by high-energy drink Red Bull, which presumably considers itself to be the equivalent of 'rocket fuel for humans'.

It was a shrewd move by Red Bull as Baumgartner's stunt prompted over 8m simultaneous live streams of the event on YouTube, which broadcast the mission with a time delay of around 20 seconds.

At the time, sceptics expressed concern that the massive investment required by Red Bull to have carried out such an audacious stunt would not actually deliver a return in incremental sales of its high-energy drink. But the sceptics were proved wrong.

'The sponsorship transcended sports and entertainment into pop culture, hitting new consumers that Red Bull doesn't usually capture and on a global scale,' observed Ben Sturner, CEO of Leverage Agency, a full-service sports, entertainment and media marketing company. 'The value for Red Bull is in the tens of millions of dollars of global exposure and Red Bull Stratos will continue to be talked about and passed along socially for a very long time to come,' he added.

Sturner believes that Red Bull Stratos was one of the greatest marketing stunts by Red Bull to date and perhaps the greatest marketing stunt of all time, given that all coverage carried the brand as central to the global news story.

In the 12 months that followed, Baumgartner was rolled out as Red Bull's key brand ambassador, supported with dramatic video images of his freefall filmed on a GoPro camera and numerous appearances on chat shows all over the world. To put things into perspective, Baumgartner declared: 'Sometimes you have to go up really high to understand how small you are.'

In many respects, brands such as Red Bull, Coca-Cola and ANZ are 'thought leaders' in their respective market segments and are engaged in content marketing.

'Content marketing' is a term that best describes 'thought leadership in action' and can include some or all of the following activities:

- breakthrough ideas
- events, presentations, conferences
- reports/books
- research studies
- white papers
- video/film
- music

All of these activities are capable of being sponsorship-driven, such as events, research studies and white papers. According to the Content Marketing Association (CMA): 'Content marketing is the discipline of creating quality branded editorial content across all media channels and platforms to deliver engaging relationships, consumer value and measurable success for brands.'

'Thought leadership' means different things to different people depending on their point of view. At one level, it is something completely new, unfamiliar to their market segment and hard to get their minds around. To others, it is a series of white papers or a research programme put together at relatively short notice to show off their expertise. In yet other cases, it is a major part of public relations with a desired group of potential customers or clients. At other times it is seen as a precursor to new business development or the creation of a massive new market.

However it is regarded, though, it has got to be about the *pursuit of a unique insight* that should not be constrained by having to go through the prism of making money, although clearly there must be a commercial advantage or business case for wanting to embark on the content marketing journey in the first place. In my experience, the attitude and knowledge of people involved in thought leadership of any description affect their approach to it and have a massive bearing on the expected outcomes as a result.

There can often be friction between the prioritisation of publisher metrics, such as engagement, on the one hand, and marketing metrics, such as click-through rates and sales conversions, on the other. According to Clare Hill, managing director of the Content Marketing Association in the UK: 'Too often conversations about content marketing can go down a direct marketing route. I don't doubt analytics tools are going to get more sophisticated, but sometimes they force us to focus too much on what we can measure and we miss the big picture. We can prove the return on investment position, but that's not the same as understanding why someone wants to buy something.'

Reputation is a critical component of content marketing and is one reason why major consultancies such as McKinsey, IBM, Accenture, PwC and Deloitte place great store on the production of thought leadership outputs, as these are often picked up by the media and influential bloggers as evidence of movements, trends and fresh ideas in market segments. It is a great way to showcase intellectual capital.

'Useful, credible and engaging content is a powerful trigger for calls to action. Implement them thoughtfully and try to ensure that they strike a balance between being easy to do and aligned to your business goals. Lean heavily on a data- and feedback-driven approach to determine which calls to action work best before implementing them,' advises Ethan McCarty, director of IBM Marketing and Communications Labs.

In such a complex environment, knowing what content to create and how to disseminate it can be a challenge. For example, how can the imperative to increase click-through rates be reconciled with the need to create useful content? Should content be created with search engine optimisation (SEO) or social sharing in mind? A related problem arising from an excessive focus on SEO or social search is 'content deluge' – bombarding consumers with large amounts of low-quality content. This is counterproductive, as consumers will turn off and the brand owner will quickly start to find that its campaigns fail to achieve their objectives.

'The notion you can create a single campaign and send it out in the world and that's it are over. Content marketing initiatives need to be living, breathing things that change over time with social media, events, and PR becoming larger components of an overall sponsorship strategy, requiring collaboration and group effort covering so many different facets of the campaign,' explains David Messenger, co-head of the agency division of Creative Artists Agency in Los Angeles.

An excellent example of this 'thought leadership in action' and taking content marketing to a new level is the programme developed by Samsung in 2014.

Case study: Samsung and 'Launching People', 2014

Having fought a hard battle against Apple to establish its technology and design credentials, Samsung embarked on a new brand strategy that it hoped would add personality to its products and engage with the millennial generation in a completely different way.

The South Korean giant recruited actor and producer Idris Elba, singer-songwriter Paloma Faith, Sunday Times cook Gizzi Erskine and photographer Rankin in a nationwide search for up-and-coming talent. And it has used Facebook to reach these audiences and customer segments.

Andy Griffiths, president of Samsung UK and Ireland, explained: 'Everyone knows Samsung for launching products and every day we're inspired by people who use those products to achieve amazing things. "Launching People" is all about doing just that – launching people's potential through technology, whatever their stage in life. We hope to give people with passion, ambition and a hungry mind, a launch pad for their bright ideas and change their lives in a positive way.'

Entrants made a two-minute video pitch about their idea and uploaded it to the site, where the lucky winner was chosen to be mentored by the celebrity depending on their interest in film-making, music, photography or cooking.

There was also a 'People's Choice' winner per category, voted for by the public on Facebook, who also received Samsung products that supported them in pursuing their dreams. Such is the strength of the creative idea that Sky 1 HD came on board to create a TV show showing the celebrities choosing one person each to mentor and followed their journeys as they collaborated on a project and spent £7m on promoting the show.

Conferences, events, seminars and trade events

Presentations at conferences, events, seminars and trade events are an excellent and powerful way to communicate thought leadership within desired customer and client segments. A subject matter expert who presents convincingly at a conference can add to the viral diffusion of an idea. It works really well in my experience, because there is a rational and an emotional dynamic to it.

The rational component is the quality of information and insight demonstrated by the presentation. The emotional dynamic is subtle but results from the environment. It can stimulate interest and prompt people to look at other aspects of a thought leadership programme, such as reports or web portals.

This type of sponsored content can be used to achieve a number of objectives:

- enhanced reputation
- achieving a position within a desired market segment
- demonstrating what you deliver, not merely what you offer
- moving into emerging markets
- creating the new 'intelligent buyer' of tomorrow
- stimulating latent markets
- creating new business models
- supporting change.

The skill of modern sponsorship planning is to design the right blend of different media and different techniques to reach and influence the desired customer and client segments. By working out an integrated approach to managing thought leadership, a much bigger impact can be achieved.

For example, the customer or client might receive an invitation to an event one day; see a newspaper article the next; notice an email with a link to a white paper, which might also invite this to be shared among other colleagues.

Table 5.1 Integrated approach to sponsored content

	J	F	M	A	M	J	J	A	S	O	N	D
Seminar programme												
Event												
Digital communications												
PR waves												
Viral programme												
Collateral launch and use												
Industry associations												
Internal communications												

If the thought leadership content is aligned with a professional organisation or institute, then again the perceived value of this content is also higher. Frequency, cumulative impact and style of message being communicated through different media all need to be carefully choreographed.

By planning an integrated approach and managing various agencies to deliver it, a concerted effort can be made by a sponsor to share the thought leadership content with the appropriate audiences (see Table 5.1).

Media sponsorship

Our world is changing at an unprecedented rate, with emerging technologies revolutionising how we conduct our lives, what we do and where we do it.

According to research carried out in 2014 by the Institute of Practitioners in Advertising (IPA), we British consumers still consume the majority of our media through the traditional platforms: 97% of our television viewing is via a television set, 88% of our reading occasions are via print and 94% our listening occasions are via radio – however, emerging platforms are changing how we consume media. Just over half of us now have a smartphone, while 24% own a tablet and 38% have access to one within our household.

We are using our smartphones for a number of new purposes. For example, 22% of us use them to look for local deals, offers and vouchers, 30% to locate places using GPS and 8% to scan QR codes. For national newspapers, their apps and website audiences add an extra 22% of net adult reach to their print-based audience – this increase is highest for the quality broadsheets at 48%. This is up considerably from two years ago, when the comparative figures were 11% and 24% , respectively. We are watching more video on demand, with 38% of us using VoD services each week – this rises to 56% among 15- to 24-year-olds.

Double-screening and accessing online user-generated video content are also particularly popular among 15- to 24-year-olds. Seventy-nine per cent of them double-screen (use the Internet while watching television) over the course of the week, compared with 54% of all adults, while 80% of 15- to 24-year-olds are accessing online user-generated video content, compared with 14% of all adults.

More than half of us – 54% – are now using social networking sites, up from 44% in 2012, and for longer. We connect for almost ten hours on average each week, up considerably from 6 hours, 39 minutes in 2012. The average adult now has 194 Facebook friends, while 15- to 24-year-olds have an average of 326. Although 32% of us assign 'likes' to friends in a week, only 7% assign them to brands.

Thirty per cent of us use Twitter each week. We follow an average of 109 people and have an average of 133 followers. We are also LinkedIn to 86 people on average. Ten per cent of our shopping occasions are now online, compared with 8% in 2012. Half of our online shopping is done via a computer; the other half is split equally between mobile and tablet.

The research concluded on a happy note that our moods are mainly positive. We feel OK/fine for 39% of our time, relaxed for 15% of our time and happy for a further 13% of our time. A growing area of media sponsorship is advertiser-funded programming (AFP) and product placement.

Advertiser-funded programming (AFP)

Advertiser-Funded Programming or, as it is sometimes referred to, content partnership or branded content is not a new idea and can be traced back to the 1930s, when original daytime dramas in the US were funded by washing powder manufacturers such as Proctor & Gamble and Colgate-Palmolive, and the 'soap opera' has remained with us ever since. The key to a successful AFP strategy all those years ago was for the brands to give their customers the entertainment they wanted during the day. The brand would be associated and so appreciated. It was less about brand values and more about the brand as benefactor. This simple and effective approach of putting viewers first when producing TV content should remain at the heart of any AFP initiative today.

Several major brand owners such as Unilever, Proctor & Gamble, Adidas and Vodafone have now deep experience of using AFP to reach existing and new audiences in a creative and engaging way.

Given that TV viewing is just as popular as it ever was, but now on a variety of devices and on a time-shifted basis, a brand's close association with broadcast content remains a compelling opportunity.

With respect to AFP, this provides the opportunity for brands to participate in the phenomenon that a successful TV show can be; on air, off air and online. AFP can be described as 'any means by which an advertiser can have a deeper relationship with programming product beyond traditional media activity'.

By this definition, there must be a funding relationship (full or part) with the programme or series. Put another way, it is 'sponsorship plus', where the brand owner's financial support goes directly into production and leads to a degree of content ownership. It is programming that would not exist without the brand owner/sponsor as a partner, subject to certain legal conditions, as we shall discuss in Chapter 7.

The AFP is not a glorified commercial for the brand over an extended period of time. It is also not an 'infomercial' extolling the benefits of using a particular product or service. The nature of the relationship with programme makers is one based on respect for editorial independence and trust that the programme makers really do understand what the audience likes – and equally, what it does not like too in order to get the balance just right. An early example, often referred to in any discussion about AFP, is the success of 'Gillette World of Sport', which delivered brilliant sports content without ever showing a razor or shaving foam product in the process.

A TV sponsorship campaign, done well, can yield real benefits for a brand, if the right show is available, at the right time; if it can be secured; and if there is sufficient time to plan and coordinate the exploitation before it goes to air. However, this is not always possible, which is where AFP has its place in the marketing mix. Through AFP, brand owners both maximise the potential of TV sponsorship on their own terms and garner a number of significant benefits from having a deeper relationship with programming and with broadcasters and producers.

However, it does require deeper pockets and also the ability to know where to draw the line with respect to ensuring the audience is not being 'taken for a ride'. And this requires brand owners to think imaginatively and creatively.

AFP can also remove the anxiety of being part of a bidding war with other brands for TV sponsorship and, of course, an AFP format cannot be copied by a competitor, as it is protected by copyright laws.

Another advantage is synchronicity, as an AFP can be broadcast at a time that is likely to engage with desired audiences when the propensity to purchase a product could be at its highest point in the day or night. Advertiser-funded programming tends to require longer lead times and will require more work in terms of planning and budgeting in order to be part of an integrated campaign that is both online and offline. However, brand owners are rewarded by creating a deeper and more immersive experience for the audience that can last 30 or 60 minutes and where all the content is helping to shape the attitudes, values, perceptions, beliefs and behaviours of consumers watching the show.

There are also many other media sponsorship benefits, such as title rights and credit integration, product deals, promotional appearances and international barter. The widespread adoption of broadband by households, coupled with the hosting of television properties on new platforms and the enthusiasm of viewers for more of the right content related to their favourite programmes, is of considerable incremental benefit for sponsors.

Moreover, since the advent of product placement, some brands have successfully combined AFP with the additional benefits of product integration. A highly innovative and creative example of AFP combined with product placement is the online sitcom devised by Domino's Pizza aimed at TV football fans.

Case study: Domino's Pizza and TV football fans, 2013

One of the most popular fast foods in the UK is pizza. And for many young men a slice of pizza and a beer is the best way to enjoy an evening watching their favourite football team on TV. Domino's Pizza has assiduously courted the attentions of this customer segment but also wanted to appeal to families that tend to have larger orders but purchase less frequently without alienating its core customer segment. 'We didn't want to lose sight of our core "social snacker" 16-24-year-old male audience. We needed to defend our position, keep them on side and ultimately drive more loyalty,' explains Nick Dutch, head of digital at Domino's. The brand decided to combine football and social media for this digital-savvy audience. 'The strategy was to spend just 3% of the Domino's budget on the creation of football content for social snackers – content that had to be topical and entertaining in order to fuel engagement, conversation and shareability,' explains Nick Dutch.

Previously, Domino's had launched its own film-streaming service via its online channel. Customer analytics showed that young men were an audience that was now spending more time than ever watching and sharing digital content among friends, especially around that favourite pastime, football.

Domino's allocated a £300,000 budget for the creation of video content about football, with the aim of boosting engagement, conversation, online sharing and, most importantly, incremental pizza sales among this core customer segment. Domino's worked with agency Arena and video production company Zodiak on the 12-week video campaign. The production team created a series of 'webisodes' accessible on YouTube called 'The Support Group', written and produced by Chris Little and Jonathan Stern, who also created the British cult TV show *The Inbetweeners*. The campaign opted for this creative team because of the irreverent tone of *The Inbetweeners*, which charted the chaotic escapades of four teenage boys, and such an approach would have strong appeal to Domino's core customer segment. 'They had the credibility to create content that was going to add value. We didn't want to risk spending money on content to find out that nobody found it very funny or relevant,' explains Henry Daglish, managing director of Arena.

The show was set in a typical workplace and centred on the daily lives of football- obsessed work colleagues. The challenge was to create content that was totally relevant to the Domino's audience and was dynamic enough to change every week so as to ensure that they kept tuning in.

Every Monday, the scriptwriters' meeting would discuss a new episode where the main characters engage in teasing, taunting banter in reaction to actual stories from that week's football news, which also added to the relevancy of the content for the audience. 'It was all around what football personalities had been up to. For example, what John Terry had done the weekend before? There was a small love story but it basically revolved around boys' banter,' says Henry Daglish.

The sitcom also flagged Domino's football pre-order service, which was created to bolster the campaign. The episodes were promoted via email to the Domino's database and on the order confirmation page on the brand website. The show was also promoted via social media channels such as Twitter and Facebook, and video content was placed on editorial platforms read by the same audience.

The campaign ran for 12 weeks and generated nearly 1m views. By the eighth week, sales directly generated by the campaign had covered all production and media costs and, critically, research showed that the audience purchased pizza more frequently. On average, a 'social snacker' tends to order a pizza once every six weeks with an average spend of £20. This increased by 15%– to a purchase cycle approximately every 5½ weeks. According to Domino's, the results showed that click-through rates were five times higher than other competitors' content, while interaction and share rates were three and five times stronger respectively than those of rivals – a significant digital dividend for Domino's. The campaign also attracted editorial partners at no additional cost when the content was picked up and placed on the websites of *The Sun* and *Loaded*, which appealed to this customer segment.

In future, Domino's will look to working more with franchisees and in particular those based in the same locations as the football teams in the sitcom. For example, when Bradford City FC made it to the League Cup Final in 2013, it would have been ideal to involve the Bradford Domino's franchise in the promotion of the sitcom. 'But trying to get something like this to filter through to franchisees in such a short period of time isn't that easy,' adds Henry Daglish, as the content would need to be uploaded more quickly in order to maintain relevance.

Another setback emerged when Manchester United FC performed so well that viewers knew the team had won the Premier League even though there were ten weeks left of the season. This reduced the excitement normally associated with the event. Nick Dutch also felt the content in the AFP could have been more cutting-edge. 'We were relatively safe in the type of humour used. It's a fine line for brands – we didn't want to be in the position where people are critical of you for being crude. But in hindsight, we could've been a bit more daring,' he concludes.

Another ground-breaking example of the collaboration between professional film directors and producers and brands is a special series created by Anthony E. Zuiker, writer/director/producer of the US hit TV crime drama *CSI*.

Case study: Symantec and sci-fi crime series Cybergeddon, 2012

Cybergeddon was a nine-part sci-fi series hosted on the Yahoo! site and followed the story of agent Chloe Jocelyn as she investigates a slew of seemingly unrelated cyber-attacks with fellow agent Frank Parker and incarcerated master hacker Chase 'Rabbit' Rosen. Chloe and her team must crack the worldwide cybercrime ring led by Gustov Dobreff before it is too late. In a world where everyone is connected, everyone is at risk.

Although the concept offered security software firm Symantec, owner of the Norton antivirus brand, a means of conveying the dangers of cybercrime in a new, engaging way, the series was also an independent piece of programming free from overt marketing messages. 'There are no product placement shots in *Cybergeddon* or conversations where people talk about how to download the latest security software. It's much more subtle than that. The brand simply provides the context that it wants to be associated with,' explains Dan Watt-Smith, Yahoo!'s head of video in the UK.

A convert to this approach to storytelling on behalf of a brand is, in fact, the creator of the series itself, Anthony E. Zuiker, who says:

> Let me give you the simplest example. Forget about numbers. Do we want to get a lot of views? Sure. Will views be important like ratings are important? Absolutely. But there's something going on beyond the bean-counting of it all, which is this: there was a time when a 30-second spot on a hit TV show would cost one million dollars. What you're getting for a million dollars on a TV spot is 30 seconds that comes and goes, or is sped past by TiVo, or ignored entirely and will never see the light of day ever again. It doesn't live on a DVD. It can't be repurposed. That money has come and gone. So unless you have that attention for 30 seconds, that money is in the ether.
>
> Let's take the same philosophy with a web series. If a brand partner puts in a million dollars, what do you get from that? Well, not only do you get product placement inside the movie and a level of entertainment and also edutainment about your product, but all of the interactive content online – tie-ins to the app, Netflix, Epix, video on-demand, the ability to download – I mean, the lifespan of that investment over the course of the next 20 or 30 years has far more global value and far more global reach of awareness than 30 seconds could ever dream of. And that's the major way going forward. We are working with brands to give them real staying power.

This was not Zuiker's first foray into online content. The writer-director-producer has been a leader in the world of multimedia content for years, having previously released the 'digi-novel' series *Level 26*, which combined a traditional novel with online videos called 'cyber-bridges' to enhance the story. Zuiker is also a partner in the BlackBoxTV YouTube channel, which features original short sci-fi and horror films. He says:

> There's a need for brands to think outside the box, to think about where to put their money to have the proper staying power. When you think about Norton in terms of being in the entertainment business, it doesn't seem like a fastball fit, right? But when you think about Norton being involved in a cybercrime movie, suddenly it makes sense. So would Norton be better to launch a 30-second spot on CSI on CBS, or would they have a better chance of accomplishing their goals of awareness by being involved in a movie as big as this, with this kind of global scale? Our hope obviously is that we can convince other companies with other particular projects to buy into this philosophy – 'Where do you want to put your money? Here or there?' – and hopefully it's with us.

The attraction for Zuiker is starting to spread to other writers, directors and producers who may at first been sceptical about how much independence they actually have over the content of such shows, given that the sponsor is putting up the finance for it in the first place and the old adage 'he who pays the piper calls the tune' could so easily apply here. But, in fact, the reverse appears to be the case.

'A lot of film-makers and producers enjoy the creative freedom they experience in this environment. TV production studios and broadcasters take a very scientific approach to the process of creating a TV show, whereas brands tend to be a lot more hands off. If the subject matter and the theme is something they're happy to be associated with, then brands tend to give a lot more creative freedom to the person they want to work with,' adds Dan Watt-Smith.

The online platform opens up a host of interactive possibilities for *Cybergeddon*, including character biographies, behind-the-scenes footage and social media feeds that are accessible alongside the main video.

Symantec's marketing is done as an adjunct to the online series with click-throughs and sponsored articles that appear elsewhere on the Yahoo! site. The software company also worked closely on the development of the storyline to ensure its authenticity, given that it is in the business of protecting people from the dangers of cyberattacks. Andrew Ford, marketing director at Symantec, explains: 'It was really important for us to emphasise how real the threat is. When it comes to the realities of cybercrime, we've built up a huge amount of knowledge over many years which our experts were able to share as the script was put together.'

The role of Yahoo! is also beginning to change as a result of these creative collaborations between brand owners and the film industry. In the past, with an original online series, Yahoo! generally acted as the digital distribution partner, although increasingly it is getting involved in shaping the content too. So rather than just being a neutral partner that provides the platform to deliver the content, Yahoo! is now beginning to help shape the content in order that it fits in with what it is doing elsewhere and that it's happy to promote it. 'A series like *Cybergeddon* is a particularly integrated approach, because we're looking at doing things in technology from an editorial standpoint. We already have a relationship with Symantec, and in conjunction with the launch we pulled all of that together with articles on our front page about online security, which is a big area of interest for Yahoo!'s audience,' explains Dan Watt-Smith. In addition, what also appealed to Zuiker was the fact that there was a day and date release, which meant that the series was rolled out simultaneously around the planet.

'That all ties in to the central creative concept behind the series, which is about somebody effectively crippling the planet because of a cyber-bug they release. So the idea you can roll this out with a platform like Yahoo! and distribute it globally is something that a lot of directors love the idea of, which also works for the brands,' concludes Dan Watt-Smith.

Product placement

Like AFP, product placement is not new. In fact, luxury brand Chanel signed a contract with film studios Metro-Goldwyn-Meyer back in the 1920s, as Sam Goldwyn thought he could increase box-office receipts by showing Paris fashions to a US audience hungry for escapism from the Great Depression.

By the 1950s, films started to look like shop fronts full of highly desirable outfits that clung seductively to its leading ladies such as Audrey Hepburn, Lauren Bacall and Jane Russell. And fashion designers including Hubert de Givenchy became as important as the Hollywood director Blake Edwards who directed Hepburn in the 1961 classic *Breakfast at Tiffany's*.

Since then there has been no end of fashion brands wanting to turn entertainment into a successful marketing tool as consumers move increasingly towards on-demand channels such as Netflix or the Web to consume content where they can avoid the 30-second ad spot.

Product placement has been a fact of life for cinemagoers and TV viewers in most countries around the world for over 60 years.

In 1949, NBC launched America's first daily TV news programme, the *Camel News Caravan*, featuring a newsreader smoking a Camel cigarette and a policy that banned footage of 'no smoking' signs and anyone puffing on a cigar, including Sir Winston Churchill!

Today, brand and product tie-ins are less brazen, but equally effective, as a weapon for achieving sales and marketing advantage over competitor brand owners' above-the-line marketing efforts.

The James Bond film franchise is credited with having started the current fashion of placing well-known branded products in the centre of the action, with brands such as Aston Martin and Omega taking high-profile roles on screen. For example, in *Skyfall* (2012) actor Daniel Craig is seen drinking a Heineken beer. Typically, this type of marketing activity is supported by heavy above-the-line advertising spend as well as online and social media interaction with fans so as to create the cut-through required.

Successful franchises like *Mission Impossible* always attract a raft of big brands, such as Coca-Cola Zero, which wants more than just a one-off relationship with a big blockbuster film. Growth of product placement globally is estimated to increase by around 12% and could top USD 10 billion in 2014, with around a 20% increase in India and Russia, although the US still accounts for around 60% of the total spend globally. Critics of product placement are plentiful and various, and include consumer groups frightened that editorial and creative independence have been sold to the highest bidder and church groups that worry the corrosive effect of commercialisation of TV content is projected to millions of viewers in their living rooms.

Even the esteemed Writers Guild of America, the union representing, among others, TV scriptwriters, has jumped on product placement practices, alleging that its members are being forced to write advertising copy disguised as storylines and that 'Tens of millions of viewers are sometimes being sold products without their knowledge, in opaque, subliminal ways.'

US campaign group Commercial Alert has labelled product placement an 'affront to basic honesty' but this has not dented the enthusiasm amongst successful British TV producers such as Peter Bazalgette of *Big Brother* fame from launching his own embedded advertising company, and he predicts the UK market could be worth in excess of £100m a year in revenues.

US experience of product placement

Research in 2013 in the US shows that covert product placements in TV programmes can increase brand recall by consumers as well as shape their attitudes towards those brands.

According to three joint studies led by the University of Colorado Boulder, consumers who watch TV sitcoms and see product placements through covert marketing have better memories of the products and better attitudes towards those brands.

'Frankly, we were a bit surprised at the power of covert marketing across a variety of studies,' said Margaret Campbell, Professor of Marketing at CU-Boulder's Leeds School of Business and lead author of an article in the *Journal of Consumer Psychology*. 'Even though most US viewers know that marketers pay to get their brands in front of consumers surreptitiously, consumers are still influenced by covert marketing efforts.' However, if prior to watching the show people saw a disclosure that sponsored product placements were included in the programme, the research seemed to indicate they were *not* more likely to list the brand in their top three choices, although they still reported a higher liking for the brand.

The studies also found that the disclosure of paid product placements in a sitcom decreased the influential effects, especially when the disclosure occurred after the consumer was exposed to the marketing. In one of the studies, people watched a sitcom including a few seconds of exposure to a breakfast cereal. Later, when asked to list the first cereals that came to mind, people who had seen a brand name cereal during the sitcom were more than three times as likely to include that cereal in their top three, as compared with those who had seen a fictitious cereal. 'Disclosures after the placement appear to alert people to the impact that covert marketing efforts can have, in which case they are less likely to be influenced,' Campbell said.

There have been calls to require disclosure of covert marketing in the US to be consistent with other requirements for disclosure of sponsorship. In the US, around USD 4bn is spent annually by brand owners in product placement activities on film and TV (see Table 5.2).

Some brand owners such as Apple have a special department that is responsible for 'seeding' Apple products into mainstream shows, such as smash-hit medical drama *House*, starring Hugh Lawrie.

Exponents of the art of product placement prefer to remain in the shadows of their famous brands, which tends to give the appearance of something a bit surreptitious or underhanded in the way product placement works.

Table 5.2 Top-ranked shows in the USA with product placement

Rank	Programme	Network	Total number of occurrences
1	*American Idol*	FOX	577
2	*The Biggest Loser*	NBC	533
3	*The Celebrity Apprentice*	NBC	391
4	*Dancing with the Stars*	ABC	390
5	*The X Factor*	FOX	312
6	*Extreme Makeover: Home Edition*	ABC	224
7	*America's Got Talent*	NBC	220
8	*Friday Night Lights*	NBC	201
9	*America's Next Top Model*	CW	178
10	*The Amazing Race: Unfinished Business*	CBS	161

Source: Kolah (2013)

In some cases, product placement can blur the boundaries between advertising and content for the unsuspecting viewer. The benefits of bringing entertainment and brands closer together appropriately are well established through our experiences with TV sponsorship and more recently with branded content.

Consumers' positive feelings for entertainment content – their interest in a favourite programme or character – can rub off on a product featured within this content. This, in turn, can build key brand metrics. Product placement works in a similar way to other forms of sponsorship and is often used to complement other sponsorship activities and to influence brand affinity incrementally.

Also, like other forms of sponsorship, the brand follows the content as the programme is viewed across channels and platforms after its first run (+1 channels, VoD, etc.).

Product placement has been proved to boost awareness and purchase consideration. It is a great way of educating viewers about the brand through usage and dialogue, and has the power to change perceptions.

Another key benefit of product placement is that it can help to normalise a brand and help it to be seen, used and understood in a natural context. Product placement works best when part of an integrated solution. Market researchers Nielsen found that spot ads paired with product placement generated double the recall and double the purchase intent. Product placement agency Liquid Thread said 'We have found that product placement is at its most effective when it is supplemented by further brand integration across a programme's supporting digital platforms. When we placed Samsung tablets and phones in *The X Factor*, we also created online video diaries of the contestants.'

UK experience in product placement

Product placement was made permissible on British commercial TV in 2011 and is accompanied by a PP logo when a brand works with editorial and production partners to place their product or service into the fabric of a TV programme. This could be a product that is used (like a mobile phone or a cash point machine), is part of the set (like washing powder on a supermarket shelf) or appears as a poster.

Product placement has been on British TV screens for some years, appearing within acquired programming from overseas or as legitimate prop provision – a natural part of making TV programmes. Since February 2011 certain programmes have also been able to contain paid-for product placement as long as they comply with Ofcom's rules (see Chapter 7).

Since then, advertisers have taken advantage of this opportunity to get their brands woven into the editorial of TV programmes in order to get closer to their viewers, and some gratifying results have been achieved.

The vast majority of product placement deals so far have been linked to a sponsorship or advertiser-funded programme (AFP). Recent research from Channel 4 also suggests that the cross-platform approach is the best approach for product placement.

Broadcasters, independent producers, talent, advertisers, media agencies and specialist content agencies all have their roles to play in the success of product placement. However, the existence of so many interested parties is also indicative of its complexity as seen from a standing start.

Add potential international distribution issues to this, and some long timelines, and there are plenty of questions to be asked. For example:

- How do I find out about placement opportunities?
- Who will set the price and do the deals?
- How will a placement be valued?
- What sort of process and management will be involved from first meeting to broadcast?
- Should I be looking for frequency or prominence?
- How will my brand sit alongside other brands?
- How can I use placement to turbocharge my sponsorship or advertiser-funded programming or to amplify my spot ads?

Dolce Gusto coffee machine on the set of ITV 1's *This Morning* was the first instance of British product placement allowable under the new Ofcom Broadcasting Code (2011). Apart from that it is pretty unremarkable!

Research by PQ Media shows that brand owners significantly increased global spending on paid-for product placement in TV and film to USD 7.4 billion in 2011 and this could top USD 20bn in 2014. Product placement is increasingly being used as part of a multimedia campaign where a key objective is to place or integrate brand names, logos or specific products within the non-ad content of various media including TV, film, Internet, mobile, videogames and music.

The ultimate goal of brand owners is to place prominently or integrate creatively products into particular story lines or a scene in order to promote brand awareness and generate favourable consumer attitude that translates into brand preference and ultimately influences purchasing behaviour. In many respects, this is not that dissimilar to the way in which other types of sponsorship work but product placement tends to be more overt with respect to the way it integrates with TV and film content.

ITV has carried out research on their *Coronation Street* product placements with viewers, reporting that:

- Relevant PP does not detract from or interrupt the viewing experience.
- It can add depth and reality (when done well) to a programme.
- A majority (91%) of viewers of treated episodes agreed that seeing the placements made no difference to their enjoyment of the programme, with some (7%) stating that it enhanced their viewing.
- Viewers enjoy PPs, with the lack of disruption to the viewing experience being an important quality.

This viewer research also highlighted certain editorial implications for product placement:

- Relevant PP does not detract from or interrupt the viewing experience.
- PP must always fit the storyline – right time, place, product and programme.
- PP's are seen as 'natural additions' to programmes and make things seem 'more real'.
- The consistency of PP across episodes is important, frequent product changes (e.g., cereals) will be noticed, but outdoor advertising placements could be changed.
- Other research projects, particularly those by Nielsen and YouGov, have yielded similar findings.

Channel 4 commissioned Work Research to summarise the current knowledge on product placement. It identified five reasons why product placement works and how it differs from other advertising:

1   We have para-social relationships with characters on TV. In the same way, brands can inform opinions of people in reality, and they can shape our perceptions of people on TV. If we see characters using brands that do not fit, it feels weird. These para-social relationships can reinforce opinions of brands, or for new brands, can build brand associations.
2   What we know about one thing informs our view of another. So a known character using a brand will inform our knowledge of that brand, and this effect is increased when the association is repeated over time.
3   Product placement helps normalise brands. TV often reflects the real world, so seeing brands exist in a 'real-life' context helps them look like a normal part of life, particularly if we often and consistently see them in a programme.
4   Product placement provides an implicit route to learning. Non-verbal cues can be stronger in shaping opinion because, put simply, they are 'felt' rather than 'thought'. Once a brand has built up a set of associations, simply seeing the brand again can trigger and reinforce these associations.

5   Product placement does not prime consumers in the way that traditional ads do. By placing brands in a natural context, product placement equalises the consumer/ brand relationship.

Sky Media demonstrated this in its research (2014) into how product placement works. This study involved over 6,000 respondents and over 300 hours of programming across a variety of sectors.

The research revealed that product placement had a positive impact among viewers in general, but when non-viewers (those who have not watched the programme with the PP) were compared with viewers who recalled the PP, there were significant uplifts in metrics from spontaneous brand awareness to talkability and purchase intent. Sky found that product placement is an important additional brand touch point; from outdoor and social to retailer point of sale. To make it effective, authenticity is key. If the right sort of brand is used in the programme, then the product placement is acceptable to viewers. The placement needs to be natural and not contrived.

For example, Amazon struck a deal with Sky for its Kindle Fire to be used by the stars of Sky 1's *Got to Dance*. Sky's research showed viewers exposed were more aware of Kindle – 80% awareness versus 73% of non-viewers following the campaign – and brand consideration was markedly greater – 32% versus 22%. Other recent product placement deals between big brands and prime-time shows include Yeo Valley and Uncle Ben's in *Jamie's 15-Minute Meals* on Channel 4.

Case study: Nokia Lumia and Hollyoaks, 2014

Mobile phone handset manufacturer Nokia Lumia achieved success in prompted and unprompted awareness of its handsets as a result of product placement in Channel 4's soap *Hollyoaks*. Prior to broadcast, spontaneous mentions of models that characters would use for Nokia Lumia were at 5%, but rose to 12% after, with prompted mentions increasing from 18% to 31%. Product placement is also having a significant impact on Nokia's brand image. Since the Lumia handsets have featured in the show, there has been 25% uplift in the amount of viewers who said a Nokia phone would be their next choice and more than half said they would like to buy a Nokia Lumia.

With more brand owners seeking similar returns on investment, the product placement market in the UK could be on track to be worth up to £120m in the next 4 years.

Mobile and social networks in sponsorship

During London 2012, Olympic partner Coca-Cola employed mobile as a location-based marketing tool in all 100 nations where it ran campaigns in support of its sponsorship of the 'greatest show on earth'. 'It was the first time mobile was an integral part of an integrated sponsorship campaign and it far exceeded our expectations in that we were able to successfully show mobile could be part of the over-arching story,' explains Kim Siler, mobile brand strategist for Coca-Cola.

Optimising content for an increasingly complex digital ecosystem is a critical part of the creative process. Dual and triple screen viewing is now the norm and if content is not formatted to be viewed on mobile and tablet devices, then brand owners are wasting the opportunity to engage with desired customer segments. Simply producing a fantastic bit of engaging and optimised content is not the end game.

The impact of mobile and social networks is absolutely critical in making the exercise deliver a return on investment for the sponsor. Going viral may be the marketer's dream come true, but it does not happen every day of the week, so the chances of content reaching a substantial audience solely on the basis of its inherent quality and nothing else is close to impossible. Instead, the content needs to be created with a clear view of the audience the brand owner wants to engage with and who are likely to engage further with the message being delivered. 'A great way of achieving this is to collaborate with existing popular YouTube channels and talent to bring in an audience,' advises James Doncaster, search marketing and seeding manager at British digital agency Whitespace.

Regularly uploaded content can also boost audience numbers, much in the way that frequently adding new content to a website is looked on positively by Google. YouTube algorithmically promotes new content and partners who upload regularly, so a recurring schedule with at least one new video a week is important in order to not fall off the Google radar. The final step in ensuring your video content becomes a blockbuster rather than a box- office flop is to integrate it with the rest of the brand's marketing strategy.

Video should never be used as a stand-alone piece and should be fully integrated into the mix. This will take creative and editorial judgement in order to ensure that the content hangs together and that the time spent by the audience exposed to this content is a valuable experience for them.

There are some very simple rules that brand owners should follow when thinking creatively about content for mobile and social networks (see Table 5.3).

Without doubt, mobile is the biggest enabler of social media, as a person's handset is rarely ever a metre away. More than half of all activity on Facebook and Twitter now happens on a mobile device which was why Facebook made the purchase of Instagram a key strategic move. Despite the fact that it had just 13 employees and had never made a profit, it was bought for a cool £1bn.

From a sponsorship perspective, marketing within the developing world requires FMCG brand owners to ensure that mobile becomes the centre of their connected world and those of its consumers. For example, in a country such as India with a population of 1bn people and 900m handsets, the reach of mobile is vastly superior to that of TV and is the primary way consumers in those markets connect with the Internet. In addition, since many of these places are 'TV-dark', mobile is the primary way that major sponsors like Unilever engage with consumers, as mobile has usurped TV as the mass medium for reaching these audiences.

Table 5.3 Six simple rules for creating content for mobile and social networks

Rank	Rule	Description
#1	Optimise content for all possible platforms.	Video now accounts for around 50% of all mobile Web traffic according to ByteMobile, so it is critical content displays perfectly on smartphones and tablets.
#2	Add interactivity.	The technology exists to embed an entire e-commerce or lead generation system in a video. Do not miss the opportunity to capitalise on audience engagement.
#3	Make it for sharing.	Video content is some of the most shareable content. For example, 1,000 videos a minute are shared on YouTube Promote content to social media followers to amplify its reach.
#4	Do not treat video content as advertising.	Overtly commercial content is a big turn-off. The key is to understand what your desired audience segment is interested in and deliver what it wants.
#5	Keep it simple.	Avoid the temptation to overload video content with too many messages, as this will cause confusion and lack focus. Much better to have one message and deliver this in an engaging and entertaining way that encourages engagement.
#6	Think about context as well as content.	Context is often as important as content, so think about the context in which the video will be watched. Also consider what other channels are being used and how the video content supports these other content marketing activities.

Source: Kolah (2015)

Mobile is affecting the way consumers engage with the world and as a result it is only natural that it has changed the way brand owners engage with them. Creativity sits at the heart of this shift from 360-degree communication to a 365-days 'always-on' approach. 'We are already able to tell a consumer when he's walking in the park, as we know his location, whether it's a hot day, as we know what the weather is like there, and where the nearest place is to buy a Magnum ice-cream and send him a code for a discount. Just think of what we might be able to so in five years' time,' observes Keith Weed, Chief Marketing and Communications Officer at Unilever.

The company has one of the biggest stable of brands involved in sponsorship and has put mobile at the centre of its thinking in terms of activation. 'Consumers are always on the move. And as a result, companies like ours need speed and immediacy of data just to keep up with the consumer. People want information now, they want to interact now, they want to buy now, and they want all this on the go. The concept of immediacy has transformed mobile into a tool of action and transaction in a single swipe, click or tap. Our communication must take into account that whenever we reach a consumer, he or she will talk not with their feet, as we used to say, but with their fingers – and unless we are ready to capture that action, then we will be missing an opportunity,' adds Weed.

Despite the enormous resources that a global company like Unilever has at its disposal, it still has to seek out experts in the mobile field in order to expand its own understanding of the art of the possible and explore new ways of working, planning and engaging with consumers. For example, Unilever works closely with mobile and content providers, such as gaming companies, in order to unlock the magic of its brands by leveraging mobile and social together and also to explore innovative ways to co-create content and to achieve distribution at scale.

This type of approach has been adopted by other major brand owners, such as Anheuser-Busch in the USA.

Case study: Budweiser and NFL sponsorship, 2015

In order to engage with NFL fans who watch the sport on TV screens in bars and restaurants across the USA, Anheuser-Busch, owners of Budweiser (NFL sponsor) embarked on an interesting experiment in 2012 whereby normal beer tap handles in bars and restaurants were replaced by interactive ones that flashed and displayed messages to mark sports highlights.

The technology was developed as a result of collaboration between Anheuser-Busch, Sprint and Mesh Systems and the flashing tap handles have been used to celebrate touchdowns and home runs with the objective of integrating social media to deepen fan engagement via mobile phones.

Using Sprint's wireless machine-to-machine expertise and Mesh Systems' cloud-based Internet of Things/machine-to-machine platform, a test of the interactive application was first performed in 100 bars and taverns in Denver in the autumn of 2012 and at Bud Light Hotel in February 2013.

Connected World Magazine recognised the technology in June 2013, when it presented Anheuser-Busch, Sprint, Mesh Systems and Microsoft with a Gold Value Chain Award in the M2M and Connected Devices category for Consumer Packaged Goods. 'This type of integration shows Anheuser-Busch's focus on innovation and their understanding of the need to enhance the on-premises experience in a unique and relevant way. This also shows the future state of mobile marketing where there's a strong integration between digital and physical experience,' comments Tom Edwards, senior vice president at the Marketing Arm, a digital agency in Dallas, Texas.

The experiment was so successful that Budweiser is now rolling out the new tap handles across 8,000 bars and restaurants across the USA in 2015, where this is permissible under state law. The brand has not stopped there and has further developed the technology so that fans can be targeted with relevant sports team content depending on the location of the bar or restaurant as well as displaying specific promotional messages. The brand owner also intends to permit fans to be able to interact through mobile devices with these new beer tap handles in order to deepen the immersion experience between NFL football and other sports, such as basketball and motorsports, and their fans.

As one of the biggest sports sponsors in the US, Budweiser's mobile forays are a way for the brand to extend the reach of its sponsorships. In 2014 Budweiser leveraged a new Twitter voting mechanism as part of its 2014 FIFA World Cup Brazil promotion, enabling football fans to view side-by-side player photos before casting their vote for each game's top player.

It made sense for Budweiser to leverage Twitter to activate its sponsorship of the FIFA World Cup 2014, as fans and attendees of major live events increasingly look to the platform to engage in real time with related content. And with much of this activity happening from a mobile device, it is critical for brands such as Budweiser to ensure that such activations work seamlessly on mobile.

Mobile has always been an important element for sponsorship activation. Budweiser and Anheuser-Busch understand that the role of mobile has expanded and they are constantly looking for new and innovative ways to connect with consumers in a relevant and contextual way. 'The focus on integrating below-the-line on-premises activation and connecting that with above-the-line campaigns in a seamless way that provides local relevance is another example of how they're focused on innovation that ultimately drives the business,' observes Edwards.

Using public relations to create brand differentiation in sponsorship

Anywhere you may travel in the world where English is a second language or hardly spoken at all, there are two words that have become ubiquitous in just about any mother tongue – Manchester United!

From a public relations (PR) perspective, this is incredibly powerful for both the club – arguably the most famous football team in the world – and, of course, its sponsors.

Case study: Manchester United FC, 2015

One of the club's biggest challenges is turning its 659 million followers on social media into addressable individuals and joining the dots for sponsors so that they can connect with these customer segments in Asia, Europe and the Middle East more profitably. 'It's all about working with our partners to activate not just globally in terms of visibility but making it locally relevant to every market and all the fans we have around the world. Using online and mobile we can develop more intimate relationships, because with every interaction we build up knowledge about who that fan is and what type of content they like to consume,' explains Matt Scammell, associate global sponsorship sales director at Manchester United FC.

Public relations has always been incredibly important to the club, and it has used social media as one of the most effective channels for boosting engagement with fans globally, having generated more than half a billion interactions on Facebook alone since joining the platform in 2010 – one of the key ways it looks to build customer data. 'It's all very well having 60m fans on Facebook but we really need to know more about them so we can interact with them and share their contact details with our partners. That makes truly valuable followers and means we can have more successful digital campaigns,' adds Scammell.

The club is currently facing its first season without European football in more than two decades after a poor finish in the Premier League in 2013–14 but despite its lacklustre performance on the field, its performance off the field continues to go from strength to strength, having signed up an impressive 20 brand partnerships in the year to 30 June 2014.

Regional deals with brands include STC in Saudi Arabia and PepsiCo in parts of the Middle East and Asia as well as global deals with Nike, Aon and DHL, all of which helped push sponsorship income up 67% from £90.9m to £135.8m in 2014. This is also set to increase in subsequent years in the wake of a £50m a season shirt sponsorship deal with Chevrolet and from 2015, a record £75m a season kit deal with Adidas, which displaced its long-standing kit manufacturer Nike.

Sponsorship at the club is an important contributor to its bottom line, delivering £433.2m for the period, up from 21% a year earlier. When Sir Alex Ferguson retired in 2013, the club did not miss a golden PR opportunity to get fans to express how they felt about one of the most successful football managers in history and provide a fitting tribute to the great man. Fans were encouraged to write farewell messages and share their details before the PR team at the club selected the best comments for publication in a special commemorative book presented to Sir Alec Ferguson. 'That delivered over 100,000 responses from fans, so there was a really strong level of engagement. We captured the information of all those people and this helped turn them into addressable individuals,' adds Scammell.

The way in which information is acquired also dictates how the club chooses to communicate with fans in future, because it will target a 65-year-old season ticket holder based in Manchester differently from a 17-year-old fan in Asia who interacts with the club using Facebook on a mobile device. 'How we acquire an email address might dictate how we communicate with that individual. We can then see who communicates with what and what the conversion rate is, so we continually refine what we're doing. This applies not just to our communications at Manchester United but for our partners too. By building up more information on every one of those email recipients, we can understand what type of promotion is going to work best for each individual contact. The more we do it, the more information we pull together and the more successful we can be,' he says.

The club uses a range of platforms including Exact Target, Buddy Media and Radian 6 to achieve this view of its fans and customer segments. The different components in this communications strategy help it to enhance the way it communicates with its followers, and tapping in across multiple platforms makes it simple and practical for the club to deliver everything from one place and time zone in Manchester. 'We are able to target people in different languages and across different demographics . . . and we can communicate with them much more effectively as we treat them as addressable individuals, which means we are capable of providing better digital campaigns with our partners,' concludes Scammell.

Manchester United FC can claim to have a strong lens on fans and customers largely as a result of how it uses PR to create a deeper relationship with these segments. In the UK, the mobile phone company O2 can also claim to have achieved remarkable success in adopting a very similar and brave approach in the way it has differentiated its brand in a highly competitive and cluttered sector.

Case study: O2 and building the UK's most successful telecoms brand, 2015

It is strange to think that O2 started life as BT Cellnet, the mobile business of BT. As part of the British government's desire to deregulate the industry and make it more competitive, BT Cellnet was spun off as a separate legal entity in 2002 and rebranded as mmO2. The very name was designed to bring 'a breadth of fresh air' to the industry. However the *Financial Times* in London branded the company 'BT's unwanted orphan', saying the name was daft and the brand was practically worthless.

Six years later, Telefónica acquired it for £17.7bn and by 2008 O2 had overtaken its parent to become the biggest provider of telecom connections in the UK and fourth best-loved brand in the UK.

This 'rags-to-riches' story of an orphan brand did not happen by luck or chance but began with a classic approach to customer insight, having a clear point of differentiation in its market segment, aligning its values both with its customers and employees and then taking a bold approach in all of its communications.

A major turning point for O2 was its relationship with Apple and bringing the iPhone into the UK market. 'There was no economic advantage or financial incentive for Apple to choose O2 over any other teleco in the UK. What motivated them to partner with us was that O2 was the brand that had more of their type of customers in it and the brand that they felt was most aligned to their own experience. Apple is a very different company from us, but in their own way they approach their market in a very similar way to us. Everyone now is trying to find an iPhone "killer".' Apple did not try to build a Nokia killer or a BlackBerry killer; it just decided to define the space and then let everybody else compete with them. 'We've tried to do the same thing in our space, which is to say we'll try and set the rules by which we think the game should be played and then others can choose to compete as they wish. As a result we've been very attractive to partners who are attracted to brands that are both innovative and very experientially driven,' explains Tim Sefton, senior vice president for strategy and development at O2.

Sefton admits that O2's relationship with AEG and the Millennium Dome represented a bold move on its part to take a 'white elephant' and put its name above the door. 'But the key thing is we didn't just put our name above the door; we entered into a partnership with a company who have a reputation for being the leading live entertainment provider in the world. We now together have our name above the door of the world's most successful live entertainment venue by ticket sales and we have created a priority ticket category for our customers. If we'd just been sponsoring a building, then frankly we would never have done it – we would have exposed ourselves to potentially a huge reputational risk. But we partnered with an experience company who had a track record,' says Sefton.

On the face of it, O2 had no licence from the public to be regarded as an entertainment brand but through the O2 Arena it has become inseparable from the entertainment world and can claim to be in the experience business. 'If you define yourself as being in the mobile phone business, there's no logic to it. So the mindset which says we're in the business of creating experiences liberates us to do an awful lot of things, so it's a great opportunity for us to change the rules,' Sefton adds.

Ronan Dunne, CEO, O2 concludes: 'To build a trust relationship with customers you have to be really clear in your communication. You have to be bold to change the rules of the game. You have to take risks. And that means having the courage of your conviction. Most organisations talk about customer loyalty when what they really mean is customer retention, all too often achieved through erecting barriers to exit. True loyalty comes from the organisation being loyal to its customers by giving them value they can't get anywhere else and then making it easy for them to leave. And guess what? Just as in any affectionate relationship, they don't. Simplicity and fair deal are two O2 propositions that liberate the customer from the restrictive practices of the industry.'

By having a tight lens on its customers, O2 has demonstrated that it can leverage value from niche social networks such as those connected with its rewards programme 'Priority Moments'.

Niche networks tend to be about helping passionate people do what they care about and for a brand owner this is a means rather than an end. The sponsor can create content that is original and credible but that ultimately requires promotion in more established channels in order to achieve scale.

And, of course, large social platforms can work well for the niche networks themselves, as well as the brands that are active on them.

Sites such as Instagram and Pinterest have done this with huge success. Ensuring there is strong connectivity and ample opportunity for users to share content from their niche network onto a more recognisable one delivers exposure to a larger audience. And tapping into this via a solid engagement strategy will deliver an improvement in the performance of sponsorship.

Chapter 5 at a glance

1   Sponsorship is about intelligent activation and about how the budget is spent rather than the size of the activation budget. In this hyper-connected world, it is not enough for a sponsor brand to be seen or heard. It has to be experienced.

2   Social and mobile sit at the heart of effective sponsorship activation and increasingly sponsors and rights holders are looking for the 'digital dividend' as a return for their activation efforts. Brands must continually seek to connect creativity with technology.

3   Insight and analysis are one of the foundations of successful sponsorship activation. A major shift has occurred from searching for 'home truths'; a brand

owner must now put their brands into a relevant social context so that it creates value for the audience as well as those who have influence over them.

4   No campaign is complete without using YouTube, Facebook, Twitter and Instagram, where the need to engage and cross-communicate is essential. Global brand owners such as Coca-Cola and Unilever have rewired how they look to activate their sponsorship investments creatively in this way.

5   Blatant advertising and over-commercialisation have been replaced by the need to create compelling content that is both relevant and meaningful for the audience.

6   Brand owners need to take risks and think laterally when looking to engage with desired audience and customer segments. What Absolut Vodka and Lady Gaga have achieved is an interesting template for how to push the boundaries of creativity to new heights.

7   Brand owners should not feel constrained for fear of upsetting people or be timid in the support of causes that really matter, such as diversity, inclusivity and sustainability. But they need to mean it and not do this in order to curry favour with the public. Internally, they must practice what they preach.

8   The options for getting creative are only constrained by the imagination of those entrusted to deliver a cut-through campaign. Some of the best examples are a combination of bought, earned and owned media.

9   Content marketing activities, such as sponsorship of a White Paper, need to have high value for the audience that they are intended for and not be a vehicle for simply advertising a service or product or extolling its virtues. The focus should be on the customer, client, support segments and what is of relevance and meaning in their lives.

10 In the UK, brands are now much better equipped to undertake media sponsorship, such as advertiser-funded programming (AFP) and product placement, as these techniques are now sufficiently mature in order to help deliver against key brand communication, relationship and sales objectives.

11 Sponsorship activation using mobile and social networks and sending content on a real-time location basis will become much more commonplace from 2015 and beyond.

12 Public relations is now much less about gathering media coverage than actually engaging with the public in a personal way wherever the fans and consumers may live.

Questions for discussion

1   What is the starting point to consider for how to inject more creative thinking into the sponsorship activation process?

2   Why have mobile, social and digital become so important for rights holders and brand owners in the activation of sponsorship?

3   Think of a major sponsorship programme and look at how it uses mobile, social and digital in order to connect with its desired audiences and customer segments. Think of ways in which it could improve the performance of sponsorship by getting more creative.

4   Consider how you would create an advertiser-funded programme for a brand of your choice. What elements would you choose? Describe how you would go about the process. What would be the objectives of such a campaign and how would you measure its success? What are the legal issues that you would need to take into account and how would you navigate around these?

Further reading

Fisk, P (2011), *Creative Genius*, Capstone
Isaacson, W (2011), *Steve Jobs*, Simon & Schuster
Kolah, A (2014), *High Impact Marketing That Gets Results*, Kogan Page
Lovell, N (2014), *The Curve*, Penguin Books
Schmitt, B (1999), *Experiential Marketing*, Free Press
Smith, S and Milligan, A (2011), *Bold – How to be Brave in Business and Win*, Kogan Page

Websites

Brands and films [accessed 4 November 2014]: http://brandsandfilms.com
Campaign [accessed 30 October 2014]: http://www.campaignlive.co.uk
Forbes [accessed 30 October 2014]: http://www.forbes.com
IEG [accessed 30 October 2014]: http://www.sponsorship.com
Lady Gaga Twitter page [accessed 4 November 2014]: https://twitter.com/ladygaga
Liquid Thread [accessed 4 November 2014]: http://www.liquidthread.com
Marketing Magazine [accessed 1 November 2014]: http://www.marketingmagazine.co.uk
Mobile Marketer [accessed 30 October 2014]: http://www.mobilemarketer.com
Move to the Beat with Mark Ronson [accessed 4 November 2014]: http://youtu.be/_bgVbBvp4X8
PQ Media [accessed 5 November 2014]: http://www.pqmedia.com
PR Week [accessed 30 October 2014]: http://www.prweek.co.uk
Red Bull [accessed 4 November 2014]: http://www.redbull.com/cs/Satellite/en_INT/Video/Exclusive-What-Felix-Saw-Red-Bull-Stratos-Live-Jump-POV-021243270932859
Samsung 'Launching People' [accessed 4 November 2014]: http://www.samsung.com/uk/launchingpeople/
SportBusiness International [accessed 2 November 2014]: http://www.sportbusiness.com
Sports Insight [accessed 30 October 2014]: http://www.sports-insight.co.uk
WARC News [accessed 30 October 2014]: http://www.warc.com/News

Reports

Content – Business critical or the Emperor's New Clothes?, published by CorpComms (2014)
Football clubs and Chinese social media, published by Mail Man Group (2014)

Journals/magazines

The Marketer, published by the Chartered Institute of Marketing

6 Ethical issues in sponsorship

In this chapter

- Corporate and individual responsibility within sponsorship
- Ambush marketing and sponsorship
- Corporate hospitality and sponsorship
- Gambling and sponsorship
- Food-and-drink brands and sponsorship
- Brands in the classroom
- Alcohol and sponsorship
- Tobacco and sponsorship
- Codes of practice
- Codes as they relate to children and young people

Introduction

Global firms including Starbucks, Google, Microsoft, Amazon, BAT, Arcadia Group, Boots, Virgin, Vodafone and even Her Majesty's favourite grocery store, Fortnum and Mason in Mayfair, London, have all come under fire in recent years for avoiding paying taxes on their British sales. What these companies and others like them have done over the years is not illegal. Many such companies have complex tax structures and are headquartered outside the UK in order to avoid paying British company tax. But the tide of public opinion has turned and whereas a company's tax affairs would barely register any interest on the business pages, say, a decade ago, it is now a matter of national interest.

What this represents is a sea change in what consumers and the public alike deem important. And that is the ethical behaviour of these companies in being prepared to make money but also in paying their fair share on the gains generated in the UK. It is also one reason Google felt obliged to pay £20m in 'tax' voluntarily, because it was 'named and shamed' as a result of the invective it received from all sides of public opinion, including the 'establishment'. As the public has come to understand better what corporate tax avoidance is, there is a clear sense of outrage that is going well beyond a small group of protesters – it is something that the public feels is really not right with the current system.

Discussions of the ethics of tax avoidance are now everywhere and are likely to be a hot political issue in the run-up to the UK's general election in 2015. What all of this indicate is that companies – and sponsors of some of the biggest high-profile properties on the planet – need to be much more conscious of acting ethically.

Younger consumers have grown up in a world in which values count and will take to social media when they feel values and ethical standards expected of sponsors are being flouted. For any sponsor to ride roughshod over, or ignore the power of, public opinion is potentially very dangerous. For example, the amount of criticism that Coca-Cola, McDonald's and Dow Chemical attracted in their role as sponsors of the London 2012 Olympic Games and then the Sochi Winter Olympic Games 2014 bears this out. Attitudes towards these and other brand owners that seek some sort of 'halo effect' as sponsor of a major global event have changed partly because of the economic downturn over the past few years, when the global economy seemed more like a ride in a Disney theme park and consumers sought refuge in tried and trusted brands that had always been there in good times and bad. They did not take it lightly when this trust was shaken by the errant behaviour of greedy corporations that could be perceived as exploiting the situation. 'When many people hear the phrase corporate social responsibility, they think about charitable giving and community involvement and employee volunteering and so on. But people understand better now . . . that it's about responsibility for core business behaviours,' observes David Grayson, Professor of Corporate Responsibility at Cranfield School of Management in the UK.

Clearly directors of big organisations do not want to be in the spotlight for all the wrong reasons and boards are generally very sensitive about appearing to do the right thing.

'They're acutely aware – and there's big media pressure too – that if you do act unethically . . . that can have very serious implications,' adds Professor Grayson.

One of the biggest examples of corporate failure on a monumental scale is BP, which was rocked to its core over the Deepwater Horizon disaster in the USA in 2010 that killed 11 people, injured 17 others, tipped more than 200m gallons of crude oil into the Gulf of Mexico – the biggest oil spill in US history – and was fined USD 4.5bn for criminal failure, which claimed the scalp of its British CEO Tony Hayward.

Although ethics and values are openly discussed more than ever, it does not mean that there is always a consensus view on how these should shape corporate or individual behaviour. In 2013, Cranfield School of Management and the charity Business in the Community published new research that revealed that boards do not always have a collective mindset about ethics and there can often be conflicting opinions between directors. Anthony Hilton, city commentator for the *Evening Standard* explains: 'Many organisations are often too big and too complex to manage, often because reporting systems are clogged up with the routine and with process that what's important isn't easily visible or indeed not there at all.'

Board papers rarely give directors the information they need to be on top of what matters. This is doubly the case given that almost all reports are numbers-driven;

yet the real risk to companies these days is reputational and caused by aberrant human behaviour that no system devised by an accountant will ever pick up. 'So it's obvious that some jobs are now too big for one person, given the increased amount of scrutiny, the 24-hour rolling news schedule, the inflated expectations of the public and the increased intolerance not just of failure but of any human weakness – particularly these days when the running is made in social media and on Twitter, where there's a level of vitriol even newspapers find hard to emulate,' muses Hilton.

Professor Grayson agrees with this assessment, highlighting that the question of ethical standards goes right to the heart of the organisation and is not just left as a discussion topic for the board. 'It's a fine line between challenging constructively and pushing an issue you feel strongly about and not being perceived as just being awkward for the sake of it,' he says. In the case of BP, a former senior executive had misled the public and the Securities and Exchange Commission (SEC) in the USA by ignoring at least 11 pieces of evidence of internal data that showed the company had dramatically underestimated the true size of the oil spill, claiming it was between 5,000–6,000 barrels a day, when, in fact, the flow rate was at least 70,000 barrels a day. The SEC ruled that 'BP misled investors by misrepresenting and omitting material information known to BP regarding the rate at which oil was flowing into the Gulf and thus the resulting liability for the spill.' BP also tried to share the blame for the disaster with its partners, which included the owners of the rig, the manufacturer of the blowout preventer that failed to cap the well as well as the contractor that carried out the flawed cementing work on the drill.

But such a move had little impact on shifting the question mark that now hangs over the ethics of the company that oversaw such operations carried out in its name. Reparations have created a state-of-the-art oil slick control system and provided compensation for the Louisiana communities that bore the brunt of the disaster. But such measures will not necessarily reverse the damage that has been done to BP's reputation, which could take at least a decade to rebuild. Research carried out in the same year by global law firm Freshfields Bruckhaus Deringer analysed 78 crises with reputational implications for companies caught in the middle of the storm.

The study found that behavioural crises prompted by reports of questionable conduct by either the company or an employee led to the greatest one-day falls in share price compared with other disasters, such as operational or liquidity issues. But it is not all doom and gloom. In the context of ethics, sponsorship can be seen a massive trust builder with internal audiences. According to the University of Western Sydney, sponsorship can help shape employees' citizenship and engagement behaviour.

The researchers of the 2013 study published in the *International Journal of Sports Marketing & Sponsorship* concluded that their findings highlighted the need for business 'to consider strategies that involve their employees in sponsorship choices and to internally market their sponsorship activities. Businesses may, therefore, wish to consider sponsorship of an activity that their employees consider important.' The research tended to demonstrate that companies engaged in sports sponsorship of an event, team or sportsperson portrays an image as a socially responsible entity as opposed to just a profit-making organisation. 'However, the culture and environment of a socially responsible organisation can also shape attitudes of employees and transform their personal position to match with overall organisational values,' concluded the report's authors, with an important caveat that employees needed to be familiar with the nature of the sponsorship in the first place.

Reputation management is important with both external and internal audiences and, of course, the ethics of an organisation have a lot to do with how successful it can be in that regard. However successful a sponsorship programme may be, building a good reputation does not ensure that a brand owner is safe forever, as examples in this book demonstrate. As no company or organisation is immune to a crisis, the issue is not about whether a crisis will happen but how it is dealt with, how quickly the management team can get to the heart of the problem and then how quickly it can rebuild the trust it may have lost along the way.

Corporate and individual responsibility within sponsorship

Brands are sensitive to public opinion and arguably need to act in an ethical way that is expected by their customers, their own employees and, of course, the fans and supporters of the rights holder.

Case study: Wonga and Newcastle United FC, 2014

When pay-day lender Wonga decided to become the team sponsor of Premier League club Newcastle United FC in 2012, the blogosphere went into overdrive with questions about how a pay-day loan company with questionable ethics could be allowed to advertise its brand on the shirt of a football club where many supporters had financial or debt problems. And also what message did that send to children about such companies, particularly as Wonga uses childlike puppets in its high-profile TV advertising, much to the consternation of MPs of the Business Select Committee, who failed to get Wonga's advertising banned on children's TV. Since the start of 2014, Wonga has been looking to repair its tarnished reputation in the wake of the departure of its chairman and CEO, which left the company in the hands of a new management team.

The sponsorship deal has been severely condemned by Nick Forbes, leader of Newcastle City Council, who has accused Newcastle United FC of acting in the pursuit of profit 'at any price' and said he was sickened and appalled that the club had decided to do a deal with a 'legal loan shark'. Incoming Wonga group chief executive Andy Haste admitted the company had made 'serious mistakes' in the past and said the business needed to undergo 'significant change', even though this would hit profits in the short term. Haste said he was 'very aware' of criticism of its current advertising and marketing campaign, and said he would 'be reviewing all of our advertising and marketing to make sure that we don't leave any impression that we are trying to influence or target the very young or the vulnerable'.

His appointment came in the wake of Wonga paying £2.6m in compensation after chasing struggling customers with fake legal letters. Haste said the company, which has been strongly criticised by MPs over excessive interest rates, must review rates, fees and charges, and no longer be seen as targeting the young and the vulnerable. 'This is a sector and Wonga is a company that needs to go through significant change if it's to have a sustainable future. Some serious mistakes have been made. The company admitted those mistakes and it has apologised for those mistakes. Wonga has understandably faced a lot of criticism and I know that we need to repair our reputation and regain our right to be an accepted part of the financial services sector.'

The new chairman pointed to the rapid growth of the company, which has more than a million customers, after being founded 7 years ago and admitted 'some of our systems, our processes, our controls, haven't kept pace' and he promised the company would review all of its products and ensure it lent money only to those who could reasonably afford to repay its loans. He also promised that Wonga would become 'a more customer-focused, and inevitably in the near term, a smaller and less profitable business. We are determined to make the necessary changes and serve our customers in the right way, to repair our reputation and become a business with a long-term future and an accepted place in the financial services industry.'

Academic research into the team-sponsor relationship published in the USA in 2010 indicates that a sponsor enjoys a degree of reputation protection when it is accepted by fans, even when there are negative media headlines circling around its head. However, the caveat to this was how the team reacted to the sponsor's negative media coverage and whether it wished to continue with the sponsorship relationship or terminate it.

Some sponsors fall far below the ethical standards expected of them and in one spectacular example the company's global CEO turned whistle-blower after being sacked from the company, which then precipitated an investigation by the Serious Fraud Office and the FBI in one of the biggest meltdowns in corporate history.

Case study: Olympus, 2008–12

Today, Japanese optical precision instruments manufacturer Olympus is a powerful company, employing 40,000 globally, and has around 70% market share of gastrointestinal endoscopes, and annual sales of around USD 4bn. Back in January 2008, Olympus signed a six-year title sponsorship deal for tennis for the US Open and US Open Series. The sponsorship was meant to be the key sales and marketing platform for the brand in the USA and was meant to cement a relationship with the powerful US Tennis Association (USTA) and the US Open. But that same year, the company started to run into financial difficulties and total operating income slumped from USD 1bn to only USD 400m.

In April 2011 the company made global headlines when it dismissed its newly appointed British-born global CEO Michael Woodford, a 30-year Olympus veteran after just two weeks in the job. Woodford had sought to probe into financial irregularities and unexplained payments of hundreds of millions of dollars and in particular the USD 2.2bn deal in 2008 to acquire British medical equipment maker Gyrus Group. Thomson Reuters reported that USD 687m was paid to a middleman as a success fee – a sum equal to 31% of the purchase price, which ranks as the highest ever M&A fee ever recorded.

More revelations included sums paid out relating to the acquisition of a technology company ITX. Woodford was quick to raise these allegations with the president of the board as well as fresh revelations in the Japanese financial magazine *Facta*, which reported Olympus acquiring three other Japanese companies outside of its core business that had been written down USD 721m less than their acquisition value just 12 months previously. Following his dismissal, Woodford flew back to the UK and his wife drove him to meet the Serious Fraud Office in order to alert the authorities to the fraud he had uncovered and in doing so, he also feared for the safety of himself and his family and even sought police protection.

In November 2011 Olympus admitted that it had deliberately covered up losses since the 1990s and that the company's accounting practices were 'not appropriate'. It had been forced to come clean on one of the biggest and longest-running loss-hiding arrangements in Japanese corporate history, reported the *Wall Street Journal*. The company laid the blame for the inappropriate accounting practices on its ex-president, auditor and executive vice president, who then faced criminal charges and subsequent prison sentences.

In 2012 the company published a special edition CSR Report: *Rebuilding Trust: The First 100 Days*. The message from Hiroyuki Sasa, president and representative director, Olympus Corporation to all its customers and employees was very clear:

> At Olympus Corporation, we sincerely regret that past financial accounting misconduct has caused our customers and society enormous difficulties and undermined stakeholder confidence. With this in mind, and in keeping with our company's 'Social IN' philosophy, the new management team hereby declares our commitment as follows:
>
> 'To regain stakeholder trust and to enhance corporate value, Olympus' management is committed to complying with all laws and regulations and respecting social norms at all times.
>
> 'In the effort to achieve sustainable growth, the management team reaffirms the importance of laws, regulations and social norms and will work to foster a corporate culture where each employee, as a member of the Olympus Group, will consider what is right and act in accordance with our company's guiding principles.
>
> 'We will thoroughly investigate any violations to this commitment, past or present, taking corrective actions and implementing preventive measures as necessary. By transforming our organisation, we aim to create new value for society, to improve communication with all stakeholders and to increase transparency of our decision making. We reaffirm our basic mission of creating value for society through innovative technology, quality products and

unparalleled service, and we pledge that all employees of the Olympus Group will make a concerted effort to help people worldwide lead healthier and more fulfilling lives.'

Other sponsors are often under intense pressure to make a public statement about an issue that can affect the very activity that they have paid substantial amounts of money to sponsor.

Case study: Sochi Winter Olympic Games, 2014

Coca-Cola is one of the oldest Olympic sponsors and possibly one of the most admired brands in the world. But that was not enough to protect it from brand vandalism at Sochi 2014 Olympic Games, where it was embroiled in the controversy over the treatment of the lesbian, gay, bisexual and transgender (LGBT) community. Russian President Vladimir Putin signed the so-called 'anti-gay propaganda' law in June 2013 that banned the promotion of 'non-traditional relationships' to minors.

In response to the law and ahead of the Winter Games 2014, a gay rights organisation, All Out, organised an online petition to put pressure on Olympic sponsors, especially Coca-Cola, asking the company to 'speak out against the Russian anti-gay propaganda law and call for its repeal before the Olympics, donate funds to Russian human rights defenders, and ask the Olympic Committee to change the rules, so future Olympics can only happen in countries that fully respect equality'. More than 25,000 people signed the petition but Coke refused to be drawn on its purported tacit support for what most fair-minded people believed was a discriminatory law in a country in which the Olympic ideals of fairness and respect for the individual appeared to be being publicly flouted. Instead, Coke issued a statement about its participation in Sochi: 'We have long been a strong supporter of the LGBT community and have advocated for inclusion and diversity through both our policies and practice. We do not condone human rights abuses, intolerance, or discrimination of any kind anywhere in the world. As a sponsor since 1928, we believe the Olympic Games are a force for good that unite people through a common interest in sports, and we have seen first-hand the positive impact and long-lasting legacy they leave on every community that has been a host.'

Russia's treatment of gay people sparked off other reactions from LGBT activists and a call for a global boycott of the 2014 Sochi Winter Olympics, and an open letter to all sponsors signed by an alliance of anti-discriminatory LGBT charities as well as Amnesty International and Human Rights Watch was issued on 31 January 2014.

In its joint communiqué to every sponsor of the Sochi Winter Olympic Games 2014, the letter stated:

> We know it must surely concern you, as it deeply concerns all of us, that since being selected as the host country for the Winter Olympics, the Russian government has intensified its assault on the human rights of its lesbian, gay,

bisexual and transgender (LGBT) citizens and the IOC has stood by without strongly condemning these acts.

Russian citizens and foreigners are banned by law from publicly support-ing equality for LGBT people. Activists and journalists who have sought to investigate and denounce such human rights abuses have been secretly recorded, harassed and deported from Russia.

LGBT Russians have effectively been pushed to the margins of society and are now forced to live with daily threats to their safety in a country that is promoting state-sanctioned homophobia and transphobia. These threats come in the form of kidnappings, torture, random acts of violence, and bomb threats.

Despite these facts, Russian President Vladimir Putin and the IOC have denied that Russia's anti-gay law is discriminatory. This is simply untrue — and the law continues to have devastating effects on LGBT Russians, their families and their supporters.

As you know, a country that hosts the Olympics has an obligation to uphold the values contained in the Olympic Charter and its principle of non-discrimination, Principle 6. The Russian government has failed to do this, and the IOC has remained silent.

You are sponsors of the Sochi Games. You have invested millions in this sponsorship. Many of you are committed supporters of equality, extending protections and benefits to your LGBT employees.

This is not only good for business but it is also the right thing to do. You also understand that discrimination has an economic cost that harms busi-nesses and economies wherever it is found.

Silence in the face of discrimination also carries reputational risks. We come to you with one simple request: to use your voice to insist on changes that will make a difference in the future

- Individually or collectively, condemn Russia's anti-LGBT law;
- Use your Olympics-related marketing and advertising — both domestic-ally and internationally — to promote equality during the weeks leading up to and during the Games themselves;
- Ask the IOC to create a body to monitor serious Olympics-related human rights abuses in host countries as they occur; and
- Task the IOC with ensuring future Olympic host countries honour their commitments to upholding the Olympic Charter, including Principle 6, which forbids discrimination of any kind.

Like you, we want the Olympic Games to be a moment where the world can come together to celebrate the richness and diversity of people across the globe. Discrimination has no place in the Olympics, and LGBT people must not be targeted with violence or deprived of their ability to advocate for their own equality. We cannot be silent on how Russia's anti-LGBT law violates this very standard to which we aspire.

As all eyes turn toward Sochi, we ask you to stand with us.

US President Barak Obama, British PM David Cameron and German Chancellor Angela Merkel all decided to stay at home rather than attend the Winter Olympic Games, a move that was widely interpreted as a snub to Putin for introducing such discriminatory and draconian laws ahead of the Olympic Games.

But it was AT&T that took the first stance as an Olympic team sponsor in the face of such discriminatory behaviour against the LGBT community by issuing the following public statement on 4 February 2014:

> On Friday night, many of us will be tuned in to the 2014 Olympic Winter Games opening ceremony. It's an event that symbolizes peace and unity amongst nations. It's also a moment for us to express our pride in America and everything for which it stands.
>
> AT&T has stood proudly with Team USA at every Olympic opening ceremony since 1984 in Los Angeles. As a Proud Partner of the US Olympic and Paralympic Team for the past 30 years, we've showcased American athletes and celebrated their diversity all around the world. For these games, we're shining a light on some of the hard work and dedication that goes into training for the Olympics, and asking fans to showcase their American pride by uploading U-S-A chants through our free #ItsOurTime app.
>
> The Olympic Games in Sochi also allow us to shine a light on a subject that's important to all Americans: equality. As you may know, the lesbian, gay, bisexual and transgender (LGBT) community around the world is protesting a Russian anti-LGBT law that bans 'propaganda of non-traditional sexual relations'.
>
> To raise awareness of the issue, the Human Rights Campaign (HRC) has called on International Olympic Committee (IOC) sponsors to take action and stand up for LGBT equality.
>
> AT&T is not an IOC sponsor, so we did not receive the HRC request. However, we are a long-standing sponsor of the United States Olympic Committee (USOC), we support HRC's principles and we stand against Russia's anti-LGBT law. AT&T has a long and proud history of support for the LGBT community in the United States and everywhere around the world where we do business. We support LGBT equality globally and we condemn violence, discrimination and harassment targeted against LGBT individuals everywhere. Russia's law is harmful to LGBT individuals and families, and it's harmful to a diverse society.
>
> We celebrate the diversity of all Olympic athletes, their fans, Russian residents and all people the world over – including and, especially, our employees and their loved ones.
>
> As the games begin, we're here to support and inspire American athletes who've worked hard and sacrificed much to achieve their dreams.
>
> We also want to be on record with our support for the LGBT community, and we hope that others involved with the Olympic Games will do the same.

Very often sponsors find themselves in the eye of a media storm that is not of their own making but stems from the indiscretions of those they spend millions on sponsoring.

Case study: Tiger Woods, 2009

Golfer Tiger Woods was deemed to be the perfect role model for children around the world with his clean-cut guy image until in 2009 he admitted to having indulged in group sex and infidelity. He was forced to confirm his extramarital affairs and offer a public apology for the hurt he had caused wife Elin Nordegren and his children. Woods was to take an 'indefinite break' from the world of golf in order to fix his personal relationships with his wife, family and friends, who all felt they had been let down. Although Nike stood by their man, Gillette announced it would be 'limiting his role' in marketing to 'support his desire for privacy'.

In a statement, the sponsor said: 'In the midst of a difficult and unfortunate situation, we respect the action Tiger is taking to restore the trust of his family, friends and fans. We fully support him stepping back from his professional career and taking the time he needs to do what matters most. We wish him and his family the best.'

Arguably the biggest scandal to have affected a single sport in the past 100 years is that of cyclist Lance Armstrong's drug-taking and doping deception that led to his seven Tour de France titles being stripped from him and sponsors pursuing him for the return of multimillion-dollar sponsorship fees.

Case study: Lance Armstrong, 2012

In 2013 one of the biggest stories in sponsorship was the interview of Lance Armstrong with chat-show diva Oprah Winfrey where he confessed to have cheated his way to the pinnacle of cycling and becoming one of the most famous people on the planet, amassing a personal fortune in excess of USD 200m. Armstrong, who cheated his way to seven Tour de France victories between 1999 and 2005, claimed in his TV confession that doping was 'part of the process required to win the Tour'.

He was subsequently stripped of all his titles and had to agree out-of-court settlements with sponsors and David Walsh, the investigative journalist on the *Sunday Times* newspaper that had pursued the story for over a decade and was finally vindicated despite having lost a multimillion dollar libel trial along the way.

The achievements of USPS/Discovery Channel pro cycling team, of which Armstrong was part, were, according to the United States Anti-Doping Agency (Usada) accomplished through the most sophisticated, professional and successful doping programme that the sport had ever seen.

Armstrong was 'engaged in serial cheating' and his career on the team was fuelled from start to finish by doping. More than a dozen former teammates, friends and former team employees confirmed a fraudulent course of conduct, orchestrated by Armstrong and his bullying tactics. But he had not acted alone and had enlisted a small army of enablers, including doping doctors, drug smugglers and others within and outside the sport and his team. It was deception on a scale so big that in any other circumstances Armstrong could have been prosecuted for being the gang leader of an organised crime syndicate.

Armstrong had ultimate control over not only his own personal drug use but over the doping culture of the whole team. Those around him were entrusted with these dark secrets and became expert at predicting when Usada testers would turn up and seemed to have inside information in order to stay always one step ahead so as to remain undetected in this fraud.

With or without performance enhancers, the repair of his badly damaged personal brand is one feat that is beyond even the mercurial powers of Armstrong.

There were too many lies, too much deceit, too many lives ruined, too great an amount of damage to a revered sport and too many missed opportunities to come clean offered by the Usada, the *Sunday Times*, Nike and even his own charitable foundation, Livestrong. By wrapping up his cycling triumphs into his own inspiring fight against cancer – the ultimate impetus for his charity Livestrong – Armstrong committed the ultimate brand sin. He broke the trust of those who needed to trust him the most. He created his own myth in his best-selling autobiography, *It's not about the Bike*, published in 2001, and the deception was complete. He felt he had fooled the world.

Despite standing by Armstrong during the months when mounting speculation about his drug taking started to resurface with greater ferocity and in the immediate aftermath of the Usada 1,000-page dossier based on sworn testimony from 11 of Armstrong's former teammates, Nike decided to drop Armstrong when it was obvious 'due to the seemingly insurmountable evidence' that he took performance-enhancing drugs.

If a Nike athlete commits a misdemeanour, such as an extramartial affair, and owns up to it – as Tiger Woods did – then the worst that can happen is that the athlete is temporarily removed from Nike's advertising until the dark clouds disperse. But it seems that Armstrong's actions plumbed even lower depths after the world's largest sports manufacturer had digested the full impact of Usada's damning report. The Oregon-based company said that Armstrong had 'misled Nike for more than a decade' and it was cancelling his multimillion dollar contract 'with great sadness'. It added: 'Nike does not condone the use of illegal performance-enhancing drugs in any manner.'

This move was soon followed by Oakley, Trek and Anheuser-Busch, which also all ripped up their sponsorship and endorsement contracts with Armstrong.

US brand consultant Scott Davis observes: 'Bottom line, the emotional connection with a personal brand is so much deeper and so much stronger than that of any product or service, because it connects on a human level. Those who've built renowned personal brands are put on pedestals and admired not just for their remarkable characteristics and the values they represent, but for their consistency in staying true to them. Armstrong destroyed the very values that defined him.'

Overall, the issue of corruption in sport is of paramount importance to sponsors and marketers. 'Once the public has a widespread perception that an event is corrupt, they'll abandon it as quickly as they do last year's fashions. And if the public has begun to abandon a sport, the sponsors will be quick to follow,' concludes British investigative sports journalist Declan Hill.

Ambush marketing and sponsorship

One of the most controversial ethical issues in sponsorship is ambush marketing and in the UK this became a hot topic of discussion within the industry ahead of the London 2012 Olympic Games.

With hosting and infrastructure costs topping £10bn from the public purse, it is reasonable that the business community would want to share in some reflective benefit of the London 2012 Olympic Games being staged in the capital, particularly in the wake of a weakened domestic economy and the opportunities for benefiting from the 'bounce factor'.

That said, the International Olympic Committee (IOC) jealously protects its revenue stream from its TOP and national sponsors, some of which pay upwards of £40m for the privilege.

Of particular concern for the IOC and its partners is the threat of ambush marketing by those brand owners which have not bought a ticket but want a free ride on the back of the excitement and interest generated by the event. The IOC is so sensitive to sponsorship rights being infringed in this way that it insists that special laws are passed in the host country to protect its intellectual property (IP) rights.

As I shall discuss in more detail in Chapter 9, this is not as simple to police as it may appear, and there may be a case to be answered that the IOC may have swung too far in introducing draconian measures that effectively snuff out any legitimate opportunity for ordinary businesses to join in the fun and where the risk of actually damaging the commercial interests of IOC partners is more theoretical than real.

Corporate hospitality and sponsorship

Another area that is attracting a lot of interest as the UK economy bounces back into shape is the use of corporate hospitality as a way of entertaining customers, clients, prospects and employees. While I was working on a piece of research for a leading hospitality provider, it struck me that a small percentage of sponsors feared the risk of being in breach of the UK Bribery Act 2010 and this had created an ethical dilemma as to whether or not to entertain existing or prospective customers and clients.

As a result, there appeared to be a decrease in interest in using corporate hospitality as part of the sponsorship mix by as much as 30%. One reason that this decline can be attributed to was that many customers, clients and prospects now had internal rules that prevented them from accepting this form of entertainment, as they did not want to run the risk of feeling compromised in some way.

Less formal hospitality at a lower level did not appear to have the same ethical challenges and there appeared to be a higher degree of acceptance for this form of entertainment among invitees. More detailed discussion on the issues surrounding offering and accepting corporate hospitality is covered in Chapter 7.

Gambling and sponsorship

The relationship between sport and gambling is one that has a long and at times difficult history. Brand owners within the UK gambling industry include Bwin, 888.com and PaddyPower.

As can be seen from Table 6.1, gambling companies are significant investors as sponsors of sports teams and events in Europe. The financial support the industry offers sport through sponsorship activities has increased in recent times, with the growth of sponsorship by online gambling businesses being particularly notable. However, the promotion of gambling services through sponsorship is governed by a variety of quite different legal and regulatory regimes within Europe, and is seen by some as raising particular ethical and policy considerations.

Across the European Union, member states (and on occasion sports bodies) regulate the provision and promotion of gambling services, including over the Internet. The legality of some of the restrictions is not always clear. This uncertainty can have an adverse impact on the sponsorship market in Europe. The European Sponsorship Association (ESA) believes that it is a matter of judgement for sports rights holders and sports governing bodies as to whether they consider entering into a sponsorship arrangement with a gambling brand owner and that they should be free to make that decision.

However, not everyone within the sponsorship industry feels the same and many pressure groups are concerned that gambling and payday loan companies are getting messages across to those who are young and/or vulnerable and indirectly exploiting these audiences with exposure to messages that will encourage gambling and applying for high APR loans as being everyday activities.

ESA agrees and in its position statement on gambling sponsorship it states:

> Gambling sponsorship must not encourage problem gambling or harm or exploit children or other vulnerable persons. ESA believes that successful and responsible sponsorships will be those which target suitable events or properties with an audience appropriate to the sponsor's brand and where activation is clearly directed at an adult audience cognisant with both the risks and rewards of gambling.

ESA advises that there should be no display gambling-related branding on children's replica kits, that there should be adequate provision of details of help and support available to those who may have concerns about their gambling habit or that of their family and that sponsors obtain the appropriate accreditation from organisations such as Gamcare.

Food and drink brands and sponsorship

The average American consumes 22 teaspoons of sugar a day and 8.5g of salt, far more than the recommended amount. About 36% of adults and 17% of children are obese and 26m Americans have diabetes. In the UK, the incidence of

Table 6.1 Gambling brands and sponsorship

Gambling brand	Sponsorship category	Property
PokerStars	Broadcast	PokerStars Sunday Million
	Sport	Aston Martin racing
	Sport	Goodwood Festival of Speed
	Broadcast	World Series of Poker Champions
Full Tilt	Entertainment	Sundance Film Festival Premiere Film and Music Lounge
	Entertainment	House of Hype hospitality (MTV film awards)
	Sport	Winky Wright vs. Jermain Taylor boxing fight
	Entertainment	Stuff Magazine Kentucky Derby Party and Poker Tournament
	Broadcast (AFP)	Learn from the Pros on Fox Sport Network
888.com	Broadcast	ITV1 and 2 comedy package broadcast sponsor (Monkey Trousers, Shane, Frank Skinner Show, Baddiel and Skinner Unplanned and Mike Bassett – England manager)
	Sport	FC Sevilla
	Sport	British Superbikes
	Broadcast	WRC Rally Championships ITV1
	Sport	Middlesbrough FC
	Sport	888.com World Snooker Championship
	Sport	FIM Czech Republic Speedway Grand Prix
	Sport	Premier League Darts, including World Dart Champion
Sportingbet	Sport	Grand Prix Americas
	Sport	American Le Mans Series
	Sport	National Lacrosse League
	Sport	CART Champ Car World Series
	Sport	Euroleague basketball
	Broadcast	Official online gaming sponsor at six boxing events televised by HBO Latino
	Entertainment	Radio music awards
Bwin	Sport	FC Barcelona
	Sport	AC Milan
	Sport	SV Werder Bremen
	Sport	Portugal's first and second soccer leagues
	Entertainment	Red Bull air race
	Sport	FEI world equestrian games
	Sport	Kitesurf Pro
	Sport	Spanish, German, Portuguese and Valencia MotoGPs
	Sport	World Touring Car Championship
	Sport	IIHF World Ice Hockey Championships
	Broadcast	Bundesliga TV rights
	Sport	Real Madrid
	Sport	Bayern Munich
32Red	Sport	Aston Villa FC
Mansion	Sport	Tottenham Hotspur FC
PaddyPower	Sport	Manchester City FC
	Sport	Swansea City FC

childhood obesity is the highest in Europe and only slightly behind that of the USA – 26% of adults and 16% of children are obese. It therefore comes as no surprise that one of the biggest ethical debates in sponsorship today concerns the large number of food and drink brands that sponsor major sports events, such as Coca-Cola's partnership with the Olympic Games and McDonald's substantial investment in the FIFA World Cup.

Will Coca-Cola and McDonald's be forced from the sponsors' podium within the next decade as a legacy of poor diet threatens to send an entire generation to an early to grave? And will these sponsors go the same way as tobacco companies, which were banned from sponsorship in 2005?

Doctors, health groups and parents have started to lobby for restrictions on the way such brands are allowed to promote their products in such high-profile ways to children before it is too late. In his book *Fat Chance*, the American paediatric endocrinologist Professor Robert Lustig argues that sugar, not fat, is one of the main causes of childhood obesity. He argues that sugar is as addictive as nicotine, because it switches on the same hormonal pathways that 'reward' behaviour. Low blood sugar affects mood, concentration and the ability to inhibit impulse. Eating or drinking something sugary reverses the effect, but if the pattern is repeated for long enough it results in insulin resistance type 2 diabetes, heart disease and obesity. Professor Lustig believes it is not possible for most people to quit through willpower, because that has been eroded by the cycle of craving.

Part of the problem of childhood obesity is with parents who feed their children processed foods with a high sugar content or products with a large amount of trans fats: a cheap industrial substance that prolongs the shelf life of products such as cereal, doughnuts, processed meat, ready meals and crisps and gives them more bulk or texture.

Even low-fat products can contain high levels of sugar and refined carbohydrates, including hydrogenated fats. Some low-calorie drinks also contain high-fructose corn syrup which has been linked to diabetes, insulin resistance and obesity, because people drink so much of this stuff and because fructose is converted into fat in the body very easily.

Case study: Coca-Cola, 2013

In 2013 Coca-Cola decided that its future lay in not ignoring a ticking health timebomb that could detonate and make a massive hole in its gigantic profits and £45bn brand anytime soon and started to include health warnings within its own iconic TV advertising. 'All calories count. No matter where they come from. Including Coca-Cola. If you eat and drink more than you burn off, you'll gain weight. Obesity concerns us all,' gushed the voice over. And so starts its damage limitation exercise.

For its part, McDonald's has put calorie counts on all its menus and even given away bags of fruit with its Happy Meals to its customers in the wake of its repositioning as the 'people's restaurant' during the London 2012 Olympic Games.

Case study: McDonald's and London 2012 Olympic Games

The company was already über-sensitive to the charge that it was part of the problem of creating a nation of obese children rather than being associated with messages about fitness and health conferred on it by its global sponsorship of the 'greatest show on earth'. London 2012 gave it the opportunity to bury this perception of its brand and replace it with the image of being the people's restaurant during the Games. 'The event was definitely a good fit for us,' explains Alistair Macrow, vice president marketing and food UK at McDonald's.

This strategy was backed by a campaign that celebrated the Olympic volunteers and supporters. During London 2012, customers celebrating the Games were encouraged to upload their own videos and photographs onto McDonald's Facebook page. The best content was incorporated into TV advertising during the closing ceremony along with outdoor advertising. 'I think people will want to remember what they were doing during the Games and we created a campaign around these people,' explains Macrow.

But his enthusiasm for the brand is not shared by all of his potential customer segments. For example, the Children's Food Campaign published the report *Obesity Games*, which criticised the IOC's decision to allow fast-food and soft-drinks companies as sponsors. The report's authors noted that while 'junk food' sponsors contribute only around 2% of the Olympic income, 'sponsors like McDonald's are given an unrivalled platform to promote their unhealthy brands and products'.

During that time, IOC president Jacques Rogge admitted that Olympic chiefs had questioned the fast-food giant's ongoing sponsorship of the Games and MediaCom's brand reputation tracker monitoring Twitter sentiment towards the 25 official sponsors of the London 2012 Games registered McDonald's as lagging at the bottom.

McDonald's frequently claims it provides high-quality food to a very high standard and safety and delivers this in a really good customer-service-centric environment. 'That's what makes us a perfect partner,' defends Macrow.

It is not clear whether London 2012 helped to transform the fast-food giant into the wholesome food restaurant it sees itself when it looks in the mirror. Perceptions are sometimes impossible to shift and this has plagued McDonald's more than many other brand owners in its market segment.

In 2001 Eric Schlosser criticised McDonald's in his book *Fast Food Nation* for using its political influence to increase its profits at the expense of people's health and the conditions of its workers. In 2004 filmmaker Morgan Spurlock delivered another blow to the brand with his acclaimed film *Super Size Me*, which highlighted the stark effect that he says a regular diet of McDonald's had on his physical and psychological well-being. As obesity statistics have risen, McDonald's has come to symbolise the national health crises. But the company is fighting back against the perception of perpetuating poor diet and lifestyle choices for its customers by providing a wider choice of healthier foods including wraps, deli sandwiches and porridge. It also has a 'healthy' carbonated drink called Fruitizz, which, it claims, counts as one of the five fruit and vegetables that a person should consume as part of a balanced diet.

Other brand owners have also responded to the threat to public health by reducing salt content, as PepsiCo has done with its popular Frito-Lays snack food because of increased risks of cardiovascular disease as a result of higher salt intake. The brand owner has a significant sports sponsorship portfolio that includes the NFL, MLB, the International Cricket Council as well as a host of individual athletes and stars, including football and fashion icon David Beckham.

Sales of carbonated drinks are on the decline but the lawyers who took on and beat the big tobacco companies have now set their sights on food and drink brands. Don Barrett, whose fight against cigarette manufacturers was portrayed in the film *The Insider*, starring Russell Crowe, has filed class action lawsuits against some of the biggest food firms involved in sponsorship. Barrett claims these companies deliberately misled the public by mislabelling food as 'natural' or 'healthy'. Big food, he says, will suffer the same fate as big tobacco and will have to pay billions in compensation not just in the USA but around the world. 'People assume food producers are telling the truth about their products, just as in the past they thought tobacco companies were telling the truth. When it comes to food, the false labels are the only proof we need.'

Predictably, all the big food and drink brands strenuously deny any suggestion that they misled consumers but such arguments are starting to wear thin.

Case study: PepsiCo, 2013

In 2013 PepsiCo agreed to settle out of court for USD 9m over a class action lawsuit that alleged 'natural' and 'non-GMO' claims on its Naked smoothies range were misleading, since they were made with GMO ingredients as well as synthetic and 'unnatural' additives. PepsiCo had given the false impression that the beverages' vitamin content was due to the nutritious fruits and juices, rather than the added synthetic compounds such as calcium pantothenate, Fibersol-2, fructo-oligosaccharides and inulin.

Michael Moss, author of *Salt Sugar Fat: How the Food Giants Hooked Us*, claims that food scientists regularly use cutting-edge technology to create addictive 'bliss points' in sugary drinks and enhance the pleasing 'mouthfeel' of fat by manipulating its chemical structure. He points to a strategy employed by food and drink brands to defuse concerns about the health risks of their products, which was the same technique used by the tobacco companies in the past. 'They dial back on one ingredient, say, fat, and pump up another, say, sugar, and then tout the new line as "healthy" when it isn't.' Moss is equally scathing about Coca-Cola's attempt to portray itself in its TV advertising as a concerned corporate citizen.

He argues that Coke's ad campaign mimics steps taken by other big companies that have come under threat from health campaigners:

> First, they deny culpability for any health problems. Second, they try to delay any effort by government or health authorities to intervene on behalf of consumers. Finally, when consumers start to act by not buying as much of a product, they seemingly embrace the concerns.

Coca-Cola always wants to feel it is on the side of the consumer and such thinking is behind its current labelling strategy of putting common first names on the face of its bottles. Stuart Kronauge, vice president in charge of its US carbonated drinks business says: 'There's a really important conversation going on out there about obesity, and we want to be part of it because our consumers are telling us they want us to be a part of it.'

The question of whether Coca Cola wants to recast itself as being part of the solution rather than the problem is an interesting ethical one which could backfire in the same way as when it attempted to launch New Coke only to find that consumers hated it. 'Saying you're now making your products healthier is a slippery slope. It invites consumers to ask whether your products were unhealthy in the first place and ask why you didn't tackle the problem sooner. It also invites consumers to think again about drinking sodas, which could hit sales of Coke's key product,' concludes Moss.

Brands in the classroom

There has been continued growth in recent years in commercial activity targeted at schools, which has given rise to some ethical issues. Sponsorship of materials used in a classroom is starting to become much more widely accepted by teachers and parents in the UK as a result of the pressure on resources coupled with teachers needing anything that could help with lesson plans that can bring the curriculum alive for their pupils and students.

Well-thought-out and appropriately executed marketing and sponsorship programmes can add value to school life and the curriculum – as well as providing welcome resources in the classroom. Ethically this is totally defensible – both from the provider's and the recipient's perspectives. In the USA and Australia, there is a long history of schools accepting corporate sponsorship, for example, in return for granting the naming rights to a sports gymnasium or playing field. Such deals are not that uncommon, particularly where the brand owner is located in the region and is seen as being part of the local community. However, in Europe such deals are much less frequent, as there has been an element of hostility to sponsorship in the playground or in the classroom. This has stemmed largely from fears of undue commercial influence or over-commercialisation of the national curriculum, even though there are strict codes in place that are largely observed by brand owners to ensure that sponsorship within an educational context is done in an ethical way.

As school's finances come under increasing pressure, so too does the need to be more open to discussing appropriate sponsorship opportunities. Another key driver for change in Europe is that pupils and young people are increasingly brand-conscious and socially connected, which makes them a massive influence on their parent's attitudes, values, perceptions, beliefs and behaviours.

Case study: Green Schools Revolution, 2014

The Green Schools Revolution is one of the most innovative educational sponsorship programmes in the UK and could signal a new way for brand owners to engage with children and their families and turn traditional business-to-consumer (B2C) sponsorship on its head.

Award-winning education marketing agency Hopscotch Consulting has been working with the Co-op on a rebrand mission that looks like being rolled out across all of its grocery stores in 2015.

The agency employs educationalists and teachers to ensure that any of its sponsored materials destined for the classroom meets educational standards irrespective of who is paying the bill. Sam Mercer, co-founder of Hopscotch Consulting, explains:

> We set up the agency a couple of years ago to help brands in connecting with primary and secondary schools and then once through the school gates we wanted to extend that influence with the families of those children in a relevant, meaningful and ethical way where the educational experience of this journey was of paramount importance.

The challenge facing the Co-operative was to create an impactful corporate social responsibility (CSR) programme, bringing together disparate community and social programmes under one roof in order to deliver better outcomes. 'We needed to capture the imagination of a highly distracted and demanding audience of 4–18 year olds that are increasingly media literate and also highly cynical of brands that are simply trying to "advertise" to them,' explains Mercer.

Apart from lesson plans and teachers' resources delivered through a specially created microsite, the education sponsorship programme differed from others in the UK because it was rooted in behaviour of children in grasping and putting into action the concepts being taught at school. So the 'Walking Bus Kits' are part of the Green Revolution, encouraging parents to leave their gas-guzzlers at home and allow children to get to school by walking together. This may sound simple but it is incredibly effective in getting the message of sustainability into the home.

And there are funded school trips under the 'From Farm to Fork' part of the sponsored education programme whereby children gain a deeper understanding about the food chain as well how fair trade can help support rural communities on a global basis. Over 7,000 teachers registered to be part of the Green Revolution and since the programme was launched it has engaged with over one million primary and half a million secondary school children across the UK. 'This hasn't just been about recruitment of schools, teachers, and children and their parents but part of a much broader picture that at its core is about adding value to the national curriculum in a flexible way and ultimately about influencing ethical behaviour and a conversation with the Co-operative at its centre,' concludes Mercer.

UK utility companies are also attracted to using the classroom as a route to getting their brand messages into millions of homes, as well as helping to shift largely negative perceptions about profiteering, where household bills have continued to rise despite a fall in wholesale prices for gas and oil. Demonstrating that they are good corporate citizens has become increasingly important in the face of a barrage of criticism from regulator Ofgem as well as consumer groups angry that cost savings have not been passed on to their customers.

Case study: British Gas, 2013

British Gas was sensitive to these criticisms but wanted to counteract this by stressing its strong green credentials. The problem was that its own research showed that consumers were not yet aware of its track record in this area.

So, in 2008, British Gas launched its 'Generation Green' initiative to establish its strong environmental credentials with local communities, schools and consumers. Its desired audience segments were children, housewives with children and ABC1 adults. By completing green activities, children, teachers and parents earned 'green leaves', which were then redeemed as rewards for participating school.

British Gas wanted to push the message that being 'green' was at the core of everything that it did by raising awareness of its project. The company's first step was to get parents and children involved. However, British Gas was faced with another challenge – engaging children can be quite difficult, especially on environmental issues. So, it decided to use TV to help and turned to ITV for help. The broadcast sponsorship strategy was to get the interest of young people through their passions of fun TV and gaming.

In 2013, British Gas and media buying agency Carat worked with ITV to develop the 'Green Up Your Life' campaign, which consisted of ten five-minute TV programmes in which children competed in 'green challenges' and which were broadcast daily at 15.50 on CiTV (Children's ITV) for one month. And because the series was ad-funded, British Gas was entitled to branded break bumpers. There were also carefully placed spot ads, which furthered the association with British Gas.

A credit promo at the end of the show drove children to the CiTV website to get more information and watch themed advertorials. From there, they could go on to play an online game on children's gaming website (www.Popcorn.co.uk) and become more engaged with 'Generation Green'. The show was also promoted on itv.com, the Friends Reunited website and through press, TV, cinema and online ads. In summary, the objective of the broadcast campaign was to reinforce to consumers the message that 'green' is at the core of everything that British Gas does by raising awareness of the 'Generation Green' project ahead of its launch and by encouraging parental and school 'Energy Savers Report' sign-ups.

There were six components to the education sponsorship:

Leaf goal – every school that registered was awarded a leaf goal. To reach their goal, schools had to earn the appropriate number of leaves.

Tasks – further leaves could be earned by completing simple tasks such as appointing a light monitor for each class.

Family and friends – those outside the classroom could also participate by completing an Energy Savers Report and pledging to be more energy-efficient, which in turn would earn extra leaves for the school.

Lesson plans – leaves could also be earned by following lessons plans that integrated with Key Stages 2 and 3 of the national curriculum.

Rewards – when each school reached their leaf goal, they were able to choose to exchange the leaves for a selection of green rewards.

The games room – further engagement with children was created through a cartoon character 'Professor Green', who needs to recruit eco-rangers and stop 'Baron Fossilosis' from wasting the world's energy.

Each component of the campaign was supported by online, offline and broadcast activations in order to deliver messages across all of these channels.

The ad-funded show *Green Up Your Life* consisted of ten five-minute segments that were broadcast on CiTV and were developed by TV game show experts Endemol. In each show, children competed in a series of green challenges. Messages were reinforced through a series of bumpers, advertising and sponsorship end credits.

CiTV also integrated the broadcast aspect of the campaign across its online assets by running splash pages, a rip banner, game hosting, and homepage promo button and display ads. On Popcorn.co.uk there were branded characters, video, game hosting, homepage button and display ads. On the itv.com and Friends Reunited websites the 'Generation Green' messaging was delivered on display ads. The results of the educational sponsorship over the campaign period were as follows:

- 'Green Up Your Life' achieved an average audience of 47,000 children, with a high of 82,000 watching episode three.
- A total of 544,000 individuals and 310,000 children were signed up to the campaign.
- The series of ad-funded programmes generated 9.7% share of viewers aged 4–9 years old and 2.05% up on the slot average on CiTV.
- Viewers were 108% more likely to see 'Generation Green' as an example of positive action for the environment and 43% were more likely to see British Gas as an environmentally friendly company.
- 100% of those who watched the programme and played the game responded that they had learnt something new about the environment.
- Over 7000 schools signed up for 'Generation Green' campaign, exceeding an original target of 3,000 schools by 57%.
- 17m leaves were donated for schools to redeem prizes.

Alcohol and sponsorship

The ethical debate on alcohol has been running for as long as the sponsorship industry has been in existence. In August 2014 a leaked document from the British Labour Party discussed whether an outright ban on all alcohol-related sports sponsorship should be phased in during the course of parliament.

Such a measure, if adopted, is expected to lead to a loss of income for sports rights holders of around £300m a year and would affect 11 Premier League football clubs as well as F1 teams and other events, such as tennis and sailing, that have a long history of drinks sponsorship with Champagne brands. It would also effectively spell the end of Budweiser's sponsorship of the FA Cup, Heineken's branding of the European Cup rugby tournament and Crabbie's support of the Grand National.

Should the UK decide to legislate, it would follow in the footsteps of the Irish government, which has proposed a series of controls under the Public Health (Alcohol) Bill, which is designed to protect children and young people from 'powerful and sophisticated' influences on their drinking behaviour and expectations.

The Irish government wants the voluntary code that governs sports sponsorship to be replaced with a statutory code and at the time of writing a taoiseach working group is due to report on the value, evidence, feasibility and implications – including the public health consequences for children and young people – of regulating sponsorship of major sporting events by alcohol companies. The working party considerations are also expected to include the financial implications and alternative sources of funding for Irish sporting organisations to replace potential lost revenue arising from any such regulation.

Health groups are also pressing for a change in UK law as they feel alcohol abuse has become a national pandemic and that self-regulation by the drinks industry has failed to curb the health and societal problems caused by alcohol misuse. It points to a worrying trend for binge drinking among young people called 'Neknomination', where drinkers are encouraged to film themselves downing alcoholic drinks – including excessive quantities of spirits – quickly and posting a video of themselves online. These videos are akin to a modern-day chain letter, as they are shared and spread on social media with participants being urged to carry on the trend, fuelled by interactions on Facebook and Twitter.

Campaigners warn that such behaviour reinforces the dangerous message that it is 'normal' and also 'fun' to get drunk, and the way it spreads though social media by 'nominations' also means that many young people who may not have considered doing something like this are now coming under considerable peer pressure to put themselves in danger. Around 1.2m people a year are admitted to hospital because of alcohol-related illness, with liver disease among those under 30 years of age now double compared with 20 years ago. It is estimated the cost to the British taxpayer in terms of alcohol-related health treatment and crime is in excess of £2.1bn a year, according to a report published in August 2014 by the All Party Parliamentary Group on Alcohol Misuse.

In a separate study, conducted by PRWeek/One Poll (2013), which surveyed the attitudes of 2,000 UK respondents, 70% felt that the problem of alcohol abuse is growing and that 75% felt that the drinks industry should be doing more to tackle the issue. More women (46%) than men (35%) were in favour of an all-out ban on alcohol advertising.

In Australia, a study published in May 2013 showed there was a correlation between alcohol-related sports sponsorship and the take-up of drinking among university sportsmen and women. Researchers concluded that sports administrators should consider action to reduce the harm associated with excessive alcohol consumption and the drinks industry's sponsorship in sport.

A similar study was repeated in the UK and the results published in May 2014 showed a striking similarity across a bigger sample size of 2,450 university students who participated in sports. The conclusion of the researchers was equally blunt: 'University students in the UK who play sport and who personally receive alcohol-related sponsorship or whose club or team receives such sponsorship appear to have more problematic drinking behaviour than UK university students who play sport and receive no alcohol industry sponsorship. Policy to reduce or cease such sponsorship should be considered.'

Some academic studies have even suggested that sports such as cricket and rugby actively promote alcohol consumption because of the relationship between the drinks industry and fans of these sports, who tend to consume large quantities of alcohol at such events. In the early 1990s France was one of the first countries in Europe to introduce substantial restrictions on broadcast advertising of alcohol and a complete ban on the drinks industry from sponsoring cultural and sports events that often appeal to young people.

The All Party Parliamentary Group on Alcohol Misuse also wants the UK to adopt a similar rigorous approach by bringing in statutory controls. It says in its Manifesto 2015:

> Children growing up see alcohol marketing on a daily basis and are more familiar with alcohol brands than with leading biscuit or ice-cream brands. Compared with adults, children and young people are exposed to significantly more alcohol adverts than expected, given their viewing habits – 51% more in the case of advertising for ready-mixed alcopop drinks.
>
> Sport, and football in particular, is hugely popular with children and young people, with alcohol sponsorship sending contradictory messages about the health benefits of participation. Viewers of top-flight football are exposed to two alcohol references every minute and during the FIFA World Cup 2010, Carlsberg – the 'official beer of the England football team' – expected to sell an extra 21m pints.
>
> Children can't make responsible decisions about their drinking if they grow up bombarded by excessive alcohol marketing. Yet our marketing regulations are failing to protect the youngest in society. Regulation must be statutory and independent of both the alcohol and advertising industries. The regulator needs meaningful sanctions, such as fines, that deter non-compliance.

In the UK, the Portman Group oversees a self-regulatory system that is consistent with the guidelines set out by the Advertising Standards Authority (ASA) with respect to the marketing and promotion of its members' products.

The Portman Group's position is that a blanket ban on sponsorship would be disproportionate and that the industry is already compliant with the strictest rules to prevent alcohol being marketed to children or in a way that might appeal to them.

This view is supported by the European Sponsorship Association (ESA), which has produced its own guidelines for rights holders regarding alcohol sponsorship, associated marketing and promotion and consumption of alcohol at events.

The 22 ethical principles that rights holders should follow as currently advised by ESA are:

1   Rights holders will comply with all relevant national and local laws and should be aware of all voluntary codes and guidelines that relate to sponsorship and alcohol.

2   Rights holders should use their best endeavours to ensure that all external consultants, agencies and media engaged in activities related to alcohol sponsorship or the supply of alcohol should also comply with all relevant national and local laws and be aware of all voluntary codes and guidelines.

3   Rights holders should support campaigns that promote responsible drinking and if allowed by law, will give reasonable prominence to responsible consumption messages within communications linked to any alcohol sponsorship.

4   Rights holders should encourage responsible consumption awareness within their associated organisations, memberships, clubs, participants and supporters, such as through educational programmes or display responsible drinking messages.

5   Rights holders should respect the choice of consumers not to drink alcohol and should never portray abstinence or moderation negatively.

6   Rights holder will only allow sponsorship by alcohol companies where the substantial majority of the audience is reasonably expected to be adults older than the legal purchase age.

7   Rights holders will not allow sponsorship by alcohol companies of organisations, events, teams or individuals with particular appeal to people under the legal purchase age rather than those over the legal purchase age. This does not prevent alcohol sponsorship of events and teams that include participation of a person or persons under the legal purchase age.

8   No alcohol sponsorship will be permitted of individuals under the legal purchase age or use of them individually in any promotional or marketing activities linked to sponsorship. Care should be taken when sponsoring an individual over the legal purchase age if they might appear to be under the legal purchase age.

9   Particular care should be taken of alcohol sponsorships where motorsport is involved and, in such cases, appropriate messages regarding responsible drinking should be communicated.

10   No sponsorship or associated marketing should imply that it is acceptable to consume alcohol before or while participating in a sports activity, or that it enhances social or sexual success.

11   No sponsorship or associated marketing should imply that alcohol enhances social or sexual success.

12   No implication should be made within any alcohol sponsorship or associated marketing that inappropriate anti-social, aggressive or dangerous behaviour is condoned.

13   Rights holders and venue owners should take particular care with alcohol signage and marketing materials at facilities and events where the participants are predominately under the legal purchase age, even if the substantial majority of the audience is over the legal purchase age. Any alcohol brand

signage or other materials should not imply that the alcohol company sponsors underage individuals or uses then in connection with its marketing.

14 Only people over the legal purchase age will be allowed to participate in competitions run by alcohol sponsors for gifts or tickets, including those offering hospitality and serving alcohol.

15 No alcohol marketing messages or imagery should be used on or within any promotional activities or games linked to the sponsored activity that are primarily aimed at those under the legal purchase age, which may include replica sports shirts, toys, mascots, online games or licensed products.

16 The number and volume of samples of alcohol products given to adults should be limited and no samples should be given to anyone under the legal purchase age.

17 Alcohol may be sold or provided at events and sponsored activities provided that all applicable national and local laws and voluntary codes and guidelines are followed.

18 Rights holders will not allow alcohol to be sold, given or to be consumed by anyone under the legal purchase age.

19 Rights holders should use reasonable endeavours to ensure that all staff working at events are fully trained in responsible service and do not serve anyone under the legal purchase age or anyone who appears to be intoxicated. Care should be taken to ensure there is sufficient staff at events.

20 Wherever alcohol is served non-alcoholic options should also be available.

21 Anyone carrying out alcohol sampling activity must comply with current licensing legislation.

22 Rights holders should consider the availability of adequate public transport in order to alleviate attendees from having to drive to events particularly if there is alcohol on sale or provided to spectators.

Tobacco and sponsorship

This is probably the most contentious and controversial ethical issue in global sponsorship today, as the tobacco industry has again become involved in sponsorship, including sports, through a back-door route, according to many commentators and anti-tobacco campaigners.

According to the latest World Health Organisation (WHO) statistics, tobacco kills almost 6 million of its users each year. The tobacco industry needs to attract new customers to replace those who die or manage to quit in order to maintain and increase tobacco sales and profits. The tobacco industry is largely credited with creating modern sponsorship practice particularly through sponsorship in motor racing and F1.

UK experience

In the UK, its association with sport came to an abrupt end when the European Union decided to ban all tobacco advertising and sponsorship in 1998 and passed the EU Tobacco Advertising Directive 2002.

The EU Directive comprehensively bans the advertising and promotion of tobacco products, including the use of brand sharing and sponsorship of cultural and sports events. Regulations also make it unlawful for the promotion of tobacco brands on items such as clothing, baseball caps, lighters and jackets.

Sports such as F1, motor racing, snooker and cricket were given until 31 July 2005 to regularise their sponsorship arrangements in order to comply with the Tobacco Advertising and Promotion Act 2002. For example, F1 teams such as BMW Williams had made a virtue of not being sponsored with money from the tobacco industry and instead received sponsorship from GSK in promoting its smoking cessation product, NiQuitin CQ. And McLaren F1 signed a £30m sponsorship deal with Intel in 2005, replacing primary sponsor West, owned by Imperial Tobacco.

In the UK, sponsorship in all other sports came to an end in 2003. Today, the tobacco companies have responded to the clampdown on the public sale of cigarettes through giant health warnings on packets and a steep rise in VAT by publicly talking about the need to find the 'safer smoke' for its customers. And this has led to tobacco companies making massive investments in e-cigarettes. But are e-cigarettes a way of weaning smokers off smoking or do they simply substitute one nicotine delivery system for another in order to protect the market share and massive profits of their producers – the tobacco manufacturers?

The discussions about e-cigarettes on the blogosphere and in vaping chatrooms are currently dominated by impassioned accounts from former smokers encouraging others to follow in their footsteps as the first step on the road to quitting. Early data on e-cigarettes shows them to be as good as or marginally better than nicotine replacement therapy (NRT) in helping smokers give up, and the effectiveness of such alternatives has as yet to make any real dent in the lives of the millions of people who continue to smoke and run the risk of cancer and respiratory diseases as a result of using these products.

But that has not stopped tobacco companies like BAT publishing scientific papers detailing the results of clinical trials showing how e-cigarettes produce lower amounts harmful by-products than the regular kind.

The big issue is whether we trust the motivations that sit behind this form of supposed corporate social responsibility (CSR) shown by the tobacco companies towards their customers. Well, not everyone is convinced. The alternative view is that this latest move by tobacco companies is protect their business empires in raking in billions from a habit that many millions of people around the world find impossible to quit.

The reputation of the e-cigarette industry depends on future independent scientific studies examining whether vaping uptake serves to keep a significant number of smokers smoking who would otherwise quit, not just immediately, but soon enough to reduce substantially their risk of premature death and serious disease. And such an effect would need to be balanced against the quitting volume achieved in any calculation of net population benefit in order to arrive at any balanced conclusion as to the net health benefits of e-cigarettes.

However, there was a growing sense towards the end of 2014 that e-cigarettes were starting to persuade critics that they should be treated very differently from tobacco products and this was reflected in the way e-cigarettes can be lawfully promoted, advertised and marketed. Crucially, e-cigarette brands are able to engage in sponsorship activities that are not permitted for tobacco brands.

Case study: Doncaster Cup, 2014

Doncaster became the first horse racecourse in the UK to carry the name of a cigarette-associated product in a race title since tobacco sponsorship was outlawed in 2003. Socialites Electric Cigarettes became the title sponsor of one of the world's oldest continually run race, the Doncaster Cup, for the next three years.

As part of the sponsorship deal, Socialites is permitted to hand out free packets of e-cigarettes to those who want to try the product and are over 18 years of age (although it is not illegal for anyone under 18 to smoke).

Previously, Rothmans Royals had sponsored the St Leger race for four years to 2002 until the impending advertising ban forced the manufacturer to pull out. According to Doncaster racetrack managing director Mark Spincer, the sponsorship tie-up with an e-cigarette brand is a bit of coup for the horse racing industry:

> Socialites were looking to get into racing and we were in the right place at the right time. We've been working with Socialites for four months and they've become one of our partners in the old weighing room that has been converted into a restaurant, and then they were looking for something high profile and we had the Doncaster Cup available, which they've taken, which is great news for us and racing.

Previously, Chesterfield-based Socialites had been involved in sponsorship and advertising with their local football league club but this is the company's first venture into horse racing. Socialites head of marketing Andrew Payne said:

> It's a great opportunity for us because Doncaster is relatively local, it's our nearest racecourse and the St Leger Festival is a prestigious event so for us it's very exciting.
>
> It doesn't put us off that smoking – or vaping in the case of e-cigarettes – isn't permitted indoors at the racecourse. Obviously quite a few places don't allow it, but I think that's something that will change in time as there's no smell, no passive smoking and no odours with e-cigarettes, and our product can be used outside.

Under UK law, nicotine-containing products (NCPs) that are presented for cutting down, quitting or reducing the harms of smoking are considered to be medicinal products by the Medicines and Healthcare Products Regulatory Agency (MHRA), the body that is responsible for regulating NCPs that are medicinal products, including electronic cigarettes.

The acceptance of this form of product has also attracted support from the anti-smoking lobby. For example, campaign group Action for Smoking and Health said it had no problem with Doncaster's sponsorship deal. ASH director of research and policy Hazel Cheeseman explained: 'It's important to remember that electronic cigarettes are not tobacco cigarettes and evidence suggests that they're helping people to quit smoking. We would not want to see these products marketed to children or non-smokers. However, sponsorship and advertising targeted at adult smokers is a different matter. We would say if you're thinking about quitting, while electronic cigarettes can help, the best proven route is to visit your local stop smoking service.'

US experience

A report by the US Centres for Disease Control and Prevention in 2012 showed a steep rise in the use of e-cigarettes among middle-school (1%) and high-school (2.8%) students, amounting to 2m users of these products, which prompted calls for greater regulation of e-cigarettes in the USA.

Only e-cigarettes that are marketed for therapeutic purposes are currently regulated by the US Food and Drug Administration (FDA) Center for Drug Evaluation and Research. Currently, the FDA Center for Tobacco Products (CTP) regulates:

- cigarettes
- cigarette tobacco
- roll-your-own tobacco
- smokeless tobacco.

In 2014 the FDA issued a proposed rule that would extend the agency's tobacco authority to cover additional products that meet the legal definition of a tobacco product, such as e-cigarettes in order that the next generation becomes tobacco free. Under the proposed rule change, manufacturers of e-cigarettes would be required to:

- register with the FDA and report product and ingredient listings
- only market new tobacco products after FDA review
- only make direct and implied claims of reduced risk if the FDA confirms that scientific evidence supports the claim and that marketing the product will benefit public health as a whole
- not distribute free samples.

In addition, under the proposed rule, the following provisions would apply to newly 'deemed' tobacco products:

- minimum-age and identification restrictions to prevent sales to underage young people

- requirements to include health warnings
- prohibition of vending machine sales, unless in a facility that never admits young people.

'Tobacco remains the leading cause of death and disease in this country. This is an important moment for consumer protection and a significant proposal that if finalized as written would bring FDA oversight to many new tobacco products,' explained FDA Commissioner Dr Margaret Hamburg. 'Science-based product regulation is a powerful form of consumer protection that can help reduce the public health burden of tobacco use on the American public, including youth.'

The FDA proposes different compliance dates for various provisions so that all regulated entities, including small businesses, will have adequate time to comply with the requirements of the proposed rule.

Products that are marketed for therapeutic purposes will continue to be regulated as medical products under the FDA's existing drug and device authorities in the Federal Food, Drug and Cosmetic Act 2011. The proposed rule is currently still within a period of public consultation at the time of writing and the FDA is currently seeking answers to many public health questions posed by e-cigarettes, which do not involve the burning of tobacco and inhalation of its smoke, as the agency develops an appropriate level of regulatory oversight for these products.

In the meantime, tobacco companies that own such businesses are ramping up their promotion and marketing efforts to new levels that are having an appeal to youth audiences that cannot be targeted by conventional cigarette promotion. From a sponsorship perspective, these tactics include:

- using celebrity endorsements and celebrity-inspired styling at glamorous events such as New York Fashion Week
- using sports and cultural sponsorship to reach potential users
- using social networking through competitions, discounts and price promotions on Facebook and Twitter
- using PR to help build trust in the product.

Researchers in the US warn corporate sponsorship of sports teams leads young people to absorb marketing messages and influences purchasing decisions. Young people are pulled into the market, as nicotine is being boosted but cessation and NRT messages are being overshadowed and the anti-smoking message at the same time is being undermined. Earned media are also playing a role, as journalists discuss the promotion of e-cigarettes in magazines with a typical youth audience.

Case study: Vapor sponsorship of South by Southwest, 2014

In 2014 the RJ Reynolds Vapor Co brand sponsored the South by Southwest music and technology confab in order to build awareness among adult smokers in advance of the product's national rollout in the US. The Reynolds American subsidiary company launched Vuse in Colorado in 2013 and then Utah in January 2014.

In addition to building visibility, the tobacco giant is using the South by Southwest event to promote the e-cigarette's digital qualities and has positioned the product as 'the first and only digital vapor cigarette' that incorporates a microprocessor-based control system and computer chip to regulate and monitor puff count, puff duration and other product characteristics. Stephanie Cordisco, president of the RJ Reynolds Vapor Co., enthused:

> With a culture of innovation and focus on emerging trends, South by South-west is the ideal setting to showcase the state-of-the-art digital technology in Vuse that makes it a game-changer for the vapor industry.

As an official sponsor, Vuse had booths on the fourth floor of the Austin Con-vention Center, while those handing out samples engaged with age-verified adult tobacco consumers at the Interactive Opening Party and the Outdoor Music Fes-tival at Butler Park, among other events.

Tobacco companies have been quick to exploit the current position of these smokeless tobacco products in order to help build market share among both smokers and non-smokers.

In 2010 Lorillard bought out independent US e-cigarette company Blu, which now has around 49% of e-cigarette market share.

Case study: Blu e-cigarettes and use of sponsorship, 2014

Actress Jenny McCarthy is the female face of Blu and actor Stephen Dorf is the male face of the brand, fronting ironically styled 1950s posters that once glamo-rised smoking as being 'cool' under the slogan 'Take back your freedom'. In one TV commercial, Dorff says: 'It's time we take our freedom back,' before going on to say that Blu e-cigarettes can be smoked 'at a baseball game . . . in a bar with your friends . . . virtually anywhere'. Inhaling with a swagger, he adds: 'Come on, guys, rise from the ashes.'

Far from being a NRT, Blu is an advocate for encouraging smoking and its current campaign at the time of writing is 'Smoking Redefined', which associates smoking the e-cigarette with the real thing and with being cool.

Codes of practice

International Chamber of Commerce (2011)

The International Chamber of Commerce (ICC) Code sets the ethical standards and guidelines for brand owners and is relevant in the context of international sponsorship. The ICC Code is a foundation code for many other codes such as the Advertising Standards Authority (ASA) Code on advertising, marketing, sponsorship, and online and offline communications in the UK.

Developed by experts from a wide range of market and customer segments around the world, the latest version of the ICC Code is a globally applicable framework that harmonises best practice from the Americas, Africa, Europe, the Middle East and Asia Pacific. The ICC Code applies to marketing communications in their entirety, including all words and numbers (spoken and written), visual treatments, music and sound effects, and material originating from other sources.

The code is voluntary but has been incorporated by industry regulators across the world. It is often referred to in legal arguments as well as by the courts, where prevailing best practices and standards in the global sales and marketing industry need to be referred to in order to settle disputes. The ICC Code is particularly relevant from a business-to-consumer (B2C) perspective and takes account of social, cultural and linguistic factors. For example, when judging communications addressed to children, the ICC Code provides that the natural credulity and inexperience of children should always be taken into account in any determination as to the appropriateness of those communications.

Assumptions made by the ICC Code

The ICC Code makes a number of assumptions:

- from a business-to-consumer (B2C) perspective, individual customers and prospects are assumed to have a reasonable degree of experience, knowledge and sound judgement and to be reasonably observant and prudent when making purchasing decisions
- from a business-to-business (B2B) perspective, companies and professional organisations are presumed to have an appropriate level of specialised knowledge and expertise in their field of operations.

These same assumptions are applied in the Committee of Advertising Practice (CAP), Broadcast Committee of Advertising Practice (BCAP) and Direct Marketing Association Codes of Practice in the UK.

The ICC Code is structured in two main parts: general provisions on advertising and marketing communication practice that contain fundamental principles and then a series of detailed sections that cover particular activities such as direct marketing, sponsorship and sales promotion.

General provisions of the ICC Code

BASIC PRINCIPLES

All marketing communications should be legal, decent, honest and truthful; should be prepared with a due sense of social and professional responsibility and should conform to the principles of fair competition as generally accepted in business (Article 1). The ICC Code adds that no communication should be such as to impair public confidence in marketing. These are the foundation principles on which the rest of the ICC Code is based.

DECENCY

Marketing communications should not contain statements or audio or visual treatments that offend standards of decency currently prevailing in the country and culture concerned (Article 2).

HONESTY

Marketing communications should be framed so as not to abuse the trust of consumers or exploit their lack of experience or knowledge. Relevant factors likely to affect consumers' purchasing decisions should be communicated in such a way and at such a time that consumers can take them into account (Article 3).

SOCIAL RESPONSIBILITY

Marketing communications should respect human dignity and should not incite or condone any form of discrimination, including that based on race, national origin, religion, gender, age, disability or sexual orientation.

In addition, such activities should not without justifiable reason play on fear or exploit misfortune or suffering, or appear to condone or incite violent, unlawful or antisocial behaviour, or play on superstitious beliefs (Article 4).

TRUTHFULNESS

Perhaps the most important principle in the ICC Code and one that goes to the root of all marketing communications is that all such activities must be truthful and not misleading (Article 5).

Marketing communications should not contain any statement, claim or audio or visual treatment which directly or by implication, omission, ambiguity or exaggeration, is likely to mislead the consumer.

The ICC Code spells this out in some detail and although not exhaustive the following is a useful checklist as to what 'truthfulness' means in practice:

- Characteristics of the product that are material in influencing the consumer to make a purchase, for example, the nature, composition, method and date of manufacture, range of use, efficiency and performance, quantity, commercial or geographical origin or environmental impact must be clear.
- The value of the product and the total price to be paid by the consumer must be clear.
- The terms for delivery, exchange, return, repair and maintenance of the product must be clear.
- Other information including terms of guarantee, intellectual property (IP) rights and trade names, compliance with international and national standards, awards and the extent of benefits for charitable causes as a result of making a purchase must be truthful.

USE OF TECHNICAL/SCIENTIFIC DATA AND TERMINOLOGY

In much the same way as Article 5 provides for 'truthfulness', this principle (Article 6) captures situations in which marketers may 'sail close to the wind' without actually being dishonest and may be tempted to be economical with the truth. In practice, marketers should not engage in the following activities:

- misuse technical data such as research results or quotations from technical and scientific publications
- present statistics in such a way as to exaggerate the validity of a product claim
- use scientific terminology or vocabulary in such a way as to suggest falsely that a product claim has scientific validity.

USE OF 'FREE' AND 'GUARANTEE'

This is perhaps unusual, as it is a specific rather than a basic point of principle, but it addresses marketers' liberal use of the words 'free' and 'guarantee' within a sales and marketing context, as this has been open to much abuse.

In order to stem underhanded and oblique sales and marketing activities, the ICC Code provides that the use of the term 'free', as in a 'free gift' or 'free offer', should only be used in very limited circumstances (Article 7):

- where the 'free offer' involves no contractual obligation whatsoever
- where the 'free offer' involves only the obligation to pay shipping and handling charges, which should not exceed the cost estimated to be incurred by the marketer itself
- where the 'free offer' is in conjunction with the purchase of another product but provided that the price of that product has not been inflated to cover all or part of the cost of the 'free offer'.

Such a provision closes the door to many 'sharp practices' where the consumer is led to believe that there is a value-added benefit (for example, a significant financial saving) when in fact there is nothing of the kind and instead the marketer is treating the consumer as gullible to such a tactic.

The provision also states that marketing communications should not state or imply that a 'guarantee', 'warranty' or any such expression gives the impression that the consumer will enjoy additional rights over and above those provided by national laws. The terms of any guarantee or warranty, including the name and address of the guarantor, should be easily available to the consumer and any exclusion clauses or limitations on consumer rights or remedies must be clear, conspicuous and in accordance with national and international laws.

SUBSTANTIATION

Sales and marketing often includes claims, descriptions or illustrations that are communicated to consumers in order to influence them in making an informed choice – what is commonly known as 'evidence-based marketing'. The ICC Code provides that such claims, descriptions and illustrations should be capable of both verification and substantiation (Article 8). In the UK, the CAP and BCAP Codes are consistent with the ICC Code, which provides that such substantiation should be available so that evidence can be produced without delay and on request when required.

IDENTIFICATION

About a decade ago or even longer it was the fashion to place 'advertorials', which were paid for advertising but made to look like editorial with the veneer of 'independence' about the content in the advertisement. The ICC Code specifically states that such activity should be clearly distinguishable as such, whatever the form or medium used.

When an advertisement appears in a medium containing news or editorial matter, it should be readily recognisable as an advertisement and the identity of the advertiser should be immediately apparent (Article 9).

Marketing communications should not misrepresent the true commercial purpose and as a result, copy that is promoting the sale of a product, for example, should not be disguised as 'market research', 'consumer surveys', 'user-generated content', 'independent blogs' or 'independent reviews', when, in fact, these are far from being an unsolicited or independent point of view.

IDENTITY

This is linked to Article 9 and the ICC Code provides that the identity of the marketer should be apparent in marketing communications and where appropriate should include contact information to enable the consumer to get in touch without difficulty (Article 10). This does not apply to 'teaser promotions', which will be followed up with other communications activities that will reveal the identity of the brand owner.

COMPARISONS

The ICC Code provides that any comparison advertising must not mislead and must comply with the principles of fair competition (Article 11). Points of comparison should be based on facts that can be substantiated and should not be unfairly selected.

DENIGRATION

Marketing communications should not denigrate any person or group of persons, firm, organisation, industrial or commercial activity, profession or product or seek to bring it or them into public contempt or ridicule (Article 12).

TESTIMONIALS

Testimonials and case studies are some of the most powerful ways of getting a message across to a desired market and customer segment, as they have a quality of independence about them.

The ICC Code recognises the potency of such communications and provides that marketers should not use or refer to any testimonial, endorsement or supportive documentation unless it is genuine, verifiable and relevant, as to do otherwise would be dishonest (Article 13). The ICC Code adds that testimonials or endorsements that have become obsolete or out of date and therefore misleading through the passage of time should be removed from all marketing communications.

PORTRAYAL OR IMITATION OF PERSONS AND REFERENCES TO PERSONAL PROPERTY

The roots of this principle lie directly in the need to protect the personal privacy of citizens, and the ICC Code provides that marketing communications should not portray or refer to any persons, whether in a private or a public capacity, unless prior permission has been obtained; neither should marketing communications without prior permission depict or refer to any person's property in a way likely to convey the impression of a personal endorsement of the product or organisation involved (Article 14).

EXPLOITATION OF GOODWILL

In the same way as Article 14 is a principle about respect for privacy, the ICC Code on exploitation of goodwill spells out that marketers should not make an unjustifiable use of a name, initials, logo or trademarks of another firm, company or institution (Article 15).

IMITATION

Marketing communications should not in any way take an unfair advantage of a brand owner's intellectual property (IP) rights or goodwill in the absence of consent (Article 16).

This principle effectively forbids a marketer from unfairly riding on the coat-tails of another brand in its market sector – a principle upheld by the courts in recent cases (see Chapter 7).

Marketing communications should not imitate those of another brand owner in any way likely to mislead or confuse the consumer, for example through the general layout, text, slogan, visual treatment, music or sound effects.

Where a marketer has established a distinctive marketing communications campaign in one or more countries, other marketers should not imitate that campaign in other countries where the marketer who originated the campaign may operate, thereby preventing the extension of the campaign to those countries within a reasonable period of time.

SAFETY AND HEALTH

Marketing communications should not without justification on educational or social grounds contain any visual portrayal or any description of potentially dangerous practices or situations that show a disregard for safety or health as defined by national laws and standards (Article 17).

Instructions for use of products destined for consumers should include appropriate safety warnings and where necessary, legal disclaimers over liability for misuse of the product.

Within the context of advertising, children should be shown to be under adult supervision whenever a product or an activity involves a safety risk, such as a climbing frame for the garden, which could potentially pose a hazard for children if not supervised by an adult. Information provided with the product should include proper directions for use and full instructions covering health and safety aspects, whenever necessary. Such health and safety warnings should be made clear by the use of pictures, text or a combination of both.

CHILDREN AND YOUNG PEOPLE
The principle applicable here (Article 18) is discussed in detail below.

PRIVACY POLICY
This principle is in alignment with the data protection principles of the country in which the marketing is taking place. The ICC Code provides that those who collect data in connection with marketing communication activities ('data controllers') should have a privacy policy and the terms of this should be readily available to consumers (Article 19).

The data protection policy should provide a clear statement if any collection or processing of data is to take place, whether this in itself is evident or not.

Appropriate measures should be taken to ensure that consumers understand and exercise their rights to opt out of marketing lists (including the right to sign on to general preference services), to require that their data is not made available to third parties for their marketing purposes and to rectify data that is held and is inaccurate.

Where a consumer has expressed a wish not to receive marketing communications using a specific medium, whether via a preference service or by other means, this wish should be respected.

Particular care should be taken to maintain the data protection rights of the consumer when personal data is transferred from the country in which it is collected to another country. When data processing is conducted in another country, all reasonable steps should be taken to ensure that adequate security measures are in place and that the data protection principles set out in the ICC Code are respected.

RESPONSIBILITY
Observance of the rules of conduct laid down in the ICC Code is the primary responsibility of the brand owner. Other parties also required to observe the ICC Code include advertising and marketing agencies, publishers, media owners and other subcontractors to the brand owner (Article 23).

Agencies and other practitioners should exercise due care and diligence in the preparation of marketing communications and should operate in such a way as to enable the brand owner to fulfil its responsibilities.

Publishers, media owners and subcontractors who publish, transmit, deliver or distribute marketing communications should also exercise due care in the acceptance of them and their presentation to the public.

Employees of any of the above who take part in the planning, creation, publication or transmission of a marketing communication are also responsible – commensurately with their pay grade – for ensuring that the rules of the ICC Code are observed and should act in the spirit and letter of the ICC Code.

The ICC Code applies to the marketing communication in its entire content and form, including testimonials and statements and audio or visual material originating from other sources. The fact that the content or form of a marketing communication may originate wholly or in part from other sources does not justify non-observance of the ICC Code rules.

EFFECT OF SUBSEQUENT REDRESS FOR CONTRAVENTION
Subsequent correction and appropriate redress for a contravention of the ICC Code by the party responsible is desirable but does not excuse the contravention of the ICC Code (Article 24).

IMPLEMENTATION
The ICC Code and the principles enshrined in it should be adopted and implemented nationally and internationally by the relevant local, national or regional self-regulatory bodies (Article 25).

RESPECT FOR SELF-REGULATORY DECISIONS
No marketer, communications practitioner or advertising agency, publisher, media owner or subcontractor should be party to the publication or distribution of an advertisement or other marketing communication which has been found unacceptable by the relevant self-regulatory body (Article 26).

Specific principles under the ICC Code, 2011

SPONSORSHIP
This section of the ICC Code applies to all forms of sponsorship relating to corporate image, brands, products, activities or events of any kind run by commercial and voluntary organisations. It includes sponsorship elements forming part of other marketing activities, such as sales promotion and direct marketing, or in conjunction with a corporate social responsibility (CSR) programme.

A consistent theme of this section is respect for the rights holder, the sponsorship property, the sponsor, the supporters/fans, participants and spectators.

Codes as they relate to children and young people

ICC Code (2011)

As previously discussed, the ICC Code (2011) lays down a number of key marketing principles that have become adopted by or incorporated into various national bodies' codes including the CAP and BCAP Codes in the UK.

The ICC Code on children and young people (Article 18) is one of the most detailed and provides that special care should be taken in marketing communications directed to or featuring children and young people.

The following provisions of Article 18 apply to marketing communications – including sponsorship – addressed to children and young people as defined in national laws and regulations relevant to such communications:

- Such communications should not undermine positive social behaviour, lifestyles and attitudes.
- Products unsuitable for children and young people should not be advertised in media targeted to them and advertisements directed to children and young people should not be inserted in media where the editorial matter is unsuitable for them.
- Material unsuitable for children should be clearly identified as such.

Marketing communications and sponsorship should not exploit the inexperience or credulity of children and young people.

While the use of fantasy in marketing communications is appropriate for young as well as older children, it should not make it difficult for them to identify the distinction between reality and fiction.

Marketing communications directed to children should be clearly distinguishable to them as such. Marketing communications should not contain any statement or visual treatment that could have the effect of harming children and young people mentally, morally or physically. Children and young people should not be portrayed in unsafe situations or engaging in actions harmful to themselves or others or be encouraged to engage in potentially hazardous activities or behaviour. Marketing communications should not suggest that possession or use of the marketed product will give a child or young person physical, psychological or social advantages over other children and young people or that not possessing the product will have the opposite effect.

The ICC Code also raises a number of other ethical and moral points that marketers need to observe when constructing communications with children and young people:

- Such activities should not undermine the authority, responsibility, judgement or tastes of parents, with regard to relevant social and cultural values.
- They should not include any direct appeal to children and young people to persuade their parents or other adults to buy products for them ('pester power' is expressly forbidden).
- Prices should not be presented in such a way as to lead children and young people to an unrealistic perception of the cost or value of the product, for example, by reducing the size of the recommended retail price relative to other sales and marketing information – in other words, such an advertisement should not imply that the product is immediately within the reach of every family budget.

- Communications inviting children and young people to contact the brand owner should encourage them to obtain the permission of a parent or other appropriate adult if any cost, including that of a communication, is involved.

ASA regulations on sales and marketing to children

CAP CODE 5, BCAP CODE 5

The UK CAP and BCAP Codes on sales and marketing to children are similar to those set out in both the ICC Code (2011) and the DMA Code of Practice (2012) and include special sections on advertising to children.

The CAP and BCAP Codes define a child as anyone under the age of 16 and provide that ads and promotions addressed to or likely to appeal to children should contain nothing that is likely to result in their physical, mental or moral harm.

For example, advertisements should not include the following:

- children entering into strange places or talking to strangers
- children being shown in hazardous situations or behaving dangerously or using or being in close proximity to dangerous substances or equipment, without direct adult supervision
- encouragement to children to copy any practice that might be unsafe for a child.

Promotions addressed to or targeted directly at children:

- must make clear that adult permission is required if a prize or an incentive might cause conflict between a child's desire and a parent's or other adult's authority
- must contain a prominent closing date if applicable
- must not exaggerate the value of a prize or the chances of winning it.

Promotions that require a purchase to participate and include a direct exhortation to make a purchase must not be addressed to or targeted at children.

The CAP and BCAP Codes also include scheduling rules on advertising age-restricted computer and console games to prevent TV commercials appearing around programmes made for or likely to appeal particularly to children.

In addition, the BCAP Code prevents TV commercials from exploiting the trust that children and young people place in parents, teachers or other people.

Chapter 6 at a glance

1   Ethics is now a major business issue for all companies and organisations – it is less about complying with legal obligations and much more about how a company or organisation makes a contribution to the wider society as part of its commercial and non-commercial activities.

2   Ethical behaviour has a linear relationship with the reputation of a company or organisation.
3   Brands are sensitive to public opinion and arguably need to act in an ethical way that is expected by customers, employees, fans and supporters.
4   Ambush marketing is an ethical issue in sponsorship and is dealt with in detail in Chapter 9.
5   Corporate hospitality is an ethical issue in sponsorship and is dealt with in detail in Chapter 7.
6   Gambling brands involved in sports sponsorship are a controversial ethical issue because of the influence on children and young people who follow sports teams and personalities.
7   Food and drinks brand owners such as Coca-Cola and McDonald's have to take responsibility for the debate about 'calories in, calories out' in order to protect their reputation as sports sponsors.
8   Brands in the classroom are a less controversial issue than they were a decade ago, as sponsorship of materials used in the classroom is starting to become much more widely accepted by teachers and parents in the UK as a result of pressure on resources together with teachers needing anything that could help with lesson plans that can bring the curriculum alive for their pupils and students.
9   Alcohol brands involved in sports sponsorship may suffer the same fate as tobacco brands in being prevented from supporting such activities in the future. In the UK, the Labour Party appears to moving in the direction of banning alcohol brands should they be elected to power in 2015.
10 The link between alcohol brands such as Guinness and rugby have endured for a substantial period of time and breaking this relationship between drinks brands and sports will represent a significant funding risk, warns the European Sponsorship Association.
11 Tobacco brand owners sponsorship is a highly controversial issue and tobacco companies' acquisition of electronic cigarette brands provides a 'back-door' entry for these businesses to return to sponsorship.
12 Health campaigners argue that these companies are less interested in nicotine replacement therapy (NRT) and more interested in protecting their lucrative sales streams from tobacco-related products that they can now promote legally without the restrictions placed on cigarette products.
13 The International Chamber of Commerce (ICC) Code of Practice provides a global framework for ethical marketing and sponsorship of products and services to consumers as well as children and young people.

Questions for discussion

1   What are the issues for brand owners in managing corporate and individual responsibility within sponsorship?
2   Can ambush marketing be defended on an ethical basis?
3   Should gambling brands be permitted to sponsor football teams that are followed by children and young people?

4   Should sponsors stand up for the values they believe, even if this could cause embarrassment for the rights holder?
5   Should sponsors expect a higher ethical standard of behaviour of high-profile personalities and insist on standards of behaviour below which they will cancel their sponsorship arrangements with that athlete/celebrity in the event of these being transgressed?
6   Should fast-food brands be banned from sponsorship of sports events?
7   Should alcohol brands be banned from sponsorship of sports events?
8   Do brands in the classroom have a pernicious influence over children and young people or should commerce and the world of work be regarded as a part of the mainstream education experience?
9   Should there be more restrictions on e-cigarettes in the same way as for tobacco brands?
10 What are the key codes of practice that provide an ethical framework for sponsors interested in engaging with children and young people?

Further reading

Bush, A J, Martin, A C and Bush, V D (2004), Sports celebrity influence on the behavioural intentions of Generation Y, *Journal of Advertising Research*
Connor, J and Mazanov, J (2010), The inevitability of scandal: lessons for sponsors and administrators, *International Journal of Sports Marketing & Sponsorship*
Davies, F (2009), An investigation into the effect of sporting involvement and alcohol sponsorship on underage drinking, *International Journal of Sports Marketing & Sponsorship*
Hill, D (2010), A critical mass of corruption: Why some football leagues have more match-fixing than others, *International Journal of Sports Marketing & Sponsorship*
International Chamber of Commerce (2011), Advertising and Marketing Communication Practice Consolidated ICC Code, ICC
Jones, S (2010), When does alcohol sponsorship of sport become sports sponsorship of alcohol?, *International Journal of Sports Marketing & Sponsorship*
Khan, A, Stanton, J and Rahman, S (2013), Employees' attitudes towards the sponsorship activity of their employer and links to their organisational citizenship behaviours, *International Journal of Sports Marketing & Sponsorship*
Kolah, A (2006), *Advanced Sports Sponsorship Strategies*, SportBusiness Group
Kolah, A (2013), *Essential Law for Marketers*, 2nd edn, Kogan Page
MacNiven, R and Kelly, B (2012), Sports sponsorship and kids' health: Who are the real winners?, *The Conversation*
Parker, H and Fink, J (2010), Negative sponsor behaviour, team response and how this impacts fan attitudes, *International Journal of Sports Marketing & Sponsorship*
Pettigrew, S, Rosenberg, M, Ferguson R, Houghton, S and Wood, L (2013), Game on: Do children absorb sports sponsorship messages?, *Public Health Nutrition*
Portman Group (2014), *Code of Practice on Alcohol Sponsorship*, 1st edn, Portman Group
Solberg, H, Hanstad, D and Thøring, T (2010), Doping in elite sport – Do the fans care?, *International Journal of Sports Marketing & Sponsorship*

Websites

AlcoholAction Ireland [accessed 16 August 2014]: http://alcoholireland.ie

Centres for Disease Control and Prevention [accessed 19 September 2014]: http://www.cdc.gov/

Institute of Alcohol Studies [accessed 16 August 2014]: http://www.ias.org.uk

Medicines and Healthcare Products Regulatory Agency [accessed 19 September 2014]: http://www.mhra.gov.uk/

US Food and Drug Administration [accessed 19 September 2014]: http://www.fda.gov/NewsEvents/PublicHealthFocus/ucm172906.htm

Reports

All Party Parliamentary Group on Alcohol Misuse, Manifesto 2015

Chartered Institute of Marketing (2011), Ambush Marketing and the Law

European Sponsorship Association (2012), Guidelines for Rights Holders Regarding Alcohol Sponsorship, ESA Publications

European Sponsorship Association (2012), Legal Clauses for Rights Holders Regarding Alcohol Sponsorship, ESA Publications

European Sponsorship Association (2014), Policy Paper on Ambush Marketing, ESA Publications

European Sponsorship Association (2011), Position Statement on Gambling Sponsorship, ESA Publications

World Health Organisation (2013), Banning Tobacco Advertising, Promotion and Sponsorship – What you need to know

7   Legal principles of sponsorship

In this chapter

- Nature of sponsorship agreement
- Rights and obligations of the property owner (rights holder)
- Rights and obligations of the brand owner (sponsor)
- Management of intellectual property (IP) rights
- Broadcast sponsorship regulatory framework
- Bribery and corruption legislation

Introduction

The sponsorship agreement is a marketing tool for the brand owner/sponsor as well as being an important funding stream for almost any type of sponsorship activity. The objections to the involvement of sponsors in sport used to be a controversial issue guaranteed to send games organisers into a tailspin.

This type of reaction has not totally evaporated but has been tempered in the wake of massive decreases in funding going into organised sports across the world as governments around the world struggle to balance their budgets and priorities in addition to the rising costs of staging major sports events.

The nature of sponsorship involvement in the arts, education and the environment is no less controversial because of concerns regarding undue influence over what is taught to children and young people; the use of corporate social responsibility (CSR) as a shield from the media, which may look to attack a poor environmental or safety record or indeed the over-commercialisation of 'art', which has made it 'safe' in order to attract funding from sponsors who are more concerned with not wanting to cause some sections of the public to be offended.

The key mechanism for regulating the relationship between the rights holder, property and brand owner is the sponsorship agreement. On one level, it is about the sponsor taking advantage of the goodwill associated with a particular individual, cause, event, league, team or activity. In simple terms, the sponsorship agreement is a commercial relationship. If there is not a contractual nature to the agreement that sets out rights and obligations, on both sides as well as defining the economic value of those rights and obligations, then it is unlikely to be a sponsorship agreement.

In the past, sponsorship agreements were largely concerned with leveraging goodwill, profile and the use of branding, merchandising and licensing rights for the intellectual property owned by the rights holder. Today, it is much more complex and often the rights involve relationships with third parties, unique content, and, of course, access to data about customers, prospects and fans, as well as using promotions, prizes and competitions that have been 'officially' sanctioned by the rights holder.

Nature of a sponsorship agreement

There are principally ten types of sponsorship arrangement that are commonly entered into:

- venue sponsorship
- exclusivity sponsorship
- multi-partner sponsorship
- secondary sponsorship
- personality sponsorship/endorsement
- broadcast sponsorship
- editorial sponsorship
- hybrid sponsorship – advertiser-funded programming (AFP)
- community-linked sponsorship
- official supplier status.

Venue sponsorship

Venue sponsorship is a relatively new development in the UK and is often referred to as naming rights and only applies to a physical structure or building. These types of sponsorship arrangement are more common in Europe and the USA. Notable examples in the UK include the Emirates Stadium in London and the former Millennium Dome which is now the O2 Arena in the London Docklands and was used as a venue at the London 2012 Olympic Games, although the O2 signage was covered as a result of the clean stadiums policy of the International Olympic Committee (IOC).

In essence, venue sponsorship is a hybrid of advertising and sponsorship rights, where the sponsor's name is physically attached to the stadium or building and sits on top of a pyramid of other tangible and intangible rights. For example, all broadcast of content from the venue is likely to include the name of the sponsor and all tickets, merchandise and publicity for the venue is also likely to carry the sponsor's brand identity, logo and trademarks.

Exclusivity sponsorship

The promotional value of being an exclusive team sponsor, such as Shell and Ferrari F1, can be extremely powerful, given the amount of broadcast media coverage that F1 attracts. In football, Barclays is the exclusive sponsor of the Premiership

League and this has opened up new communications opportunities with fans, customers and prospects on a scale that could not have been achieved in the absence of the sponsorship investment.

Multi-partner sponsorship

A multi-sponsor format involves several sponsors benefiting from a basket of identical sponsorship rights or having different levels of sponsorship rights commensurate with the amount of sponsorship fees, benefits-in-kind and value-in-kind invested by the sponsor.

Examples include the Victoria & Albert Museum, which has a host of sponsors from Apple to Viking River Cruises and the Indian Premier League (cricket), which has Pepsi (title sponsor), official partners Vodafone, Star Plus, Yes Bank, and official broadcast partners Sony Max and Sony Six.

These types of sponsorship work particularly efficiently where a brand owner wants to reach a consumer audience on a global basis and relies heavily on broadcast coverage to do the job. In the case of the Olympic Games, which does not permit any form of branding on athletes or hoardings within the line of camera view, sponsors must be creative in activating their sponsorship rights in other ways, such as on merchandise and at the point of sale within a retail environment.

From a rights holder's perspective, sponsorship clutter needs to be avoided. For example, the UEFA Champions League currently limits the number of its sponsors to six in order to deliver a higher level of media exposure for Heineken, PlayStation, Mastercard, UniCredit, Adidas and Ford of Europe.

Secondary sponsorship

This describes that status of a sponsor that provides lower-level cash that is counterbalanced by a larger benefit-in-kind or value-in-kind contribution to the rights holder.

For example, Heineken enjoys primary sponsorship of the European Rugby Cup (the 'Heineken Cup') with a range of secondary sponsors, including FedEx, Amlin, Adidas and EDF, supporting the event.

Personality sponsorship/endorsement

Many superstars have individual sponsorship deals in place by which they endorse a particular product or service. For example, Hollywood actor George Clooney has a global endorsement deal with Nescafé for a range of its coffee products and coffee machines. And Mercedes-Benz has a multiplatform global marketing partnership with the 16-time Grand Slam champion Roger Federer that covers the use of his image, personal appearances and product placement in a partnership that makes the tennis star a global ambassador for the brand.

Tiger Woods went into the record books as the highest paid sportsman in history in groundbreaking deal with long-time sponsor Nike in 2013.

Broadcast sponsorship

Broadcast sponsorship is typically the sponsorship of a TV or radio broadcast on a commercial channel or the channel itself. In the case of the broadcast sponsorship of an event, the broadcast sponsor will enter into a separate arrangement with the broadcaster and may therefore be different from the event sponsor.

The event organiser may either license the right to broadcast the event to a production company, which will then sublicense these rights to broadcasters, or the rights holder may commission a producer but sell the broadcast rights itself directly to broadcasters. Television and radio rights are commonly sold on an individual territory basis and often before sponsors have been acquired. This is common in the case of TV broadcasts, as a sponsor will usually make TV exposure a condition of entering into any sponsorship agreement, as in the case of UEFA's Champions League.

Broadcast sponsorship of a programme or series will confer on the sponsor rights to associate itself with each programme in 'bumpers' around the opening and closing credits as well as in the ad breaks and must comply with strict Ofcom regulations.

Editorial sponsorship

Editorial sponsorship is a bit like an 'advertorial', although the copy is not generated by the brand owner but by a journalist working for the newspaper, magazine or website.

Hybrid sponsorship – advertiser-funded programming (AFP)

In the future, AFP will become much more commonplace than it is at present, as viewers reject the old interruption model of TV advertising. Within the industry there is often talk about the loss of editorial 'ownership' but this ignores the fact that AFPs are subject to the same Ofcom broadcasting code rules as conventional sponsored programmes.

Crucially, the sponsor must not influence programming content or scheduling in such a way as to affect the editorial independence or responsibility of the broadcaster, and the commercial relationship must be transparent to the viewer.

However, during the initiation phase, before deciding to invest their collective time and money in the programme idea, the broadcaster, producer and advertiser will have discussed and agreed the following critical details:

- programme format and script outline
- cast outline, including presenter
- sponsorship credits.

As to 'ownership', the extent to which any additional approvals are awarded may depend on the extent to which the brand owner is funding the project: for example, this could be fully funded or a co-production with rights shared by the broadcaster or producer.

These AFP rights may include:

- platforms and territories for distribution, for example, mobile, online and geographic regions
- any third-party licensing rights, for example, logos, use of copyright by others
- marketing and PR activity in support of the programme/ content.

An advertiser can have more influence on the co-creation and deployment of off-air and multiplatform brand content assets. According to Thinkbox, the body set up to help promote TV advertising in the UK, this framework helps to define the various roles and protect the editorial independence and integrity of the production. In so doing, it creates a powerful platform for brand content marketing – programmes that viewers will want to watch, from people who know how to make them.

Through brand content programming, advertisers have the opportunity to engage with consumers in the context of entertainment that reflects their brand values, and to turn that engagement into dialogue.

A deep relationship with good TV programming creates a hub around which a plethora of promotional tools can spin, both on air and off air. These include online and mobile applications, events, merchandise, PR, trade hospitality, point-of-sale licensing and other media promotions. Non-broadcast platforms are an excellent means of amplifying the broadcast commission.

Community-linked sponsorship

To some extent this is corporate social responsibility (CSR) but under a different name (see also Chapter 9). The nature of this type of sponsorship is different from other forms of sponsorship because it satisfies a range of sponsor objectives that are more community-rather than commercially based. In this respect, a community-linked sponsorship, such as a brand owner funding a healthy-eating programme in schools through educational literature, helps put a 'halo' around the brand rather than necessarily driving incremental sales; although the latter may occur as a result of the activity where messaging about healthy eating extends beyond the school gates and into the homes of families, where it can then influence their purchasing behaviour.

Official supplier status

Under such an arrangement, an existing sponsor can receive enhanced rights as 'the official supplier' of a product or service category it wishes to associate with the event for marketing purposes. Alternatively, 'official supplier' status can be conferred on a brand owner that is not a full-blown sponsor of the event or property. This indicates a lower level of commitment.

For example, 'official supplier' status will almost always include category exclusivity such as kit supply agreements often entered into with sports brand owners such as Nike and Adidas.

Rights and obligations of the property owner (rights holder)

With respect to a single event, the rights holder will typically accept the following non-exhaustive legal obligations to:

- make all the necessary arrangements for the event to take place
- ensure that the venue has the necessary facilities to enable performance of all its obligations
- comply with applicable regulations, whether national or particular to the type of event (for example, regulations of a sports governing body)
- not materially alter the format or schedule of the event in a way that would impact the value of the rights acquired by the sponsor
- fulfil all its obligations to third parties who provide goods, services or facilities for the event
- not incur any unnecessary expense or liability for the sponsor outside any implied, usual or actual authority given by the sponsor to act on its behalf
- use its sales and marketing capabilities to promote the event to agreed market and customer segments
- guarantee that a particular level of TV coverage will be provided
- allow access by the sponsor to the venue before the event to install agreed display, product and/or sampling opportunities
- provide special access for the sponsor and its guests to VIP areas and also include privileged parking rights near to where the hospitality is taking place
- appoint secondary sponsors, where appropriate, to work alongside the main sponsor
- indemnify the sponsor against any expense or liability arising from breach of any warranties given under the terms of the sponsorship agreement
- maintain necessary insurance cover, for example, for the cancellation or postponement of the event and for third-party liability
- not assign the benefit of any of the obligations under the sponsorship agreement to a third party without the agreement of the sponsor.

Rights and obligations of the brand owner (sponsor)

As I have already mentioned, sponsorship is a basket of tangible and intangible rights that the sponsor will need to activate in order to unlock the value of that sponsorship investment (see Table 7.1).

The rights and obligations of a sponsor will largely depend on the objectives it is trying to achieve as a result of becoming or continuing as a sponsor. The provision of sponsorship funding does not automatically entitle a sponsor to any proprietary rights or control over a marketing opportunity. In order to maximise

Table 7.1 Tangible and intangible rights for a sponsor

Tangible rights	Description	Intangible rights	Description
Media exposure	This may be as a result of broadcast coverage of the sponsorship property and can be measured in terms of hours, minutes and seconds of broadcast media coverage.	Positive brand perception among desired audience and customer segments.	This is important for all sponsors, as the perception of the brand among key stakeholder groups can have a dramatic impact on sales of its products and services.
Tickets	This is very often the easiest of rights to measure from a financial perspective, as each ticket has a face value, and typically this will be discounted as part of the sponsorship package sold to the sponsor.	Tickets are the currency for networking opportunities with influencers, authorisers and specifiers hosted by the sponsor.	Good, old-fashioned face-to-face contact is extremely important in a 'wired world' where relationships are still important. Inviting an existing customer or client by providing them with a ticket to an appropriate event can open the door to some strong ongoing networking opportunities.
Hospitality	Corporate entertainment at a venue or event is extremely powerful for customer relationship management.	Networking with customers and prospects can help oil the wheels of business development.	These activities are subject to the Bribery Act 2010, which places a higher standard of ethical behaviour on organisations and its officers.
Advertising and signage	This is very important within a stadium or facility, where such signage can help to brand the location and demonstrate a link with the sponsor and the property in a high-impact way.	Prestige and reputational enhancement.	Part of the allure of sponsorship for the brand owner is the feeling of prestige of being part of something that arouses passion among audiences it wants to reach.
Database access	Data about fans and prospects is extremely valuable but must be collected on a permission basis.	Open dialogue with audience and customer segments in a more meaningful way and on the back of something that they are genuinely passionate about.	Given the long-term nature of sponsorship, there is a good opportunity for developing the database of customers and prospects in the future, subject to the Data Protection Act 1998.

Specialist knowledge/ expertise	For example, if the sponsorship is in sport, education, environment or the arts, then it is likely the sponsor will have access to specialist knowledge and expertise that it would not have enjoyed in the absence of the sponsorship.	Teamwork with the rights owner that empowers the sponsor and deepens the relationship between the parties.	There is a lot that business can learn from sponsorship in terms of teamwork, leadership and performance, and involving the coach of a successful sports team to work with the management of the sponsor can be an enlightening and fulfilling experience.
Conference/ meeting and product showcase facilities	Facilities at the venue, such as a stadium, will have a commercial value and be part of the sponsorship package.	Convenience of location and access to facilities that saves the sponsor time and money.	Given that there is an existing relationship between the sponsor and the rights holder, using conference facilities at a stadium for internal and external events should be much easier to organise.
Sampling and pouring rights	These are particularly valuable rights for an FMCG sponsor in order to avoid a competitor's products being served or sampled at the venue.	Exclusivity and prestige.	The opportunity to run sampling among a highly targeted customer segment, as well as positioning the product within an exciting and engaging environment without any competitor distractions, can be uplifting for the brand.
Personal appearances of celebrities, individuals and team members	This is another valuable tangible benefit, as high-profile athletes and celebrities can often be a big draw for clients and employees and add the 'wow' factor.	'Money-can't-buy' experiences using high-profile athletes and celebrities in their fields when engaging with customers and clients can be extremely memorable for the guests.	Building good relationships with employees and third parties that are important to the business.
Content production	This is becoming extremely important, particularly 'behind the scenes' video material, as well as user-generated content by fans and others.	Building a strong relationship with supporters/fans.	Making content exclusive to an audience by viral and mobile channels can be very powerful in keeping customers engaged with the brand and for building loyalty.
Marketing communications	Many sponsors expect to see a proportionate amount of activity by the rights holder in helping to activate the sponsorship in order to unlock its benefits.	Sounding board for ideas and buy-in to the 'brand world' of the sponsor by the rights holder.	Sponsorship is all about great teamwork – and working with the rights holder's own in-house team or external agency or agencies can be extremely cost effective for the sponsor in its own marketing communications activities.

the marketing and brand-building opportunities, a licence to use proprietary rights for certain purposes must therefore be acquired.

The IP rights to be licensed are diverse and include the name of the sponsored property, for example, the team, event or venue and logo for promotional and merchandising activities. In addition, in some cases, the image or personality rights of sports personalities and celebrities may also be licensed to the sponsor. The following is not an exhaustive list of the rights and obligations of a sponsor but covers those terms most likely to be found in a sponsorship agreement:

Exclusivity

Sponsors may expect different levels of exclusivity depending on the level of sponsorship investment. It is possible for the rights holder to grant and the sponsor to receive a certain degree of exclusivity. Many rights holders will offer sponsorship opportunities in various packages, which may involve title sponsorship rights for one brand owner along with various designations and a package of secondary or ancillary rights for other sponsors.

In other cases, there may be a number of deals at one primary level (for example, 4–8) and a similar number of second-level deals. In this situation, which is typical of international events, the rights packages will differ significantly in terms of costs and benefits delivered to the sponsors, as well as the territory that those rights are restricted to. It is in the sponsor's best interests to ensure that rights holders do not offer such packages with impunity and they are given some comfort on the number of partners and a degree of exclusivity which they are granted in the sponsorship agreement.

Obviously the considerations here vary enormously and will depend on the relative bargaining power of the rights holder and the profile of the property concerned. Within global sports events, a sponsor may be able to obtain complete exclusivity and ensure that no other sponsors are appointed for any number of reasons, including the amount of rights fee paid, the popularity of the event, and the availability of broadcast coverage.

The fact is that most rights holders will be unable or unwilling to grant total exclusivity to one sponsor, as this will curtail other opportunities for engaging with other potential sponsors and limit the sponsorship revenues that can be achieved for the rights holder. Although it is unlikely the sponsorship agreement will give the rights holder complete freedom to appoint other sponsors, it will usually be able to do so if there is an agreed well-structured package of rights and sensible exclusivity provisions with sponsors. It is unlikely that any sponsors will consent to a package of rights being granted to one of its competitors within its market segment.

Duration of the agreement

The sponsorship agreement may or may not have a defined duration. In the case of a specified term, the circumstances and terms on which the period can be extended should be defined. For example, in sports sponsorship, the average length of a football shirt sponsorship deal is three years. Other examples include a club season or the period of an annual event or competition.

In contrast, a naming rights deal on a new football stadium could be as long as 15–20 years. With respect to an event or TV broadcast, a sponsor will want to ensure there are timetables specified for the occurrence of the relevant event or broadcast of the sponsored programme. Where there is a fixed term sponsorship agreement, this will expire on an agreed date subject to any options to renew or any other extensions to the agreement. Although the precise length of a sponsorship arrangement will be subject to a number of commercial factors, the actual provisions of the agreement relating to the term tend to be reasonably straightforward. The sponsor should ensure that it obtains the rights for a sufficient length of time to leverage its association with the rights holder and to build up a certain amount of goodwill to exploit the sponsorship successfully.

For a sponsorship based on relationship and association, such as a club or team sponsorship, then three years would be a fair functional minimum. The same may apply to a sponsorship of an annual competition. A more 'project-specific' sponsorship could be much shorter.

Termination

The termination date of the sponsorship agreement should take account of all the opportunities the sponsor wants to exploit from the relationship. For example, if the sponsor wants to sell merchandise after the event has taken place, it should expressly reserve the right to exploit its association with the rights holder for 90 days or longer after the event has ended.

The sponsor should also retain the right to terminate the sponsorship agreement prematurely if the rights holder goes into liquidation or fails to fulfil some or all of its obligations, such as failing to spend the sponsorship income on specified items, not obtaining additional sponsorship, not staging the event within a specific timescale or if one event in a long-term campaign does not meet specified criteria.

Any compensation payable in such a case must be expressly stated in the agreement. The consequences of termination or post-termination restrictions must also be specified carefully. A sponsor may also wish to include a provision to terminate if the sponsored property has changed its image, for example, if a famous athlete has tested positive for the use of banned drugs and a full investigation corroborates this finding.

Where certain elements of a sponsorship agreement are of the 'essence' of the sponsorship, for example, the appearance of certain sports personalities at an event on specified TV coverage, the sponsor should reserve the right to terminate the sponsorship agreement if these elements are not delivered. The fundamental matters giving rise to the sponsor's right to terminate should be cited as essential conditions within the body of the sponsorship agreement. If these fundamental matters remain unfulfilled, the right to terminate should be stated to be automatic and immediate. The alternative is to allow the rights holder a specified time to remedy the fundamental breach. If a condition is not phrased in this way, damages for breach of contract may be held to be a sufficient remedy.

Any notice required to be given should allow both parties time to put alternative arrangements in place. In the event of termination, there should be provisions preventing the parties from continuing to promote their connection with each other and other provisions dealing with the handover of materials, logistics and any forward commitments made by the incumbent sponsor that may bind the new sponsor.

Payment structures

The sponsorship agreement may structure the payment method in a number of ways depending on various factors such as cash flow, risk assessment and tax effectiveness.

Different methods of funding sponsorship include the following:

Fixed amount

The sponsorship fee may be payable upfront or at fixed intervals, for example, in the case of F1, where payments are made for each of the individual grand prix races held.

Repeat fees are normally subject to an annual increment calculated according to a specific formula or are renegotiable following an agreed period.

Brand owners should avoid payment of the whole sponsorship fee in advance if a marketing opportunity is new and there is no guarantee that it will deliver as agreed or at all. In such a case, the brand owner should obtain an agreement to retain a proportion of the sponsorship fee until the agreed criteria have been fulfilled.

Conditional

This arrangement is often appropriate where the sponsor wishes to be satisfied that certain participants will attend, certain performance targets are met, or specified TV coverage is obtained.

The sponsorship agreement must therefore cater for failure of one or more of the rights holder's obligations. A specified consideration should be attached to each of the key rights to be received by the sponsor so that if one or more is not received, the sponsorship fee is reduced accordingly or a refund is due to the sponsor.

Variable

The sponsor may wish to provide additional funds to the sponsored party if certain events occur; for example, a bonus is payable on the team securing promotion to the Premier League. However, a cap on the maximum payable by the sponsor should be considered if this arrangement is chosen.

Value in kind

This involves the sponsor providing something that the rights holder would have had to buy in any event, such as IT or certain facilities that have a clear economic value. For example, for many years IBM has supplied the technology and man-power behind the Wimbledon Tennis Championships as part of its sponsorship of the tournament.

The sponsorship agreement should specify any maintenance or insurance requirements, as well as what will happen to any products or equipment after the event.

Event sponsorship rights

Given the huge choice of potential events available, the first decision a brand owner must take is whether to sponsor a single event, a seasonal or annual event or a one-off long-term project. In some cases, the decision will already have been made by cash constraints, provided the brand owner has been realistic about its cash-flow requirements in each year of the event.

Subject to cash restrictions, the choice will depend on whether the target benefits are to be achieved within a short period or the intention is to make a long-lasting impression. If the latter is the objective, the event must be capable of sustaining a prolonged marketing communications campaign. In order to take full advantage of the sponsorship of an event, it will often be necessary to obtain licences from more than one party. In particular, regarding a sports event, the relevant international or national sports federations may hold certain rights separately from the league organising the event, the participating clubs and individuals and the venue owner.

In addition to the exclusive or non-exclusive right to associate itself with the event and use the rights holder's trademarks in connection with its promotional activities, the sponsor may seek to gain added value from additional activities.

Such additional rights may include any of the following:

- rights to the appointment of a sponsor's representative to the board of the event
- rights to be involved with the organisation and management of the event
- rights to supply and to insist that participants wear particular clothing
- additional advertisements in the event programme, on boards and banners in and around the venue, preferably within view of TV cameras, and product display facilities
- rights to take and publish its own photographs of the event, having obtained the consent of any individuals prominently featured
- rights to use and publish official photographs of the event in marketing campaigns. In such a case a licence of the copyright in the photographs will need to be acquired (along with the consent of the individuals)
- personal endorsement (personality rights) agreements with participating individuals

- right to award prizes and trophies at major events
- guaranteed TV exposure
- sponsorship of TV and/or radio broadcasts
- free tickets, hospitality rights and free parking
- marketing and merchandising rights in respect of the event name and logo.

Hospitality rights

The sponsor will typically be granted the non-exclusive right to use the event's hospitality facilities, including entrance tickets, reserved seating and the use of office, catering and other facilities at the event venue.

Such a right may or may not be at the expense of the sponsor and the right may include access for corporate guests to meet sporting heroes or the cast of a film at a post-launch premiere party.

The sponsorship agreement should also set out any rights and limitations the sponsor may have in the resale of tickets, for example, to the sponsor's customers or clients or in the use of tickets for unconnected promotional activities, such as a competition with a national newspaper, magazine or radio station.

Postponement rights

Unless the date of the event is expressed in the agreement as 'essential', the rights holder may be entitled to postpone the event. If, as a consequence of postponement, it is necessary to amend the material contract terms, the sponsor should be allowed a reasonable period of time to review its position and if necessary withdraw from its sponsorship. Third-party contracts may also need to be extended or renegotiated.

A sponsor should consider insurance to cover any costs incurred as a result of the postponement of an event because of bad weather or an act of war (force majeure), which is unfortunately more than a theoretical risk today.

Duration of the agreement

In the case of one-off events, the sponsorship agreement will usually cover the event and any postponement, plus any post-event period during which the sponsor may continue its association with the event. Periodic events may be treated in the same way or as a series of events with the sponsorship agreement also covering any period of inactivity in between events.

Cancellation rights

Whether cancellation of the event constitutes a breach of contract depends on the wording of the sponsorship agreement. A breach may entitle the sponsor to:

- recover damages for wasted expenses incurred as a result of a campaign to promote its products and services in connection with the event

- all or part of any sponsorship fees paid, depending on whether it can be shown to have received some benefit from these already
- damages for lost opportunity, if that can be clearly demonstrated and they are recoverable in law.

Renewal rights

If an event is seasonal or annual, the parties may wish to maximise the return on their investment in the relationship by agreeing to maintain their relationship for a minimum number of years or seasons. For example, Emirates deal with Arsenal FC was signed in 2004 and is expected to run past 2021.

It is, therefore, important to specify the minimum number of years or seasons up front and if relevant include a provision in the agreement such that at the end of the initial period there is a recalculation of the sponsorship fees on renewal by reference to a specified formula.

Matching option rights

If the sponsor wants to have an ongoing relationship with a particular event but is not prepared to commit up front, then the sponsor should consider including an option to renew the sponsorship either on payment of an increased fee or through a matching rights option which is designed to establish the market value of the event. In simple terms, the sponsor is granted an option to match the highest offer obtained by the sponsored party from any other bona fide potential sponsor.

Such options need safeguards to ensure that rights owners cannot simply obtain a false offer from a third party in a bid to inflate a potential offer from the incumbent sponsor. Where the sponsor has effectively helped create and fund a new event and build it into something prestigious, matching option rights are a particularly effective method of achieving a return on investment and a marketing advantage over its rivals by locking them out of entering into a fresh agreement with the rights holder, should the sponsor wish to renew.

Clauses giving the sponsor a first 'right of refusal' to renew the sponsorship contact must be carefully drafted to prevent a rights holder attempting to circumvent its terms.

In order to protect the sponsor, the option must include the following key clauses:

- a clear statement of precisely what it is the sponsor has the first option to accept
- a time frame for negotiations – these should begin before the expiry of the existing agreement to enable a new agreement to be made
- a deadline for the acceptance of the new sponsorship package.

Management of intellectual property (IP) rights

Sponsorship is a complex web of (IP) rights that belong to the rights holder, sponsor and increasingly broadcasters of an event that needs to be coordinated and managed. Figure 7.1 provides a schematic of some of the IP rights involved in a televised football match.

Some of the most valuable IP rights are trademarks, copyright and personality rights.

Trademarks

The rights holder and sponsor should ensure that their respective trademarks are registered in all territories relevant to the event, particularly if this is broadcast internationally. The event logo and identity and other marks should be registered separately.

If the event logo was created by independent designers, assignment of their rights in the mark should be made to the event rights holder.

The sponsor will require a licence to use the rights holder's logo or event name on its products and marketing literature and in promotional and advertising campaigns.

In return, the event organiser will want a non-exclusive licence to use the sponsor's trademark for specified purposes, which typically include advertising promotions and related public relations activities.

Licensees of official licensed merchandise may also be interested in using both the event logo and the sponsor's trademark and such deals need to be carefully negotiated, for example, to ensure that the brand guidelines and sign-off procedures for the use of those marks are followed.

Copyright

A sponsor may also want to use photographs or film footage in a future promotional marketing campaign but will need to ascertain who owns the copyright in such works in order to start to negotiate a licence for the use of that content.

Personality/image rights

The publication of photographs featuring star players and celebrities requires careful consideration. Personality rights are recognised in a number of jurisdictions outside the UK, including the USA, France, Italy and Germany, where greater protection is available for celebrities with respect to the use of their image.

There is no such legal protection for privacy under UK law, although many lawyers argue that the protection of privacy exists through the back door as a result of the Human Rights Act 1998.

As I have discussed in previous chapters, the unauthorised use of a person's image may also be actionable under the tort of passing off, defamation and in an action for malicious falsehood.

In the USA, however, the situation is very different. For example, in New York, an individual's personality rights are protected as well as her right of publicity.

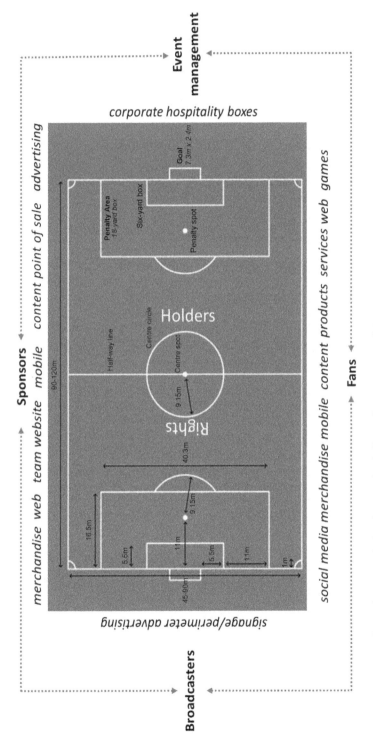

Figure 7.1 Key intellectual property (IP) rights in a football match on commercial TV

Source: Kolah (2015)

The safest route for a marketer is always to get written permission for the use of the photograph or broadcast material for its own marketing and promotional purposes, although a copyright licence fee for the use of such material may be required.

Various industry codes of practice contain guidance on the use of an individual's image. For example, the Broadcast Committee of Advertising Practice (BCAP) Code provides that living persons must not be portrayed or referred to in TV ads without their permission.

Marketers must be careful when using 'stock' or 'library' footage of celebrities or sports personalities, as the copyright in the image is one issue; the use of the image or likeness of a famous person and the commercial context of that use are a completely separate matter.

IP rights in an event itself

In terms of IP rights, performances of a dramatic nature that include works of dance or mime are protected by copyright, but there is no IP right in sport, as this is not generally considered to be dramatic works under the Copyright Designs and Patents Act 1988.

Instead, sponsorship rights are 'controlled' contractually through the agreements entered into by the organiser of the event (the rights holder).

Competition law

Article 101 of the Treaty on the Functioning of the European Union (TFEU) (formerly Article 81 of the EC Treaty) prohibits agreements which prevent, distort or restrict competition in the EU and which have an appreciable effect on trade between EU member states. Provided sponsorship is organised in a fair, open and transparent way and the rights owner does not abuse a dominant position in the market, there will generally be no grounds for intervention under EU competition rules.

Nevertheless, one particular issue that will give rise to competition concerns is a requirement that only equipment or goods of a certain manufacturer may be used during an event. Sponsorship should not result in the grant of an exclusive right for a manufacturer to supply a market with its products in such a way that excludes competitors. So, for example, a league or championship could not enter into a sponsorship with the supplier of certain sports equipment and insist that every player and team had to use that brand of equipment in order to compete in the league or championship.

The European Commission takes the view that unless the 'official supplier' label can be justified on technical grounds, then granting the right to its use may mislead consumers by unjustifiably attributing a label of quality to the products. It must be clear from the label that the relationship concerns a sponsorship/supply arrangement, and does not close off the market to other manufacturers.

Broadcast sponsorship regulatory framework

In the UK, regulator Ofcom is responsible for ensuring that Section 9 of the Broadcasting Code (2011) is observed by broadcasters as it applies to commercial references in TV programming, which includes sponsorship of TV content by a sponsor. Sponsorship is not permissible on the BBC, as this is funded through the TV licence fee and sponsorship of its programmes would be incompatible with its public service broadcasting remit.

Terminology used in the Broadcasting Code, 2011

- 'TV programming': This is taken to mean all broadcast content apart from spot advertising and teleshopping.
- 'Sponsor': This is any public or private undertaking or natural person other than the broadcaster or programme producer who is funding the programming with a view to promoting its products, services, trademarks and/or its activities.
- 'Sponsor reference': This is any reference to the sponsor's products, services or trademarks.
- 'Sponsored programming/channel': This is programming that has had some or all of its costs met by a sponsor and includes advertiser-funded programmes (AFP). Sponsored programming covers a single programme, a single channel, a programme segment or block of programmes.
- 'Sponsorship credit': This is an announcement that informs the viewer when content is sponsored and by whom.
- 'Costs': In relation to broadcast sponsorship, this refers to any part of the costs connected with the production or broadcast of the programming.

Current position as to TV sponsorship

Subject to certain rules, programme and channel sponsorship is permitted where the primary purpose of the sponsor is the promotion of its products, services, trademark or activities.

Under the rules, sponsors can fund programmes at any stage of the production process; for example, a broadcaster may sell the sponsorship of a programme that it has commissioned or produced itself or an advertiser may directly fund the production of content on that channel (AFP).

In addition, sponsors now have the flexibility to fund blocks of programmes, programme segments or entire TV channels. The rules attempt to strike a balance between allowing a brand owner the promotional benefit of being associated with the content it is sponsoring while at the same time ensuring that sponsorship arrangements do not lead to a blurring of the boundaries between editorial and advertising that surreptitiously or otherwise can be taken as a form of 'viewer deception'. For example, the line is drawn preventing a sponsored programme overtly promoting a sponsor's individual products and services.

The rules require broadcasters to retain editorial independence over sponsored content, as well as ensuring the audience is told when content is sponsored and preventing unsuitable sponsorship from reaching the small screen.

When a reference to the sponsor within a sponsored programme meets the definition of 'product placement', then Ofcom licensees must comply with the rules on product placement.

What has not changed under the new regime is that sponsorship of news and current affairs is not permitted. However, short specialist reports that accompany news, such as sport, travel and weather reports can be sponsored, provided that such content does not itself comprise material that constitutes news or current affairs.

Such programme inserts should also look distinct from the rest of the news output and this can be achieved by using different presenters and a different set so that viewers are not under any misapprehension as to the sponsored content that is being presented within the show.

Compliance issues

Both the Broadcast Committee on Advertising Practice (BCAP) and the Committee on Advertising Practice (CAP) Codes provide a list of prohibited categories of advertisers that are barred from undertaking any form of programme or channel sponsorship and these include:

- political parties
- tobacco brands
- prescription-only medicine brands
- guns and gun clubs
- adult sexual services.

In addition, the BCAP Code prevents any deviation from the content and scheduling rules. For example, a children's programme may not be sponsored by a product that is high in fat, sugar or salt.

Commissioning of programmes that attract sponsorship

Brand owners can legitimately get involved in the commissioning and creation of programmes, although such arrangements should not lead to the creation of content that is a vehicle for the purpose of nakedly promoting its commercial interests or the distortion of editorial content for that purpose.

The broadcaster must ensure that it retains ultimate editorial control over the programmes it transmits in order to prevent the viewer from being exploited by such overt commercialisation of TV programme content.

Reference to the sponsor within programming

There are limited circumstances in which a sponsor or its interests may be referred to during a programme as a result of a commercial arrangement with the broadcaster or programme maker. For example, in the case of a product placement arrangement or when the sponsorship arrangement is identified, it must also comply with the relevant product placement rules as I discussed in Chapter 5.

An incidental reference to the brand owner that is not part of any commercial arrangement is also caught by Section 9 of the Broadcasting Code (2011) – for example, when a product is acquired for use as a prop or when a reference to one of the sponsor's products is unintentionally included in a programme as a result of filming on location.

Advertiser-funded programming (AFP)

In the case of AFP, where the sponsor has been involved in the creation of the programme, any reference to the sponsor or its commercial interests is likely to be considered to be deliberate and therefore subject to the product placement rules.

References to generic products or services that are associated with the sponsor may also be treated as product placement depending on the circumstances. For example, a generic reference to a product that is synonymous with the brand owner is more likely to be treated as product placement than a generic reference to a product that is not associated with a particular brand.

Programme credits

Broadcast sponsorship must be clearly identified by means of sponsorship credits and these must make clear:

- the identity of the sponsor by reference to its name or trademark
- the association between the sponsor and the sponsored content.

Viewers should be told when a programme is sponsored and the identity of the sponsor. The sponsor's association with the sponsored content must be clear to the audience in all sponsorship credits.

Broadcasters are free to use various and different creative messages to identify sponsorship arrangements, for example: 'sponsored by . . .', 'in association with . . .', 'brought to you by . . .' and other such phrases.

However, care should be taken to avoid ambiguous statements that may lead to viewer confusion over the nature and purpose of the announcement. Sponsorship messages should not suggest the sponsorship arrangement has in any way compromised the requirements of the BCAP Code.

To ensure viewers are made aware when a programme is sponsored, credits must be broadcast at either the beginning, during or end of the programme. To help ensure transparency, credits may be broadcast at each of these junctures as well as the 'bumpers' in the programme. The rules on undue prominence apply and excessively long sponsorship credits or frequent internal credits are likely to be unacceptable under the BCAP Code.

For sponsored content other than programmes, such as programme segments or TV channels, sponsorship credits should be broadcast at appropriate points during the schedule to ensure viewers are able to identify sponsored content. For example, where a programme segment or item is sponsored – such as a cookery spot in a magazine format or a sports programme – credits could be broadcast at the time the segment or item is shown.

Distinction between sponsorship and editorial content

Viewers should be able to distinguish at all times between editorial content and paid-for commercial references. As a result, particular care is required when a sponsorship credit is broadcast during a programme to ensure that it is not confused with editorial content.

The rules permit the use of programme elements in sponsorship credits and this can include a presenter or character actor appearing in sponsorship credits but broadcasters must exercise caution to avoid blurring the distinction between sponsorship credits and editorial content.

Sponsorship credits must be distinct from advertising

The rules provide that:

- sponsorship credits broadcast around sponsored programmes must not contain advertising messages or calls to action
- sponsorship credits must not encourage the purchase or rental of the products or services of the sponsor or a third party.

Sponsorship credits are an intrinsic part of the sponsored content (albeit distinct from editorial) and their purpose is to identify sponsorship arrangements: they are not a platform for a sponsor to sell its products or services to the viewer.

The focus of the credit must be the sponsorship arrangement itself. Such credits may include explicit reference to the sponsor's products, services or trademarks for the sole purpose of helping to identify the sponsor and/or the sponsorship arrangement.

Article 10(1) (b) of the Audio Visual Media Services Directive 2010/13/EU provides that sponsored programmes 'must not directly encourage the purchase or rental of goods or services, in particular by making special promotional references to those goods or services'. Sponsorship credits should therefore fulfil the role of identifying the sponsorship arrangement and not be capable of being confused with advertising by focusing on the products or services of the sponsor.

Ofcom adjudication of Aviva sponsorship of ITV 1 drama Downton Abbey, 2011

The sponsorship credits featured a 'mini-drama' involving a character called 'Gary'.

Each credit throughout the episode reflected a development in the storyline of Gary's motorbike accident, his recovery, his inability to return to work and his decision to retrain for a new career. One of the sponsorship credits consisted of the following: Gary and his wife are sitting on the sofa. Gary is reading a document. His wife asks: 'What are you doing now?' Gary responds: 'It's my insurance policy. I think I'm still covered if I do that course!' His wife asks: 'Will you have to wear a uniform?' and Gary laughs. The Aviva logo and the caption: 'Aviva Income Protection Sponsors Drama Premieres. Reconstruction. Inspired by actual events' appeared on a yellow strap across the bottom of the screen.

Ofcom ruled that the sponsorship credit was in breach of Rule 9 of the Broadcasting Code (2011), as it referred to a benefit of Aviva's Income Protection Policy and so it was an 'advertising message'.

Channel sponsorship

The BCAP Code permits the sponsorship of programmes, programme segments and channels. Ofcom recognises that the sponsorship of entire channels may raise specific issues in relation to compliance with the sponsorship rules and has produced guidelines to assist broadcasters when entering into channel sponsorship arrangements.

There are certain rules that may render the sponsorship of some channels unacceptable, such as a news and current affairs channel like Sky News. However, channel sponsorship is possible where that channel broadcasts some news and current affairs content, such as ITV1.

However, broadcasters need to ensure that channel sponsorship arrangements do not result in the sponsorship of programmes that may not be sponsored or appear to apply to such programmes.

When assessing whether a channel may be sponsored, Ofcom will take into account the following factors:

- the amount of content to be sponsored on the channel
- where a channel broadcasts content that consists wholly or mainly of programmes that may be sponsored.

In the above example of ITV1, channel sponsorship may be permitted. As a rule of thumb, programmes should normally account for around 75% or higher of the channel's output.

Channels that broadcast a significant amount of programme content that is incapable of being sponsored (25% or higher) are unlikely to be capable of being sponsored by a brand owner.

Identifying channel sponsorship arrangements

The BCAP Code requires sponsorship to be clearly identified and it is important that credits for channel sponsors make clear what is sponsored – the channel and not the programmes – and the identity of the channel sponsor.

Unlike most TV programmes, channels do not have a clearly defined beginning and end at which credits can naturally be placed.

Broadcasters will need to exercise judgment when and where to identify channel sponsorship to ensure that Section 9 of the Broadcasting Code (2011) and the BCAP Code requirements on transparency and distinction are met, while avoiding undue prominence for the sponsor. For example, natural breaks in the broadcast schedule such as after commercial breaks and between programmes would provide suitable junctions at which to place channel sponsorship messaging.

However, care needs to be taken to avoid confusion if a programme sponsorship credit is also broadcast near to a channel sponsorship credit. Channel sponsorship credits, like programme sponsorship credits, must be distinct from both editorial and advertising content. Channel sponsorship may be identified when channel 'idents' are broadcast. However, the size and duration of credits should be limited to avoid giving undue prominence to the sponsor.

Bribery and corruption legislation

One of the many reasons for brand owners undertaking sponsorship is to entertain their key customers, clients and stakeholders. Outside brand image, awareness and credibility, hospitality is an important benefit. For example, in cultural and arts sponsorships in particular, where name awareness and media promotion levels are traditionally much lower than those provided by high-profile sports sponsorships, the ability to offer exclusive entertainment opportunities is often crucial.

Providing tickets and hospitality to a memorable event and creating a 'money-can't-buy' experience for guests are priceless for long-term relationship building. Not least, these occasions also offer something that is more attractive and outstanding than anything done by a brand owner's peers in its market segment.

Yet, despite its obvious attractions, legislators are tightening up the rules on hospitality for fear of the spread of bribery and corruption, although the approaches taken are not always consistent, given the cultural differences that exist throughout the EU and beyond. For example, offering hospitality and gifts is very much part of the tradition in the Middle East and Asia but is less acceptable in a western culture, where, in some cases, it may even be illegal.

An organisation set up to fight global corruption, Transparency International, defines bribery as the 'offering, promising, giving, accepting or soliciting of an advantage as an inducement for an action which is illegal, unethical, or a breach of trust. Inducements can take the form of gifts, loans, fees, rewards or other advantages (such as taxes, services and donations).'

In the UK, the Bribery Act 2010 required commercial organisations as well as those in the public sector to have in place an anti-fraud and bribery policy together with codes of practice for the prevention of bribery by 1 July 2011. This sent a shudder through many marketing and communication departments responsible for managing corporate hospitality and sponsorship, as initially it was thought that influencing clients to gain new deals or retain existing contracts could be considered an illegal activity.

The timing could not have been worse – bosses had started to measure the success of sponsorship not just in terms of how many decision-makers and at what level were being entertained as guests but also what business leads and new business were being generated as a result. However, most of the provisions in the Bribery Act 2010 will make not the slightest difference to any reputable company. They will not have to spend millions of pounds on new control systems, which the compliance industry will tell them they need.

Bribery Act, 2010

Many of the offences under the Bribery Act 2010 refer to 'improper performance' and broadly the test is how a reasonable person in the UK would expect a person to behave, ignoring any local custom or practice unless the law of the relevant country allows or requires that practice.

There are two general bribery offences that can be committed by a person or organisation:

- offering a bribe
- accepting a bribe.

The Bribery Act 2010 only deals with bribery and not other forms of white-collar crime.

The relevance from a hospitality perspective is that an offence will be committed if a person:

- intends to influence the official in his relevant capacity
- intends to get or keep business or a business advantage
- offers or promises, directly or indirectly, a bribe to the official (or another person at the official's request or with his agreement) and the written law that applies to the official does not allow or require him to be influenced.

A brand owner commits an offence if it allows anyone connected with it ('an associated person') to bribe another person intending to get or keep business or a business advantage for the organisation. An 'associated person' is defined as 'a person who performs services by or on behalf of the relevant commercial organisation', such as a public relations or sponsorship agency. However, it is a defence for a brand owner to prove it had in place adequate procedures to prevent persons associated with it from engaging in this conduct.

It is also an offence to bribe a 'foreign public official' and, broadly speaking, this means any person outside the UK who holds any legislative, administrative or judicial position, exercises a public function for any country or public agency or enterprise or is an official or agent of a public international organisation.

The maximum penalty for an offence under the Bribery Act 2010 is ten years' imprisonment and/or an unlimited fine. In the case in which the brand owner fails to prevent a bribery offence from being committed and has not taken reasonable steps to prevent such activities from taking place so that on the balance of probabilities bribery and corruption was likely to occur, then the court will impose a fine.

The Ministry of Justice has laid out six principles to help brand owners in complying with the new duties and obligations under the Bribery Act 2010.

Principle #1: proportionality

The action to be taken by a brand owner should be proportionate to the risks it faces and to the size of its own business.

On this basis, a brand owner might need to carry out a thorough audit to prevent bribery if its organisation is large and operates in an overseas market where bribery is known to be commonplace, compared with a brand owner that has a much smaller organisation and operates in markets where the incidence of bribery is exceptionally rare.

Principle #2: top-level commitment

Those at the top of an organisation are in the best position to ensure their organisation conducts business without bribery. The executive management team running the business will want to show that it has been active in making sure that all employees, as well as the key people who do business with it, understand that it does not tolerate any form of bribery.

Principle #3: risk assessment

A brand owner will need to consider the bribery risks it might face. For example, it may want to do some research into markets and customer segments in terms of customs, traditions and culture to protect itself from being implicated in activities that could be in breach of the Bribery Act 2010.

Principle #4: due diligence

The Ministry of Justice guidance states: 'Knowing exactly who you are dealing with can help to protect your organisation from taking on people who might be less than trustworthy. You may therefore want to ask a few questions and do a few checks before engaging others to represent you in business dealings.'

Principle #5: communication

Communicating ethical and anti-corruption policies and procedures to employees and others who will perform services for the brand owner will raise awareness and help to deter bribery by making clear the basis on which the company or organisation does its business. It may be prudent to provide additional training or awareness-raising among all employees.

Principle #6: monitoring and review

The risks faced and the effectiveness of procedures may change over time and so a brand owner may want to keep an eye on the anti-bribery steps it has taken so that it can keep pace with any changes in the bribery risks it faces when it enters new market segments.

The Ministry of Justice guidance on the issue of hospitality states: 'Bona fide hospitality and promotional or other business expenditure which seeks to improve the image of a commercial organisation better to present products and services or establish cordial relations is recognised as an established and important part of doing business and it is not the intention of the Bribery Act 2010 to criminalise such behaviour.'

In other words, hospitality will be acceptable if it is reasonable and proportionate depending on the circumstances. It should not be overlooked that providing sponsorship itself could be taken as a form of bribery if it is judged to be an undue influence or providing a benefit to a foreign public official related to obtaining or retaining business.

One notable case that caused controversy occurred in 2007, when Nike sent a couple of tickets to the opening match of the Rugby World Cup in Paris to the European Commission's trade office in Geneva, along with the offer of free transport in its company van to Paris.

Adjudication by the European Ombudsman in the Nike case, 2007

In September 2007 Nike offered two officials working for Peter Mandelson, the European Commissioner for Trade at that time, VIP tickets to see the opening game of the Rugby World Cup in Paris. The officials were allowed to accept the offer and also travelled in a car provided by Nike staff from Brussels to Paris.

In December Friends of the Earth wrote to the European Commission asking whether the decision was in line with staff rules. The organisation was not satisfied with the EC's response and brought a complaint to the European Ombudsman, arguing that the two officials could be involved in a conflict of interest because they had been working on anti-dumping duty cases involving sports shoes made in China and Vietnam.

Friends of the Earth pointed out that the EC's own guidance for staff stated that 'as a general rule of thumb you decline all such offers that have more than merely symbolic value'. The European Ombudsman found that the evidence did not suggest that accepting gifts had led to an actual conflict of interest and accepted that the decision to impose anti-dumping duties on imports of sports footwear from Asia was taken a year before the tickets were offered by Nike and there were no ongoing anti-dumping investigations directly relevant to the company.

Nonetheless, he found there was an 'apparent conflict of interest', because it could not be ruled out that the two officials would deal with anti-dumping cases in future. In a letter sent on 20 April 2007, the European Ombudsman Nikiforos Diamondouros offered the EC, as an alternative to a verdict of maladministration, a 'friendly solution' that involved the EC admitting that it should not have allowed the two officials to accept the invitation and also undertaking to change its internal staff rules so that officials would not be allowed to accept such hospitality in the future.

For its part, the EC issued a statement, saying it 'understood the need to guard against both real and apparent conflicts of interest in order to maintain public trust and confidence and to protect staff from unjustified suspicion'.

It should be noted that most anti-bribery legislation like that enacted in the UK has extraterritorial aspects and this is important in relation to multinational sponsorships by a brand owner with a global operation.

The key question is whether the hospitality is provided with the relevant criminal intention at its root. The 'lavishness' of any hospitality is only one factor to be taken into account in determining relevant criminal intent. The safest approach to take is that corporate hospitality should not be lavish or too frequent and be appropriate to the business relationship with the attendees.

The Ministry of Justice guidance note does provide some helpful examples in making such an assessment. For example, an invitation to foreign clients to attend a Six Nations match at Twickenham as part of a public relations exercise designed to cement good relations or enhance knowledge in the organisation's field is extremely unlikely to be a breach of the Bribery Act 2010.

However, the outcome may be different if the invitation were to a foreign public official, as the required intention is different, as can be seen in the Nike case.

The following checklist for brand owners will assist in keeping hospitality within a sponsorship programme legal:

- Establish a company policy on ethical behaviour, including the giving and receiving of hospitality and gifts, based on the principles of transparency, honesty and openness in such dealings.
- Consider imposing limits on the value and type of hospitality to be provided to guests so that it is compatible with the scale and prestige of the sponsored event.
- Ensure recipients clearly understand hospitality is provided on a no-obligation/no-expectation basis.
- Ensure payment for hospitality is made to the services supplier rather than making cash reimbursements to the invitees.
- Consider any hospitality to foreign public officials very carefully and question whether this should be done at all.
- Create a standard procedure for handling requests from within the company or organisation for tickets and hospitality as part of the company's sponsorship programme – this should cover the motivation for the hospitality, whether it is standard practice, who is invited, whether it may impact on any decision-making in the future, whether it is in alignment with company policy to offer such hospitality and whether such provision would stand up to public scrutiny or court of law.
- Consider training all employees and incorporating these procedures into the staff handbook.

- Ensure that all marketing communications agencies know and acknowledge in writing that they will follow the procedures as they relate to sponsorship and hospitality on behalf of the company or organisation.
- Ensure that all dealings with customers and prospects are clearly logged so there is a paper trail of all correspondence and contact linked to the sponsorship activity.

Chapter 7 at a glance

1 The most common types of sponsorship agreement are venue, exclusive, , multi-partner, secondary, personality, broadcast, editorial, advertiser-funded programming, CSR-type sponsorship and official supplier status.
2 One of the key obligations of a rights holder of a televised sponsored event is to guarantee that a particular level of TV coverage will be provided.
3 One of the most valuable rights that a sponsor will look for is exclusivity within its own market segment.
4 There are typically four payment structures that will apply to most sponsorship agreements: fixed amount, conditional, variable and value-in-kind.
5 The most valuable intellectual property (IP) rights in a sponsorship agreement are trademarks, copyright and personality rights.
6 Broadcast sponsorship has been slow to take off in the UK but will gain more acceptance in the form of advertiser-funded programming (AFP) as viewers switch off from traditional advertising, which is increasingly seen as the old interruption model of brand communication. However, regulation in this area is likely to get tighter.
7 The guests of sponsors have tended to react conservatively when receiving an invitation to attend an event at the expense of a sponsor for fear of falling foul of the Bribery Act 2010. Client companies have also brought in draconian internal policies by which any form of hospitality being offered by a sponsor will automatically be turned down. Over the coming years, these entrenched positions are likely to become more flexible and be evaluated on a case-by-case basis.

Questions for discussion

1 What are the most common types of sponsorship agreement likely to be entered into in the UK?
2 What are the key rights and obligations of the rights holder (property owner) under a typical sponsorship deal?
3 What are the key rights and obligations of the sponsor (brand owner) under a typical sponsorship deal?
4 What do sponsors need to do in order to comply with the Broadcasting Code 2011 if they wish to fund a programme on commercial TV?
5 Can a news and current affairs programme be sponsored by a brand owner?
6 What are the main intellectual property (IP) rights in a sponsorship deal?

7   What are the main content rights involved in a televised football match where the teams are sponsored?
8   What are the main provisions of the Bribery Act 2010 and what practical steps should sponsors take to ensure they comply with its provisions?

Further reading

Collett, P and Fenton, W (2011), *The Sponsorship Handbook*, Jossey-Bass
Ferrand, A, Torrigiani, L and Povill, A (2007), *Routledge Handbook of Sports Sponsorship*, Routledge
Kolah, A (2006), *Advanced Sports Sponsorship Strategies*, SportBusiness
Kolah, A (2013), *Essential Law for Marketers*, 2nd edn, Kogan Page
Kolah, A (2001), *How to Develop Effective Naming Rights Strategies*, SportBusiness
Kolah, A (2004), *Maximising the Value of Hospitality*, 2nd edn, SportBusiness
Kolah, A (2003), *Maximising the Value of Sponsorship*, SportBusiness
Kolah, A (2007), *Sponsorship Works: A Brand Marketer's Casebook*, Electric Word

Websites

European Sponsorship Association [accessed 7 June 2013]: http://www.sponsorship.org
The Global Anti-corruption Alliance has useful information on its website [accessed 18 June 2013]: http://www.transparency.org
The Ministry of Justice has published a Guide to the Bribery Act 2010 [accessed 18 June 2013]: http://www.justice.gov.uk/ guidance/bribery.htm

Journals, etc.

Guidance Notes: Commercial references in television programming (2011), Ofcom
Journal of Brand Strategy, published by Henry Stewart Publications

Cases and judgments

Adjudication by the European Ombudsman in the Nike case (2007) is reported on the news website European Voice: http://www.europeanvoice.com
Adjudication by Ofcom in Aviva broadcast sponsorship of ITV 1's *Downton Abbey* (2011)

8 Ambush marketing

In this chapter

- Definition
- Different types of ambush marketing
- Is there room for guerrilla marketing in sponsorship?
- Preventing ambush marketing
- Legal issues
- Future of ambush marketing?

Introduction

One of the hot topics guaranteed to get debate going amongst sponsorship practitioners is the subject of so-called ambush marketing. The phenomenon tends to afflict some of the biggest sports events on the planet, including the FIFA World Cup, F1 and, of course, the Olympic Games. Other property types attract nothing like the problems encountered by sports rights holders and sponsors with respect to ambush marketing activities, so this chapter focuses on examining ambush marketing through the lens of sports sponsorship.

At the outset, it is useful to bear in mind that there are two schools of thought on the subject.

First school of thought

Ambush marketing is a perfectly acceptable form of marketing activity for a non-sponsor to be engaged in, provided it breaks no ethical codes of conduct that may be in place to regulate sales, marketing and communication activities in its territory and provided that such activities do not infringe the intellectual property (IP) rights of others or break the law in the territory. Defenders of the practice call this 'smart marketing', where the objective of ambush is implied by those who sneer at the practice but may find themselves incapable of doing anything to stop it once it has taken place.

Second school of thought

On the other side of the debate are those who have much to lose from so-called ambush marketing activities – the games' organisers, sports rights holders of events and properties and their official sponsors and partners that have spent a small fortune for the privilege of association with the sponsored event.

Not surprisingly, with so much at stake, as the sponsorship investments made for the Winter Olympic Games 2014 in Sochi, Russia, demonstrate, this vociferous group sees ambush marketing activities as 'parasitic' – a brazen attempt to feed off the goodwill, reputation and interest that are created by the rights holder and its sponsors to the detriment of or damage to the Olympic Games and the benefits it wants to deliver to a wider pool of stakeholders.

In many instances, the strategy of rights holders is to take the moral high ground in order to sway public opinion against the culprits (there is usually more than one!). But as will be discussed in this chapter, it is not a black-and-white issue, as some rights holders, such as the International Olympic Committee (IOC) or FIFA, would lead us to believe and certainly the jury is out as to whether ambush or smart marketing damages brand reputation in the long term irrespective of the negative headlines that may circulate at the time of the ambush marketing.

That said, there are clearly instances where the line between legal and unlawful ambush marketing is crossed that can trigger legal enforcement proceedings. It should also be noted that official sponsors often unwittingly ambush one another, particularly with respect to rights granted for a product category at the beginning of the sponsorship programme. For example, a mobile phone manufacturer such as Samsung could easily find that its promotion of its sponsorship of a global event or property treads on the toes of an electronics equipment manufacturer like Panasonic.

Both are Olympic partners, where the possibility for 'sponsorship rights creep' is evident in the case of the Korean conglomerate that manufactures an increasing array of equipment where different technologies converge, effectively changing the product category in which the rights originally applied to.

Getting sponsors to stay in their box can be quite a challenge.

Definition

There is widespread debate by what is meant by the term ambush marketing. For some, ambush marketing is a strategy by which an organisation indirectly associates with an event in order to obtain the same benefit as the official sponsor. An example often given is the 1984 Olympic Games, with Eastman Kodak strategising an association with the Games, although its rival Fuji had secured the rights to be the official sponsor. In those times, Kodak was able to seize the broadcast sponsorship rights on the US TV network, ABC.

Four years later, at the 1988 Summer Olympic Games in Seoul, Korea, the family of official sponsors witnessed at least one of its rivals employ ambush marketing activities. For example, hamburger chain Wendy's ambushed McDonald's;

American Express ambushed Visa; Quality Inns ambushed Hilton; and Fuji took revenge on Kodak, which had secured the sponsorship rights this time round by throwing its weight behind the US swimming team.

Today, it is much harder to pull off this type of ambush marketing, but not impossible.

Chartered Institute of Marketing definition

There is no official definition of what constitutes ambush marketing but the Chartered Institute of Marketing (CIM) provides this definition:

> Ambush marketing is when a company that hasn't paid to be a sponsor of an event, gets free publicity by unofficially communicating their brand in places where spectators, cameras or reporters will see them. Additionally, and somewhat more subtly, it is when a company seeks to create an association between their brand and a sporting event, in order to create positive publicity for their own products or services.

This tends to indicate that ambush marketing is a meticulously executed strategy, and it is rather expensive, given that it mostly relies on outdoor media and possibly print and TV broadcast activities in order to be pulled off and create the desired impact by 'spoiling' the carefully prepared plans of the official sponsor.

European Sponsorship Association definition

The European Sponsorship Association (ESA) provides an alternative definition:

> Ambush marketing is any kind of marketing activity undertaken around a property by an entity that is not a sponsor, where the entity seeks commercial benefit from associating itself with the property without paying sponsorship fees.

In other words, the ESA view is that it is some sort of 'corporate shoplifting' taking place, where a brand owner is 'stealing' something for nothing, when others have paid their way.

Although both definitions do a reasonable job in attempting to define the term ambush marketing, some opponents do not see the point and feel the concept of ambush marketing is meaningless.

Why should we be making a big deal about it in any event, they say? Is it not in reality two competitors slugging it out to communicate similar messages through similar channels in similar places, where each has a right to do so? No one writes articles about car brands buying ad spots during the broadcast of a popular TV show and, of course, comparative advertising is a legal form of this type of competitor activity, which should be labelled smart rather than ambush marketing.

This point of view is understandable. But ambush marketing is not in every case a bit of fun that involves an audacious story of how a plucky challenger brand stuck out its tongue to the establishment. It is not always David versus Goliath. For example, McDonald's has worldwide sponsorship rights to the Olympic partner (TOP) programme. That did not stop rival Subway signing an endorsement deal with Olympian gold medallist swimmer Michael Phelps ahead of London 2012 Games, however.

But should Subway be labelled an ambush marketer? It does not agree with such a label. The argument goes that Subway is ambushing the Olympic Games and not just McDonald's by running ads that suggest a connection to the event.

But wait a minute.

Is not any brand owner that signs a deal with an Olympic athlete, a national team or a single sport's governing body, such as US Gymnastics, connected with the Olympics and should have the right to market that connection so long as it stays within the law? The arguments are not always so clear-cut.

The key to whether or not ambush marketing should be permissible is in direct proportion to the value of goodwill that could be damaged as a result. Recognising that goodwill has a custom-raising value means that its theft is potentially unlawful.

International Olympic Committee definition

In the eyes of the IOC, ambush marketing has a wide definition:

> Any attempt by an individual or an entity to create unauthorised or false association (whether or not commercial) with the Olympic Games, the Olympic Movement, the IOC, the National Olympic Committee of the Host Country or the Organising Committee of Olympic Games (OCOG) thereby interfering with the legitimate contractual rights of official marketing partners of the Olympic Games.

The Olympic Games is the only property class in the world that forces national governments to pass laws that prohibit the use of words, logos, images and associations unless officially sanctioned by the IOC and the local organising committee of the Olympic games.

Different types of ambush marketing

Whether some competitor marketing activity is deemed to be an ambush of the rights of an existing rights holder or sponsor will largely depend on the precise nature of the activity, the contractual relationship between the parties and the laws prevailing in the relevant jurisdiction. However, there is a growing tendency for national governments, in response to pressure from sports rights holders wishing to protect their events and sponsorship arrangements to introduce specific anti-ambush marketing laws.

These go beyond the traditional protections offered by trademark law, unfair competition/passing off, copyright, competition law, human rights legislation and ticket terms and conditions.

One of the most high-profile examples of a government-sanctioned clamp-down on ambush marketing was in South Africa ahead of the Cricket World Cup in 2003, when the government made it a criminal offence to gain promotional advantage for a brand by association with certain designated events. The penalty included a term of imprisonment!

Ambush marketing can take many forms, although, generally, it falls into two main areas of activity.

Infringement of intellectual property rights

These are usually actionable in law and include violation of intellectual property rights such as trademarks, copyright and could also involve passing off. Equally, it could also extend to false claims by suppliers of being officially linked to the event or the use of copyright broadcast material on a website or mobile device.

Counter-marketing strategies

These are a range of activities that may be lawful but designed to confuse consumers into thinking that the non-sponsor is in some way connected with the event and/or to distract attention away from official sponsors' brand communication activities. Such activities include:

- unofficial publications
- online and offline advertising
- text marketing
- mobile marketing
- public relations stunts
- unofficial hospitality
- staging and sponsorship of alternative events in parallel but on a smaller scale to give an impression of 'official status'
- theatrical screening of an event to an invited audience as part of a hospitality event.

These activities are more than simply annoying for the rights holder. Over a sustained period, they can start to erode the value of IP rights granted to official sponsors to such an extent that the sports rights holder faces substantial deflation in value of those rights unless it can demonstrate how those IP rights will be protected.

Arguably, ambush marketing also increases the sponsor's activation costs for fear of being hijacked by a competitor brand owner and also diverts resources into policing and safeguarding those IP rights as opposed to spending these on other value-added activities, such as measurement and evaluation.

The litmus test is not whether the property has significant viewership, attendance, or participation among the target audience but whether the property will generate increased sales and increase brand equity for the sponsor. Failure of a brand owner to activate its investment effectively in a sports property leaves the door wide open for ambush marketers to steal the sponsor's thunder, and there are many sponsors who buy rights, sit back and wait only to find that it has eroded the value of its own investment.

In the words of one former anonymous Nike executive, if companies are not aggressive in promoting their sponsorships, then they should be ambushed. Sponsors should dominate all the public relations, advertising and promotions. Blitz the town where the event is held and buy up all the billboards. Make sure that everyone *knows* you are the sponsor. Do this and the ambusher looks like a bit player. If you are sloppy, then maybe an ambush will force you to become a better marketer.

Is there room for guerrilla marketing in sponsorship?

The London 2012 Olympic Games is possibly the best example of two sides of the argument and spawned several highly creative executions that 'sailed close to the wind' but did not appear to fall foul of the Olympic Brand Police. In some senses, this is 'guerrilla' marketing.

Table 8.1 Examples of non-sponsor marketing for London 2012

Brand	Nature of the campaign	Media used
Tetley Tea (Tata)	Launched a light-hearted social media campaign to leverage the popularity of London 2012 for TeaGB using the Tetley Tea Folk characters that have become synonymous with the brand in the UK. The posts turned actual Olympic events into tea-and-cake-themed competitions, such as the Ar-cherry event, which saw Victoria Sponge pitted against Bakewell Tart. Fans chose nominees and voted on the winners.	Twitter and YouTube
Nike	'Find Your Greatness' was a campaign focusing on the athletic greatness taking place in other places with the name London rather than the one in England. The advertising featured Londoners from South Africa, Jamaica, Nigeria, the USA and other countries in a one-minute TV commercial, as well as a series of sport-specific shorter films, to demonstrate that even if you play far away from the dazzle of the Olympics, your greatness is no less important.	TV advertising, Twitter and YouTube videos alluded to the Olympics but did not name them.
Nike	Outdoor Nike ad campaign 'Greatest Doesn't Only Exist in SW19'.	Outdoor 48-sheet posters

(Continued)

Table 8.1 (Continued)

Brand	Nature of the campaign	Media used
Nike	Nike sponsors all but one of the players on the US basketball team and uses players to commentate spontaneously in real time on the game.	Twitter
Puma	London's Puma store featured Usain Bolt, as it sponsors the athlete, although Adidas was the official sponsor of the London 2012 Games.	In-store
Puma	Brought an array of musical talent to its Puma Yard venue in Brick Lane in East London. Sets were performed by professor Green and Groove Armada.	In-store social club, food stalls serving Jamaican cuisine and a 'beach' bar
BrewDog	To coincide with London 2012 the craft brewery based in Scotland launched 'Never Mind the Anabolics', a beer made with eight substances that would get an athlete banned from the Games. Brewdog claimed it was launched to protest against the Olympics selling out to sponsors with unhealthy products. The company had a PR coup on its hands.	New product, Twitter, Facebook, YouTube
Specsavers	Quick to respond to the South Korean flag mix-up by LOCOG when North Korea was playing Colombia. An ad appeared in newspapers the next morning: 'Should have gone to Specsavers'.	Ran a full-page ad in national newspapers.
Oddbins	The wine retailer poked fun at LOCOG rules with an in-store promotion offering a 30% discount for Nike-wearing, Vauxhall-driving, RBS MasterCard-holding, iPhone-using, British Gas bill-paying, Pepsi-drinking, KFC-eating consumers – all of which were not Olympic sponsors.	Oddbins window displays highlighted that it was not allowed to refer to London 2012 in its marketing.
PaddyPower	Irish bookmaker proclaimed itself as the 'Official sponsor of the largest athletics event in London this year! There you go, we said it (ahem, London, France, that is)'.	Billboards at railway termini and on Facebook
Dr Dre	The rapper superstar sent Team GB athletes his Beats headphones with Union flag colours, skirting strict rules on ambush marketing by LOCOG. Olympic medallist Tom Daley was seen wearing his ahead of the diving competition, an event watched by seven million viewers on BBC. Tennis player Laura Robson tweeted about receiving her headphones.	Sending a gift to athletes
Red Bull	Created a documentary in support of Australian pole vaulter Steve Hooker.	Documentary on YouTube and Facebook
Virgin Media	Increased its ad spending by 37% in the lead-up to London 2012 in the face of official Tier 1 sponsor BT. Several executions featuring celebrities such as Usain Bolt in its 'Keep Up' campaign.	TV and print ads

A cursory look at Table 8.1 seems to reveal no sinister overtones and, indeed, one could argue that these brand owners have brought their own brand of creativity to the table without any unfair exploitation of the rights of London 2012 sponsors.

Nike and ambush marketing at London 2012 Games

Widely recognised through the media as the most prominent 'non-sponsor' to take to the streets in celebration of the 'Greatest Show on Earth', Nike has virtually turned guerrilla marketing into an art form. And, at the London 2012 Games, it did this with the help of an amazing yellow-green neon shoe.

In focus groups of amateur, college and professional athletes that had been shown the shoe in different colours, there was unanimous support for the Volt, as yellow-green neon is the most visible colour to the human eye. The man behind the Volt Shoe was 37-year-old Martin Lotti, Nike's global creative director for the Olympics.

The advertising industry 'bible' *Ad Age* ran the cover story: 'The beautifully crafted, incandescent kicks that whizzed by on the feet of 400 Olympic athletes including USA's Ashton Eaton and Trey Hardee, Great Britain's Mo Farah and France's Renaud Lavillenie'.

Painting Nike's Flynit shoe Volt in such a vivid way was a stroke of genius, as it created a kind of informal 'Team Nike'. Previously, the colour of the shoe had matched the colour of individual athletes' kit and, of course, that made it blend in with everything else.

At the London 2012 Games, hundreds of athletes from different countries wore the same vivid colour. And that was the tipping point. The result was a wave of attention that has taken something so simple and effective into the pages of marketing textbooks. Without doubt, Nike's move was really smart. It had used marketing assets that belonged to it alone and those assets gave them a pretty unique opportunity to take advantage of the Olympic rules.

London Olympic Games and Paralympic Games Act, 2006

The London Olympic Games and Paralympic Games Act 2006 created the London Olympic Association Right, which gave LOCOG the power to grant licences to authorised sponsors to use the symbols, words and logos of the event.

By all accounts, LOCOG delivered one of the most successful Olympic Games in history and extreme concerns of ambush marketing failed to materialise. These fears were of course well founded, as, if we look back at other events, such as the FIFA World Cup, it is easy to see the paranoia of official sponsors, given that the rights fees commanded by major sports properties have grown steadily at a far greater rate than inflation for the past 25 years. The current assumption that ambush marketing is, on the face of it, a bad thing, needs to be addressed.

Back in the early 1990s, Jerry Welsh, the former Global Marketing Head of American Express was reported to have said: 'Ambush marketing, correctly understood and rightly practiced, is an important, ethically correct, competitive tool in a non-sponsoring company's arsenal of business and image building weapons.' Welsh has been credited with coining the term ambush marketing, which, of course, is at variance with the definition we read earlier in this chapter provided by the IOC.

According to Welsh, there *is* room for guerrilla marketing in sponsorship, particularly where there is no intention to mislead the public. 'In buying a sponsorship, a company buys only that specific packaged product [. . .] the company doesn't thereby purchase the rights to all avenues leading to the public's awareness of that property and more importantly it doesn't buy the rights to the entire thematic space in which the purchased property is usually only one resident. In other words, when you own and license Kermit, you have only given the rights you own to one specific frog – not all frogs, and maybe not even to all green ones. Anything not specifically licenced in this way is up for commercial grabs,' he said. For Welsh, this is how it should be in sponsorship and how it is in the larger world of commerce and in life itself.

In the future, it is possible that we could see challenges to the legality of preventing ambush marketing. Getting the balance right means protecting investment and not unnecessarily penalising businesses. Forty years ago, cities had to be persuaded to host the Olympic Games: at the time of the 1980 Moscow Olympics the IOC was on the verge of a financial crisis. Of course, the situation is very different today and the London 2012 Games have demonstrated beyond doubt that there are significant commercial and promotional advantages for a host city if they get their sums right.

There does seem to be something of a 'sledgehammer to crack a nut' about how the likes of Coca-Cola and McDonald's seek the full protection of draconian laws to protect themselves from much smaller companies merely wishing to trade harmlessly on the back of what is a national and cultural event and make this the exclusive preserve of a few brands that have deep pockets.

From a pragmatic perspective, it is to be hoped that common sense prevails and that legal action will be taken against ambushers that indulge in deliberate attempts to mislead the public, whereas those that indulge in guerrilla marketing where no goodwill has been unfairly infringed do not face legal proceedings.

Preventing ambush marketing

With an event as successful as the Olympic Games, the FIFA World Cup or, indeed, the Wimbledon Tennis Championships, it is little wonder that many companies want to find ways of taking advantage of the buzz that is generated at the time of these major occasions. Table 8.2 provides some high-profile examples of ambush marketing from the past.

Protecting official sponsors by policing the activities of ambush marketers is a complex undertaking and it is fair to say there are more holes than plugs in the rules governing sponsor protection, although various governing bodies have attempted to reduce the risks of ambush marketing of their own events very successfully.

Table 8.2 Examples of high-profile ambush marketing tactics from the past

1984	Kodak sponsors TV broadcasts, despite Fuji being the Los Angeles Olympics' official sponsor; Fuji returns the favour at the Seoul 1988 Games.
1992	Nike sponsors news conferences with the US basketball team; Michael Jordan accepts the gold medal for basketball and covers up his Reebok logo.
1994	American Express runs ads claiming Americans do not need 'Visas' to travel to Norway for the Winter Olympics.
2000	Qantas Airlines' slogan 'Spirit of Australia' coincidentally sounds like the Games slogan 'Share the Spirit' to the chagrin of official sponsor Ansett Air.
2010	Dutch brewer Bavaria creates a publicity stunt with women wearing orange mini-dresses in the stadium during the South Africa World Cup; Budweiser was the authorised beer.

Wimbledon Tennis Championships

One of the All England Lawn and Tennis Club's (AELTC) key objectives is to enhance the unique character and image of the Championships by keeping its courts and grounds relatively free of commercial sponsorship and product placement – hence the lack of overt advertising around the grounds.

This helps to give the event and the Wimbledon brand a special resonance that TV and commercial companies around the world wish to be associated with, and enables the club to derive revenue which goes towards the funding of the Championships and British tennis.

Over the years, there has been a sharp increase in the amount of free unauthorised commercial advertising material that is distributed to the Wimbledon queue and ticket holders in order to obtain free advertising in the grounds or on TV.

This practice often consists of free sunhats, free rain capes, free umbrellas, free suntan creams, free radios, free water bottles, etc., all bearing heavily branded commercial messages. It is an issue similar to that faced by other rights holders and the AELTC is not alone in taking a firm stance that includes either temporarily confiscating those items that it knows or has reason to believe are part of an ambush marketing campaign or refusing entry to spectators who are not prepared to surrender such items.

However, the organisers draw the line at spectators who want to bring their own branded food and beverages into the grounds, for example, items that have been purchased from normal retail outlets. Similarly, branded clothing purchased for normal personal use, with no obvious ambush potential, is also entirely acceptable.

The AELTC also does its best to ensure that its security staff are fully conversant with the issue and are able to apply the policy with tact, common sense and good judgement in order to avoid negative headlines in the media for being overbearing with tennis fans who want to come and enjoy the fortnight every year without the fear of being stopped and searched.

FIFA World Cup Rio, 2014

The preparations for staging the FIFA World Cup Rio 2014 began many years in advance of the event, where the focus was not merely on the logistics and infrastructure and stadium development required but also on building the FIFA World Cup Brazil brand. For example, this includes the official emblem, official look programme, official mascot, official slogan, official poster, host city posters and much more.

From the early days of the event preparations through to the final dramatic moments when the Jules Rimet Trophy is presented to the winning team, the whole event needs a strong brand that captures the essence of the event and the host country, while forging strong emotional links between the FIFA World Cup and fans all over the world.

FIFA's view on ambush marketing

According to FIFA, 'Ambush marketing can be defined as prohibited marketing activities which try to take advantage of the huge interest and high profile of an event by creating a commercial association and/or seeking promotional exposure without the authorisation of the event organiser.'

The two areas of concern for FIFA are where ambush marketers attempt a direct association with the event through advertising or promotions, such as ticket giveaways, or the use of the tournament designations and other marks without authority. The other area of concern is an indirect association with the

Table 8.3 FIFA 2014 ambush marketing rankings

Ranking on the Brand Affinity Index (BAI)	Brand	Sponsor of FIFA World Cup 2014 (☑) or ambusher (☒)	BAI
1	Continental	☑	538.20
2	Beats	☒	461.95
3	KFC	☒	365.49
4	Bridgestone	☒	356.50
5	Nike	☒	353.61
6	McDonald's	☑	348.93
7	Sony	☑	342.40
8	Adidas	☑	270.98
9	Coca-Cola	☑	231.86
10	P&G	☒	225.58
11	Visa	☑	154.76
12	Red Bull	☒	138.25
13	Budweiser	☑	56.71
14	Johnson & Johnson	☑	56.17
15	Heineken	☒	52.43
16	Mastercard	☒	46.19

Source: Global Language Monitor (GLM) 2014

property without making a direct link, such as executing a creative campaign aimed at creating the perception of a link to the World Cup (see Table 8.3).

Marketing activities by non-sponsor brand owners that seek to take advantage of the huge public interest in the event through physical on-site presence can also be categorised as prohibited. The common denominator in such prohibited marketing activities is that they primarily seek free advertising.

The reason that FIFA considers prohibited marketing as a priority in its brand protection work is that it puts FIFA's commercial programme directly at risk by trying to devalue official sponsorship. Companies engaging in prohibited marketing fail to appreciate that the FIFA World Cup is the result of FIFA's significant investment in developing and promoting the tournament, something that would not be possible without the financial support of FIFA's commercial affiliates.

Ambush marketing is an attempt to take advantage of the goodwill and positive image generated by the FIFA World Cup without contributing to its organisation and, of course, is outside of the spirit of fair play that transcends the tournament. FIFA runs a global licensing programme that gives a wide range of licensees the opportunity to produce official licensed products for the FIFA World Cup. However, there are also companies that seek to produce items featuring FIFA's official marks without purchasing the required licence. These counterfeit products can severely impact the profitability of official merchandise sales, even though they bear incorrect authentication features such as hang tags, official sew-in labels, incorrect use of trademarks, get-up and other product features.

In FIFA's case, counterfeit products can range from footballs to caps, from clothing to toys, and from footwear to miscellaneous items such as pins, keychains, World Cup Trophy replicas and other items that feature FIFA trademarks. For the 2014 FIFA World Cup, FIFA is working together with Brazilian authorities including the police, customs and host cities of the FIFA World Cup to be able to use existing structures and know-how in the joint battle against counterfeit products.

Once FIFA is informed of the production, importation or sale of products that bear unauthorised reproductions of FIFA's official marks, FIFA is obliged to take corresponding action, including any legal measures at its disposal, to bring the activity to a halt. This is an undertaking that FIFA has given to its licensees, which have paid substantial sums to be an official manufacturer and retailer of FIFA merchandise.

It is worth pointing out that official licensed products bear a quality guarantee in relation to standards of product quality, ethical business practices and working conditions, which ensure that practices such as child labour are excluded. The same cannot be said of counterfeit merchandise and consumers need to be aware of that.

Such guarantees also apply with regard to the materials that have been used to fabricate a specific product in comparison with counterfeit products, which could pose serious health risks in the light of the absence of any such quality guarantee.

IP rights requiring protection

FIFA's intellectual property primarily consists of trademarks such as FIFA, World Cup, COPA 2014, BRAZIL 2014; designs (both registered and unregistered) and copyright as subsisting in works such as the official poster, emblem, mascot and look artworks. FIFA has developed and protected an assortment of logos, words, titles, symbols and other trademarks that it will use, or allow others to use under a formal agreement, in relation to the 2014 FIFA World Cup.

FIFA is obliged to take action against any unauthorised reproduction of its marks in a commercial context. If FIFA did not follow up on any infringements of its trademarks and copyrighted works, it would risk losing its legal right and title to such works, thereby endangering the foundation of its commercial programme.

And as I mentioned earlier, FIFA's commercial affiliates (licensees) will only invest in the 2014 FIFA World Cup if they are provided with this exclusivity for the use of the marks and for any other kind of association with the event.

If anyone were free to use the official marks without cost and create an association with the 2014 FIFA World Cup, there would be no reason to become a commercial affiliate. This would mean that FIFA could not appoint any commercial affiliates and would, therefore, not receive the revenue required to maintain the high standards expected of the FIFA World Cup.

An example of the strength of FIFA's intellectual property assets is reflected by recent research in seven key global markets where the FIFA World Cup Trophy recorded an average recognition level of 83% (99% in Brazil). These levels are significantly higher than for any other sporting trophies.

Non-sponsor companies increasingly try to target fans going to FIFA World Cup stadiums by means of promotional teams, branded vehicles, branded items and on-site advertising and mobile marketing tactics.

These companies aim to obtain promotional exposure on the site of the event and thereby to the billions of TV viewers around the world through large numbers of fans displaying their brand. These actions knowingly play on the fans' enthusiasm for wearing fancy dress and exploit such enthusiasm for the commercial advantage of the non-sponsor company.

It is worth noting that the marketing activities of FIFA's commercial affiliates are subject to prior approval from FIFA, with the emphasis on enhancing the fan experience of the FIFA World Cup rather than excessive branding exercises where over-commercialisation starts to impact the spectacle of the tournament.

First and foremost, FIFA tries to increase awareness regarding the official marks that enjoy legal protection as well as on the restrictions that apply in relation to commercial association with the FIFA World Cup. To avoid 'accidental' unauthorised use of the official marks/commercial association with the FIFA World Cup, FIFA engages in extensive awareness campaigns to ensure that the general public, the business community, ticket holders and any other potential stakeholders have access to information setting out the regulations that apply in this regard.

On detection of an infringement, FIFA's brand protection team assesses the most effective way of quickly bringing the situation to an end, without having to resort to disproportionate enforcement actions.

There are several elements to FIFA's brand protection work that are aimed at identifying infringements of FIFA's rights. For example, FIFA actively engages with customs authorities on a global level to detect shipments of counterfeit products. FIFA also actively monitors intellectual property registers across the world in order to safeguard and preserve the exclusivity of its brands and marketing assets.

One further element is the enactment of commercial restriction areas (CRAs) around the stadiums that host matches of the FIFA World Cup and other official sites. A CRA is specifically intended to identify easily and deal effectively with marketing activities that focus on the physical presence of non-sponsor companies in and around event sites such as stadiums. A CRA is not curtained by a physical fence but an imaginary line that is outlined on a map and included in local laws in order to provide additional legal protection against prohibited marketing activities around the stadium, unauthorised traders, counterfeit goods and ticket touts.

The impact on local businesses located within the CRA is typically limited by applying a 'business as usual' principle. As a consequence, any commercial activity that is not specifically targeting the event or its spectators to obtain a promotional benefit should not be limited by the enactment of the CRAs.

In fact, many local businesses around the stadium and other official sites, such as bars, restaurants and convenience stores, benefit from the CRA, as it effectively excludes non-local businesses, including opportunists from other countries, seeking to cash in on the sudden surge in the number of spectators at the expense of local businesses. In return, FIFA asks that local businesses commit to fair play with regard to FIFA and its commercial affiliates in their activities that seek to profit from the high number of visitors without engaging in prohibited marketing activities.

Education rather than the courts

FIFA's approach to brand protection focuses on education and guidance, rather than enforcement by means of legal threats and sanctions. FIFA prefers direct personal contact in order to bring infringements to an end by speaking to the business in question, explaining why the specific situation is problematic and seeking cooperation in solving the issue.

In more serious cases, where there is a clear intention to take a free ride on the goodwill vested in the event and the public excitement about it, FIFA may need to engage in court proceedings to halt an infringement and to claim financial compensation for the damages suffered. However, FIFA will only resort to such action on the back of in-depth analysis of the intention, scale and commercial impact of the matter at hand.

Legal issues

One of the key issues for any brand owner that is looking to become a sponsor, partner or licensee of a sports rights holder, such as FIFA or the IOC, is to have a complete picture of the rights landscape – the relevant IP rights for the event, team, player, league or personality.

No brand owner should become involved in any form of commercial deal without a clear idea of the rights landscape of the proposed commercial deal that is being negotiated with the rights holder. For example, the sports rights holder may appoint a main sponsor as the 'title' sponsor. As a result, this brand owner will have the rights to name the competition, to be featured on all PR material, possibly to design the trophy, to have its logo featured on all broadcasts of the event in an agreed form, as well as a bundle of other IP rights that identify it as the exclusive main title sponsor of the event.

With respect to large events, there may well be six to ten subsidiary 'partners', each of whom enjoys exclusive rights within a certain product or service category and enjoys effective parity among the other partners with the same basket of IP rights. For example, these rights may include signage at a ground that is in the line of broadcast cameras, the right to include the competition name and logo and footage on advertising and promotional media, the right to refer to themselves as 'official partner' and the right to have signage on a backdrop board where interviews are conducted.

All these rights are fertile areas for potential ambush, both from within the groups of sponsors and partners as well as from those not in a contractual relationship with the rights holder.

At its most blatant, ambush marketing can take the form of an actionable wrong, such as trademark infringement or passing off. There may also be trade descriptions offences that can be dealt with in the UK by officials from the Trading Standards Office and the rights owner acting in unison.

Unauthorised use of IP rights

This may involve the manufacture and sale of merchandise products bearing the name and logo of the event or some or all of the participants in the event. Typically, an event organiser and some of its participants will appoint official merchandise kit suppliers who will be authorised to use identified IP rights (such as a registered trademark). The unauthorised infringer will make its own merchandise and will sell this in contravention of the IP rights held by the official licensee.

In certain circumstances, an injunction may be sought or else search and seizure using various criminal remedies contained in the Trade Marks Act 1994 and the Copyright, Designs and Patents Act 1988.

Future of ambush marketing

As rights fees increase, brand owners will expect a higher degree of certainty that those rights are unlikely to be infringed because the rights holder has gone to enormous lengths to protect the integrity of those rights by registering them and being prepared to enforce trademark protection across all relevant jurisdictions. Part of this deterrent to would-be infringers will be some form of PR campaign that alerts anyone who may fancy their chances that there is a zero-tolerance policy towards such activities.

As a result, ambush marketing in its most obvious form is likely to dissolve and in its place competitor brand owners are more likely to engage in smart marketing, which will have the desired effect of distracting audiences away from the messages emanating from official sponsors and partners.

Chapter 8 at a glance

1 Ambush marketing is viewed as 'smart' by some where it keeps within the law and illegal where it infringes the intellectual property (IP) rights of rights holder.
2 The main area of ambush marketing activity tends to be in sports.
3 The main types of ambush marketing involve the infringement of IP rights such as copyright and trademarks.
4 An ambush marketer looking to create a perception that there is a connection with an event, team, league or personality could face civil and criminal sanctions that can include injunctions, damages and delivery up of the offending goods for destruction.
5 Some brand owners, such as Nike, have turned ambush marketing into an art form by sailing close to the wind.
6 Rights holders such as FIFA and the International Olympic Committee invest substantial sums of money in protecting their logos, symbols, words and marks from being used by non-authorised parties.
7 Ambush marketing can sometimes occur as a result of 'category creep' among sponsors for an event.
8 Rights holders tend to favour education rather than the courts in order to enforce their IP rights but will also work with law enforcement agencies to prevent the illegal shipment of counterfeit goods from flooding local markets.
9 Ambush marketers are going to be smarter in the future by indulging in tactics that distract audiences away from the official sponsors and partners but stop short of infringing IP rights.

Questions for discussion

1 How would you distinguish between ambush marketing and smart marketing? What are the main implications of this difference for the global sponsorship industry?
2 What are the different types of ambush marketing and which tend to have more severe economic consequences for rights holders and sponsors?

3   What does ambush marketing deliver to a brand owner that it is not able to achieve as an official sponsor or licensee?
4   What are the major dimensions used to analyse whether it is worth considering undertaking some form of ambush marketing?
5   What practical steps should rights holders and sponsors take to protect themselves against ambush marketing tactics?
6   Why does the sponsorship industry continue to be divided on the issue of ambush marketing?

Further reading

Ad Age (2012), Nike's high-voltage marketing at London 2012. http://adage.com/article/special-report-marketer-alist-2012/nike-s-high-volt-age-marketing-results/238417/ (accessed 17 March 2013)

AELTC (2013), Protecting the Wimbledon brand. http://www.wimbledon.com/en_GB/visitor_a_to_z/201205141337004580049.html (accessed 17 March 2013)

Amis, J and Cornwell, B (2006), *Global Sport Sponsorship*, Berg

Andrews, Jim (2012), Blog: Time to put ambush marketing to rest. http://www.sponsorship.com/About-IEG/Sponsorship-Blog/Jim-Andrews/August-2012/Time-to-End-Ambush-Marketing.aspx (accessed 17 March 2013)

BBC (2012), Tackling ambush marketing at London 2012. http://www.bbc.co.uk/news/business-18628635?print+true (accessed 17 March 2013)

CIM (2011), *Ambush Marketing and the Law*, Chartered Institute of Marketing

Davis, J (2012), *The Olympic Games Effect*, Wiley

The Drum (2012), How Nike pulled off brilliant ambush marketing in the Olympics. http://www.thedrum.com/news/2012/08/22/how-nike-pulled-brilliant-ambush-marketing-olympics (accessed 17 March 2013)

European Sponsorship Association (ESA) (2010), Position Statement on Ambush Marketing. http://www.sponsorship.org/content/esaPressDetail.asp?id=816 (accessed 17 March 2013)

Ferrand, A, Torrigiani, L and Povill, A (2007), *Routledge Handbook of Sports Sponsorship*, Routledge

FIFA (2013), FIFA World Cup brand. http://www.fifa.com/worldcup/organisation/marketing/brand-protection/world-cup-brand/index.html (accessed 17 March 2013)

The Guardian (2012), Non-Olympic brands push ambush marketing rules to the limit. http://www.guardian.co.uk/media/2012/jul/25/non-olympic-brands-ambush-marketing/print (accessed 17 March 2013)

Klein, N (2001), *No Logo*, HarperCollins

Kolah, A (2006), *Advanced Sports Sponsorship Strategies*, SportBusiness Group

Kolah, A (2013), *Essential Law for Marketers*, 2nd edn, Kogan Page

Kolah, A (2005), *Maximising the Value of Licensing and Merchandising*, SportBusiness Group

Sutherden, A (2011), Laying the law down on ambush marketing, *Journal of Sponsorship*

Ukman, Lesa (2012), *Ambush Marketing*. http://pinterest.com/lesaukman/ambush-marketing/ (accessed 17 March 2013)

Verow, R, Lawrence, C and McCormick, P (2005), *Sports Business Law, Practice and Precedents*, Jordans

9 Corporate social responsibility and sponsorship

In this chapter

- Definition of CSR
- Current thinking in CSR and its relationship with sponsorship
- How Unilever has embraced CSR and made it indistinguishable from its business

Introduction

There is a view that companies are built to do only three things: make profits, pay taxes and obey the law. The rest is window dressing. Well, those brand owners who subscribe to that point of view are probably now retired. The business world is increasingly expected to take a lead role by its customers, clients and employees in making a net contribution to society rather than simply taking as much as it can for the benefit of its shareholders and investors.

Consumers like to know that business cares. And in its own way, this is big business, too. A recent survey, published in October 2014, showed that Fortune 500 companies spent more than USD 15bn on corporate social responsibility (CSR) activities. The research, carried out by economic consulting firm EPG, found that there was a clear difference in how US and UK companies approached CSR, but that, on both sides of the Atlantic, spending was dominated by only a handful of groups.

In-kind donations, such as donating free drugs to health programmes or providing free software to universities accounted for 71% of the USD 11.95bn spending on CSR in 2013. Oracle, for example, which is one of the biggest CSR spenders, grants its software to secondary schools, colleges and universities in about 100 countries around the world. Cash contributions were just 16% of the US total, with employee involvement and fundraising making up the remaining 13%.

In the UK, while donating goods and services in kind was the largest component of the USD 3.25bn CSR activity, it totalled just 46% of the total. Employee volunteering and fundraising made up 34% and cash contributions 20%.

There are a wide range of CSR activities that Corporates roll up their sleeves to become involved with. For example, British life assurance group Prudential involved employee volunteers in delivering an education programme to children in an impoverished community in central Jakarta. Drugs companies are also particularly active, with Merck and Johnson & Johnson being among the six groups providing almost two-thirds of the US CSR spend, while London-listed AstraZeneca and GSK were two of the four companies accounting for more than three-quarters of the British total.

Companies often prefer to direct their CSR activity to areas with which they are familiar and this appears to be a factor in why spending on health CSR far outstrips that on education.

On a global basis, more money needs to be channelled into education projects particularly in Africa and Latin America.

The Fortune 500 survey decided to choose a narrow definition of CSR spending, with the aim of excluding corporate activity that was not genuinely philanthropic. But some academics believe that in doing so researchers missed the full scope of business social activity as well as accounting for CSR within the context of a sponsorship programme.

Such limitations in the research notwithstanding, the findings of the survey will give fresh impetus to the continuing debate about how far brand owners can persuade shareholders and investors to see the value in CSR activity outside a purely commercial context.

In 2013, a survey of 1,000 chief executives by the UN Global Compact and management consultancy firm Accenture suggested that the landscape had become harsher.

In that year, 37% of industry leaders said the lack of a clear link to business value was a critical factor in deterring them from faster action on sustainability – about twice the number who had cited the failure to identify such a link back in 2007. Clearly there can be a wide range of investor reaction to sustainability initiatives, but long-term shareholders increasingly see environmental and social governance as a key indicator in terms of investment.

And the call for a more self-enlightened approach is most definitely on the corporate agenda. For example, back in the 1990s, analysts might put a 'sell' recommendation on companies with a strong CSR rating, as they saw it as wasting investors' money. But that negative perception has for the large extent been neutralised in recent years and indeed some analysts now view CSR activity more positively. The caveat is provided CSR spending is aligned to the company or organisation's business model; investors can see it is a matter of enlightened self-interest. And they are not the only group that needs to be convinced of CSR as being a force for good and being good for business.

As I said earlier, consumers also expect a lot more today, too. They are different from previous generations of consumers and have their own distinctive attitudes, values, perceptions, beliefs and behaviours. They are optimistic and feel empowered to be able to make a difference rather than sitting back and waiting for something to happen.

According to Steve Overman, author of *The Conscience Economy: How a Mass Movement for Good is Great for Business*, this new breed of consumer 'rejects everyday choices in ways that defy traditional logic. They're questioning everything from the notion of career consistency to the value of money itself. They're hacking everything from government policy to genome.' And signs of this newfound consumer self-confidence is all around us. 'The global wave of young entrepreneurs are an indicator not only of an increase in personal self-belief and empowerment but also a sign of the growing optimism that there's a better way to work, produce and live in the world today,' reflects Overman.

As I have explained at length in this book, sponsorship can be seen as giving something back to fans, customers, clients, supporters, employees and the wider community. This is not at variance with other objectives that are commercially driven. Fundamentally, sponsorship is a commercial agreement between the rights holder and the brand owner where the sponsor is seeking a measurable return on investment for its efforts.

But that does not mean there is no space for non-commercial objectives to be satisfied at the same time as commercial ones. In many respects, having CSR objectives that run in parallel with commercial objectives helps to elevate sponsorship to new heights. This is largely because the level of engagement with desired audiences and customer segments is that much deeper and the sponsorship programme itself is much less self-serving as a result, creating a 'triple bottom-line' impact for the brand owner, its desired customers/clients and wider society.

This new paradigm in sponsorship can be accurately described as 'enlightened self-interest' and is definitely shaping the agenda. For example, many global brand owners, such as Unilever and the Olympic partners, including Coca-Cola and McDonald's, have not just paid lip-service to this principle but have staked their future commercial success on achieving a position in which the enterprise is built on the values of sustainability, improved well-being, care of the environment and enhancing the quality of life for millions of people around the world.

Another notable exponent of 'enlightened self-interest' is Tata, one of the most successful multinational organisations in the world – and this is an organisation that is built on ancient Zoroastrian values that place contribution to the wider community on an equal basis with wealth creation and profit. In many respects, CSR has ceased to exist outside sponsorship in today's modern business world and, rather than being an add-on, CSR is increasingly seen as intrinsic to the enterprise and to modern global sponsorship.

India and developments in CSR

The principle of 'enlightened self-interest' was taken a step further in 2014 when India became the first country in the world to enact a law making it mandatory for companies to invest 2% of their net profits in social development.

Ratan Tata, former chairman of Tata Sons, the holding company of the USD 100bn Tata Group remarked: 'We have a phenomenon which is meant to be good but is going to be somewhat chaotic . . . we don't as yet know what kind of monitoring there'll be in terms of how well this money is used.'

He was right to raise the issue of transparency – not something that India is well known for, and the risk is that such a measure could inadvertently precipitate a 'tick-box' culture among Indian business leaders or worse still spawn more imaginative tax avoidance schemes or even corrupt business practices that obviate the need to make such a contribution to wider society in the first place.

It is to be hoped this does not happen and that Indian-based organisations such as Tata and others show that being a force for good is also good for being a force in business. On conservative estimates, around 6,000 Indian companies will be required to undertake some form of CSR projects within the next 12 months in order to comply with the new guidelines, which could result in CSR spend tripling to £1.8bn a year.

Helpfully, the Indian government has set out specific guidelines on how CSR activities should be handled. For example, these guidelines stipulate that CSR activities need to be implemented by a CSR committee that includes independent directors. This committee will be responsible for preparing a detailed plan on CSR activities, including the expenditure, the type of activities, roles and responsibilities of various stakeholders, and a monitoring mechanism for such activities. The board is required to approve the CSR policy for the company and disclose its contents in a CSR report as well as publish details on its website.

Acceptable CSR activities include measures to eradicate hunger, promote education, environmental sustainability, protection of national heritage and rural sports, and contributions to PM Narendra Modi's relief fund. The enterprise can implement these CSR activities on its own, through its non-profit foundation or through independently registered non-profit organisations that have a record of at least three years in delivering similar outcomes.

The sanctions for non-compliance look feeble – a public explanation as to why the company failed to invest 2% of its profits on such activities. Clearly not all organisations are like Tata in having this CSR philosophy embedded in their company DNA, so it is one thing making it a requirement and quite another ensuring that it is actually delivered in practice. One key success factor for the future will be how Indian sponsors align various CSR activities in order to create tangible outcomes for the communities they serve, alongside those social measures being pursued by the Indian government.

This also has implications for western brand owners looking to build profitable businesses in India for their products and services in that they may be tempted to use sponsorship as a channel for customer engagement. For example, the success of the Indian Premier League and Pepsi is likely to accelerate interest in the use of commercial sponsorship and with it CSR, which could help support grass-roots development of the game.

However, one question mark remains: is CSR just a passing trend or is it something that will reshape the business of sponsorship?

According to UN Global Compact, it is hoped it will be the latter rather than the former outcome.

United Nations and CSR policy

UN Global Impact is a strategic policy initiative for businesses that are committed to aligning their operations and strategies with ten universally accepted principles in the areas of human rights, labour, environment and anti-corruption (see Table 9.1).

By doing so, business, as a primary driver of globalisation, can help ensure that markets, commerce, technology and finance advance in ways that benefit society as a whole. In addition, UN Global Compact has identified four key trends that indicate that CSR – and with it sponsors – can help make a real difference:

Trend #1: greater transparency

As with technological change, transparency is an irreversible force. Reporting and disclosure will undoubtedly continue to grow, driven by ever lower barriers to information access, higher public interest and regulatory changes. Already over 5,000 corporations disclose their environmental, social and corporate governance (ESG) performance on an annual basis and this number is bound to grow.

Table 9.1 UN Global Compact's ten principles

Number	Area of activity	Principle
#1	Human rights	Businesses should support and respect the protection of internationally proclaimed human rights.
#2	Human rights	Businesses should make sure that they are not complicit in human rights abuses.
#3	Labour	Businesses should uphold the freedom of association and the effective recognition of the right to collective bargaining.
#4	Labour	Businesses should uphold the elimination of all forms of forced and compulsory labour.
#5	Labour	Businesses should uphold the effective abolition of child labour.
#6	Labour	Businesses should uphold the elimination of discrimination in respect of employment and occupation.
#7	Environment	Business should support a precautionary approach to environmental challenges.
#8	Environment	Businesses should undertake initiatives to promote greater environmental responsibility.
#9	Environment	Businesses should encourage the development and diffusion of environmentally friendly technologies.
#10	Anti-corruption	Businesses should work against corruption in all its forms, including extortion and bribery.

Source: United Nations Global Compact (2015)

Trend #2: building greater trust

The ever-growing impact of business on society means that citizens and consumers expect corporate power to be exerted responsibly. As citizens become more sceptical, self-organised and prone to challenge authority, brand owners will have to raise their game in understanding how to build and maintain trust. The result is that tomorrow's company will become increasingly proactive and thorough in how it views its responsibilities and impact on the wider society and then show how it manages its operations accordingly.

Trend #3: building deeper community participation

Business is expected to do more in areas that used to be the exclusive domain of government – from health and education to community investment and environmental stewardship. For example, environmental issues and sustainability are now on the business agenda for many global FMCG companies such as P&G, Unilever and a host of energy suppliers. The world's natural resources are now recognised as being finite and under stress. What was once unthinkable is now a reality – clean water and an unpolluted atmosphere come with price tags.

Brand owners that actively seek to collaborate with scientists, civil society and public regulators and show early on that they are part of the solution will come out ahead of their competitors by being able to build deeper community participation. And it is here that CSR in sponsorship has a role to play.

Trend #4: accessing new markets responsibly

Business is moving from being the consumer of precious resources to building sustainable market capacity. With economic growth migrating southwards and eastwards, foreign direct investment (FDI) is becoming more about building and gaining access to new markets and less about simply exploiting low-cost inputs.

Overcoming barriers to growth, such as civil violence, an uneducated workforce and unsustainable sources of energy, water, minerals and soil, is now in the interest of business.

Sponsorship, if used appropriately and with clear measurable objectives, can deliver results for brand owners where trust with market and customer segments is strengthened by CSR and where these companies can be seen as good corporate citizens.

Definition of CSR

The concept of CSR refers to the general belief held by growing numbers of citizens that modern business has a responsibility to society that extends beyond its obligations to shareholders or investors.

The obligation to investors, of course, is to generate profits for the owners and maximise long-term wealth creation. Other societal stakeholders include consumers, employees, the wider community, government and the natural environment.

The CSR concept applies to organisations of all sizes and geographies but discussions about CSR have tended to focus on large organisations, because these tend to be more visible and have more financial resources for making a difference in society. And, of course, with this financial muscle power comes responsibility. Jeremy Hobbs, executive director of Oxfam International, observes:

> Some companies recognise the business case for sustainability and have made important commitments in that regard. No brand is too big to listen to its customers and if enough people urge the big food companies to do what's right, they've no choice but to listen.

There is a school of thought that says that unless CSR leads in some way to corporate social performance (CSP), then it is actually a meaningless exercise and at best is window dressing. CSP is a more rigorous approach for companies to take, as it focuses on the outcomes achieved as a result of CSR activities rather than getting stuck at showing general business accountability or talking about vague notions of responsibility to society, where there is very little substance behind such claims.

Many sponsorship practitioners naturally assume that CSR will lead to results or outcomes, but this is not always a given.

It is a simple truth, but words need to be matched by deeds; otherwise it is empty rhetoric. The definition of CSR has evolved over many decades, generally becoming more precise as to the types of activity and practice that might be subsumed under such a concept.

Early definitions were often general and ambiguous but more recently the definition of CSR has reflected these concerns and as a result has become much tighter. For example, the European Union definition of CSR is 'a concept whereby companies integrate social and environmental concerns in their business operations and in their interaction with their stakeholders on a voluntary basis'. Some of the features of modern CSR include:

- seriously considering the impact of the actions of an enterprise on others
- the moral and ethical obligations of managers to protect and improve the welfare of society as a whole
- meeting economic and legal responsibilities and extending beyond these obligations.

Perhaps a more encompassing definition of CSR is that it includes economic, legal, ethical, discretionary or even philanthropic expectations that society has of organisations at a given point in time.

Such a definition favours four different but interrelated categories of responsibilities that business has towards society. Such an approach also attempts to place the traditional economic and legal expectations of business in context by combining them with more socially oriented concerns such as ethics and corporate philanthropy. Stewart Lewis, researcher at Ipsos MORI, observes:

> Healthy business requires a healthy community, and should be contributing to its creation and maintenance. The public increasingly wants to know about companies that stand behind the brands and products presented to them. And they use their power to reward 'good' companies and punish the 'bad' ones.

With respect to ethical responsibility, the behaviour of a brand owner is one that society expects it to follow and this extends to actions, decisions and practices that are beyond strict legal requirements.

Perhaps a big growth area that needs to be better understood is corporate philanthropy, the sister discipline of sponsorship. Whereas sponsorship is commercially driven, the CSR component of a sponsorship programme is not saddled with the same considerations of helping to drive profits for the enterprise. Instead of focusing on communicating the 'what' and the 'how' of the brand proposition, CSR can help to communicate something much more powerful and perhaps at a deeper level – the 'why'.

No matter what definition is used, CSR is all about business performance in a variety of societal and environmental topic areas that usually embrace issues of diversity, philanthropy, socially responsible investment, environment, human rights, workplace issues, business ethics, sustainability, community development and corporate governance.

Looking down the list of developing countries in Table 9.2, we can see that CSR tends to have the following basic features:

- CSR is formally practised by internationalised national and multinational firms and these firms mostly set the local CSR agenda.
- CSR codes, standards and guidelines tend to be issue-specific, such as HIV/AIDS, poverty or literacy.
- CSR is commonly related to corporate philanthropy or charity.
- Firms perceive making an economic contribution, such as investments and job creation and provision of social services, such as housing or healthcare, as the most effective way of making a social contribution.
- The practice of CSR is strongly influenced by traditional community values and religion – for example in Africa (*ubuntu*), in Japan (*kyosei*) and in China (*xiaokang*).

Although academics have had an interest in CSR for over half a century, global business has only just started to take the issue much more seriously and websites such as Business Ethics (http://www.business-ethics.com) now cater for corporate interest in this area, and global organisations such as Business for Social Responsibility (BSR) seek to support companies implementing CSR policies and practices that contribute to sustainability and responsible commercial success.

Table 9.2 CSR agenda on a country basis

Country	CSR understanding	Key CSR issues	Key environment CSR issues
Argentina	CSR is a relatively new concept in Argentina. The economic crisis of late 2001 highlighted the social problems affecting even relatively prosperous segments of the population. The active role played by NGOs became particularly noticeable, which increased dramatically over the past few years. This, in turn, has prompted companies to show more social commitment.	Poverty and unemployment	Water pollution and air quality
Australia	CSR is commonly described by its promoters as aligning a company's activities with the social, economic and environmental expectations of its 'stakeholders'. It has become a multibillion dollar public relations speciality in the business world.	Employment, environment and indigenous groups	Sustainability, climate change, conservation and invasive species
Brazil	CSR is firmly established on the corporate agenda as one of the most important reputation and image risk management factors. Companies have become proactive and social players of change.	Value chain, poverty, inequality and transparency (anti-corruption)	Climate change, water and deforestation
Canada	CSR is a concept with a growing currency in Canada and closely resembles the business pursuit of sustainable development and the triple bottom line.	Poverty, climate change and youth at risk	Air pollution, conservation and climate change
China	CSR has led to Chinese consumers paying more attention to goods produced by sweatshops. To redeem their reputations and enhance investor confidence, multinational companies in China are now taking the lead in establishing their own codes of conduct.	Poverty and malnutrition	Pollution, carbon emissions, water resources and desertification
Ecuador	CSR is conceived of as a new way of doing business. Some business people see it as a fashion but others see it as a pure way of doing business. The government is implementing actions to motivate companies to put into practice good practices of CSR, but unfortunately more than 50% of companies still do not add this concept to their business.	Education, health and access to services	Animals in danger of extinction and the low control of carbon emissions

Country	CSR understanding	Key CSR issues	Key environment CSR issues
Egypt	So far Egypt has attached relatively little importance to CSR.	Poverty	Aridity, uneven population distribution and pollution
El Salvador	CSR is a strategic imperative that allows a business to incorporate policies and practices to benefit stakeholders, community, environment and all its supply chain through the alignment of its core activities with ethics and transparency principles, so that it is changed into a competitive agent that helps towards economic and social development.	Poverty, violence and illiteracy	Climate change (e.g., floods), deforestation and air pollution
Hong Kong	CSR strategy is a very important part of the overall success of companies. The key issues include transparency and accountability, taking account of workplace and community issues, as well as ensuring strong development and opportunities for employees.	Living wage, minimum wage, poverty, unemployment, HIV, drug use, prostitution and human trafficking	Absence of nature conservation policy, the pillaging of reef fish, sharks and other seafood
India	CSR is perceived as more of a community engagement initiative. Charity and philanthropy are migrating towards a CSR strategy that is being embedded in the business strategy of the corporation. CSR had, historically, been part of Indian business tradition as established by pioneers such as the Zoroastrian industrialist Jamsetji Tata	Education among the poor, poverty, health, living conditions, displaced communities	Pollution, greenhouse gas concentration, climate change, global warming, waste management, water contamination, air quality and land use
Iran	Philanthropic and charitable donations are the main focus of Iran-based firms – with a lack of multinational firms they do not have the more mature concepts of CSR that come from Europe or the USA.	Rural employment, disadvantaged groups from ethnic, religious or language backgrounds who are excluded from housing, education and employment	Air pollution, overexploitation of natural resources and droughts
Israel	Concepts of CSR are developing in Israel, with the banking and communications sectors being at the forefront of CSR reporting. However, the general view in terms of transparency and CSR reporting is that many firms in Israel fail to see the need to develop and provide such information.	Youth education, health and welfare issues	Waste, water resources and air pollution

(Continued)

Table 9.2 (Continued)

Country	CSR understanding	Key CSR issues	Key environment CSR issues
Japan	Almost all the listed companies in Japan address CSR strategies and initiatives by, for example, producing their annual CSR report, implementing CSR programmes, etc. CSR is now an issue for SMEs.	Ageing society, work–life balance and unemployment	CO_2 reduction, recycling and reusing
Mexico	CSR is still in the early stages of development in Mexico, with the need to move beyond the embedded idea that CSR refers to corporate philanthropy rather than a direct engagement with Mexican society. Most Mexicans have a hostile view of the corporate community. However, the European concept of CSR is slowly being integrated into the corporate strategy of some firms in Mexico, normally in the form of a simple set of guidelines to ensure a limited CSR policy is being followed.	Poverty, unemployment and violence	Lack of water, deforestation, lack of recycling programmes and high levels of CO_2 emissions from cars and industries
New Zealand	Increasing awareness, understanding and implementation of a wide range of CSR activity beyond just environmental and philanthropic initiatives.	Unemployment, personal and community safety (including domestic violence and drug abuse) and sustainable economic development	Government policy and regulatory control, non-sustainable farming practices, depletion of fish stocks, upsetting marine ecosystems and equilibrium
Nigeria	CSR plays no important role in Nigeria and has not been the subject of a wider public discussion.	Poverty, public health, lack of money for medicines, and illiteracy	Sea-level rise, fiercer weather, more frequent storms, floods, hurricanes, droughts and water scarcity
Pakistan	CSR is very much in the initial stages of development in Pakistan. Several NGOs are pushing CSR and awareness is growing.	High illiteracy, poverty and political tensions	Water scarcity, deforestation and pollution
Panama	There is a growing interest in CSR from companies. The transition from philanthropy to CSR is still in process. Activities or projects for the community are common in businesses and best practices are often not called 'CSR'. Nevertheless, some companies have already developed complete CSR programmes.	Safety, education and poverty	Recycling, clean production, sustainable development, and the lack of knowledge of existing environmental laws

Country	CSR understanding	Key CSR issues	Key environment CSR issues
Peru	CSR is used to define the responsibility of business regarding its social and environmental responsibility.	Employment opportunities, housing improvement, contributing to local infrastructure and services and other basic needs of the population	Climate change, mining, environmental liabilities and industrial waste disposal
Philippines	CSR is vibrant and there is an active community of companies practising and promoting CSR, which makes it one of the most developed CSR countries in Asia.	Poverty reduction, education, health, access to water and other basic services	Sustainable development, environment management and preparing for climate change, impact at the community level affecting farmers and fishermen, the poor and those living in rural, agricultural communities
Russian Federation	CSR is still in its infancy with some companies engaging in social issues, especially with regard to children, drawing on expectation and a culture of social responsibility from the Soviet period. However, much of this work does not relate to wider international concepts of CSR, with companies not linking it to their corporate strategies. Overall, the impression is that companies publicise their CSR activities in order to attract media attention without actually being able to prove their involvement.	Housing, healthcare, medicines, drug abuse and organised crime	Environmental degradation, acid rain and greenhouse gases
Singapore	CSR entails businesses paying back to society and tends to be driven by corporate philanthropy.	Fair employment, volunteerism, widening income gap, decline in fertility and ageing population	Water scarcity, public health, clean technology, renewable energy for economic growth and sustainable development

(Continued)

Table 9.2 (Continued)

Country	CSR understanding	Key CSR issues	Key environment CSR issues
South Africa	South African businesses have more actively pursued a CSR focus, moving towards measurement of their triple bottom line (economy, society and environment). Socially responsible investment is a concept in its infancy and is slowly being integrated into corporate policies, especially in an attempt to compete against global players.	Poverty, HIV/ AIDS and inequality	Dearth of water, as less than 10% is usable as surface water, one of the lowest rates worldwide, air pollution and water pollution
South Korea	CSR is playing an increasing role in Korea. Associations, the media and NGOs have taken up this topic more and more in recent years, while politics remains largely content to observe.	Ageing population, rural poverty	Air pollution, carbon emissions and the fact that Korea has no energy resources of its own
Taiwan	CSR is playing an increasing role in Taiwan.	Unemployment, the education of children from poor families and the lack of sustainable income generation in rural areas	Greenhouse gas emissions, vulnerability from extreme climate change, water shortage, soil and groundwater contamination and e-waste and illegal chemical use
Thailand	CSR in Thailand is well received and many corporations, both Thai and international, are eager to become involved in meaningful projects.	Lack of sustainable income generation in rural areas, poor and under-resourced education and inadequate oversight and management of infrastructure projects in rural areas	Deforestation, smuggling or illegal trading of endangered animals
UAE	CSR has grown worldwide into an interdisciplinary area of study and is reshaping the way in which businesses act. While the field has been a subject of extensive study worldwide, it has received little attention in the Middle East.	Indentured servants and gender inequality because of sharia law	Urbanisation, industrial development, overfishing and overgrazing

Country	CSR understanding	Key CSR issues	Key environment CSR issues
United Kingdom	CSR has developed into a sophisticated discipline among global brand owners.	Education, environment, grass-roots sports, health/diet of children, obesity, and welfare	Greenhouse gas, pollution, erosion of coastline, overfishing
United States	CSR is a well-defined concept with firms developing CSR strategies in response to the growing importance of issues such as sustainable investments, and with companies using CSR policy in their marketing output. CSR is used to develop brand awareness and give legitimacy to a firm.	Cost of living, universal healthcare and the inequity of the educational system	Climate change, greenhouse emissions and energy use
Uruguay	CSR is conceived as a wide set of policies, practices and programmes integrated in the core business of the company that support the decision-making processes and are explicitly recognised by the administration. The process of CSR expansion as a normal issue has been the result of pressure from consumers, suppliers, community, shareholders, NGOs and other social actors.	Unemployment, poverty and unequal welfare	Cellulose factories, conservation and solid residues in urban areas
Vietnam	CSR remains new and relatively undeveloped in Vietnam.	Poverty, living wage, unemployment, education, HIV, drug use and human trafficking	Wastewater, misuse of underground water and the rise of the sea level and flooding as a result of global warming

Source: Kolah (2015)

Current thinking in CSR and its relationship with sponsorship

One of the closest relationships between sponsorship and CSR activities is in the field of sports sponsorship, according to research conducted by SMG-Insight/YouGov in 2013 (see Table 9.3).

The survey questioned in excess of 19,000 UK respondents and revealed that high-profile sports sponsors have maintained their grip on the UK public's imagination when it comes to associating their brands with grass-roots sports.

Barclays scores highest among male respondents, with 25% mentioning the brand compared with 19% of female respondents, while the opposite trend is the case with Nike: 29% of female respondents associate the brand with grass-roots

Table 9.3 Brands most associated with grass-roots sports, 2013

Rank	Brands most associated with grass-roots sports	Overall percentage (%) of mentions by respondents
1	Nike	24%
2	Barclays	22%
3	Adidas	19%
4	McDonald's	16%
5	Coca-Cola	16%
6	Aviva	11%
7	RBS	8%
8	O2	8%
9	Lucozade	7%
10	Mars	5%
11	None of these	5%
12	Lloyds	5%
13	Guinness	4%
14	Carlsberg	4%
15	Nationwide	4%
16	Sky	4%
17	NatWest	3%
18	Carling	3%
19	Tesco	3%
20	Sainsbury's	3%
21	Umbro	3%
22	Vodafone	3%
23	Santander	2%
24	Red Bull	2%
25	British Gas	2%
26	National Lottery	2%
27	Reebok	2%
28	Visa	1%
29	BT	1%
30	Samsung	1%
31	EDF Energy	1%

Source: SMG-Insight/YouGov (2014)

sports compared with 20% of male respondents. Barclays also achieves strong recognition from the 55+-year-old segment at 29% recognition for grass-roots sports support but that association drops off dramatically among 18–34-year- old segment (15% recognition).

Adidas was third overall in the survey, linked to grass-roots sport by 19% of respondents and McDonald's and Coca-Cola sit in joint fourth place with 16% each. After this, there is a considerable dip in brand association, with insurance giant Aviva being mentioned by 11% overall and then each of the remaining brands in the Top 10 being mentioned by under 10% of all respondents.

As well as being the overall most mentioned brand in relation to grass-roots sport in general, Nike is also the brand most frequently associated with the development of specific sports at grass-roots level. For example, scores recorded in July 2013 showed 65% of respondents associated Nike with the development of basketball, 45% with golf and 38% jointly with both tennis and athletics. Adidas also achieved strong association with grass-roots sports, with 43% of respondents linking the brand with the development of grass-roots badminton, 40% with tennis and 29% with boxing.

Frank Saez, MD of SMG-Insight/YouGov, comments: 'These figures show significant opportunities available to previous London 2012 Sponsors to promote their grass-roots activities and to strengthen the relationship with key customer segments.'

Even where the association of grass-roots support has dropped, as in the case of McDonald's to 16%, nonetheless other sports-related programmes in the wake of London 2012, such as the Kickstart Community Programme, helped to maintain the brand's share of recognition by providing funding to local clubs.

The SMG-Insight/YouGov research tends to indicate there are four core reasons for a brand owner to consider grass-roots sports as part of the CSR component of sports sponsorship:

- More so than cultural sponsorship, sports sponsorship and the CSR component have the potential to reach a wide group of fans and simultaneously offer the sponsor a platform for social commitment to children and young people.
- Provided that the sports are not tainted by drug scandals or widespread cheating, these sports offer invaluable potential to communicate values such as respect, tolerance and fairness. These values are also essential for social integration as well as economic success for society.
- Employee volunteering can also be easily combined with sports. For example, in many sports clubs and associations, such as the Scouts, where sports and outdoor activities are a core component of the programme and development, adults already volunteer to train children and adolescents, offering emotional and social support provided they have been cleared by legal safeguarding checks.
- CSR for the environment and society requires increased visibility but also comprehensibility, which sports can often provide. CSR must be applied in the core business of the enterprise and whenever this is the case, sport can be the force that brings together customers, employees, and other stakeholder groups that can be inspired to get involved and to take part, and the activity, for example, creating more spaces for sports in urban and deprived areas, can have a transformative impact for the local community.

The motivations for brand owners to get involved in CSR as part of their sponsorship activities can vary between sectors and, of course, between competitive brands in those market sectors.

Research on CSR in English, Swiss and German top national league football clubs, 2011

This research study looked at the CSR component of football sponsorship pro-grammes in England, Switzerland and Germany and found 11 key motivations for sponsors to embed CSR in their sports sponsorship programmes (see Table 9.4).

The research also suggested that there is always a risk that, because sports sponsorship is often perceived as being about image, advertising and sales, the credibility and motivation of activities represented as CSR endeavours can often be open to question.

A key factor for brand owners undertaking CSR activities with these clubs was the ability to implement CSR programmes strategically within the context of football sponsorship as well as to make CSR activities communicable and measur-able so that these are seen in a positive light rather than being some new form of company rhetoric.

The research found a high degree of consistency but also differences in terms of the approach in using CSR as part of sports sponsorship. For example, Premier League clubs in the UK were recognised as being the most advanced in Europe in terms of embedding CSR as part of their sponsorship programmes, whereas in Switzerland football clubs tend not to get involved in CSR activities, largely as a result of limited resources, and in Germany there is a high level of involvement. CSR activities pursued by the football clubs in the individual national leagues can be seen in Table 9.5.

Table 9.4 Motivations of brand owners for incorporating CSR as part of football sponsor-ship

Sponsor motivation	Expected corporate social performance (CSP)
Improvement of image, reputation, and brand value	Increased consumer confidence/satisfaction
Creating confidence and legitimisation	Higher employee retention
Risk management	New investors
Improved use of resources	Fewer business risks
Access to financial capital	More successful innovations
Avoidance of state regulation and political pressure	More efficient cost structures
Establishment/maintenance of relationships with stakeholders and partners	Higher advertising impact
Increasing employee motivation and attractiveness for new employees	A better environmental balance/safer working conditions
Promoting innovation and new ways of thinking	Strategic brand differentiation
Development of new markets	Better cooperation with suppliers
Transmission of organisational culture/ values	Better crisis prevention/defence against attacks from competitors

Source: Journal of Sponsorship (2011)

Table 9.5 Typical CSR activities in football sponsorship (UK/Switzerland/Germany)

Education	Environment
Health	Ethics/racism
Social work	Drugs/violence
Fan efforts	Disabled
Sports/exercise	Former players
Children/youth	Family

Source: Journal of Sponsorship (2011)

Football club managers who were surveyed generally understood the differences in objectives between sponsorship and CSR, although they recognised that the relationship between CSR and football had become much stronger in recent years. In summary, football club managers revealed some interesting insights from their perspective:

• Revenue is generated from sponsorship and other intellectual property rights owned by the club. Given that CSR requires expenditure, some football clubs' economic goals are in conflict with social goals, even if there is a marketing concept associated with CSR.
• For some football club managers, there needs to be a clear boundary delineated between CSR and sponsorship and in some cases CSR is not managed by the marketing department, although it is an issue in marketing.
• There is strong contact between CSR and sponsorship and the balancing act between commerce and social commitment that tends to be reflected in the marketing of CSR measures, where clubs must tread very cautiously and where social commitment must take priority.
• Sponsorship is perceived as attracting a bigger spotlight on the club than CSR activities and so CSR activities cannot be pursued at the expense of sponsorship performance.
• Sponsorship is a commercial agreement with rights and obligations and needs to achieve a win–win outcome. CSR activities are in addition to sponsorship activities and CSR partners must not feel they have been used for achieving purely commercial rather than societal objectives. Sponsorship must not be sold as if it is CSR.
• CSR and sponsorship are of equal importance to football clubs. The view of some football managers is that CSR is not supported by sponsorship (only the club is) but, on the other hand, CSR is important for the club in order to sustain commercial sponsorship.

'Increasingly, sport is being used to create social progress. The link between sport and social progress is found in two of the biggest trends in business today – social media and "corporate social opportunity". People seek out brands that deliver both great value and great values, so companies need to communicate their values. Sports – with its built-in fan base, media coverage and attention-grabbing athletes – is the highest profile channel for companies to promote their values,' says Lesa Ukman, founder of IEG, the world's largest sponsorship research and consultancy organisation.

Beyond cash, awareness and conversation, sponsors are in a unique position to trigger significant shifts in consumer behaviour and have the potential to leave a legacy of positive change long after a sporting event is over. Two examples stand out for different reasons of how the relationship between CSR and sponsorship can be a force for good and good for business.

Case study: Coca-Cola and London 2012 Olympic Games

As a global beverage company, Coca-Cola is a leader in integrating its corporate social agenda into its sports partnerships and has made sustainability one of its key business objectives. It recycled all clear plastic waste at the London 2012 Games and turned it into new Coke bottles, back on the shelves within 6 weeks. To achieve this, Coca-Cola built western Europe's largest food-grade plastic recycling facility and it also invested in biogas trucks to deliver product for London 2012 and incorporated sustainability into its supply chain. None of this would have happened without its Olympic partnership. The sponsorship was a catalyst for mobilising action with environmental benefits well beyond the Olympic Games.

Case study: Proctor & Gamble and London 2012 Olympic Games

One of the other most successful CSR/sports sponsorship campaigns was delivered by global household and consumer products giant Proctor & Gamble as part of its sponsorship of the London 2012 Olympic Games.

The CSR/sponsorship campaign 'Thank You, Mom' was phenomenally successful because of the simplicity of the message and its execution. In essence, the campaign was all about celebrating what mothers do and thanking them for their efforts, their care and their achievements.

The campaign came to life with the short film *Best Job*, which tugged at emotional heart strings and celebrated the role that mothers play in raising Olympians and great children. There were also videos of the mothers of some of the 150 athletes sponsored by P&G brands. For example, a mother was shown watching her child excel through an exceptional sporting performance or achieving success in an event.

The campaign was promoted through a host of online and offline media channels and a companion in-store worldwide retailer programme was rolled out five months ahead of London 2012 and involved four million retailers. It was tied to an effort to raise USD 25m to support youth sports programmes that would aid both the Olympics and mothers everywhere. The promotions involved some 34 P&G household brands, including Tide/Ariel, Pantene, Pampers and Gillette.

There was a 'Thank You Mom' mobile app that allowed people to thank their own mothers with personalised content in the form of a video message, photo or text. The CSR/sponsorship programme was a winner on several levels as well as helping P&G generate USD 500m in incremental sales. 'There are universal human insights that really not only unify our brands and company from a creative standpoint but also bring people together,' remarks Marc Pritchard, global chief marketing officer at P&G.

The CSR/sponsorship campaign provided the prestige and energy of being involved in the London 2012 Olympics plus the 'feel-good' aspect of supporting youth sports and the connection with real mothers provided a sense of authenticity tinged with emotion. 'It's easy to empathize with moms that have fed babies, provided lunches, supported at swim meets, bandaged skinned knees, attended recitals and shared in the joy of winning gold at the Olympics. Everyone has a mother, and everyone can relate to the best aspects of a mom's role. If your firm has the all-too common problem of attempting to achieve synergy when there are multiple brands, most of which also span products and countries, you might look at the P&G "Thank You, Mom" program for inspiration,' advises US brand guru David Aaker. Aaker sees the P&G campaign as a brilliant effort to draw on a universal human value to create a programme with energy, relevance and emotion that spanned brands and countries and has endured well beyond the life of London 2012 Olympic Games. He points to the challenges facing brand owners today in delivering brand messages to multiple local markets via the Internet. Aaker adds:

> A brand that has different local positions can become confused and the necessary scale of advertising, promotions, and big idea brand building are virtually unavailable when local brand building dominates. So brand owners need to deal with this silo issue by overlaying co-ordination and communication between silos. The brand building answer is to find driving ideas in the form of human values that are universal and that everyone can relate to. That answer could be found in education, health issues, water conservation or others, but it needs to apply to all silos and be capable of maintaining relevance over time.

How Unilever has embraced CSR and made it indistinguishable from its business

Outside the area of CSR/sport sponsorship, multinational company Unilever has embraced sustainability as its key platform for brand communication and the way it does business across the world.

In some respects, Unilever has made the term 'CSR' redundant and has avoided falling into the silo trap as described by Aakers by embracing ethics and social responsibility and wrapping this around the whole enterprise.

Case study: Unilever and the Sustainable Living Plan, 2010–15

Unilever's global CEO Paul Polman views the legacy of Lord William Lever as one of the most valuable assets that the company owns today. And that legacy inherited from its founder is the principle of 'responsible capitalism'.

Lever had pioneered the Victorian model of paternalistic business, going further than the Cadbury and the Rowntree families, who were staunch Quakers with a strong sense of corporate philanthropy.

At a time when disease and malnutrition were widespread in Britain, Lever's products were famously marketed for their health benefits. His employees were decently housed in a purpose-built company town, Port Sunlight, on Merseyside, Liverpool. Lever campaigned for state pensions for the elderly and even provided schooling, health care and good wages at palm-oil plantations in the Congo – something that no other industrialist had done on such a scale before, although George Cadbury had also supported rural communities of people who worked harvesting cocoa beans for the company in its plantations in Ghana and other African countries.

Today, Unilever has continued to build its global business on the values laid down by Lord Lever by paying close attention to its environmental and social impact. This form of enlightened self-interest was the basis for the company's Sustainable Living Plan, which aims not only to reduce Unilever's environmental footprint and increase its 'positive social impact' but also to double sales and increase long-term profitability.

Rather than simply focusing on maximising shareholder value and investor returns, Polman has higher ambitions for the company and wants sustainability to be at the core of its business, rather than something that appears as corporate rhetoric on its website and in news releases. So far, Polman's efforts have been universally welcomed and in a recent survey Unilever was ranked as the world leader in this field by a wide margin (see Figure 9.1).

Unilever is generally reckoned to have the most comprehensive strategy of enlightened capitalism of any global firm. The company also stands out for the way it has tried to institutionalise its efforts according to Alice Korngold, author of *A Better World, Inc.*, a book on corporate do-gooding.

The Unilever board scrutinises the Sustainable Living Plan and executive pay is linked to its targets. According to *The Economist*, the plan has helped to boost employee satisfaction, not just Polman's pay packet and it has also positively impacted the company's share price since it was unveiled in November 2010 by more than 40%. And this was during a period when its biggest rival, Procter & Gamble of America, lost its way and ultimately its boss.

However, Unilever may have reached a critical point, as some analysts are starting to question whether the Sustainable Living Plan will actually deliver the double-digit growth promised by Polman.

In 2014, Unilever's annual results disappointed the markets, and the share price dropped below what it had been a year earlier. Shareholders remain cautious and are looking for bigger returns in 2015 and beyond.

'Unilever has built a strong niche position with investors who focus on environmental concerns,' says Martin Deboo of Jefferies, an investment bank. 'But for mainstream investors, it's a modest positive at most, and then only so long as it doesn't cost much.' So despite the leadership Unilever has shown, there are still question marks over its sustainability strategy, for example, whether it can

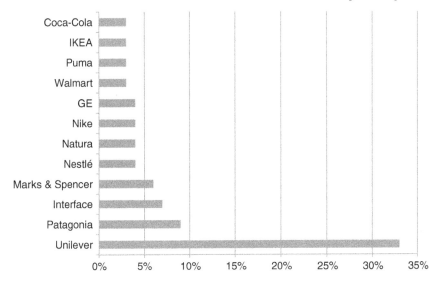

Figure 9.1 Leaders in sustainability (% of analysts polled)
Source: GlobeScan/SustainAbility Survey (2014)

achieve the targets set out in its plan and whether this will help to raise the share price. Polman remains committed, as does the Unilever board, to seeing this through, although it may take more persuasion to get shareholders, and investors' backing for sticking to the Sustainable Living Plan.

Unilever defines sustainability as including not just environmental factors but also improving the lot of customers and workers – its own employees and those in its supply chain. It also aims to contribute to society as a whole.

These CSR goals are seen as necessary to maintain the firm's 'licence to oper-ate' in an age in which companies are under increasing public scrutiny.

By 2020, Unilever aims to 'help a billion people to take steps to improve their health and well-being'; halve the environmental impact of its products; and source all its agricultural raw materials sustainably, which means that it should meet requirements covering everything from forest protection to pest control.

Progress on energy use and waste reduction – which the company directly controls – has been impressive. Through recycling and efficiency drives, 75% of Unilever's manufacturing sites now send no non-hazardous waste to landfills. Carbon emission in its manufacturing operations is 33% lower than in 2008, through a combination of cleaner technologies and greater efficiency. Newly established best practices have spread faster than expected through the company largely as a result of a central corporate team dedicated to spreading the word; previously this had been left to individual factories.

In many respects, this is evidence of joined-up CSR thinking, although Unile-ver never describes what it does as CSR, of course, because its ethics and business practices wrap around the whole enterprise. The company has also gone a step further and established a 'small actions, big differences fund' to invest in cost-saving ideas proposed by its business units as a way of encouraging greater innovation in its business. In some respects, such activities have opened the door to a new wave of corporate sponsorship. For example, the company has signed up to certification schemes run by the Rainforest Alliance, a non-governmental organisation, to improve farming practices in cocoa that is used in its ice cream brands such as Wall's and Ben & Jerry's, and in tea used by Lipton's. Rainforest Alliance schemes also have an educational component and Unilever has trained more than half the small farmers of Kenya who grow in tea, the country's largest export crop, and it has budgeted USD 5m for expanding the scheme to other parts of Africa and to Vietnam. Other major brand owners such as Coca-Cola, SABMiller and Wal-mart also have similar schemes for training small farmers, as this improves incomes at the bottom of the pyramid and makes farm supplies more secure by reducing environmental threats such as water scarcity.

Although Unilever may be able to buy its own raw materials from sustainable sources, it alone is rarely big enough to make a difference to any given commodity worldwide.

As a result, Polman spends a lot of time trying to persuade his peers and rivals to act more sustainably too. A big test of his effectiveness will come with palm oil, a crop that plays a significant role in deforestation, as tropical forests are often cleared illegally to make way for palm-oil plantations.

As impressive as these efforts appear, Unilever will ultimately fail unless it can influence and change the behaviour of its billions of consumers worldwide so that they too learn to behave in a more eco-friendly and sustainable way. At the start of the Sustainable Living Plan the company measured the carbon footprint of 2,000 of its products and found that on average 68% of greenhouse gas emissions in their life cycles occurred only after they got into the hands of consumers, mostly through the energy-intensive process of heating water, for example, for its tea bags or using its washing powder.

However behaviour change does not happen overnight and by 2015 Unilever hopes that 200m of its consumers will be encouraged to take shorter showers and by so doing reduce greenhouse gas emissions as well as conserving water – consuming more Unilever products designed to work with less liquid, which is good for its bottom line too. But can this really be achieved rather than making a great news headline when it fails to materialise, which can only weaken its efforts to continue to invest in its new business model?

Unilever has embarked on the hardest part of its new strategy – overhauling how it markets its brands.

Soon after William Lever launched Lifebuoy soap in the 1890s, he started running linked advertisements and educational campaigns. In the USA, millions of children took part in a 'Clean Hands Health Campaign' in the 1920s. In 2002 Unilever started pushing the same idea in India, offering hand-washing classes in villages and this has now been expanded across the developing world in order to help combat hepatitis and other infectious diseases.

These sponsored health education programmes have also reduced diarrhoea by 25% and, as a result, children's school attendance has also increased because children are sick less often. The challenge now is to do the same with brands that do not have such obvious health benefits as Lifebuoy.

'Unilever is taking this approach to sustainability further than other companies', says Linda Scott of Oxford University's Said Business School. But refocusing 400 brands 'on the good the product can do', she reckons, will take a long time and 'require patient capital'. And this is a lesson that Unilever may have learnt over 100 years earlier. Back in the 1920s shareholder pressure eventually forced William Lever to scale back his ambitions and Polman had the foresight to recognise this could happen again.

So, one of his earliest executive decisions was to get the company to move away from quarterly financial reporting and stop giving guidance to the markets about the company's next financial results. Instead, the company is now on a new path to encourage investors to think about the fundamentals of the business, which Polman claims are vastly improved by the Sustainable Living Plan.

What is certain is that Unilever's 'enlightened capitalism' is leading the global business community to embrace a more ethical and sustainable way of doing business while at the same time trying to change the short-term horizons of shareholders and investors. It remains to be seen whether Polman can achieve both objectives while he remains at the helm of one of the biggest global companies in the world.

Chapter 9 at a glance

1   All the evidence indicates that corporate social responsibility (CSR) has become a key issue for many brand owners such as Unilever that compete in a highly competitive global market where strong social credentials based on deeds rather than just words can provide a highly valuable competitive advantage that cannot easily be replicated.

2   Price, quality and functionality are no longer enough for success. Depending on the market segment, all of these can be replicated within days or weeks. They no longer help to maintain brand differentiation in the longer term.

3   Emotional engagement and values, by way of contrast, are much harder to develop, much harder to replicate and, once established, much more embedded and harder to shift. Investing in values and a 'bank of goodwill' pays dividends. As brand management evolves, values are becoming the key differentiator for those involved in sponsorship and CSR activities.

4   Such 'enlightened self-interest' as envisioned nearly 200 years ago by the Zoroastrian founders of Tata permeates virtually all the best examples of CSR and its relative low-cost compared with above- and below-the-line advertising has helped to make it a compelling proposition for many brand owners across the world.

5   Although CSR activation costs are usually a lot lower than those of other types of sponsorship activation activity, CSR does requires commitment,

imagination and a genuine partnership with the cause or issue to make it work successfully. And increasingly, this will also include government, as it does in India. Without this, brand owners can be seen to be paying lip service to being committed to making a difference not just for themselves but to wider society and run the reputation risk of being accused of indulging in a cynical public relations exercise designed to make the public believe that it is doing its bit for the community, when, in fact, it is unashamedly using a charity or cause for blatant self-promotion.

6   If the sole objective of the brand owner is to promote itself and its products and services, then it may be better to use straight sponsorship as a key communication platform rather than try to disguise it in the clothes of CSR.

7   Ultimately, if a brand owner wants to enjoy high levels of consumer trust, then there are three golden rules it needs to follow:

   i.   CSR must be at the heart of its business – it must be about how the brand owner makes its profits not just on how it spends its profits

   ii.   It needs to look at how customer segments receive information about its brands. These brand communication channels must be used for engaging in dialogue with the audience rather than for traditional 'push' communication activities

   iii.   The brand owner needs to respond with integrity to attacks on its reputation where these occur and must not ignore problems or concerns before they morph into serious issues that erode and damage trust, confidence – and ultimately its reputation.

8   The relationship between CSR and sponsorship is getting much closer, as evidenced in sports sponsorship as well as activities concerning health, welfare, education, environment and sustainability, which promises to open up new opportunities for brand owners in how they can make a positive difference in the lives of millions of consumers around the world.

Questions for discussion

1   What are the key differences between CSR and sponsorship? How can they be made to work better together?

2   Why should a global brand owner consider CSR as part of its sponsorship programme?

3   Is it practicable or desirable for other countries to follow the lead given by India and force companies to undertake CSR activities by making it a statutory requirement?

4   Is CSR a fad that will eventually fade away to be replaced by something else or does it have a long-term future as part of a brand's marketing and communications strategy?

5   Should CSR be managed by those not involved in marketing?

6   What are the risks facing brand owners and rights holders when embarking on a high- profile CSR programme?

7   What is the business case that can be put to a board of directors that will convince them that being a force for good is also good for business?
8   What lessons can brand owners learn from how Unilever abolished the use of the term CSR?

Further reading

Cave, A (2012), Socially responsible investment, *CorpComms Magazine*, November/December 2012

Crane, A, McWilliams, A, Matten, D, Moon, J and Siegel, D (2009), *The Oxford Handbook of Corporate Social Responsibility*, Oxford University Press

Eccles, R and Krzus, M (2010), *One Report*, Wiley

Fisk, P (2010), *People, Planet, Profit*, Kogan Page

The Guardian (2014), India's new CSR law sparks debate among NGOs and businesses, 11 August

Hoskins, T (2008), *The ICSA Corporate Social Responsibility Handbook*, ICSA Publishing

Hoverman, G, Breitbarth, T and Walzel, S (2011), Beyond sponsorship? Corporate social responsibility in English, German and Swiss top national league football clubs, *Journal of Sponsorship* 4, , 338–352

Kanter, E M (2009), *Supercorp*, Profile Books

Korngold, A (2014), *A Better World, Inc.*, Palgrave Macmillan

McCormick, A (2012), Building the company brand: Connecting CSR to the business, *Journal of Brand Strategy* 1, 2, 106–117

Overman, S (2014), *The Conscience Economy: How a Mass Movement for Good is Great for Business*, Bibliomotion

Pohl, M and Tolhurst, N (2010), *Responsible Business*, Wiley

Visser, W, Matten, D, Pohl, M and Tolhurst, N (2010), *The A-Z of Corporate Social Responsibility*, Wiley

Websites

BSR [accessed 19 October 2014]: http://www.bsr.org

Business Ethics Magazine [accessed 19 October 2014]: http://www.business-ethics.com

Can CSR change the world? [accessed 14 October 2014]: http://www.guruinabottle.com

Conference Board Paper: The link between brand value and sustainability (2013) [accessed 14 October 2014]: http://www.csrhub.com/

Getting brands through the school gates can start a green revolution [accessed 14 October 2014]: http://www.guruinabottle.com

360 Global Partner Network [accessed 15 October 2014]: http://www.csr360gpn.org/

Unilever Sustainable Living [accessed 14 October 2014]: http://www.sustainable-living.unilever.com

United Nations Global Compact [accessed 14 October 2014]: http://www.unglobalcompact.org

Reports

CSR: A Global Overview, Business in the Community International (2010)

10 Measurement and evaluation of sponsorship

In this chapter

- Six-step sponsorship model
- Importance of SMART objectives
- Methods of sponsorship proposal assessment
- Inputs, outputs, outcomes
- Budget setting
- Return on objectives
- Return on investment
- Measurement methodologies
- Role of market research
- Using external providers of measurement and evaluation

Introduction

On 29 April 2009 the *Financial Times* reported that promoting the London 2012 Olympic Games 'is probably the biggest assignment in the history of UK marketing'. A key issue was the ability of sponsors to achieve a strong return on investment (ROI) on a scale never seen before in the UK.

One of the most striking features of London 2012 – which has rarely been matched since – is the way in which the event was 'owned' by the public as well as the wholehearted and unanimous support, enjoyment and participation by the entire population. The benefit of London 2012 transcended financial and sporting considerations and has left a deep impression on the psyche of the British public for years to come, according to research by Brand Finance (see Figure 10.1).

Sponsorship managers are under increasing pressure to demonstrate a return on investment and sports rights holders are under increasing pressure to ensure that the rights sold will help to deliver a return for the sponsor. In this context, measurement and evaluation are of equal importance and value to all parties that have an investment in making sure that the sponsorship works.

Measurement and evaluation must be non-adversarial and should serve the interests of all parties to a sponsorship programme in terms of how that programme can be improved for the future as well as delivering measurable results for the sponsor and rights holder.

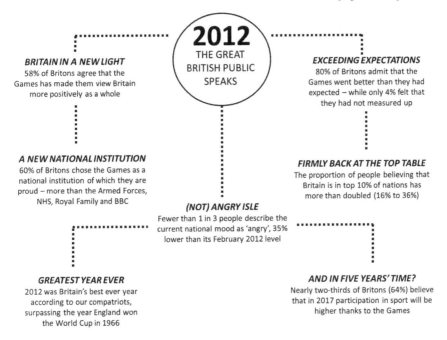

Figure 10.1 Measurement and evaluation of London 2012

Source: Brand Finance (2014)

Measurement and evaluation in sponsorship are typically used in two ways:

- Cost comparison of the money that a brand owner invests in sponsorship compared with other brand communication and marketing activities, such as advertising or direct mail.
- The impact that the sports sponsorship has had in terms of volume, price, distribution, revenue and profits for the sponsor.

Measurement and evaluation are no longer an option but a strategic discipline at the heart of improving the performance of sponsorship. Talk to any sponsorship practitioner or sponsorship manager and they will tell you that the lack of a universally accepted measurement methodology is a factor that holds back the credibility of sponsorship as a part of the marketing mix.

The good news are things are changing rapidly as sponsorship practice has matured and rights holders have risen to the challenge of delivering a return on objectives (ROO) and return on investment (ROI) for brand owners (see further in this chapter). To measure the ongoing value of a sponsorship programme effectively it is necessary to focus on inputs, outputs and outcomes. This should be done by having a transparent and accountable methodology that allows the campaign deliverables to be constantly tracked against allocated resources.

Many in the sponsorship industry now recognise that the art of setting meaningful metrics needs to be elevated to being a key driver in developing a successful sponsorship strategy and improving the performance of sponsorship.

In the past, metrics have been talked about as a consequence of the sponsorship tactics (outputs) employed in a sponsorship campaign or programme. But that alone is not enough. What must also be measured is outcomes as a result of the sponsorship campaign or programme. This subtle but critical shift in thinking about measurement and evaluation means that sponsorship managers must embrace measurement before the sponsorship strategy has been finalised.

Today, many brand owners take an almost forensic approach to setting measurement based on a complete examination of business requirements – and this will include selling more stuff – desired audience and customer segments, brand marketing and communication objectives and, of course, actual behaviour as a result of the sponsorship.

Only by fundamentally understanding and testing what desired customers, clients, and supporters are looking for can we set appropriate objectives for the resulting campaign. It is here that the metrics by which the campaign will be measured should be set out.

Irrespective of whatever methodology is used, it is important that:

- measurement and evaluation are built on analysing measurable objectives
- there is a clear research brief
- the criteria for measurement are properly explained and understood by all those taking part
- there is an understanding of how this analysis will be used in a constructive (rather than destructive) context.

Ideally, all sponsorship programmes should have an element in the budget set aside for measurement and evaluation; yet fewer than 11% of all sponsorship investments are measured and evaluated – a situation that has retarded the growth of sponsorship.

Measurement and evaluation of sponsorship are not an exact science. However, provided the process is focused on analysing the achievement of measurable objectives, it is possible to measure and evaluate sponsorship like any other form of brand communication and marketing. Measurement and evaluation tools and techniques can also help brand owners to qualify those opportunities that are more suitable and justify further investigation and financial commitment. Increasingly, sponsorship consultancies are providing this level of support for brand owners in the sponsorship planning process.

From a global perspective, most sponsorship deals are USD 150,000–USD 500,000 in value, which, in turn, means that the vast majority of sponsorships are relatively small in value terms. As a result, little effort has traditionally been made to measure and evaluate the net impact of sponsorship on the brand and on sales unless the brand owner has used sponsorship as a central platform for all its key brand communication and marketing activities on a local or international basis.

Given that sponsorship, as with other forms of marketing, is subject to greater scrutiny and accountability than ever before, sponsors' attitudes towards measuring the return on investment are starting to change – albeit slowly. One issue is separating the difference sponsorship contributes to business value and what other elements of the marketing mix contribute to business value.

The impact on desired market or customer segments is extremely important in this regard – B2B, B2C, employees, partners – as these audiences will need to have demonstrated that they understand the link between the sponsor, rights holder and the property and that this had a tangible and measurable impact on behaviour.

Several years ago, and on the basis of my own experience in the sponsorship industry, I devised a six-step sponsorship model (see Figure 10.2) to help brand owners and rights holders understand how best to measure and evaluate sponsorship investments with a high degree of accuracy and insight and this has been used extensively in my own sponsorship work. It is a logical six-step process that can apply to any property type, not just sport.

Six-step sponsorship model

The perspective of the model is deliberately from the point of view of the brand owner that may want to evaluate its move to renew the sponsorship, change the course of the existing sponsorship, not renew the existing sponsorship programme or indeed enter into a new sponsorship agreement with a completely different rights holder.

From the rights holder's perspective, the six-step sponsorship model is still relevant, as it is vital to understand the thought processes of a brand owner prior to a decision being made. As I often explain to my post-graduate students, in the vast majority of cases in which you may become involved, a major brand owner will already be engaged in some form of sponsorship, in which case the starting point for the six-step sponsorship process will be an existing activity review of the current sponsorship property.

Step 1: existing activity review

There are four parts to this process:

1 qualitative review of existing activities (for example, a review of other sponsorships that the sponsor may also be involved with)
2 establishing criteria for this review (for example, making an assessment on effectiveness)
3 environmental analysis (for example, looking at political, economic and technological issues)
4 brand audit (for example, looking at strategic objectives).

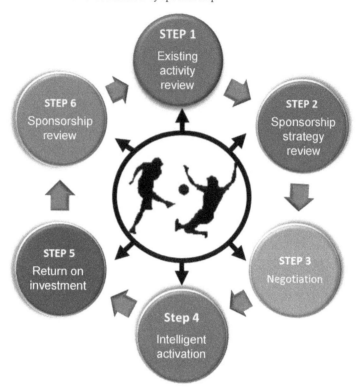

Figure 10.2 Six-step sponsorship model
Source: Kolah (2014)

The existing activity review will look at all sides of the activation of a sponsorship programme and will include online, mobile, social, interactive, advertising, direct mail, sales promotions, PR, internal communications and other activities.

The criteria used to evaluate activation of the existing sponsorship are:

- creative ingredient
- timeline
- spend
- effectiveness (out of 100%).

In the absence of an existing sponsorship, the brand owner can focus its effort on conducting an environmental analysis. Depending on the budget, the brand owner and rights holder might wish to carry out an environmental analysis.

In broad terms, this will include the following:

- market conditions, products/services
- target audiences

- experience
- problem areas
- geographical footprint for brand
- competition
- sponsorship activity of the competition (if any)
- political, economic and technological issues.

The last phase in Step 1 is the brand audit – this is extremely important in order that the brand owner can achieve a successful match with a property mapped against its core brand essence, values and brand personality:

- understanding the brand owner
- strengths, weakness, opportunities and threats (SWOT) analysis
- current strategic objectives
- brand essence
- values
- brand personality
- image.

Step 2: sponsorship policy and strategy

Assuming that there is a sponsorship policy and strategy, it is how the property is measuring up on the basis of the policy and strategy. The strategy may contain areas of uncertainty that may have been the cause for weak performance or a mismatch of expectations in the past. The sponsorship strategy may need to be updated; for example, technology may have changed with the increased importance of content for 4G mobile handsets and user-generated content (UGC) that needs to drive engagement compared with the point in time when the sponsorship strategy was first conceived.

Steps 1 and 2 may have taken place immediately before the expiry of the sponsorship programme, at a point before renewal or immediately before undertaking a new programme.

Combining the two steps of the sponsorship provides a sound basis for Step 3 – negotiation with the rights holder.

Sponsorship policy and strategy review can be triggered by a number of factors, including internal changes within the brand owner as well as external changes.

The following are the key elements that should be present in any sponsorship policy and strategy:

- measurable objectives
- audience segmentation (including internal)
- brand essence
- brand fit
- sector match (to the sport, social, arts, culture, education, association, environmental, media property)

- length/duration
- location/geography
- integration with other channels
- impact on behaviour of internal and external audiences.

Step 3: negotiation of sponsorship deal

The outcome of the negotiation step is an extension of the sponsorship pro-gramme subject to certain amendments, a new sponsorship agreement, or a termination of the relationship and negotiation with other suitable/alternative rights holders by the brand owner.

Negotiations within sports sponsorship, for example, can sometimes take weeks, months and even years, particularly where the deal being contemplated is for a long-term sponsorship in excess of three years.

Each side will have a team of specialist commercial and sponsorship lawyers whose job it is to ensure that there are no duties or obligations that are owed to the other side that have not been intended. In addition, each side will thrash out in minute detail what rights and benefits will flow from the sponsorship contract and this will be particularly important in relation to the use of intellectual prop-erty (IP) rights.

In general, there are three expected outcomes from the negotiation process:

- extension of the existing sponsorship agreement (renewal)
- amendments to the current sponsorship agreement and renewal
- termination of the agreement (or non-renewal).

There are some common features to negotiations within sports sponsorship:

- legal considerations – ease/difficulty of conducting contractual negotiations with the rights holder
- assessment of the value of promotional activities/sales and marketing outside sponsorship
- integration of the sponsorship with sales process/selling cycle
- integration of sponsorship within the marketing mix
- sponsorship as a solution to achieve brand owner's objectives.

The conclusion of Step 3 assumes there is a workable sponsorship agreement in place in order to move to Step 4.

Step 4: activation of the sponsorship

A common mistake made by some brand owners is to assume that the activation of a property is the key responsibility of the rights holder. This give rise to so-called 'self-activation sponsorship' but this is dangerous thinking!

While there is usually an obligation in the sponsorship agreement on the rights holder to do everything in its power and use its 'best endeavours' to promote the link between the property and sponsor, it is incumbent on the sponsor to ensure that it fully exploits the intellectual property (IP) rights it has acquired. For example, Coca-Cola in the USA spends upwards of four times the sponsorship rights fee in its activation of its FIFA football World Cup and Olympic Games properties. Its research shows the incremental value returned for every dollar spent on leveraging its sponsorship campaigns and using sponsorship to create Coca-Cola brand experiences is an effective means of generating brand loyalty that helps to drive sales in over 100 consumer markets across the world. The most common forms of activation of a sponsorship property are through advertising and public relations, although interactive platforms, such as mobile and social networks and broadcast channels are increasingly important.

Each channel offers its own particular advantages and the channels selected for activation of the sponsorship programme need to be evaluated in an appropriate way (see Figure 10.3).

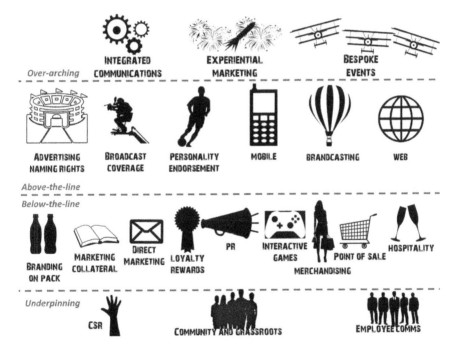

Figure 10.3 Exploitation of sponsorship
Source: Kolah (2014)

Step 5: Measuring return on investment

Brand owners and rights holders should know and measure:

- relevant audience numbers (general or niche audiences, depending on objectives)
- demographic and psychographic details on the audience that are also required before, during and after a sponsorship programme.

With respect to the data available, brand owners and rights holders should carefully monitor activities and only measure impacts against desired audience reach as opposed to all reach.

In terms of sponsorship events, brand owners and rights holders should measure:

- spectator numbers
- hospitality guests attendance
- employee tickets uptake.

In some cases, this is linked to promotions, prizes, and competitions, and so a correlation between attendance and these types of activation can be easily and accurately measured.

Media coverage is a key value for assessing the return on investment:

- TV figures – demographics by programme
- press – readership by title plus sports pages – only 50% read and mostly male
- Internet – unique visitors
- social – likes, downloads, tweets, retweets, Favourites
- radio – listening figures should be by programme rather than by station
- BARB has profiles of people watching.

Promotions and competitions are increasingly popular ways in which to activate a sponsorship, particularly across the Web and other interactive platforms:

- response rates for prize draws
- redemption rates
- revenue from mobile or other services.

Step 6: sponsorship review

Once some form of return on investment has been computed, then both the sponsor and the rights holder can have a full and frank discussion on making an overall assessment of the sponsorship programme and whether it has delivered against the objectives as well as the expectations of all parties concerned.

There are four main perspectives that need to be covered in this final step of the sports sponsorship strategic process:

1   brand owner's perspective
2   sports rights holder's perspective
3   fans and consumers' perspective
4   other stakeholders' perspective.

The sponsorship policy and strategy should have helped to segment these groups and research may be conducted on a quantitative and qualitative basis.

Once the review of the sponsorship programme has taken place, there will need to be a period of time before a second review of the sponsorship programme commences, which could be 12 months from the date of Step 6, and the process is then repeated. As you have now seen, successful sponsorship is built on two major foundations – planning and strategy. Without ensuring that attention is given to both of these aspects, the rights holder and the brand owner will enter negotiations at a distinct disadvantage and may find themselves on the wrong side of a sponsorship agreement that provides a disproportionate amount of benefit to one party at the expense of the other.

Planning is dependent on ascertaining both qualitative as well as quantitative data that is both internal and external in nature. Successful sponsorship strategy takes account of this information and provides a route map in terms of how the sponsorship can be successfully activated.

However, this cannot be achieved unless the strategy clearly defines measurable objectives from the outset as well as how these objectives will be measured.

Importance of SMART objectives

There are several important considerations that a brand owner must take into account when thinking about getting involved in a sponsorship programme:

- How can we cut through the noise and beat the intense competition that we face in our market segment?
- How do we use sponsorship as part of the brand value proposition and use it to do business on our customers' terms?
- How does sponsorship help us take an 'outside-in' rather than an 'inside-out' perspective?
- How do we articulate what we deliver in an emotional and rational way that is totally compelling, memorable and ultimately influences behaviour?
- How do we use sponsorship to help build relationships that our customer segments actually want to belong to?
- And what does it take to engage with audience and customer segments more deeply and turn them into brand advocates?

In order to achieve any or all of these, we need to apply two 'tests' to the sponsorship programme – will the sponsorship under consideration deliver a return on objectives (ROO) and a return on investment (ROI)? Should any sponsorship programme fail these two tests, then the brand owner should seriously consider whether it should invest in the programme in the first place or continue to reinvest in it.

It is important to set benchmarks *before* the activation of a sponsorship programme and even before the sponsorship is announced, so that the impact of the sponsorship on particular metrics can be clearly seen.

To improve the performance of sponsorship there needs to be a link between business and marketing performance (see Table 10.1).

Sponsorship managers need to 'move the needle' of sponsorship performance by impacting the following metrics:

- customer engagement – customer awareness, customer preference, customer affinity
- market impact – market share, customer retention, channel penetration
- marketing improvement – product innovation, brand building, market development
- financial performance – sales revenue, profitability, growth
- enhancing brand image – building a valuable brand
- increasing sales/market share – financial performance
- building awareness – fame for the brand
- increasing Web traffic – helps to drive consideration
- generating social media buzz – building a narrative.

Table 10.1 Link with business and marketing performance

Marketing performance	Business performance	What the link looks like
Marketing spend	Marketing activities	How much you spend on brand marketing, advertising and sponsorship activities (above and below the line)
Marketing activities	Purchase drivers	How brand marketing, advertising and sponsorship address the priorities of customer segments, for example, quality, price, image, etc.
Marketing activities	Customer attitudes	How brand marketing, advertising and sponsorship drive increased brand preference, perceived value, etc.
Customer attitudes	Purchase behaviour	How perceived value translates into price premium for the sponsor's products, multi-purchases, etc.
Sales results	Financial results	How sales and margins translate into operating profits and growth
Financial results	Shareholder value	How sponsor's profits and growth translate into future cash flows and business confidence

Source: Kolah (2015)

As a result, sponsorship objectives need to be SMART:

- **s**pecific
- **m**easurable
- **a**chievable
- **r**elevant
- **t**ime-bound.

Case study: Speedo global sponsorship

Back in 2008 I was appointed by Celia Muir, who was responsible for managing Speedo's global sponsorship programme, to create its first ever sponsorship toolkit. This was no easy task, as Speedo has dominated its product category for swimwear globally for nearly 100 years and has used sponsorship to build its brand marketing and communication platform effectively to drive its sales growth.

The toolkit had to reflect current and future best practice for arguably one of the most experienced sponsors on the planet. The Speedo Sponsorship Toolkit was issued to all markets globally across 64 countries and was the blueprint for how Speedo was to improve the performance of sponsorship across five levels;

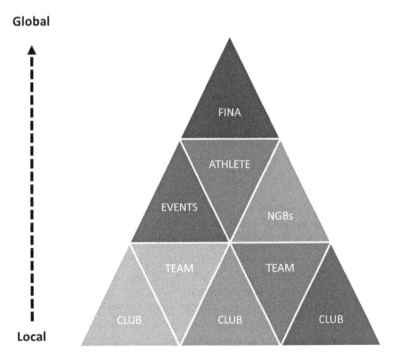

Figure 10.4 Speedo's hierarchy of sponsorship investments globally

Source: Speedo Sponsorship Toolkit (2008)

with the world governing body for swimming FINA (Fédération Internationale de Natation) at the top of the sponsorship apex and individual local swimming clubs at the base of the sponsorship apex (see Figure 10.4).

In order to understand how Speedo got involved in sponsorship in the first place, it is useful to take a brief look at Speedo's history. Speedo's founder was Alexander MacRae who arrived in Sydney in 1910 as a 22-year-old immigrant from the Scottish fishing village of Loch Kishorn. The industrious MacRae, whose descendants live in Australia today, established MacRae Knitting Mills, a modest hosiery business.

However, after a few years and with the outbreak of World War I in 1914, MacRae's manufacturing business grew rapidly as a result of demand from the Australian Army for socks. Production continued to boom after the end of World War I and by the late 1920s MacRae was able to diversify production into swimwear after spotting a gap in the market for more modern attire that would protect the modesty of women at a time when they were permitted to bathe in the sea during daylight hours!

These early products were commercially successful, as a more liberal attitude was emerging in Australia that accepted mixed public bathing as well as viewing swimming as a competitive sport. An innovation at the time was the racer-back costume and MacRae ran a competition among his employees to come up with a catchy slogan for these new products. Captain Jim Parsons won £5 in 1928 for coming up with the catchy slogan 'Speed on in your Speedos' and the brand 'Speedo' was born. As a result of the commercial success of these garments, MacRae changed the name of the company to Speedo Knitting Mills in 1929.

Over the next 40 years, Speedo became the premium brand of choice for professional swimmers and this helped to drive sales with a discerning consumer not just in Australia and by the 1960s Speedo was a dominant swimming brand in the USA; by the 1970s Speedo was the biggest producer of swimsuits in the world.

Early sponsorship deals reinforced Speedo's commitment to grass-roots swimming, particularly in the USA. In the 1970s, Speedo sponsored a 48-minute film on the Munich Olympics designed to be an educational aid to the growth of amateur swimming and it supported the Australian Swimming Union in order to develop national championships and to provide coaching camps in order to nurture natural swimming talent.

In 1976 the Australian Open Championships' installation of timing equipment was sponsored by Speedo and later that year Speedo became the driving force behind a scheme known as SOS. (State Olympic Squad) Montreal that was designed to advance Australian swimming.

Speedo's close relationship with amateur swimming attracted the attention of the Trade Practices Commission in 1989, which ruled 'the public benefit of the sponsorship out-weighed any anti-competitive factors'. A year later, Speedo sponsored the Australian swimming teams for the next five years. However, Speedo continued the tradition of providing numerous small grants to individuals, clubs, coaches and charities, which continues to this day.

At the same time, and perhaps more well known, is Speedo's philanthropic work behind the scenes in supporting less able and disabled swimmers, lifesaving, water polo and all forms of aquatic sports, which also continues to this day.

The preamble to the Speedo Sponsorship Toolkit states:

> In creating this Toolkit, we've set out very carefully to define our core sponsorship principles and apply these across *all* our markets. The Toolkit is intended for use by our worldwide marketing and sponsorship teams and focuses on universal principles of sports marketing and sponsorship which are then adapted and applied for local conditions. If we can achieve this *working with our colleagues in Business Development*, we'd have measurably improved the performance of our sponsorship investment . . . and make a positive impact on the bottom line! In short, we aim to create the environment where the sale is more likely to take place than not!

Methods of sponsorship proposal assessment

An organisation like Speedo receives literally hundreds of sponsorship proposals every day from individual athletes, local clubs and events that are eager to create an association with the world's most famous swimming brand.

As I have discussed throughout this book, there needs to be a win–win outcome for all the parties; otherwise the sponsorship programme will fail. Brand owners are now much more sophisticated buyers of sponsorship, but the basics still apply.

The process of sponsorship assessment relates to reviewing myriad sponsorship proposals and opportunities (event, team/club, athlete, grass-roots) presented by sponsorship seekers in order to ascertain which of these will best fulfil Speedo's brand marketing, advertising and sponsorship objectives.

These sponsorship proposals may be unsolicited or may have been developed as a result of proactive conversations between the local Speedo market and the rights holder.

The starting point for this assessment is to look at what brand marketing, advertising and sponsorship objectives Speedo's local markets have set.

Table 10.2 is an example of how the sponsorship objectives of Speedo were turned into selection criteria for any proposed sponsorship or endorsement programme.

Typically, there are four main methods used for sponsorship proposal assessment.

Method #1: *proactive property search*

- This is where the brand owner proactively scans the sponsorship market for a potential property that meets a specific brief.
- The choice of property available may be limited as a result of pre-existing contractual obligations to existing sponsors.
- If no suitable property can be identified, many brand owners now create their own property.

Table 10.2 Speedo's objectives turned into selection criteria for sponsorship/endorsement

General selection criteria	Relevant considerations
Activation potential	• Above- and below-the-line opportunities? • Overarching and underpinning considerations?
Athlete association	• Star of tomorrow? • Brand/athlete fit? • Possibility of personal appearances? • Which products to promote/endorse?
Availability of content (stills, audio, video, Web)	• Copyright fee? • Uniqueness? • Attractiveness for audience and customer segments?
Community impact	• Types of opportunity to engage with local communities in a way that generates positive responses?
Competitors	• Absence of category competitors – past, present, future? • Exclusivity in category? • Level of sponsorship – title, partner, supplier?
Corporate hospitality	• Tickets? • Entertaining/meeting facilities? • Exclusivity of access? • 'Money-can't-buy' experiences?
Corporate responsibility	• Property elements that demonstrate responsible/sustainable behaviour?
Database	• Size, information available? • Frequency of communication? • Methods of communication? • Potential for Speedo to undertake bespoke communication?
Due diligence	• Risk assessment of partnering with the rights holder organisation?
Employee engagement	• Volunteering opportunities? • Skills transfer? • Training opportunities for Speedo employees? • Motivation and reward opportunities?
Environmental impact	• Attitude towards pollution and energy usage? • Carbon footprint? • Actions to encourage positive fan behaviours?
Licensed merchandise	• Speedo/rights holder branding? • Royalty rates?
Media interest	• Visibility for Speedo? • Standout compared with other sponsors?
Natural fit and relevance	• Strength of intuitive link between Speedo and property? • Desirability of property? • Relevance of property to audience and customer segments? • Corporate fit?
Opinion formers	• Opportunity to involve opinion formers in the sponsorship programme? • Access to opinion formers as a result of the sponsorship programme?
Product integration	• Provision to rights holder of Speedo products?
Profile of activity	• Stature of sponsorship property?

(Continued)

General selection criteria	Relevant considerations
Resource requirements	• People? • Time? • Fees and exploitation costs? • Management and other hidden costs?
Revenue generation	• Sales opportunities for Speedo's products (on-site and off-site?) • Other opportunities? • Commercial threats?
Rights holder	• Standing/reputation? • Resources and desire to deliver on agreement? • Track record? • Financial stability? • Partnership objectives match Speedo's sponsorship objectives?
Sensitive areas	• Cultural issues? • Religious issues? • Social issues? • Gender issues? • Racial issues? • Political issues? • Ethical issues? • Moral issues? • Historical issues?
Showcase and sampling	• Opportunity to showcase and sample Speedo products?
Target audience and customer segments	• Demographic fit? • Psychographic fit? • Segmentation issues?
Technology	• Use of interactive communication channels to reach existing and new audiences and customer segments?
Timeframe	• Realistic and achievable? • Contract negotiation? • Implementation?

Source: Speedo Sponsorship Toolkit (2008)

Method #2: Web-based screening

- In your market, if you receive a large number of unsolicited sponsorship proposals you may wish to implement a Web-based filter process in order to save time/costs in replying to these offers.
- Some brand owners offer a form on their websites to be completed by a rights holder that will use algorithms to help weight the answers to a series of questions.
- Self-diagnosis tools are a more friendly way of saying 'no thanks'.
- Some potentially interesting sponsorship opportunities could be lost because the system does not exercise any discretion or leave room for discussion/ negotiations.

Method #3: spreadsheet computation

This uses the same approach as Web-based screening but the brand owner inputs data into the model using a spreadsheet.

Method #4: intuition?

- Only relevant where a small event/club or grass-roots level of sponsorship engagement is contemplated.
- Unlikely to be an appropriate method of assessment in the vast majority of cases.

Inputs, outputs, outcomes

As we have discussed throughout this book, there are three important areas of focus in sponsorship, endorsement or for that matter PR:

> Inputs – for example, the number of perimeter boards, the number of news releases issued, amount of online and offline media exposure, the demographic and psychographic profile of the desired audience and customer segments exposed to the sponsorship campaign, the number of branded marketing materials produced and distributed, the number of attendees/spectators at a sponsorship event, etc.

> Outputs – for example, changes in the preference expressed by consumers for the brand, changes in attitudes expressed by consumers for the brand, the number of participants entering the promotion, prize draw or competition, the number of customers signing up to the loyalty programme, improved B2B relationships, etc.

> Outcomes – incremental sales achieved during and after the sponsorship programme, improvements in customer purchase frequency, a reduction in customer churn, higher customer retention rates, a higher level of loyalty, commercial improvement in B2B relationships, cost savings in recruitment, product launch and sales of new product, etc.

As Pippa Collett and William Fenton (2011) state in their book, *The Sponsorship Handbook:*

> The Holy Grail of sponsorship evaluation is calculating the real outcomes from a sponsorship. Sponsorship outcomes demonstrate the reality of a sponsorship's performance. The figure that most senior managers would like to have reported is the link between sales and sponsorship activity. This is difficult because it is hard to isolate sponsorships from other elements of the marketing mix; there are external events, competitor activity, even seasonal variations that affect sales. Some tracking can nevertheless be done through promotional coupons, purchase frequency or B2B benefits.

For example, while it is accepted that this measure is a challenge, sponsorship managers should still actively pursue data relating to this outcome if a direct sales impact was a key objective of the sponsorship.

Frequency of measurement

How frequently measurements should be taken will depend on factors such as the length of the sponsorship period, the level of investment made, the budget available for measurement, the number of key performance indicators (KPIs) being tracked and the estimated speed at which the effects of the sponsorship activity should be felt.

Whatever the sponsorship or endorsement programme, it is essential as a minimum that at least one benchmark against which sponsorship performance can be measured is established in advance of implementation, in order to start assessing the real value of the sponsorship at the earliest possible opportunity. Effective evaluation also requires that a set of measurements is taken once the sponsorship has been completed, in order to facilitate a post-investment review.

These two measurements – a benchmark and a final analysis – may be all that is required if a sponsorship is of short duration.

For sponsorships lasting more than a year, best practice suggests that an annual process of measurement will give a fair balance of resources used against results gained, and quarterly reviews may be necessary, depending on your own market conditions. For reporting purposes, it is helpful to create a 'scorecard' – a one-page report that uses visual elements such as graphs, charts and other graphical devices to facilitate the absorption of key metrics.

The key to successful measurement is consistency. Consistent, comparable data is produced by:

- using the same agreed sponsorship metrics across national governing bodies, athletes, team/club and grass-roots programmes across all territories
- using the same phraseology and terminology in questions across different surveys in all territories
- using the same techniques and metrics in different markets and at different stages
- using consistent sample sizes and control groups.

It is important to note that gaining the required level of consistency can be a challenge, particularly where more than one market or customer segment is incorporated into the methodology.

Difficulties may arise as a result of different cultures and varying market maturity across Europe and other territories, as well as other aspects of 'how business gets done around here'! Over time, however, consistency of data will enable the brand owner to make robust comparisons between one sponsorship period and another, between results in different markets and between sponsorships, which helps increase the understanding of how each and all of its sponsorship investments are performing in reality.

Budget setting

The European Sponsorship Association (ESA) recommends between 5 and 10% of the rights purchase cost should be allocated for measurement and evaluation but few sponsors or rights holders spend anything like that, and the norm is closer to 1 to 2%.

Sponsors tend to do their homework by accessing a variety of information and data sources, as shown in Table 10.3, some of which carry 'no cost', when done in-house, while other sources may carry 'low cost'.

Return on objectives

Return on objectives (ROO) requires analysis in terms of whether the property type (sports, arts and culture, broadcast, education, environment or any other) is a basic fit with our brand communication, marketing and sales objectives; whether it is feasible in our time frame; and whether it can be used to drive customer loyalty as well as customer acquisition.

Should it tick all the right boxes, then the next challenge is how to bring the investment in the sponsorship property alive.

Many sponsorship practitioners make a distinction between return on objectives (ROO) and return on investment (ROI), as seen in Table 10.4

Table 10.3 Where most sponsors tend to do their homework

Type of information	Internal sources	Independent suppliers	Property-provided research
Demographics	79%	58%	55%
Psychographics	67%	48%	53%
TV ratings	54%	39%	69%
Growth trends	56%	46%	56%
Attendance estimates	80%	34%	40%
Interest level among trade (B2B)	40%	60%	36%

Source: ESA (2014)

Table 10.4 Return on objectives and return on investment

Return on objectives	Return on investment
Variety of 'currencies'	Case-based
Values outcomes in terms of how well objectives have been achieved	Values outcomes in terms of financial efficiency

Source: Kolah (2015)

There are some commentators, such as Kim Skildum-Reid, an Australian sponsorship practitioner and trainer, who talk about the fallacy of return on investment (ROI). The issue is leverage of a sponsorship programme. If leverage is done properly, then measurement is easy. To some extent, she has a point. Measurement of the activation of the sponsorship is a more accurate description of what she has in mind.

However, where I do not completely agree with Kim Skildum-Reid is that it is not just about leverage. Sponsorship is like any other marketing tool, and as a result ROI has to be about the money spent and the money generated in terms of incremental sales. I make no apologies for taking such a narrow perspective on the performance of sponsorship; otherwise it is almost impossible to justify from a business perspective, and indeed corporate philanthropy or pure corporate social responsibility (CSR) or even hospitality may be more appropriate to use in achieving certain non-specific sales goals.

I recognise that this is a narrow view but it happens to be the correct view given that sponsorship at the end of the day is about selling more stuff, a theme that runs through the thinking of improving the performance of sponsorship. Shifting awareness and perceptions are outputs, whereas in the past they may have been regarded as outcomes. But brand owners now look for much, much more and how they can monetise sponsorship.

Return on investment

In general, return on sponsorship investment can be measured against the following criteria:

- additional/incremental sales
- shifts in brand loyalty
- B2B benefits
- shifts in brand awareness
- shifts in brand image
- media value generated.

A key objective for the majority of sports sponsors is fan and consumer reach – the ability to engage with fans and consumers that draws them to the brand rather than a competitors' brand. Many sponsors often need to look past obvious promotion of an association with a sports property, such as a team, player, club or tournament, and turn this into a compelling experience for desired customer segments.

In terms of sales, new customers, incremental sales and loyalty sales can be segmented by:

- retail figures
- scanner data
- sales promotion participation

- on-site or direct sales (sales as a direct result of the sports property)
- coupon and voucher redemption
- profit margins.

A simple example of ROI is given in Figure 10.5 and, of course, will depend on getting the appropriate inputs in order to calculate the outcomes in terms of incremental new sales. This will not always be easy or even possible, and some assumptions will have to be made where this information is not available, but it is worth trying to quantify the value of the sponsorship in terms of ROI.

Attributing sales to sponsorship requires a multifaceted approach – most sales are driven by a combination of marketing messages and channels, and it is not always easy to attribute sales to a specific message or call to action or indeed sponsorship programme.

However, carrying out research before, during and after the sponsorship programme against key performance indicators (KPIs) will go a long way to getting a view on the performance of sponsorship.

It is also important to attribute a time frame for the sales (usually in terms of a period such as a year) as well as to identify above- and below-the-line marketing support, including point of sale, particularly in B2C market segments.

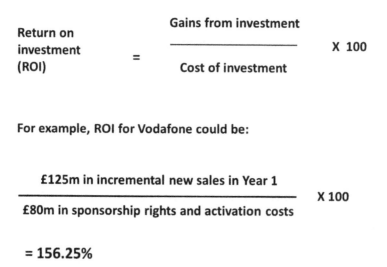

$$\text{Return on investment (ROI)} = \frac{\text{Gains from investment}}{\text{Cost of investment}} \times 100$$

For example, ROI for Vodafone could be:

$$\frac{\text{£125m in incremental new sales in Year 1}}{\text{£80m in sponsorship rights and activation costs}} \times 100$$

$$= 156.25\%$$

This is represented as 56.25% ROI as the original investment has been recouped in full plus a further 56.25% of incremental profit has been delivered by the original investment of £80m in sponsorship rights and activation costs

Figure 10.5 Simple calculation for return on investment

Measurement methodologies

The measurement and evaluation of a sponsorship/endorsement programme can be broken down into three key areas for a major brand owner:

- brand
- commercial
- relationships.

These groups of sponsorship/endorsement objectives may be different in each market or territory that the sponsorship/endorsement takes place.

Brand objectives

It is often much better to have a small number of precise brand objectives, as then you are much more able to deliver these, rather than an endless list of brand objectives that you have no hope of delivering.

Typical brand objectives include:

- advocacy
- loyalty
- bonding
- consideration
- sampling
- consideration
- favourability
- relevance
- awareness
- image perception
- association.

Remember, you do not have to include all of these as brand objectives, but it is better to choose three or five key brand objectives.

For example, when I was working with Speedo, it was notable that each market had a broad definition of possible objectives and some suggested ways of measuring performance against them. Within the framework country managers had first to outline three to five (maximum) key objectives for the sponsorship programme. They then had to locate these within the framework and review the recommended measurement methodologies before deciding which of them were most appropriate for their specific needs (see Table 10.5).

Commercial objectives

Whether the brand owner is competing in B2B or B2C market segments will determine the type of commercial objectives it is seeking to achieve.

Table 10.5 Speedo brand objectives

Brand objective	Sponsorship objective	Research type: qualitative	Research type: quantitative	Other methods	Measurement methodologies — Outline
Awareness	Create/increase/maintain awareness or recognition of Speedo brand.		✓ ✓		• Market research among target audience/customer segments, exposed and not exposed to sponsorship programme • Unprompted recall of the Speedo brand among target audience/customer segments compared with competitor brands
Association	Create/increase/maintain awareness of the sponsorship relationship between property and Speedo.		✓ ✓		• Unprompted recall of Speedo as sponsor among target audience/customer segments compared with competitor brands • Market research among target audience/customer segments, exposed and not exposed to sponsorship programme
Image perception	Change/enhance brand image by transfer of image and values from the property.	✓	✓		• Market research comparing relevant brand values as perceived by those who are aware and those who are unaware of the sponsorship programme • Focus group research to understand further the differences in brand perception between aware/unaware groups
Favourability	Create/increase/maintain level of preference for Speedo compared with competitor set.		✓		• Market research where members of target audience/customer segments identify their preferred brand from a predetermined competitive set, comparing those exposed and those not exposed to the sponsorship programme
Relevance	Create/increase/maintain perceived relevance of the Speedo brand to lifestyle of target audience/customer segments.	✓			• Use focus groups to understand how relevance may be affected by the sponsorship programme • Market research to establish absolute relevance of the Speedo brand in comparison with stated levels for our competitive set

Objective	Description	Research / measurement approaches
Consideration	Increase likelihood that target audience/customer segments will consider Speedo when next making a purchasing decision.	• Use qualitative research to explore key drivers of consideration for those audience/customer segments exposed to the sponsorship programme and how to apply these more widely • Establish stated consideration levels in comparison with stated levels for Speedo's competitive set
Trial or sampling	Encourage Speedo product trial via sampling or incentivised initial purchase.	• Establish stated trial levels for Speedo in comparison with stated levels for our competitive set • Sampling programme with in-store redeemable offer • Sales of trial-size product stock keeping units (SKUs)
Loyalty	Increase/maintain customer loyalty to Speedo brand – customer segment to purchase Speedo brand to fulfil 60% or more of total need for this Speedo product.	• Quantitative research to ascertain claimed purchase levels, comparing those customer segments exposed and not exposed to the sponsorship programme • Qualitative research to contextualize differing levels of loyalty between customer segments exposed and not exposed to the sponsorship programme • Loyalty programme purchase behaviour tracking • Share of wallet tracking via purchase panel membership • Retention rates of distributors/retailers on contract renewal between those exposed and not exposed to the sponsorship programme
Bonding	Create/increase/maintain perceived 'friendship' between audience/customer segments and Speedo.	• Ascertain stated bonding levels for Speedo in comparison with our competitive set among those audience/customer segments exposed/not exposed to the sponsorship programme • Investigate how target audience/customer segments talk about the Speedo brand as an integral part of their life
Advocacy	Generate positive Speedo brand recommendations by customer segments to non-customers in target group.	• Claimed referral levels among those customer segments exposed/not exposed to the sponsorship programme • Qualitative research to contextualized drivers of advocacy among customer segments exposed compared with not exposed to the sponsorship programme • Recommend-a-friend scheme activity levels, comparing exposed with not exposed to the sponsorship programme

Source: Speedo Sponsorship Toolkit (2008)

Typically, commercial objectives irrespective of the market segment of the brand owner will include the following:

- incremental sales
- increase market share
- new market entry
- database building
- loyalty programme
- sales promotion
- competitive differentiation
- innovation
- licence to operate
- tax benefits.

Speedo has some sophisticated commercial objectives (see Table 10.6).

Relationship objectives

All organisations and companies have relationship objectives – in fact, the absence of such objectives would be unthinkable. These are no less important than brand or commercial objectives and, of course, to be realistic, these objectives need to work on a long- rather than short-term timescale.

Such objectives for a FMCG brand owner could include any of the following:

- B2B relationships
- employees
- corporate social responsibility (CSR)
- alliances
- third parties
- government lobbying
- reputation management
- community relations
- co-sponsor relations
- internal communications.

Speedo has built its brand on a global basis by ensuring that it is engaged with communities at all levels and also by ensuring that governments and others know it gives something back, as this is important when government may be lobbied to help reduce red tape and even local taxation that could affect jobs and profits (see Table 10.7).

Robust measurement itself is, of course, not the end of the story! It is a means to an end. When thinking about improving the performance of sponsorship we need to be more interested in the insights we are able to glean as a result of this evaluation.

Table 10.6 Speedo commercial objectives

Commercial objective	Sponsorship objective	Research type: qualitative	Research type: quantitative	Other methods	Outline (Measurement methodologies)
Product sampling	Allow target audience/customer segments to experience Speedo product(s) to increase likelihood of purchase.			✓	• Number of samples distributed/used/consumed at sponsored events, compared with sampling at other locations
				✓	• Number of coupons redeemed compared with other promotional coupons
				✓	• Measure of pre- and post-event sales among target customer segments compared with a control group's behaviour during the same period
			✓		• Exit poll interview versus control group sampled in non-sponsorship environment
Product showcasing	Demonstrate Speedo product(s) capabilities to increase likelihood of purchase.		✓		• Tracker study: cross-tabulation of those audience/customer segments exposed to the sponsorship programme versus not exposed on intention to purchase
			✓		• Number of visitors to Speedo retail outlets when sponsorship featured versus not featured
			✓		• Exit poll awareness of key Speedo product attributes compared with control group where Speedo products are in a non-sponsorship environment
				✓	• Number of qualified sales leads gained via sponsorship-associated channels versus other marketing initiatives

Table 10.6 (Continued)

Commercial objective	Sponsorship objective	Research type: qualitative	Research type: quantitative	Other methods	Outline
Increase in sales	Increase product sales, either for new Speedo product(s) or to boost established Speedo lines.			✓	• New Speedo brands: sales data, but with limited scope to differentiate between sponsorship-related sales and sales related to other marketing initiatives
				✓	• Established Speedo brands: sales data compared with previous figures and trends, to establish impact
			✓		• Stated purchasing among those exposed/not exposed to the sponsorship programme
			✓		• Purchase panel information on those exposed versus those not exposed
				✓	• Increased requests for Speedo product(s) received (especially if specifically coded against the sponsorship programme)
				✓	• Increased footfall, especially of those customer segments presenting a sponsorship-related/coded leaflet/flier
				✓	• Sales of Speedo product(s) based on a sponsorship-related offer
				✓	• Coupon redemption patterns – those distributed in sponsorship environment versus non-sponsorship environment
Increase in market share	Increase/maintain market share.			✓	• Market place analysis – growth, trends, dynamics, competitors
				✓	• Market penetration – number of customers versus potential total
				✓	• Customer 'quality': level of customer scores against key 'quality' parameters (comparing those introduced via sponsorship with those introduced via other channels)
				✓	• Stated share-of-wallet information (exposed versus not-exposed to the sponsorship programme)
			✓	✓	• Market share data
				✓	• Additional shelf space/other marketing exposure negotiated to display Speedo product(s) with sponsorship-related promotions

Objective	Description	Measurement		
Sales promotion platform	Increase sales of related Speedo product(s) over the promotional period.	Response to sponsorship-related sales promotion compared with other promotional platforms	✓	
		Stated preference for sponsorship-related promotions versus others		✓
		Response to sponsorship-related promotions versus others	✓	
Database building	Capture contact details and opt-ins for future communications.	Number of records captured through sponsorship-related sources (on-site bins, weblinks, postcards, competitions, promotions, etc.) versus other sources	✓	
		'Quality' of rights holder's database compared with other list sources measured by level of gone-aways/returned emails	✓	
Loyalty programme enhancement	Provide merchandise and activities to enhance customer loyalty programmes.	Number of sponsorship-related rewards redeemed as a percentage of total redemptions, benchmarked against pre-sponsorship rewards	✓	
		Stated interest in spending towards acquiring sponsorship-related rewards versus other rewards offered by the sponsorship programme		✓
		Redemption rates of similar items, for example, a sponsorship-related Speedo bag versus a similar Speedo non-sponsorship related bag	✓	
Distribution and supply chain incentives	Incentivise desired behaviour up- and downstream, for example, improved credit terms, increased shelf space, etc.	Desired behaviour achieved post-sponsorship-related engagement, based on benchmarks agreed with finance/sales/purchasing departments	✓	
		Feedback on impact of the sponsorship engagement on influencing change of behaviour among supply chain elements		✓
Direct sales opportunities	Secure a new sales channel directly associated with the sponsorship programme, such as exclusive new Speedo product(s) at the event or selected retail outlets.	Sales revenue/profit generated by sponsorship-related sales channels	✓	
		Sales revenue/profit generated by bespoke Speedo product(s) made for sponsorship audience/event	✓	
		Extent to which provision to rights holder is leveraged into pure provision to similar rights holders or market segments	✓	
Innovation catalyst	Shorten new product development cycle and/or increase number of developments made.	Number of sponsorship-related product developments achieved	✓	
		Relative speed or creativity of sponsorship-related NPD teams or previously accepted norms in achieving both incremental and breakthrough innovations	✓	
Tax benefits	Benefit from tax advantages where these exist.	Savings accrued	✓	

Table 10.6 (Continued)

Commercial objective	Sponsorship objective	Research type: qualitative	Research type: quantitative	Other methods	Measurement methodologies — Outline
Advertising alternative	Gain Speedo brand exposure more cost-effectively than by purchasing advertising space.		✓ ✓		• Media cost comparison between cost of purchasing sponsorship property rights and estimated costs of advertising to gain equivalent level of brand exposure • Level of brand awareness generated • Level of brand awareness and awareness of associated brand attributes among key audience/customer segments • Extent to which these were generated by the sponsorship rather than by other marketing activities, such as in-store promotions
Spoiling tactics	Securely prevent Speedo's competitors from gaining a foothold in the sponsorship programme.			✓ ✓ ✓	• Breadth of category and extent exclusivity clause in sponsorship agreement, as evidenced by degree of absence of Speedo's competitors from the sponsored event and its environs • Competitor response • Market share of those exposed to sponsorship versus not exposed • Revenues generated through the rights holder's network
Competitive differentiation	Align with rights holder to secure a unique and defendable competitive advantage.		✓		• Perceptions of Speedo within our competitive set between those exposed to sponsorship versus not exposed to the sponsorship
'Licence to operate'	Provide a platform that meets local 'investment' requirements and as a result secures Speedo a 'licence to operate'.			✓	• Number of key stakeholders engaged via the sponsorship programme
New market entry	Invest in a sponsorship platform that portrays the right social, political, cultural and sporting approach to facilitate entry into a new market.			✓	• Number of new markets entered where the sponsorship programme is active
Employee development	Use the sponsorship programme as a source of job-related training opportunities.			✓	• Level of skill among those utilising sponsorship-related training versus employees using traditional training platforms to develop similar skill sets

Table 10.7 Speedo relationship objectives

| Relationship objective | Sponsorship objective | Measurement methodologies | | | Outline |
		Research type: qualitative	Research type: quantitative	Other methods	
Reputation management	Use sponsorship to enhance the reputation of Speedo across all target market and customer segments.		✓	✓	• Positive media coverage of Speedo in the context of the sponsorship programme • Stated perceptions of the reputation of Speedo and our competitors between those exposed and not exposed to the sponsorship
Government lobbying	Use sponsorship platform to enable effective lobbying on relevant issues.		✓	✓ ✓ ✓	• Number of contacts made using the sponsorship as an introductory platform • Compare levels of support among MPs engaged via the sponsorship versus control group • Frequency of invitation and level of requests to engage on key decisions/policies affecting Speedo • Number of favourable legislative outcomes/NGO policies further to sponsorship-related engagement
Community relations	Convince those local to Speedo that we are a good neighbour.		✓	✓ ✓	• Reduction in the number of complaints received from local communities • Stated preference for Speedo as a good local employer by those exposed versus not exposed to the sponsorship • Increased requests to engage with local community events

(Continued)

Table 10.7 (Continued)

Relationship objective	Sponsorship objective	Measurement methodologies			Outline
		Research type: qualitative	Research type: quantitative	Other methods	
Corporate social responsibility (CSR)	Ensure all stakeholders perceive Speedo as investing in the wealth and well-being of the wider community.	✓ ✓ ✓	✓ ✓	✓	• Rating of Speedo as a good corporate citizen in pools/omnibus surveys • Sponsorship-related comment in Web chatrooms and blogs • Analysts' commentaries relating to sponsorship and good corporate citizenship • Customer feedback via focus groups comparing those exposed/not exposed • Research among each stakeholder group to assess perceptions comparing those exposed with those not exposed • Input from community panel members
B2B relationships	Develop relationships with key B2B customers to encourage positive purchase decisions.	✓		✓ ✓ ✓ ✓ ✓ ✓	• Number of guests invited versus refusals compared with non-sponsorship-related invitations • Systematically collected anecdotal feedback from Speedo account managers regarding impact on B2B customer relationships and sales • Increased number of preferred supplier agreements arranged with entertained B2B customers versus levels among those not entertained/engaged with the sponsorship • Increased referrals by B2B sponsorship-related corporate hospitality guests versus those not entertained • Stated preference for doing business with Speedo versus our competitors • Sales data tracking

Category	Objective	Metrics
Co-sponsor alliances	Create value through interaction with other sponsors involved with the same rights holder.	• Number of projects undertaken as a result of being co-sponsors • Value of projects undertaken as co-sponsor
Employee engagement	Improve productivity, reduce turnover, increase employee satisfaction, increase integration of Speedo team within Pentland Group.	• Levels of sponsorship awareness and understanding of rationale for the sponsorship programme via internal questionnaire • Percentage take-up of sponsorship-related programmes • Detailed questioning on sponsorship and the role it plays in retention, satisfaction, etc. among different employee groups • Enhanced understanding of how the sponsorship programme affects different groups and of what could be done to increase the benefits accruable to Speedo • Productivity, quality output levels between those motivated by the sponsorship and those not motivated by the sponsorship • Regular tracking of key employee metrics comparing those highly engaged with the sponsorship programme versus those less/not engaged, including staff turnover
Potential employee perceptions	Persuade pool of potential employees of Speedo's leadership as an employer.	• Number of applicants responding to a Speedo job advertisement that includes sponsorship-related imagery/ messages versus non-sponsorship-related advertisement • Stated interest in being employed by Speedo compared with competitors cross-referenced against awareness of the sponsorship programme • Number of positive mentions of sponsorship in relevant trade press, including sponsorship-related awards won • Number of new hires surveyed who admit an attraction to Speedo as a result of a specific sponsorship programme • Number of additional high-quality speculative approaches – especially those that mention the sponsorship and impact on recruitment agency costs

Merely achieving a target is not sufficient in itself – we also need to know what achieving that target actually means for the business and whether the result is actually acceptable. In other words, what are the outcomes as a result of achieving such an objective?

For example, a non-challenging target that is easily achieved would bring in a 'result' in theory, but, in practice, there would still be significant room for improvement.

Once results are known, it is important to communicate them effectively to the relevant people. This may include senior management internally, as well as key external stakeholders, including the rights holder.

Sharing results, both positive and negative, with the rights holder should be a priority in the spirit of a partnership with shared goals. This assists in empowering the rights holder to be a significant contributor to the process of continuous improvement in sponsorship activation.

Role of market research

Research has a part to play at all points in the sponsorship selection, implementation and review process. Like the use of market research in marketing, it boils down to focusing on objectives. For example, in the context of sponsorship, a brand owner or rights holder may be interested in understanding the following:

1   passion – the need to measure this (the ideal being lifetime experience)
2   presence – breaking through the sponsorship clutter
3   need – giving something of value to customer segments/communicating appreciation for support.

Market research can also be used to understand desired audience and customer segments' reactions to potential sponsorship themes and specific properties, and thereby assist in sponsorship property selection process.

Once a sponsorship property has been contracted, research will establish key performance indicator (KPI) benchmarks from which sponsorship impacts can be measured.

Regular tracking research over long-term sponsorships provides data that assists in identifying where remedial action needs to be taken or where changes of emphasis would breathe new life into the project.

Prior to renewing a sponsorship contract, research will help to gauge whether the programme still has the potential to inspire audience and customer segments. After the sponsorship, the role of research is to establish the actual outcomes delivered by the sponsorship, to provide 'lessons learned' and maybe even to establish a benchmark for further sponsorship investments.

As in other fields, in sponsorship evaluation there are two primary types of market research: quantitative and qualitative.

There are relative strengths and weaknesses in both quantitative and qualitative approaches (see Table 10.8). In general, quantitative research is more useful for testing, benchmarking, etc., but ideally should be used alongside qualitative

Table 10.8 Advantages and disadvantages of research methodologies used in sponsorship

Quantitative research	Qualitative reasearch
✓ Top-of-mind responses	✓ More depth and understanding (why, what, who, where, how many, etc.)
✓ Representative of wider populations	✓ Focused on key audiences/individuals
✓ Statistically robust/relevant	✓ Can be quick to set up and run (but longer to analyse effectively)
✓ Benchmarking data	

Source: Kolah (2015)

research tools that can offer an insight into why people feel and behave the way they do.

Quantitative research

Quantitative research offers a numerical, consistent, statistically robust approach that can be repeated across different properties and stakeholder groups. SMART objectives are likely to be quantitative in nature, because they must be measurable. In the case of measuring the impact of a sponsorship against different brand objectives, a quantitative approach using pre- and post-sponsorship measures, with ongoing monitoring if appropriate, is considered to be the most effective.

The 'pre-' measure establishes a benchmark for each brand objective; the 'post-' measure, which should encompass the same target audience and customer segments, shows whether the sponsorship has been effective in delivering against the objectives set.

Control groups

The key with all measurement mechanisms is to define control groups. These are groups of the desired audience and customer segments that are not exposed to the sponsorship or its activation but have been exposed to the brand owner's other marketing activities. By comparing the views of those exposed to the sponsorship versus those not exposed, it is possible to isolate the impact of the sponsorship as separate from other marketing activities.

Identifying a 'perfect' control group may be challenging, but usually it is possible to reach a reasonable compromise. Defining and managing control groups may require internal discussion and agreement to ring-fence certain customers for this purpose at the outset of a sponsorship.

It has to be accepted that it is likely that control groups will have a reduced level of response to the sponsor and its other marketing messages compared with those audiences being actively targeted by a sponsorship proposition. However, this must be seen as an acceptable price to pay for understanding how a sponsorship is working in the wider context.

How to use quantitative research

Quantitative research is a structured methodology based on an identifiable sample in order to produce statistically relevant quantifiable insights into behaviour, motivations, attitudes, values, perceptions and beliefs of desired audience and customer segments.

ADVANTAGES

- Data gathering is more structured.
- Larger samples than qualitative research (thousands rather than hundreds).
- Can be more easily replicated than qualitative studies.
- Quantifies the incidence of particular behaviours, motivations and attitudes in the market and customer segment under investigation.
- Good for spotting and predicting future trends.
- Variety of proven methods.
- Statistical in nature and will typically use computer software.

DRAWBACKS

- Less flexible than qualitative research as it tends to use predefined questions that are consistently used with all respondents.
- May not generate sufficient insight.
- Dependent on the quality of the questions set, which has a direct bearing on the quality of the data received.

Survey methods

Surveying involves structured questioning of respondents and recording responses and must take account of national and international laws, such as the Data Protection Act 1998 and the EU Directive on Privacy and Electronic Communications, which apply in the UK, as well as other legal protections, such as the mail preference service, telephone preference service and fax preference service.

Quantitative surveys can be undertaken verbally, in writing or via computer-based technology. An interviewer may be used to administer the survey or the respondent may self-complete the survey. Interviewer-administered surveys are generally undertaken over the phone or through face-to-face contact in different environments, such as a sports venue.

Parameters and demographic variations can be set when using either face-to-face or telephone research, as there is a strong element of control in using these techniques compared with a self-selecting survey. The interviewer will typically use paper-based questionnaires, computer laptops and notepads or voice-recording equipment – provided the respondent consents beforehand and the material is only used for note-taking purposes. Self-completion surveys are usually delivered and collected from respondents by post, hand, fax, website, email, mobile phone and even interactive TV.

Table 10.9 Advantages and disadvantages of using face-to-face interviews

Advantages	Drawbacks
Motivate a respondent to take part and answer difficult questions when there is a direct face-to-face interaction	Generally seen as being more costly and time consuming
Convince respondent that the research and interviewer are genuine (particularly useful with senior business audience)	Interviews tend to be clustered within set geographical areas and therefore not convenient for those in more remote areas
Check and ensure respondent eligibility before interview is conducted	Training and briefing of interviewers can be more difficult as a result of geographic dispersion
Assist a respondent with a more complex questionnaire or set of questions	Quality control can be more difficult as supervisors have to travel around a dispersed set of interviewers to ensure proper interviewing standards are met
Judge interest, impatience and seriousness with which a respondent is answering a questionnaire	More difficult to motivate interviewers than is the case in a centralised telephone call centre
Improve understanding of the interviewer and respondent through non-verbal communication	Interviewer bias is more prevalent
Have control over visual elements of the questionnaire (creative work)	Dependent on the quality of recording responses

Source: Kolah (2015)

Face-to-face interviews

Face-to-face interviews are extremely valuable for getting in-depth information from respondents, particularly since there is an opportunity for showing creative concepts, visuals for new campaigns and promotions and an advertising campaign in support of sponsorship.

In addition, parameters and demographic variations can be set when using either face- to-face or telephone research, as there is a strong element of control in using these techniques compared with an online self-selecting survey.

However, according to market research company MORI, face-to-face research is rarely used in the USA. More common are telephone interviews and the use of computer- aided telephone interviewing (CATI) technology, which records results from telephone interviews directly onto a database and, of course, online surveys and questionnaires (see Table 10.9).

While both face-to-face and telephone interviews are useful research tools, you should be aware of 'respondent fatigue' in using these techniques (see Table 10.10). Best practice is to keep the methodology consistent to ensure comparability between the two techniques and in international sponsorship programmes it is often best to adapt these techniques to take account of cultural norms.

Table 10.10 Face-to-face versus telephone interview techniques

Face-to-face	Telephone
✓ Can show visual stimulus materials, test sponsorship awareness, etc. ✓ Allows interviewer to build rapport with respondent ✓ Shows respondents that their input is valid	✓ Better for busier audiences ✓ More flexible timing ✓ Easier for geographically diverse audiences ✓ Faster feedback of results ✓ Possible to interview from a central location/office

Source: Kolah (2015)

Telephone surveys

The use of telephone surveys has to be conducted with care, as many people find such methods highly invasive, particularly if they are conducted outside normal business hours and at home (see Table 10.11).

Email/online surveys

From a base of zero a decade ago, this type of quantitative survey now accounts for 25% of all quantitative data collected in Europe and the USA – mainly because of speed and cost. For example, for the same budget as commissioning four focus groups, online research can survey 5,000 respondents.

There are two main types of survey: where the questionnaire appears as text within the email and where it is sent as an attachment (see Table 10.12).

Qualitative research

Qualitative research, such as focus groups or one-to-one interviews, can also be used both before and after a sponsorship. Qualitative research can help develop an understanding of how a sponsorship may connect with a brand or generate insights into how the sponsorship might be activated.

During the post-sponsorship phase, qualitative methods can be used to put the findings of a quantitative study into context, helping to understand the motivations, behaviour, attitudes and values of customers and provide a richer appreciation of the sponsorship process in more general terms.

In the sponsorship industry, researchers frequently use intensive and immersive research methods to explore fan and customer needs. The methodology, often called 'exploratory research', takes an unstructured research approach (compared with quantitative research, as we have just seen) with a number of carefully selected individuals to produce non-quantifiable insights into behaviour, motivations, attitudes, values and beliefs.

Table 10.11 Advantages and disadvantages of using telephone surveys

Advantages	Drawbacks
Centralised call-centre location provides control, allowing calls to be monitored using unobtrusive monitoring equipment	Respondent attitudes towards being contacted by phone
Easy to supervise	Seen as a 'junk' marketing rather than serious research exercise
Quality control	Seen as trying to 'sell' something to the respondent
Cost of calls can be logged accurately	Invasion of privacy a key complaint
Control and timing of interviews	Lack of motivation to want to answer a series of questions or give up sufficient time
Not dependent on being located near to respondent	Unable to read body language and unable to check for sincerity
No travel time	Can be monosyllabic and does not provide an opportunity for an in-depth discussion in every case
Local, regional, national and international research can be managed from one central location	Easy for respondent to refuse to participate and hang up
Convenient and cost-effective	No control over the environment around the respondent
Fast and reliable and able to be recorded (with permission of respondent)	Respondent subject to distraction when answering questions
Flexibility – calls can be longer or shorter and easier to change questionnaire at will	Telephone line and other technical difficulties make it difficult to hear responses
Good for gaining reaction immediately to a sports triumph or major event	Time-bound in terms of when calls can be made and therefore not that flexible from this perspective

Source: Kolah (2015)

Table 10.12 Advantages and disadvantages of using email/online surveys

Advantages	Drawbacks
Shorter turnaround times	Can be regarded as spam and easily deleted
Easy to complete – usually a series of tick boxes that take a few minutes to complete	Respondents are largely self-selecting – as they choose to complete the survey, they are likely to be more positive
Lower cost than other methods	Does not allow for in-depth follow-up of respondents' answers compared with face-to-face or telephone surveys
Can provide a mix of questions and therefore more flexible	Quality control can be more difficult, as supervisors have to travel around a dispersed set of interviewers to ensure proper interviewing standards are met
Targeted reach	Not good for tracking behaviour online
Good for busy respondents	No way of testing truthfulness or double-checking responses
Flexibility over timing	Less control over when email/online survey is completed

Source: Kolah (2015)

Qualitative research is more flexible than quantitative research and does not depend on a predefined question-and-answer format.

The two most common approaches are depth interviews and group interviews, each with respective strengths and weaknesses.

Depth interviews

Advantages

- Respondent is centre of attention and can be probed at length to explore remarks made, which may provide critical insights.
- Respondent cannot hide behind other respondents' comments or discussions and does not have to compete for time to talk.
- Peer pressure is eliminated.
- Respondents may feel less inhibited about talking about sensitive issues.
- Deeper and more penetrating insights.
- Can be conducted at the respondent's location.
- Group facilities are not required.

Drawbacks

- More time-consuming (typical interviewer will conduct four interviews per day).
- Less convenient than group interviews.
- Potentially more expensive, because more visits involved.
- More difficult to verify what is said.
- Not measurable.

Group interviews

Advantages

- Better targeting and selection of respondents.
- Involves small samples of individuals who are not necessarily representative of larger populations.
- Good for testing stimulus, such as a new campaign, sponsorship or other brand communication or marketing programme.
- Allows for discussion between other respondents that can produce additional insights.
- Group discussions allows interaction and observation between respondents.
- Useful to see how respondents shift their opinions during the course of a group interview as a reaction to the opinion of others.
- Moderator could do two groups of 16–20 people in one day.
- Good for using projective techniques, such as word association, that can be used to enhance the quality and quantity of material produced.

Drawbacks

- Needs more organisational time commitment and resources.
- More time-consuming to set up.
- Peer pressure is present (which may be unwanted, depending on the objectives of the research).

Advances in qualitative research

Neuroscientists in the UK are currently investigating how marketing messages work on the brain, spurred by the knowledge that the tiny capacity of the working memory means that the vast bulk of information must be processed by the unconscious part of the brain.

Portable electroencephalography (EEG) technology is used to measure human responses to a broad range of marketing stimuli, which has given birth to a new qualitative research approach termed 'neuromarketing', which tests responses to a broad range of marketing stimulus material, such as:

- advertising (audio and visual)
- packaging
- new product development
- concepts, ideas and propositions
- brand imagery
- media types (print, digital, TV, radio, etc.)
- retail and leisure environments (store, shopping malls, bars, etc.).

Great sponsorship is about combining sponsorship discipline in terms of ROO with creativity to unleash innovation where it really matters most.

To create difference and engage people in the world, it often seems that all the best ideas have already been taken. And the bar is increasingly getting higher, not lower. We need new ideas for new sponsorship solutions. We need new ideas to exploit existing markets and customer segments better. And we need new ideas to do it more effectively. Sponsorship managers cannot afford to get complacent and must constantly strive to innovate in order to ensure all of their sponsorship investments stay relevant and compelling.

It is only by taking a rigorous approach to planning, measurement and evaluation that we can channel the necessary resources and investment to the areas delivering the greatest return on our sponsorship investments.

Using external providers of measurement and evaluation

There are several advantages to using external measurement and evaluation providers, such as SMG Insight/You Gov, an excellent agency that I have worked with closely on a number of projects, as well as Ipsos MORI and Sports Marketing Surveys.

Each of these and other measurement and research agencies has extensive experience in optimising the return on objectives and return on investment by:

- evaluating the existing sponsorship portfolio to determine the sponsorship objectives and return on investment
- determining the optimum sponsorship strategy to achieve corporate and brand marketing objectives
- ensuring that the most appropriate properties are selected to meet corporate objectives, brand fit, target market and budget requirements
- establishing achievable and distinct objectives for each sponsorship, with measurable and meaningful key performance indicators (KPIs)
- designing and providing a holistic evaluation system to monitor performance and provide actionable feedback.

All of this expertise and experience has been gained in working extensively with brand owners across the world, as well as through having an in-depth understanding of sports and entertainment content in helping brands drive their brand marketing and communications activities across online and offline media environments.

Another organisation that is arguably the world's leading sponsorship measurement and evaluation agency is IEG, based in Chicago, USA, which is led by the brilliant Lesa Ukman. IEG (part of WPP) works with some of the world's leading rights holders and brand owners and provides a range of products and services, including:

- survey research that tracks brand metrics and awareness
- Web analytics/digital research that can determine how best to increase site visits, average stays, click-through rates, etc.
- earned media tracking (PR) by evaluating the impact on reach, target audience and sentiment
- social media analytics that look at measuring the effect on buzz, interactions and positive sentiment
- broadcast exposure analysis that looks at maximising on-screen exposure via logos, signage and mentions
- linking sponsorship to overall business performance through analysis of business metrics, including sales leads and new accounts.

Chapter 10 at a glance

1   Sponsorship managers are under increasing pressure to demonstrate a return on investment and rights holders are under increasing pressure to ensure that the rights sold will help to deliver a return for the sponsor.
2   In this context, measurement and evaluation are of equal importance and value to all parties that have an investment in making sure that the sponsorship works. Measurement and evaluation must be non-adversarial and should serve the interests of all parties to a sponsorship programme in terms of how

that programme can be improved for the future as well as deliver measurable results for the sponsor and rights holder.

3   There are two ways in which measurement and evaluation are used in sponsorship:

  i.   cost comparison of the money that a brand owner invests in sponsorship compared with other brand communication and marketing activities, such as advertising, online or direct mail

  ii. the impact that the sponsorship has had in terms of volume, price, distribution, revenue and profits for the sponsor.

4   Objectives go to the root of measurement and evaluation in sponsorship. Some of the most typical include:

  i.   customer engagement – customer awareness, customer preference, customer affinity

  ii.   market impact – market share, customer retention, channel penetration

  iii. marketing improvement – product innovation, brand building, market development

  iv.   financial performance – sales revenue, profitability, growth

  v.   enhancing brand image – building a valuable brand

  vi.   increasing sales/market share – financial performance

  vii. building awareness –fame for the brand

  viii. increasing Web traffic – helping to drive consideration

  ix.   generating social media buzz – building a narrative.

5   The six-step sponsorship model was created to assist brand owners as well as rights holders to understand how best to manage the sponsorship investment:

  Step 1: existing activity review
  Step 2: sponsorship strategy review
  Step 3: negotiation
  Step 4: intelligent activation
  Step 5: return on investment
  Step 6: sponsorship review.

6   One of the biggest global brands in the world – Speedo – keeps a tight focus on inputs, outputs and outcomes in managing its portfolio of sponsorship investments across the world, which has helped to drive incremental sales in over 62 markets.

7   Despite the importance of measurement and evaluation in sponsorship, few sponsors or rights holders spend anything like 5–10% of the rights purchase as recommended by the European Sponsorship Association (ESA), and the norm is closer to 1–2%.

8   The simple ROI calculation is to divide the gains from sponsorship investment by the cost of sponsorship investment multiplied by 100.

9   Measurement and evaluation of a sponsorship programme can be broken down into three key areas:

  i.   brand
  ii.   commercial
  iii. relationships.

10   Quantitative research offers a numerical, consistent, statistically robust approach that can be repeated across different properties and stakeholder groups. SMART objectives are likely to be quantitative in nature, because they must be measurable.

11   Qualitative research, such as focus groups or one-to-one interviews, can also be used both before and after a sponsorship. Qualitative research can help develop an understanding of how a sponsorship may connect with a brand or generate insights into how the sponsorship might be activated.

12   Using external agencies and suppliers may provide deeper capability and expertise in measurement and evaluation that may not exist within the rights holder or brand owner and also delivers a high level of objectivity in the process.

Questions for discussion

1   Why are measurement and evaluation critical for improving the performance of sponsorship?

2   What commercial justification can you provide for spending more resources on measurement and evaluation from the perspective of the sponsor and the rights holder?

3   Describe how you would advise a rights holder and brand owner on evaluating the performance of an existing sponsorship programme?

4   How would you calculate the return on investment? What inputs and outputs will you require in order to calculate the outcomes of a sponsorship programme?

5   How would you measure the return on investment in the following sponsorship programmes:
   • Visa and FIFA World Cup
   • Barclays and the Premier League
   • Budweiser and NFL Super Bowl
   • H&M and David Beckham
   • Accenture and Six Nations
   • Felix Baumgartner and Red Bull
   • Compare the Market and *Coronation Street* (ITV1)
   • Salton and George Foreman
   • Nike and Tiger Woods
   • BP and the Tate Gallery
   • AON and Manchester United FC
   • Speedo and Athletes
   • Coca-Cola and the Olympic Games
   • Nissan and UEFA Champions League

Further reading

Collett, P and Fenton, W (2011), *The Sponsorship Handbook*, Wiley
Kolah, A (2013), *High Impact Marketing That Gets Results*, Kogan Page

Websites

European Sponsorship Association (ESA) [accessed 11 May 2014]: http://www.sponsor-ship.org
Financial Times online [accessed 11 May 2014]: http://www.ft.com/cms/s/0/e8ec69ba-3456-11de-9eea-00144feabdc0.html?siteedition=uk#axzz31PlgYpey
Speedo [accessed 11 May 2014]: http://wwww.speedo.com

Index

Page numbers in **bold** refer to figures, page numbers in *italic* refer to tables.

Aaker, David 259
Absolut Vodka 123–4
accountability 269
accounting periods *105*
Action for Smoking and Health 179
activation 270, 272–3; budgets 29, 62, 273; planning 117; popular meathods **116**
activity review 269–71
Adiba, Patrick 50
Adidas 52, 56, 58, 131, 254
Adidas Underground campaign 121–2
advertiser-funded programming (AFP) 83–4, 131–6, 140, 197–8, 213
advertising xvii–xviii, 13, 81–3, 89, 90, *104*, **xx**
advertising equivalent value 3, 88
Advertising Standards Authority (ASA) 174; Code of Practice 182, 190
advertorials 185
Agüero, Sergio 79–80
aims 10
alcohol abuse 173
alcohol-related sponsorship 172–6
All England Lawn and Tennis Club's (AELTC) 232
All Party Parliamentary Group on Alcohol Misuse 174
Amazon 142
ambush marketing 163, 223–38; aims 235; balance 231; and brand reputation 224; counter-marketing strategies 227–8; definition 224–6, 233; ethics 223–4, 225–6, 231; future 237–8; impacts 227–8; infringement of intellectual property rights 227; legal issues 237; London, Olympic Games, 2012 228, 228–9, 230–1; prevention 231–6; promotional exposure 235; tactics *232*; types 226–8; zero-tolerance policy 238
Anheuser-Busch 145, *145–6*
ANZ Bank 124–5
Apple 117, 138, 148
apps 130
Argentina 37, *248*
Armstrong, Lance 161–2
Arnold, Bob 125–6
arts and culture sponsorship 16, **17**, *17*
Asia 39–40, 216
associations and professional bodies' sponsorship 19, *19*
AT&T 155–62
atmosphere, negotiation 110
Atos Origin 49–52
attitude, negotiation 107, **108**
audience: and brand narrative 11–2; emotional connection 122; engagement xxv, 3; focus 29; fragmentation xxv; segmentation 65–6; strategy 122–5
Audio Visual Media Services Directive 214
Australia 42, 169, 173, *248*
Aviva 214–5
awareness 45

Bahrain 35, 36
Barclays 4, 5, 75, 84–5, 195–6, 253–4
bargaining 111–2
Barrett, Don 168
Baumgartner, Felix 11, 126–7
Bazalgette, Peter 138
behaviour, negotiation 107, **108**
behaviour change 262
benchmarks 276, 283

benefit-in-kind 104
benefits 61, *61*; intangible 86, 93, 94;
   premium 86, 91–3, *91*, *92*; tangible 86,
   89, *89*; value 106
big data 7–8, 15
blogs and bloggers 3
Blu e-cigarettes 181
BMW 82–3
Bose, Mia 4–5
bounce factor 163
Bournville College, Birmingham,
   sponsorship audit 86–96, *88*, *89*, *90*, *91*,
   92, *94*, *95*, *96*
BP 153, 154
Brand Affiliation Index (BAI) 52
brand ambassadors 75, 127
brand audit 271
brand awareness 12–3
brand communication xvii
brand content programming 198
brand differentiation 6, 8, 146–9
Brand Finance 266
brand loyalty xvii, 133–4
brand message 126
brand metrics 139
brand narrative 11–2, 14
brand networks 98
brand objectives 287, 288–9
brand owners, segmentation 85, **85**
brand partnership programmes xviii
brand promotion 45
brand protection 234–6
brand stories 10
branded content 83–4
branding, celebrity 57–8
brands: core resources 73; role 24
Brazil 32, 33, 37, 248
bribery 216–21
Bribery Act 2010 163, 216, 217–21
British Academy of Film and Television
   Arts (BAFTA) 65, 76–8, *77*
British Gas 171–2
British Olympic Association (BOA) 28
British Paralympic Association (BPA) 30
Broadcast Committee on Advertising
   Practice (BCAP), Code of Practice 210,
   212
broadcast sponsorship 17–9, 80–1, 197;
   regulation 211–6
Broadcasting Code 18, 211–6
Brown, Orion 126
Browning, Chuck 67
budgets xix–xx, 61–2, *62*; setting 284
Budweiser 145–6

bumpers 18
Burn 124
business and marketing planning cycle
   69–71, **70**
business model 70
business performance, and marketing
   performance **276**
business-to-business (B2B) 182
business-to-consumer (B2C) sponsorship
   170, 182
Button, Jenson 75
buying sponsorship, questions 99–104, *104*
Byers, Sharon 118

Campbell, Margaret 138
Canada 40–1, 248
cancellation rights 207
CAP Code 82
Capri Sun 126
Carnegie, Dale 66–7
Carter, David 56
case studies 2
celebrity sponsorship: *see* personality
   endorsement and sponsorship
Chanel 143
Channel 4 83
Chartered Institute of Marketing 225
Chattopadhyay, Avik 125
Cheeseman, Hazel 179
Chevrolet 125–6
chief marketing officers (CMO) xvii–xviii,
   xxviii, 45
children and young people, protection
   187, 188–90
Children's Food Campaign 167
Chime Communications 28
China 15, 32, 33, 39–40, 248
click-through rates 128
Closing/review, negotiation 112
CO2 emissions 20
Coca-Cola 2–3, 30, 49, 79, 118, 120–1,
   149, 153, 157, 166, 168–9, 170, 242,
   254, 258, 273
codes of practice 181–90, 210, 212
Coe, Sebastian 28
Cole, Marty 8
Colgate-Palmolive 131
collaboration 6, 48, 68, 74
Colombia 38
Commercial Alert 138
commercial objectives 287, 290, *291–4*
Committee on Advertising Practice
   (CAP), Code of Practice 212
Commonwealth Games 42

communication 116–7, 218; 365-days
'always on' approach 144; corporate
storytelling 6–7; goals 50; internal 103;
results sharing 298; unpredictability in
116
community-linked sponsorship 84–5, 198
comparisons 185
compensation 203–4
competition law 210
concessions, negotiating 110–1
conferences, events, seminars and trade
events 129–30
consumer behaviour, knowledge of 121
consumer expectations xviii, 45–6
consumer journey 46
consumer relationships, importance of 8
Consumers' Association (CA) 20
content, importance of 11–2
content marketing 49, 125–9; activities
127; challenge 126; conferences, events,
seminars and trade events 129–30;
integrated approach 129–30, **130**; and
reputation 128
Content Marketing Association (CMA)
127–8
context, lack of 5–6
contracts 101
control groups 299
Co-operative, the 170
copyright 208, 235
Copyright, Designs and Patents Act 1988
210, 237
copywriting 119
Cordisco, Stephanie 181
core resources, brands 73
Coronation Street 9TV series 141
corporate hospitality: *see* hospitality
corporate responsibility 155–62
corporate social performance (CSP) 246,
256
corporate social responsibility (CSR)
21–2, 45, 84, 86, 170, 194, 198,
240–63, 285; activities 240–1,
242–3; agenda on a country basis
248–53; business integration 259–63;
community participation 245; consumer
expectations 241–2; definition 241,
245–7; direction 241; donations
240; engagement 242; enlightened
self-interest 242, 242–3; features
246, 247; importance of 257; India
242–3; joined-up 261–2; objectives 257;
principles 244–5, *244*; recognition
253–4, *254*; relationship with

sponsorship 253–9, *254, 256, 257*;
responsible market entry 245; and
revenue 257; spending 240; and sports
sponsorship 253–9, *254, 256, 257*;
stakeholders 245–6; tobacco industry
177–8; transparency 243, 244; trust 245;
UN Global Compact 241, 243, 244–5,
244; value 241; voluntary work 241
corporate storytelling 6–7
corruption 157, 162, 216–21
cost comparison 267
cost effectiveness 1
counterfeit products 234–6
counter-marketing strategies 227–8
covert marketing 138
creative content 119
creative sponsorship 115
creative thinking 119
creativity: creative fusion 119–20, **120**;
importance of 119–22; rule breaking
122–5; and strategy 115; and technology
117
credit 50
credit integration 131–2
Cricket World Cup, 2003 227
criminal intent 220
culpability 168–9
customer engagement xxviii
customer loyalty xvii, 149
customer loyalty programmes 16, 102
customer networks 98
customer relationships xvii; trust 149
cut-through 122
Cybergeddon 134–6

Daglish. Henry 133
damages 206–7
data protection 187, 300
Data Protection Act 1998 300
database marketing 103
Davis, Scott 162
Deboo, Martin 260–1
decency 183
decision-making, strategic 47–52
Deepwater Horizon disaster 153, 154
demographics xviii, 15
denigration 185
Department for Education (DfE) 20
depth interviews 304
diabetes 164
Diamondouros, Nikiforos 219–20
digital content, optimised 142–6
digital dividend, sports sponsorship 115–7
digital revolution xxviii

Discovery Channel 80–1
discrimination 157–60
Domino's Pizza 133–4
Doncaster Cup 178–9
Dow Chemical 153
Downton Abbey (TV programme) 214–5
drug abuse 161–2
Dubai 35
due diligence 218
Dunkin Donuts 78
Dunne, Ronana 155–6
Dutch, Nick 133, 134

Eastman Kodak 224
e-cigarette industry 177–81
economic conditions xxii
Ecuador *248*
editorial content 214
editorial sponsorship 81–3, 197
education sponsorship 20–1, 169–72
EE 76–8, 86
Egypt *249*
El Salvador *249*
electroencephalography (EEG) technology 305
email/online surveys 302, *303*
emerging markets 6, 32, 33
emotional connection 122
emotional intelligence 66
endorsement deals 56
engagement 51; audience xxv, 3; corporate social responsibility (CSR) 242; customer xxvii; strategy 149
enlightened capitalism 259–63
enlightened self-interest 242, 242–3
Ennis, Jessica 58
environmental, social and corporate governance (ESG) performance on 244
environmental analysis 270–1
environmental sponsorship 20
ethics 2–3, 46, 152–90; alcohol-related sponsorship 172–6; ambush marketing 163, 223–4, 225–6, 231; children and young people 187, 188–90; codes of practice 181–90; comparisons 185; corporate hospitality 163; corporate responsibility 155–62; culpability 168–9; decency 183; denigration 185; educational sponsorship 169–72; fair competition 182–3, 185; food and drink brands 164, 166–9; gambling sponsorship 164, *165*; halo effect 153; honesty 183; imitation 186; importance of 159–62; individual responsibility

155–62; liability 186; personality endorsement 181; privacy 187; redress 188; reputation management 155–62; responsibility 187–8; social responsibility 183; tax avoidance 159–60; tobacco industry 176–81; truthfulness 183; use of terminology 184
EU Directive on Privacy and Electronic Communications 300
EU Tobacco Advertising Directive 2002 176–7
EURO 2012 36
EURO 2016 38
Europe, sports sponsorship opportunities 32, 36–7, 38
European Commission 210
European Ombudsman 219–20
European Sponsorship Association (ESA) 24, 46, 164, 174–6, 225–6, 284
event sponsorship 205–6; cancellation rights 206–7; duration of the agreement 206; hospitality rights 206; matching option rights 207; postponement rights 206; renewal rights 207
EventScotland 42
evidence-based marketing 184–5
Ewanick, Joel 4
exchange theory 48
exclusivity 101, 195–6, 202
exploitation **273**
exploratory research 302
external providers, measurement and evaluation 305–6

Facebook 3, 11–2, 118, 131, 143, 146, 147, 180
face-to- face interviews 301, *301, 302*
fair competition 182–3, 185
Fast Track 28–30
Fenton, William 106
FIFA 2
Financial Fair Play (FFP) Rules, football 27, 28
Financial Times 61
Fisk, Peter 119, 120
food and drink brands, ethics 164, 166–9
football: alcohol-related sponsorship 172–3; CSR and 256–8, *256, 257*; domination **14**; Financial Fair Play (FFP) Rules 27, 28; intellectual property (IP) rights **209**; Premier League 4–5, 75, 195–6; social commitment 257; World Cup xxii, 33, 35, 37, 52, 58, 79–80, 146, 233–6, *233*

Football Association 4
Forbes 123
Forbes, Nick 155
Ford, Andrew 136
foreign direct investment (FDI) 245
fragmentation, sports sector 24–5
France 33, 38, 174
Franklin, Peter 121
Fraser, Gillian 68
full service offering 27

gambling sponsorship 164, *165*
General Motors 4
'Generation Green' initiative 171–2
Gillette 161
'Gillette World of Sponsorship' 83
glamour projects 5
Global Language Monitor (GLM) 51–2, *52*
global opportunities, sports sponsorship
    31–3, **33**, **34**, 35–42, *35*
Gold Coast 42
goodwill, exploitation of 186
government, role 24
Grammy Awards 54
Grayson, David 153, 154
Greece, ancient 13
Green Schools Revolution 169–70
Griffiths, Andy 129
group interviews 304–5
guerrilla marketing: *see* ambush marketing
Guetta, David 124
Guru in a Bottle® 65–6

halo effect 153, 198
Hamburg, Margaret 180
Haste, Andy 155
Heineken 196
Hill, Clare 127–8
Hill, Declan 162
Hilton, Anthony 153–4
Hobbs, Jeremy 246
Hollyoaks (TV series) 142
honesty 183
Hong Kong 249
Hopscotch Consulting 84–5, 170
hospitality 102, 163, 206, 216, 217–21
Human Rights Act 1998 208

IBM 7
IEG xix, xx, 306
IEG Research 16, 19
IEG/Performance Research Sponsorship
    Decision-makers Survey, 2014 53, 59,
    116

image rights 208, 210
image transfer 50
imitation 186
immediacy 144
impact 121, 267, 269; mobile and social
    networks 143; product placement 141–2
improper performance 217–21
Incorporate Society of British Advertisers
    (ISBA) 20
incremental sales 285
India 15, 32, 33, 40, 242–3, 249
India National Defence Academy 80–1
individual responsibility 155–62
information sources 284, *284*
infrastructure, technology and logistics
    providers, sports 24
inputs 282
Instagram 118, 149
Institute of Practitioners in Advertising
    (IPA) 130
intangible benefits 86, 93, *94*
integrated sponsorship 142–6, *144*
integrity 22
intellectual capital 128
intellectual property (IP) 45, 86, 99, 163;
    rights 202, 207–10, **209**, 227, 235, 237
intelligent activation 115
interactivity 6, 136
internal communication 103
International Chamber of Commerce,
    Code of Practice 181–9
International Cycling Union 2
*International Journal of Sports Marketing &
    Sponsorship* 154
International Olympic Committee (IOC)
    2, 69, 163, 167, 195, 224, 226
Internet, the 11
intuition 282
investment xviii, 27, 61–2, *62*
Iran *249*
Isaacson, Walter 117
Israel *249*

James Bond film franchise 137
Japan 39–40, *250*
Jenkins, Anthony 5
Jobs, Steve 117
joint venture partnerships 27
Jordan, Michael 55–7
justification xviii

Kellogg's 125–6
key performance indicators (KPIs) 283,
    286, 298

Kia Motors 116
Kildum-Reid, Kim 285
Korngold, Alice 260
Kronauge, Stuart 169

Lady Gaga 123, 123–4
'Launching People' campaign, Samsung
    128–9
legal disclaimers 186
Lewis, Stewart 247
LGBT community 124–5, 157–60
liability 186
Libor scandal 5
licensing rights 101
LifeSkills Programme 84–5
lift cycles 81
Lindstrom, Martin 5
LinkedIn 131
listening 67–8
Liverpool FC 78
local knowledge 26, 32
logos xvii
London, Olympic Games, 2012 xxiv, 6–7,
    24, 25, 167; ambush marketing 163,
    228, 228–9, 230–1; corporate social
    responsibility (CSR) 258–9; creative
    routes 120–2; financial returns 28; food
    and drink sponsorship 167; impact
    29–30; measurement and evaluation
    266, 267; mobile and social networks
    149; sponsors 30, 31; sponsorship 28–31,
    29, 30, 31, 49–52
London Olympic Association Right 230
London Olympic Games and Paralympic
    Games Act, 2006 230–1
London Organising Committee of the
    Olympic Games 28
loyalty sales 285
Luiz, David 79–80
Lustig, Robert 166

McCarthy, Jenny 181
McCarty, Ethan 128
McDonald's 153, 166, 167, 226, 242, 254
Mackay, Malky 2
McLaren Mercedes 75
Macrow, Alistair 167
Magnum 12–3
Malaysia 40
Manchester United FC 4, 146–8
market entry, responsible 245
market research 103, 298–9; qualitative
    298–9, 302, 304–5; quantitative 298–9,
    299–302, 301, 302, 303

market saturation 26
marketing xvii; agencies and advisors 23;
    and business performance 276; services
    providers 23–4; spending growth xx;
    sponsorship integration 52–3, 73, 73;
    and sponsorship performance 46
marketing-in-kind (MIK) 107
mass personalisation 8
MasterCard 54
matching option rights 207
measurement and evaluation 62, 266–9,
    267, 274; consistency 283; external
    providers 305–6; final analysis 283;
    frequency 283–4; methodologies 287,
    288–9, 290, 291–7, 298; outcomes
    282–3; return on investment (ROI) 68,
    284, 284, 285, 285–6, 286; return on
    objectives (ROO) 284–5, 284
MEC Access 81
media consumption 3
media exposure 88–9, 89, 94, 103, 122,
    274
media sponsorship 130–1; advertiser-
    funded programming (AFP) 131–6;
    product placement 132, 137–42, 139;
    value 135
Mercer, Sam 170
merchandise 208
mergers and acquisitions 27
message 98
Messenger, David 128
Messi, Lionel 79–80
metrics 268, 276
Mexico 41, 250
Middle East 35–6, 216
Millennium Dome 148–9, 195
mobile and social networks 142–6, 144
mobile phones 149–53
Moor, Keith 75
Moss, Michael 168–9
Mueller, Tom 48
Muir, David 48–9
multi-sponsor format 75–6, 196

naming rights 48, 87, 203; value 94, 95–6,
    95, 96
narrative 2, 14, 98
NASCAR 48
National Lottery 28
native advertising 81–3
NBA 116
needs and wants 110
negotiation 48, 58–61, 59, 60, 107;
    atmosphere 110; attitude 60, 107,

108; bargaining 111–2; behaviour 60, 107, **108**; closing/review 112; concessions 110–1; effective 60–1; essential elements 107; framework 107, **108**; needs and wants 110; offer 111; outcomes 272; preparation 108–9; process 60, 107, **108**; seven-step checklist 108–12, **109**
networking 97–9, 98
networks: mobile and social 142–6, *144*; niche 149
neuromarketing 305
New York Times 82
New Zealand 42, *250*
Newcastle United FC 155–6
NFL sponsorship 145–6
NFL Super Bowl, 2014 118–9
niche networks 149
nicotine replacement therapy (NRT) 177
nicotine-containing products (NCPs) 178
Nigeria *250*
Nike 16, 52, 54–7, 161, 162, 219–20, 228, 230, 253
Nokia Lumia 142
Nordström 53
North America, sports sponsorship opportunities 32, 40–1
Norwegian Business School 51

O2 148–9
O2 Arena 148–9, 195
obesity 166, 167
objectives 45, 62, 275–9, *276*, **277**; brand 287, 288–9; commercial 287, 290, *291–4*; relationship 290, *295–7*
obligations 194
Oceania 41–2
Ofcom 18, 140, 211, 214–5
offer: making; negotiation 110–1
Official supplier/partner status 78–9
official supplier/partner status 198–9, 210
Ohio University, Sports Administration Department 115–6
Olins, Wally 54, 77
Olympic Games 49, 69, 196; 1980 231; 1984 224; 1988 224–5; 2012 *see* London, Olympic Games, 2012 2016 xxii, 31, 37; 2020 38; 2024 35
Olympic partner (TOP) programme 46–7, 226
Olympus 156–8
online dimensions 11–2, 102
online exposure 89
onsite opportunities 101

Opinion Research 28–30
optimised content 142–6
Oracle 240
Orange 76–7
outcomes 282–3
outdoor exposure 87–8, 88
out-of-home (OOH) poster advertising 12–3
outputs 282
outside-in perspective 98
Overman, Steve 241–2

Pakistan *250*
Panama *250*
Partner Z 48
partners sponsors 237
partnership xx
passion 15
pass-through rights 104
Patrick, Kristen 79
patronage 14
Payack, Paul 52
payment structures 204–5
Payne, Andrew 178
Pepsi 79–80
PepsiCo 167, 168–9
performance: evaluation *62*; expectations 3; improvements xviii; marketing xviii; *see also* measurement and evaluation
permission-based platform 53, **53**
personality endorsement and sponsorship 16, 53–7, **53**, **55**, 79–80, 196; ethics 181; principles 57–8; reputation management 161–2; tobacco industry 180, 181
personality/image rights 208, 210
perspective 98
perspective taking 71
Peru *251*
Pfahl, Michael 116
philanthropy 14, 16
Philippines *251*
Pink, Daniel 71
Pinterest 149
planning xvii, xix, 275
pleasure 13
Poland 36
policy review 271–2
political influence 167
Polman, Paul 259, 260, 263
Portland Business Journal 56
Portman Group, the 174
post-investment review 283
postponement rights 207

potential xvii
power xxviii
PQ Media 140
Premier Range 2
premium benefits 86, 91–3, *91*, *92*
preparation, negotiation 108–9
pricing 106
Pringle, Hamish 54
PRISM 32
Pritchard, Marc 7
privacy 187
Probst-Iyer, Carolin 125
process, negotiation 107, **108**
Proctor & Gamble 7, 8, 131, 258–9
product placement 132, 137–42, *139*, 212
production requirements 104
professionalisation 13
professionalism 28
programme credits, television 213–4
promotion, spending growth **xx**
proportionality 218
Prudential 240–1
PRWeek/One Poll 173
public health 164, 166–9
public relations (PR) 7, 103, 146–9
purchase cycle 69
purpose networks 98
Putin, Vladimir 157, 158
PwC xxii, 25

Qatar 31, 32, 33, 35
qualitative research 298–9, *299*
quantitative research 298–9, *299*, 299;
    control groups 299; email/online surveys
    302; face-to- face interviews 301, *301*,
    302; methodology 300; survey methods
    300; telephone interviews 301, 302,
    302, *303*

radio 17–9, 80–1, 130, 197
Rainforest Alliance 262
Real Living (magazine) 82–3
Red Bull 11–2, 126–7
regulation 194; advertising 82–3; alcohol-
    related sponsorship 172–6; broadcast
    sponsorship 211–6; codes of practice
    181–90; gambling sponsorship 164;
    personality/image rights 210; product
    placement 140
relationship objectives 290, *295–7*
relevance 105
renewal rights 207
reputation 46, 49, 50, 128, 224
reputation management 155, 155–62

research methodologies 299
responsibility 20, 187–8, 247
responsible capitalism 259–60
results sharing 298
return on commitment xviii
return on investment (ROI) 46, 52, 61,
    267, 274, 276; measurement 68, 284,
    284, 285, **286**; product placement 142;
    social media 118
return on objectives (ROO) xviii, 68, 267,
    276, 284–5, *284*
revenue streams 83
Rich, Clive 60–1, 108
Ridderstråle, Jonas 53
right of refusal 207
rights and obligations 194
rights and obligations, brand holders
    199, *200–1*, 202; compensation 203;
    duration of the agreement 202–3; event
    sponsorship 205–6; exclusivity 202;
    payment structures 204–5; termination
    203–4
rights and obligations, rights holders
    200–1, 206
rights holders 5–6, 69, 71; bargaining
    power 202; rights and obligations 199,
    200–1; workflow 85
Rines, Simon 32
risk and risk taking 149
risk assessment 218
RJ Reynolds Vapor Co. 180–1
Robinson, Lena 65
Rogge, Jacques 167
role models 161–2
Rozario, Joel 123
Rugby World Cup 38, 39, 219–20
Russia 15, 33, 36
Russian Federation *251*

Saez, Frank 255
sales process 64–112, **97**; best practice
    67–8; buying sponsorship 99–104, *104*;
    collaboration 68; and emotion 66–7;
    listening 67–8; mistakes 72; negotiation
    107–12, **108**, **109**; networking 97–9,
    98; preparation 67; spamming' 71;
    sponsorship audit 86–96, 88, 89, *90*, *91*,
    92, *94*, *95*, *96*; sponsorship hierarchy
    99, **100**; sponsorship proposal 105–7;
    sponsorship propositions 74–86; strategy
    68–74, 85, **85**
sales strategy 85, **85**
Samsung 8, 224; 'Launching People'
    campaign 128–9

Santander 75
Sasa, Hiroyuki 157–8
Satterthwaite, Chris 32
Saudi Arabia 35, 36
Schlosser, Eric 167
school trips 170
schools, sponsorship 20–1
Schwarzkopf 81
scope 1
Scott, Linda 263
search engine optimisation (SEO) 128
secondary sponsorship 77, *77*, 78–9, 196
seeding 138
Sefton, Tim 148
selection criteria *280–1*
self-activation sponsorship 272
selling, traditional view of 68–9
seven-step negotiation checklist 108–12,
   109
Shape (magazine) 81–2
shared destiny 47
Shell 70
signage 101–2
signals 6
Siler, Kim 143
Singapore 40, *251*
six-step sponsorship model 51, 269–75,
   270, **273**
Skildum-Reid, Kim 62
Sky Media 142
Sky News 215–6
SMART objectives 275–9, *276*, **277**
smartphones 130
social context 117
social marketing 14
social media 6, 115–7, **116**, 117–9, 122,
   123, 131, 142–6, 173, 180
social networks 98
social responsibility 183
Socialites Electric Cigarettes 178–9
South Africa 227, *252*
South America 37–8
South by Southwest 180–1
South Korea 31, 33, 39–40, *252*
Speedo 287, 288–9, 290, *291–7*, 298
Speedo Sponsorship Toolkit 277–9, **277**,
   280–1, 288–9
spending xviii–xxi, 29, **xix**, **xx**, *xxi*
Spincer, Mark 178
sponsor identification 51–2
sponsored content 129–30
sponsorship: case against 3–6; evolution
   13–4; historical precedents 13; nature of
   xvii–xviii

sponsorship agreement 272; advertiser-
   funded programming (AFP)
   197–8; broadcast sponsorship 197;
   community-linked sponsorship 198;
   compensation 203; duration 202–3;
   editorial sponsorship 197; event
   sponsorship rights 205–7; exclusivity
   202; exclusivity sponsorship 195–6;
   importance of 194; multi-sponsor format
   196; official supplier/partner status
   198–9; payment structures 204–5;
   personality endorsement and
   sponsorship 196; rights and obligations,
   brand holders 199, *200–1*, 202–7;
   rights and obligations, rights holders
   198, *200–1*; role 194–5; secondary
   sponsorship 196; termination 203–4;
   types 195–9; vedor sponsorship 195
sponsorship audit 86–96, *88, 89, 90, 91,
   92, 94, 95, 96*
sponsorship credits 214–5
sponsorship fee, payment structures 204–5
sponsorship hierarchy 99, **100**
Sponsorship Intelligence 88
Sponsorship Intelligence and Zenith
   Optimedia 6
sponsorship investments, hierarchy of **277**
sponsorship lifespan **72**
sponsorship performance, and marketing
   performance 46
sponsorship policy 98, 271–2
sponsorship process, six-step model 51,
   269–75, **273, 275**
sponsorship programmes 1–2
sponsorship property: arts and culture
   sponsorship 16, **17**, *17*; associations
   and professional bodies' sponsorship
   19, *19*; broadcast sponsorship 17–9;
   as commodity 69; corporate social
   responsibility (CSR) sponsorship
   21–2; education sponsorship 20–1;
   environmental sponsorship 20;
   identification 47–9; personality
   endorsement and sponsorship 16; search
   279; selection 45–67; selling 99; sports
   sponsorship 14–6, **14**; valuation 106
sponsorship propositions 74; advertiser-
   funded programmes (AFP) 83–4;
   assessment 279–82, *280–1*; broadcast
   sponsorship 80–1; community-linked
   sponsorship 84–5; creation 105–7;
   editorial sponsorship/native advertising
   81–3; exclusive sponsorship 75; multi-
   sponsor format 75–6; official supplier/

partner status 78–9; personality
sponsorship/endorsement 79–80;
secondary sponsorship 77, 78–9; venue
sponsorship 74–5
sponsorship review 274–5
sponsorship rights creep 224
Sponsorship Toolkit, Speedo **277**, *280–1*,
288–9
sponsorship value 88, 89
sports 13; and big data 15; domination
xxii–xxiii, **xxiii**; drug abuse 2; ethics 2,
161–2; fan demographics 15; growth
xxiiv; importance of 10; live 15; market
value xxiii; one-off events **xxi**; team-
sponsor relationship 155–6; UK market
xxi, xxv
sports bodies, role 24
sports events 32, **33**
sports fans, role 24
Sports Illustrated 55
sports marketing agencies and advisors **23**
sports sponsorship: alcohol-related 172–6;
and brand differentiation 147; and CSR
253–5, *254*; digital dividend 115–7;
dominance 14–6; global opportunities
31–3, **33**, **34**, 35–42, *35*; growth, UK
26–7, 28; growth drivers 33; impact 267;
infrastructure, technology and logistics
providers 23–4; market saturation 26;
marketing services providers 23–4;
negotiation 272; professionalism 28;
role of brands 24; role of government
24; role of sports bodies 24; role of
sports fans 24; sector fragmentation
24–5; sponsorship review 275; by sport
14; sports marketing agencies and
advisors **23**; tobacco industry 176–9,
180; United Kingdom 22–7, **23**, 28–31,
29, *30*, *31*; US sector 25
spot ads 139
spreadsheet computation 282
Spurlock, Morgan 167
stakeholder relationships 74
stock value 48
storytelling 135; brand 10; corporate 6–7;
real-time 10, 12
strategic business units (SBU) 70
strategic decision-making 47–52
strategic planning xix
strategy 46; audience engagement 122–5;
and creativity 115; sales process 68–74
strategy review 271–2
Sturner, Ben 126–7
style partners 77

subliminal benefits 6
substantiation 184–5
Subway 226
Super Size Me (film) 167
super-global economies 27
surreptitious advertising 13
survey methods 300
sustainability 242, 246, 259–63, **261**
'Sustainable Living Plan' Unilever 259–63
Sweden 38
Symantec 134–6

tablets 130
Taiwan *252*
talkability 12–3
tangible benefits 86, 89, 89
target benefits 205
target customers 65–6, 147–8
Tata 242
Tata, Ratan 242–3
team-sponsor relationship 155–6
teaser promotions 185
technological change xviii, xxv, 7
technology, and creativity 117
telephone interviews 301, 302, *302*, *303*
television 80–1; advertiser-funded
  programming (AFP) 131–3, 213;
  channel sponsorship 215–6;
  commissioning 212; editorial content
  214; editorial independence 212;
  funding 131–2, 211; programme credits
  213–4; rights 17–8; sponsorship 17–9,
  197, 211–2; sponsorship credits 214–5;
  viewing figures 130, 131
termination rights 203–4
Tesco 13
testimonials 185–6
Thailand *252*
'Thank You, Mom' campaign 258–9
'Think Different' campaign 117
Thinkbox 198
Think!Sponsorship/Sponsorship Today
  30–1, *30*, *31*
third parties, pass-through rights 104
thought leadership 127–9, 130
Timberlake, Justin 54–5
timeliness 105
title rights 131–2
title sponsors 237
tobacco 166
Tobacco Advertising and Promotion Act
  2002 177
tobacco industry 176–81
top-level commitment 218

tracking research 298
Trade Marks Act 1994 237
trademarks 208, 237
Trading Standards Office 237
transition economies 27
transparency 82–3, 116, 243, 244
Transparency International 216
Treaty on the Functioning of the European
    Union (TFEU) 210
trust 149, 245
truthfulness 183
Tuckey, Mark 82–3
Turkey 31, 32, 37
Twitter 10, 116, 118, 123, 131, 143, 180

UAE *252*
UEFA 2020 38
UK Trade & Investment 26, 31–2
Ukman, Lesa 257–8, 306
Ukraine 36
UN Global Compact 241, 243, 244–5, *244*
Unilever 8, 12, 131, 145; 'Sustainable
    Living Plan' 259–63
United Arab Emirates 35; Football
    Association 36
United Kingdom: broadcast sponsorship
    18–9; childhood obesity 166; CSR
    agenda *253*; education sponsorship
    20–1; growth, sports sponsorship
    26–7, 28; infrastructure, technology
    and logistics providers 24; marketing
    services providers 23–4; product
    placement 139–42; role of brands
    24; role of government 24; role of
    sports bodies 24; role of sports fans
    24; sponsorship in xxv, **xxvii**, *xxvi*;
    sponsorship sector fragmentation 24–5;
    sports market xxi, xxv; sports marketing
    xxii; sports marketing agencies and
    advisors **23**; sports sponsorship 22–7,
    23, 28–31, **29**, *30*, *31*; tobacco
    sponsorship 176–9
United States of America: association
    sponsorship 19, *19*; Centres for
    Disease Control and Prevention 179;
    CSR agenda *253*; diabetes rate 164;
    educational sponsorship 169; Federal
    Food, Drug and Cosmetic Act 2011
    180; Food and Drug Administration
    (FDA) 179–80; personality rights 208,
    210; product placement 138–9, *139*;
    sports sponsorship 25, 41; tobacco
    sponsorship 179–81
unsaturated sports markets 26

Uruguay *253*
US National Advertising Division 82
US Tennis Association (USTA) 156
user-generated content (UGC) 51, 131,
    271–2

value 268
value added xvii
value in kind 205
value proposition 73
value services 62
value-in-kind (VIK) 107
values 153
vendor sponsorship 195
venue sponsorship 48, 74–5
Vevo 81
Victoria & Albert Museum 196
video on demand 130
Vietnam *253*
viewer deception 211
Vine 116, 118
visibility 61, 146
Vodafone 131
Volkswagen 125
Vuse 181

Wallach, Russell 124
Walsh, David 161
wants and needs
Watt-Smith, Dan 135, 136
web-based screening 281
Weed, Keith 144
Welsh, Jerry 230–1
Wembley Stadium 86
Westlake, Andy 30
Wigan Athletic FC 2
Wilshere, Jack 79–80
Wimbledon Tennis Championships 232
Winter Olympic Games 37; 2014 31–2,
    36, 157–60, 224; 2022 41
Wonga 155–6
Woodford, Michael 156–7
Woods, Tiger 55, 161, 162
Work Research 141–2
workflows 70, 85
World Cup, FIFA 230; 2014 xxii, 37, 52,
    58, 79–80, 146, 233–6, *233*; 2022 33, 35
World Health Organisation (WHO) 176
Writers Guild of America 137–8

Yahoo! 136
YouTube 3, 11, 118, 123, 126, 133, 143

Zuiker, Anthony E 135